Making Cairo Medieval

TRANSNATIONAL PERSPECTIVES ON SPACE AND PLACE

Nezar AlSayyad, Series Editor

Transnational Perspectives on Space and Place is a publication of the Series of Lexington books based on conferences, symposia, and projects organized by the Center for Middle Eastern Studies and the International Association for the Study of Traditional Environments at the University of California at Berkeley as part of their transnational initiative. Unlike comparative research, which focuses on similarities and differences between regions, transnational research examines the socio-spatial connections through which global cartographies are constituted and transformed. It is also an epistemological technique that pays attention to how concepts and discourses are produced within specific geopolitical regions and histories, and that allows knowledge of one region to be used to interrogate another.

Muslim Europe or Euro-Islam: Politics, Culture, and Citizenship in the Age of Globalization, edited by Nezar AlSayyad and Manuel Castells (2002)

Urban Informality: Transnational Perspectives from the Middle East, Latin America, and South Asia, edited by Ananya Roy and Nezar AlSayyad (2003)

Making Cairo Medieval, edited by Nezar AlSayyad, Irene A. Bierman, and Nasser Rabbat (2005)

Making Cairo Medieval

Edited by
Nezar AlSayyad
Irene A. Bierman
Nasser Rabbat

LEXINGTON BOOKS
Lanham • Boulder • New York • Toronto • Oxford

LEXINGTON BOOKS

Published in the United States of America
by Lexington Books
An imprint of The Rowman & Littlefield Publishing Group, Inc.
4501 Forbes Boulevard, Suite 200, Lanham, Maryland 20706

PO Box 317
Oxford
OX2 9RU, UK

British Library Cataloguing in Publication Information Available

Library of Congress Cataloging-in-Publication Data

Making Cairo medieval / edited by Nezar AlSayyad, Irene A. Bierman, and Nasser Rabbat.
    p. cm. — (Transnational perspectives on space and place)
    Includes bibliographical references and index.
    ISBN 0-7391-0915-4 (cloth : alk. paper) — ISBN 0-7391-0916-2 (pbk. : alk. paper)
    1. Architecture—Egypt—Cairo—19th century. 2. Achitecture,
Islamic—Egypt—Cairo. 3. City planning—Egypt—Cairo—History—19th century. 4.
Cairo (Egypt)—Buildings, structures, etc. I. AlSayyad, Nezar. II. Bierman, Irene
A. III. Rabbat, Nasser O. IV. Series.
NA1583.M35 2005
720´.962´1609034—dc22
                                        2004025668

Printed in the United States of America

♾™ The paper used in this publication meets the minimum requirements of American
National Standard for Information Sciences—Permanence of Paper for Printed Library
Materials, ANSI/NISO Z39.48-1992.

CONTENTS

1. Prologue: The Project of Making Cairo Medieval   1
   Nezar AlSayyad, Irene A. Bierman, Nasser Rabbat

   PART I: A MEDIEVAL CITY FOR A MODERN WORLD

2. Disciplining the Eye: Perceiving Medieval Cairo   9
   Irene A. Bierman

3. The Medieval Link: Maqrizi's *Khitat* and Modern Narratives of Cairo   29
   Nasser Rabbat

4. 'Ali Mubarak's Cairo: Between the Testimony of *'Alamuddin* and the   49
   Imaginary of the *Khitat*
   Nezar AlSayyad

   PART II: REPRESENTING AND NARRATING

5. Performing Cairo: Orientalism and the City of the Arabian Nights   69
   Derek Gregory

6. Nineteenth-Century Images of Cairo: From the Real to   95
   the Interpretative
   Caroline Williams

7. The Museum of What You Shall Have Been   125
    Donald Preziosi

PART III: DISCIPLINING AND MAKING

8. Nineteenth-Century Cairo: A Dual City?   143
    Heba Farouk Ahmed

9. Modernizing Cairo: A Revisionist Narrative   173
    Khaled Fahmy

10. Medievalization of the Old City as an Ingredient of Cairo's   201
    Modernization: Case Study of Bab Zuwayla
    Nairy Hampikian

11. The Cemeteries of Cairo and the *Comité de Conservation*   235
    May al-Ibrashy

    Selected Bibliography   257

    Index   261

    Contributors   265

1

Prologue:
The Project of Making Cairo Medieval

Nezar AlSayyad, Irene A. Bierman, Nasser Rabbat

Making Cairo Medieval is the result of the efforts of the Misr Research Group, which is constituted of a number of scholars who have for the last several years shared research on Cairo in public events and symposia. The Misr Group met for the first few times at the Gustav E. von Grunebaum Center for Near Eastern Studies at the University of California, Los Angeles, at the invitation of Irene Bierman, who was then the center's director. Later, at the invitation of Timothy Mitchell, the group members delivered the annual Hagop Kevorkian Lectures in Near Eastern Art and Civilization at the Near Eastern Studies Center at New York University. Our most recent meeting was a one-day conference organized by the Center of Middle Eastern Studies at the University of California, Berkeley, under the direction of Nezar AlSayyad. Each time we have met, new members have been added and our focus has shifted a bit, settling on its current form as presented in this book. Along with a few members of the initial group,[1] this book brings together scholars from various disciplinary backgrounds—urban history, architectural history, social history, cultural geography, and preservation—to provide a new look at the history of Cairo and its representations at the turn of the twentieth century.

Many books have been written about Cairo. Among them, a few deserve special mention. Janet Abu Lughod's 1971 *Cairo: 1001 Years of the City Victorious* covers the entire history of the city and remains the classic work in the field. André Raymond's *Cairo: City of History* is also a distinguished work, especially in its analysis of Cairene architectural types and the Ottoman city. Through the years, however, nineteenth-century Cairo has received very little concerted scholarly effort or historical attention that is commensurate with its significance for the study of the transformations of modernist concepts as they became entangled in the different political, social, and cultural contexts of the colonies. We hope this book will begin to remedy this situation.

Through the various cycles of history and historiography, Egypt has remained a pivotal site for the visualization of key episodes in the genealogy of civilization. Following modern European encounters with the country, the history of Egypt came to be represented as comprising two discontinuous segments: the Pharaonic and Hellenistic periods, foundational eras in the Western version of the history of civilization; and the Coptic and Islamic periods, which were assigned to the definition of modern Egypt. The chapters in this book aim at articulating the complex construction of Cairo as primarily the material manifestation of these historical trajectories with a focus on the nineteenth century.

During that century, Cairo witnessed one of its most dramatic periods of expansion and change. Ironically, the transformation process resulted in the emergence of two Cairos, as it were, developing side by side and almost in a symbiotic mode. A modern, cosmopolitan city, which was initiated by Khedive Isma'il (1863–79), was pushing westward toward the Nile from the edge of the premodern city, while the traditional, Islamic Cairo was concurrently being branded a primordially "medieval" city. The inscription of a "medieval" identity onto the old city was the outcome of selective restoration and rehabilitation practices executed by an impressive cultural infrastructure comprising art historians, architects, urban planners, conservationists, literary writers, and travelers who all poured their energies into "medievalizing" the old city's image. This double operation of modernization and "medievalization" was started several decades before Egypt came under direct British control in 1882, and it went on unabated well into the first quarter of the twentieth century. It is these crucial decades of the city's history that form the backdrop of our context.

The concept of a "medieval" Islamic Cairo first appeared in the 1867 Exposition Universelle in Paris. But it took only twenty years for the boundaries of such an imaginary place to be firmly fixed within the historic city by early conservation practices. During this time, geographic boundaries and cultural biases came together to define distinct areas such as "Islamic Cairo," which comprised the Fatimid royal city and its southern Mamluk extensions; "Old Cairo" with its churches, synagogues, and old mosques; and their urban antithesis—"Modern Cairo."

The shaping of a "medieval" Islamic Cairo, a project largely confined to European and local elites, hardly echoed the sensibilities of its residents. It did, however, affect their lives. Displacement, relocation, and the reordering of social rituals and patterns were only some of the ramifications of the making of a "medieval" Islamic Cairo. The true actors and audiences of this new geography were scholars and professionals from such newly founded disciplines of the eighteenth and nineteenth centuries as Egyptology, archaeology, architecture, and urban planning. With rare exception, they lived outside the space of "medieval Islamic Cairo," either within other areas of Cairo, or in Europe.

The process through which Cairo was "medievalized" consisted of two separate but overlapping parts. First, the representation of medieval Cairo through literary narratives, painting, photography, etc. Second, and not remote from the first, either chronologically or conceptually, came the fabrication of a "medieval" Islamic Cairo on the ground through the reorganization of the physical space of the city, the work of the Comité de Conservation des Monuments de l'Art Arab (the Comité), etc. Both parts fit snugly within the larger context of orientalism, and more specifically, they illustrate how the East has been an inextricable part of the West's self-representation as modernity's locus and history's peak. Accordingly, some of the contributors to this book show how Europeans, through representations of the architecture and urban spaces of nineteenth-century Cairo, constructed dualities like East/West and modern/medieval, which remain with us today. Other chapters focus on material practices such as conservation and restoration, and the establishment of museums, which helped to construct Cairo as "medieval." Yet others offer insight into how Cairenes understood their own city and represented their own views of what they thought the city was like.

The chapters in this book have been arranged around three different interrogative modalities. The first section, "A Medieval City for a Modern World," comprises chapters by the three editors, laying out the various competing perceptions of fin-de-siècle Cairo. The book starts with Irene Bierman's analysis of perceptual technologies employed to create a medieval Cairo. She argues that visual representations as well as on-the-ground restoration work carried out by the Comité served to "discipline the eye."

If the first chapter gives a central role to "foreign" agents in the refashioning of Cairo, those that follow by Nasser Rabbat and Nezar AlSayyad focus on other voices that helped shape the representation of the city. Rabbat's chapter shows that the *khitat* of al-Maqrizi—the great medieval historian of Cairo—occupies a central place in the contemporary discourse on the history of Egypt. As a literary work, al-Maqrizi's text, written in the fifteenth century, represents a powerful foundation for a linear historical narrative, which is suffused with self-conscious patriotism. AlSayyad's chapter uses *'Alamuddin*, the only known novel by 'Ali Mubarak—the Baron Hausmann of nineteenth-century Cairo—to interrogate the voluminous history of Cairo that Mubarak also wrote at the time. Representing the voice of the Egyptian elite, this chapter shows how turn-of-the-century Cairenes were also active agents (rather than passive receptors) of the project of "making Cairo medieval."

The second part of the book, "Representing and Narrating," starts with a chapter by Derek Gregory examining the role that literature played in shaping the experience of the Orient. Seminal texts such as Edward William Lane's *Modern Egyptians* and European translations of *The Arabian Nights* fixed the Orientalist gaze within the medieval city of Cairo and allowed Western tourists to see it as unchanged and frozen in time. Looking at nineteenth-century images of Cairo by various Western artists, Caroline Williams then demonstrates how representations of the city changed over the course of forty years. Starting with the highly documentary work of early topographical artists (Pascal Coste, Robert Hay, David Roberts) who largely painted what they saw, Williams argues that Western art about the Orient soon moved to a more interpretive phase. From providing "realistic depictions" of the other, Orientalist art moved to supplying fantasyscapes for a largely Western clientele. The third chapter in the section, by Donald Preziosi, continues this analysis of the role of Western representations in the creation of a medieval image for Cairo, specifically examining the role of museums and art history. The establishment of such institutions played an important role in creating a unified narrative out of Egypt's complex history. We would especially like to express gratitude to the University of Minnesota Press for allowing us to reprint Prof. Preziosi's chapter in this book.

Four essays, by Heba Farouk Ahmed, Khaled Fahmy, Nairy Hampikian, and May al-Ibrashy, make up the third and final part of the book, entitled "Disciplining and Making." Ahmed's chapter wrestles with the idea of nineteenth-century Cairo as a dual city. Like many of the authors in this book, she believes Western representations of Cairo eclipsed its true nature as a harmonious city in the midst of rapid expansion, restructuring, and regeneration. The chapter shows that reducing Cairo to the epithet of a "dual city" was the outcome of a "European category of thought" that was imposed onto a dynamic and indeed modern nineteenth-century city. Following on the same theme, Fahmy seeks to reverse the traditional elitist vantage point through which Cairo has been understood, and presents a narration of everyday acts of resistance by the subaltern population of Cairo against the top-down policies of modernization and medievalization targeted against them. Fahmy's chapter reminds us that while centralized power may be effective, it rarely goes unchallenged or uncontested.

Nairy Hampikian further problematizes the notion of a European modernity as separate and distinct from an Egyptian "medievalness." In her chapter on the conservation and preservation of the Bab Zuwayla district, she argues that the desire to privilege the medieval quality of certain parts of the city was ineluctably intertwined with the desire to modernize others. Finally, May al-Ibrashy's chapter is centered around the activities of the Comité—one of the main agents of change in nineteenth-century Cairo. Committed to the cause of preservation and restoration (in the nineteenth-century European sense of the term) the Comité turned buildings and spaces that were used by Cairenes into monuments of art-historical worth. The chapter exposes the tensions between local and Comité perceptions of collective memory and monumentality in the reshaping of the city at the turn of the century.

In conceiving our book, we recognize that the process of making Cairo "medieval" was one of several similar projects that went on in Europe in the nineteenth century. As such, it cannot be seen as independent of the larger trends in urban activity and the debates regarding modernity in Europe at that time. As Paula Sanders once reminded us, the Hausmannization of Old Paris ended just as the restoration of "medieval" Cairo was beginning. The process of Hausmannization, which was recorded in photographs and narrative, both intrigued and traumatized Parisians, evoking in them a nostalgia for the streets of the old city that, only a decade or so earlier, had provoked their disgust. In this sense, many European observers who came to Egypt sought to recapture a past that no longer existed in Europe, one for which they had developed a distinct nostalgia.

In Cairo, Europeans found dark, winding streets that no longer existed in Paris. What did Cairo offer the European observer, photographer, architect, or traveler? Perhaps it was a glimpse of the ruined, of the old, without the pain of loss; a view where nostalgia for the medieval could be enjoyed without the sense of rupture and catastrophe that marked the European experience of Paris after Hausmann had finished his extravagant work. Thus, even as Paris changed, its changes affected the ways in which Cairo was perceived, represented, and ultimately altered. Nineteenth-century Cairo became the "natural" receptacle of the nostalgias and desires that were erased from Paris: the "medieval" other to a "modern" Paris. Applying a transnational methodology to the historical study of nineteenth-century Cairo, this book once again serves to remind us that what went on over "here" has in effect always been shaped by what happened over "there." We believe that the transnational approach, implicitly or explicitly embedded in the different chapters of this book, offers a new and different understanding of nineteenth-century Cairo.

NOTE

1. The initial members of the group included Nezar AlSayyad, Irene A. Bierman, Derek Gregory, Donald Preziosi, Nasser Rabbat, and Paula Sanders.

PART I

A MEDIEVAL CITY
FOR A MODERN WORLD

2

Disciplining the Eye: Perceiving Medieval Cairo

Irene A. Bierman

Let me begin with two photographs taken in the last five years in Cairo. Both were shot from high vantage positions. One shows Tahrir Square from the Nile Hilton Hotel (FIGURE 2.1). The other is the street leading north from Bab Zuwayla (FIGURE 2.2). Perhaps the two images look similar: each shows a cityscape of contemporary Cairo. The disciplined eye, however, perceives one as representing contemporary Cairo and the other as medieval Islamic Cairo.[1] How a section of Cairo came to be perceived as "medieval" and "Islamic" over the course of the last two decades of the nineteenth century and the first two decades of the twentieth is the subject of this chapter. The processes by which such a perceptual transformation took place involved a complex weaving of new disciplinary understandings and categorizations of buildings and objects, new conceptualizations of the city and its parts, and the uses of new kinds of evidence. Eventually, these processes helped train a specific group, what is termed here audiences and actors, to perceive a medieval and Islamic Cairo within the modern. In so doing, they disciplined the eye.

A NEW CULTURAL GEOGRAPHY

The primary physical place of medieval Islamic Cairo is indicated on the map, although architectural elements considered medieval and Islamic are located outside its borders (FIGURE 2.3). Of course, the perception that this area was medieval and Islamic had little to do with the sensibilities of its residents as they went about their daily, turn-of-the-century modern lives. It did, however, affect them. Many of them moved, or were moved, and businesses were closed and relocated.

Figure 2.1. Tahrir Square,
Cairo, Egypt
(Source: Author's collection)

**Figure 2.2. View north
from Bab Zuwayla,** Cairo,
Egypt
(Source: Author's collection)

To designate one area of the city as medieval and Islamic was to fabricate a
space and place that was at once spatial and temporal, as well as social and religious. And to fully accomplish this, other cultural sites in the city also needed to
be fabricated and contrasted to it. Thus, "old Cairo" (*misr adíma*) was delineated
south of "medieval Cairo," and modern Cairo was shown to surround it on three
sides. Meanwhile, antiquity, Pharaonic Cairo, was designated as extra-urban.

Modern Cairo was unaccented by religion. True, the shrine complexes of
Sayyida Nafisa, Sayyida Zainab, and Sayyida Aisha on its borders were expanded,
and one might even say given fresh prominence. But Isma'il Pasha's new urban
districts were designed without the presence of even one mosque. Display and
consumerism accented this "modern" Cairo, and some of the most expensive living quarters were located within its borders. By contrast, old Cairo as represented by the presence of churches and synagogues and the oldest mosque in Africa,
that of 'Amr ibn al-'As, was characterized as an area of religious diversity.

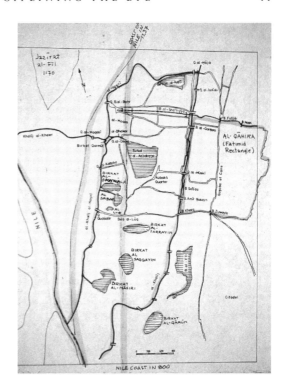

Figure 2.3. Schematic map of Cairo
(Source: Adapted by Carel Bertram)

This "myth of social place" provided an imaginary urban geography that upheld old Cairo as a symbol of a place of religious diversity. Meanwhile, Islamic Cairo was a place that belonged only to Muslims. Naturally, this myth ran contrary to the everyday life of Cairo itself, where all areas were cosmopolitan and diverse. In fact, quarters within "Islamic" Cairo had been named after their Jewish and Christian inhabitants, and were known as such well into the late nineteenth century (*harat al-yahud, harat al-nasara*).[2] Nevertheless, the activities during the forty years in focus here did in actuality produce an *Islamic* space in the practice of daily life in this section of Cairo, although not a medieval one.[3]

The production of this new cultural geography was bound up with the significant attitudes and perceptions that were part of the firm, yet shifting foundations of modernity. Its actors and audiences were one and the same: scholars and professionals from many of the newly founded or newly formulated disciplines of the eighteenth and nineteenth centuries, such as Egyptology, archaeology, geography, architecture, urban planning, and art history. Its actors and audiences also included writers, as well as statesmen and businessmen, especially those engaged in international business.[4] Painters, travelers, tourists, and photographers also numbered among them. But with rare exception, the actors and audiences of medieval Islamic Cairo lived outside that space, either within other areas of Cairo, or elsewhere in the world, but mainly in Europe and England, and in time, the United States.

Institutions of learning, especially major universities in England, Scotland, Germany, France, and Italy supported these processes of modern disciplinary classification and social ordering, inflecting these very processes with specific national character. France and England's national interests were particularly important; indeed, the special relationship of these two countries with Egypt was the larger space within which all these actions took place. Yet many of the textual discourses, visual conventions, and institutions that supported the concept of medieval Islamic Cairo, and made an Islamic Cairo tangible, transcended Egypt's colonial experience. Instead, they were part of the spatial, temporal, and social ordering of modernity itself, and as such were taken up by many nations that were neither colonized nor invaded.

As a result of these wider processes, the making of a medieval and Islamic Cairo ran parallel to similar actions taking place elsewhere.[5] Thus by 1900, the old, medieval parts of other cities had also been recognized and fabricated, e.g., in Paris, London, and even the Vieux Carre of New Orleans. But in Egypt, of course, a hegemonic order also did exist. Invaded by Napoleon in the closing years of the eighteenth century, Egypt was colonized by the British in the 1880s. For some of the practices instituted in Egypt, therefore, practices already at play in India and Algeria were as relevant as those in England and France—if indeed it is possible to separate these.[6]

TOOLS OF SEPARATION

French and English were the literary—that is, the written—languages used by these actors and audiences in delineating a medieval and Islamic Cairo. Of course, many of the participants were literate in several other languages, including Arabic; but it was French, and initially to a lesser degree English, in which this discourse of cultural geography emerged with all its conventions and hegemonic representations. English, of course, came to dominate publications about the city in the second half of the twentieth century. But French was originally the language of the documentary records detailing the architecture and the changes made to the actual city. French was also the language of the Institut d'Égypte.[7] And it was the language of the museum and exposition catalogues that explained the concepts represented in these peculiarly modern spaces.[8] In comparison, English, as Derek Gregory's work has indicated, was the language of the guidebooks clutched in the hands of most travelers as they set out on voyages to Egypt in time as well as space.[9]

If one primary tool for creating the time and space of medieval Islamic Cairo was language and its cultural conventions, the other significant tool was representations, both two- and three-dimensional. Representations were used as documentary evidence, and the uses of such evidence became part of new power relationships. Maps, line drawings, watercolors, oil paintings, photographs, panoramas, architectural drawings, ground plans and elevations, exhibitions in the World's Fairs, museum displays, and the museum-city itself all helped produce and make visible a medieval Islamic city that was to be critically viewed, discussed, and acclaimed by the actors and audiences of the French and English discourses.

Visual practices, of course, were bound up in language; technologies as well as use practices are always taught within cultural systems. In this regard, by the time of the French invasion of Egypt, academic practices for representing the ancient past were well developed, based in the École des Beaux-Arts and the French Academy in Rome. In a practice beginning in the seventeenth century, two sets of drawings (called *envois*) were required annually from those scholars in Rome receiving government stipends: an "actual-state drawing" of an antique building and an "ideal reconstruction." Different protocols pertained for these sets. One- or two-point perspectival drawings were used primarily for actual-state drawings, whereas two-dimensional sections and elevations were the mainstay of the ideal-state drawings.[10] A written description accompanied the reconstruction drawing.

In general, these separate protocols were also observed for representing Pharaonic Egypt in that first encyclopedic visual representation of Egypt, the *Description de l'Égypte*.[11] In Cairo, however, where no building was recognized as old enough to be antique, the two distinct drawing practices were blended. Unforeseen circumstances often caused such blending. Practices were also blended because most of the savants accompanying Napoleon had not been trained in the École des Beaux-Arts. Rather, they were graduates of the military engineering colleges founded on the eve of the expedition or reorganized to meet its needs. Nevertheless, the representations of Cairo they made for the *Description de l'Égypte* remained important sites/sights that were continually re-represented over the long nineteenth century, even as media and technology changed.

Visual images were used as documentary evidence only in French and English discourses about Cairo, however. During these same years 'Ali Pasha Mubarak was completing his major twenty-volume urban history of Cairo, *al-khitat al-tawfiqiyya al-jadida* without the use of any visual evidence.[12] Mubarak's Cairo was filled with buildings and streets where social interaction took place, where collective memory was at work, and in which the actions of people existed in words.[13] His text, as the title suggests, was also written in the venerable Egyptian scholarly tradition of urban history, and it brought up to date the study of Cairo begun by al-Maqrizi. In the study of *khitat*, it is important to note, some places are more richly layered than others, but no medieval or Islamic places existed separate from other areas.[14]

Visual evidence also was interpreted differently, at least initially, in French and in English discourses. Writers in French initially understood visual culture as evidence of ethnicity. Thus, buildings were indicators of Arab style, since Cairo was an Arab city.[15] Meanwhile, writers in English—and at this time the authors were mainly British—understood visual forms as expressive of the religion of the builders/users, and so the buildings were "Muhammadan."[16] These categories were not only used in Egypt to define the built environment; they were also used in French discourse about buildings in Algeria, and the category "Muhammadan" came to be applied in Egypt after its appearance in English discourse in India. After World War I, however, the term Islamic came to predominate. Until then, in Egypt, in architectural discourse (even in the languages of the minorities), "Arab" was the preferred term.[17]

ORIGINS OF THE MEDIEVAL

This inquiry about perception also requires an understanding of the term "medieval." If "medieval" is a temporal space fixed in an imagined geography, we need to ask when and where this temporal situation was perceived, and how it was represented in relation to Cairo. The image of the mosque of al-Hakim from the *Description de l'Égypte* provides a starting point for this inquiry (FIGURE 2.4). When this image and images of other buildings in Cairo were published in the *Description de l'Égypte* they represented sights/sites in what that text categorized as *modern, Arab Cairo*.[18] Understanding these buildings as part of the modern city in which they existed—although the functions of some buildings were different from the original—resonated with an understanding of urban history found in the texts of contemporary Egyptian authors writing in Arabic.

By 1867 and the Exposition Universelle in Paris, however, representations of Cairo's buildings were displayed in the Egyptian exhibit as indexical of the medieval period. The exhibit itself was divided according to a tripartite chronology: Antiquity, the Middle Ages, and Modern. Cairo's buildings were also termed Arab and Mohammadan, which indicates the processes of change in the perception of visual evidence from ethnic to sectarian that was underway at somewhat past mid-century. In the exhibit as a whole, one major building set within a series of domestic facades represented each of these ages, and was aligned along the "Street of Cairo," as the exhibit was called. This kind of three-dimensional arrangement was not peculiar to the Egyptian exhibit; it was followed, albeit on a much grander scale, for the street of medieval Paris, and for the installations of Vienna and several other cities.[19] These were after all stage settings through which visitors could wander, much as one can wander today through the national areas of Disney's EPCOT Center, a descendant showplace.

Several elements are important to note here. First, the medieval period was recognized and represented in the Exposition as a stage in both the national and

Figure 2.4. Mosque of al-Hakim
(Source: Description de l'Égypte, *1st edition)*

urban development of France and Paris—as well as for Egypt and Cairo, and for other nations and cities. Indeed, in mid-nineteenth-century France the concept of the medieval was only just coalescing as an architectural period between antiquity and modernity. Viollet-le-Duc, in particular, in his writings and practice, had sought to establish Gothic as the style native to France. It was therefore "medieval"—that is, located between antiquity and the appearance of "foreign" forms from outside France during the Renaissance. The Gothic style, its proportions and architectural elements, were maintained in architectural discourse in French as hegemonic exemplars—and the effects of this domination will be apparent below.[20] In England, of course, the paradigms for defining the medieval were different, and evoked sectarian discussions not relevant in France. They were, however, certainly relevant to those who imagined the medieval from such texts which disciplined their eyes to perceive sectarian forms in architectural expression.

In addition to recognizing the medieval as a historical moment important to both national and urban history, a second factor to keep in mind about the Exposition was that its exhibits were conceived in part to make money by selling concepts as well as souvenirs. Thus, the spaces of medieval Paris and medieval Cairo also offered entertainment to visitors: one could see jousting and the hanging of a miscreant in medieval Paris; and in medieval Cairo a procession on camels and a beheading were performed several times daily. Beyond formal differences in styles of architecture and differences in characteristic events, however, representations of "real" Egyptians were also displayed in the Cairo exhibit, whereas such displays were lacking in that of medieval Paris.

In the display of medieval Paris, workers dressed in medieval fashion mingled with the visitors dressed in contemporary clothing. Modern Paris, of course, was not within the Exposition, but outside it in the real city, and so the contemporary Parisian in modern dress was there for all to see. In the Egyptian display, however, workers in *gallabayas* and turbans moved back and forth in time from antique to modern Egypt. This spatial and temporal access to all periods of Egypt's history, which were not available to their French "medieval" cohorts, presented the *gallabaya* as a timeless Egyptian dress rather than an indicator of class and or a signifier of difference between the rural and urban. Needless to say, when the Egyptian ruler appeared in Paris for the Exposition in contemporary sartorial splendor, the public was sadly disappointed, perhaps even offended, that he would "copy" modern dress.[21] This presentation was in fact underscored by the official book on the exhibit sponsored by the Egyptian government, which highlighted the continuity and unchanging quality of the Egyptian people throughout history.

Outside the realm of the Exposition this attitude that the real Egyptian wore a *gallabaya* and was unchanging and homogeneous was supported by the very popular book *Manners and Customs of the Modern Egyptians* by Edward William Lane, first published in 1835, with continuing editions until the last decade of the twentieth century.[22] This popular text, with its often reused images, was the last major work of a genre of literature that first became popular at the beginning of the eighteenth century. The genre, as the title suggests, undertook to describe the manners and customs of numerous groups, from North Americans to (and perhaps most especially) rural residents in Europe, who were studied in a search for authentic roots by their educated urban relatives. Lane's book on the modern Egyptians, without serious regard to differences between social groups, affected scholarship and popular thought longer than any other of its genre.

Another salient aspect to keep in mind about this display at the Exposition Universelle was that it was official. Nubar Pasha, President of the Egyptian Council of Ministries, led the Egyptian commission for the Exposition, and it was managed by two Egyptians, Raphael Levy and Isaac Ben-Yacar.[23] In addition, Isma'il Pasha chose the authors for the official texts, Charles Edmond and Auguste Mariette. These texts, of course, were in French, and available as souvenirs in Paris and by gift from the ministers of state in deluxe editions. Edmond's book in particular underscored this final salient point—a point with a double-face.[24] On the one hand, the book characterized the display; and on the other, it underscored its imagined or representational qualities. And, interestingly in this regard, Edmond gave little space in his text to medieval Egypt; instead, he preferred the Antique and Modern periods. Indeed, he characterized the few buildings at the Exposition that represented the medieval period as "Arab and Mohammadan." And, importantly, these medieval, Arab, Mohammadan buildings were portrayed as "lacking a true architectural system and displaying disconnected elements."

Here in the official Egyptian government text is one effect of the hegemonic Gothic model in architecture. The few undistinguished "medieval," "Arab," "Mohammadan" buildings represented at the Exposition served as a synecdoche not for that period of Egypt's past but rather as a representation of its power relations as expressed through time and space—Gothic (unspoken Catholic) Paris in juxtaposition to medieval, Muhammadan Cairo. In reality, of course, in the middle centuries, Cairo had been known as the *umm al-dunya*, "the center of the world," because of its numerous endowed institutions that served as testimony to the endeavors of dynasties, and great (and generous) men and women.

THE CITY AS ARTIFACT

In addition to representations of the medieval at the World's Fairs, the medieval was represented within cities across the globe through the process of restoration of buildings identified as medieval monuments, especially those that served, or had served, a religious purpose. In many places these buildings were simply the ones that remained, because they were often originally built of sturdier and finer materials than those serving other purposes. In this process, such buildings often became monuments of the nation's past—what today are called *les lieux de memoire*, as studied for France in the pioneering edited work by Pierre Nora, and the more recent critical study by Francoise Choay.[25] And in the years examined here, the process by which the time and space of medieval Cairo were restored were bound up with the creation of the Comité de Conservation des Monuments de l'Art Arabe (the Comité), with the creation of museums, and with the World's Columbian Exposition in Chicago in 1893. And here I move from representations and their perception, to Cairo *dans le vrai*.

Discussion of a few broad issues regarding the restoration process in Cairo during these years will serve to highlight important elements in the fabrication of the space and place of medieval Islamic Cairo. The ideas about restoration developed in France by Viollet-le-Duc were directly influential in Egypt precisely because they informed the deliberations of the Comité. It had been established in 1881, and was composed of Egyptians and foreign nationals, mainly French, Italian, and later British, both professionals (most of whom were architects) and professional amateurs. The composition of the Comité and the influences on it did, of course, change over time. But initially, Viollet-le-Duc's theories were readily appropriatible by it, since its deliberations were in French, and were subsequently recorded in French. Only abstracts, or redactions of sessions, were recorded in Arabic.

Among other things, Viollet-le-Duc argued that only in the second quarter of the nineteenth century did "restoration" as a science come into being. Before that time it was appropriate to speak of buildings being renovated, rebuilt, or maintained. But restoration was for him a modern term that referred to a process "to reestablish [a building] in a complete condition that may never have existed." The "condition" of the building was important, and was arrived at by understanding its time and place within broad classifications that established a sense of origin and development according to basic materials (wood, stone, earth), and by a developmental style, as closely related to racial and linguistic classifications. Restoration, therefore, called for a building to be restored to a formal and material state based on stylistic classification and a comparison with the development of styles for its region and group—a comparison that included other regions and groups. France, naturally, was the base.

In the deliberations of the Comité this classification system brought to focus the need to establish "pure" styles by dynastic period—Tulunid, Fatimid, Mamluk—as comprising the period known as medieval, Arab, and Mohammadan. The deliberations of the Comité that took place concerning the restoration of the mosque of al-Salih Tala'i (1160) were emblematic of the process. To its credit, the Comité left copious photographic documentation of its work. The photograph of what remained of the mosque, basically a part of the western facade wall, when the living city was cleared away provides a starting point (FIGURE 2.5). Every stone of what remained was disassembled, numbered, and the formal articulations of the wall and its front portico were "restored" according to the process described above. Practicing that process required that the remaining jagged edge of the mosque be supplemented by comparing it to a facade of the al-Aqmar mosque, built earlier (1125), and that of the al-Salihiyya *madrassa* built later (FIGURES 2.6 & 2.7). The result is the mosque of today, which is minus the Ottoman-style minaret that had existed when the mosque was exposed, but which was torn down because it did not represent pure Fatimid style (969–1171) (FIGURE 2.8).

The discussions over the minaret, and what constituted a "pure" Fatimid-style minaret when no extant Fatimid-period minarets or parts thereof were similar in style, posed a serious question for the Comité. The discussions were heated and raged so long that world events—this time World War II—eventually intervened. No minaret surmounts the mosque today.

The effects of this mode of restoration on buildings of the Mamluk period (1250–1517) were even more apparent than on the buildings of earlier periods.

Figure 2.5. Comité photograph of the mosque of al-Salih Tala'i
(Source: Courtesy of the K.A.C. Creswell archives)

Not only were there more Mamluk buildings in the city, but the architectural forms and elements crafted for the restoration process fueled the creation of a popular neo-Mamluk style in domestic and government architecture. The task of establishing a pure Mamluk style, however, created a look that was more formally regimented than that which probably existed. In particular, banisters, awnings, railings, windows, and entrance staircases were standardized and prefabricated. Today, the apparent sameness of these architectural features may seem well founded, and is often attributed to the military quality of the Mamluk regime. But in fact it emerged from the nineteenth-century process of making the city medieval.

The establishment of a pure, medieval, Arab and Mohammadan architecture was aided in Egypt by the establishment of museums, and those aspects of museum-building that elaborated the space of medieval Cairo also need to be closely investigated. The Comité first established a Museum of Arab Art in the mosque of al-Hakim, but it then moved all the architectural elements and other objects that came to light in its restoration efforts to a newly constructed building intended for that purpose.[26] Lectures were offered to tourists (for a fee) in the museums at both sites—in French and in English—and these were advertised in the tourist hotels. But the publications of the museum existed only in French. Among other things, the establishment of this new museum meant that objects and architectural elements previously identified as "Arab" needed to be moved from the Egyptian Museum. And when the Coptic Museum was established, a new re-

Figure 2.6 (above). Facade of al-Aqmar mosque
(Source: Author's collection)
Figure 2.7 (right). Facade of al-Salihiyya madrassa
(Source: Author's collection)

sorting of objects had to be made.[27]   However, this second-order distinction between Copt and Arab, when both groups had a medieval past, made it necessary to refine distinctions between objects that were formally similar. Thus, for example, carved wooden doors and architectural panels from eleventh- and twelfth-century Cairo needed to be identified and catalogued as either Coptic or Arab and placed in the appropriate museum. (The term "Islamic" as related to the museum and its contents comes after the period focused on here.)[28]

Figure 2.8. Mosque of al-Salih Tala'i
(Source: Author's collection)

The display of the medieval past in a museum did more than classify objects by religion or ethnicity; the process of display also reinforced the purification of styles begun in the restoration process. Less pure examples of architectural elements and objects were sold in museum shops (and in jewelry shops), leaving for display only those that conformed to the stylistic range established for the given period. Thus, the medieval world, as conceived and displayed in the museums and its publications, and in the museum city, was much more homogeneous than had been the lived experience of the actual medieval world.

"MEDIEVAL" CAIRO

The Comité also set about to create a primary physical place in Cairo that had margins, a liminal space that could at once be medieval, Arab, and Mohammadan to one audience, and modern to a larger, local audience. Many aspects of the tourist industry—guidebooks, maps, and tourists themselves—were also primary actors and audiences in this space, along with members of the Comité. However, I will focus in this final section on aspects of creating the actual physical space of medieval Mohammadan Cairo, and the role that the Street of Cairo exhibit in the World's Columbian Exposition had in this fabrication.

Extensive work was undertaken to establish the boundary walls of the living museum of the medieval city. The Comité worked especially hard to establish and highlight visually the southern limits of this area. In so doing, it linked the medieval city directly with the new Arab Museum. The walls of the southern gate, Bab Zuwayla, originally built in the Fatimid period, were revealed in a multifaceted program of restoration. The first step here was to move the *zawíya* of Farag ibn Barquq, which had been built less than a meter from the western flank wall of Bab Zuwayla.

This structure was disassembled and moved back some thirty meters to its present position where it is aligned with a new road. Moving the *zawiya* disconnected its *sabil* (fountain) from its infrastructure so that it could no longer serve as a water source for nearby residents. But it also opened up the area in front of Bab Zuwayla so it could serve as a *maydan* connected directly with the new city, and a place for tourists to transit between where they lived and where they visited. Because the modern road did not overlay the medieval one, however, its construction involved negotiations with the Armenian community, one of whose major churches and earliest cemeteries occupied some land through which the new road was to be routed. The restored mosque of al-Salih Tala'i bordered the *maydan* on the opposite side.[29]

Within the adjacent medieval Islamic city, walls, facades, domes, and minarets were also all restored along a north-south spine. The Comité was able to clear the facades of the western side of the street of their shops and businesses. However, on the eastern side, only the facade of al-Aqmar mosque and the mausoleum of al-Salihiyya were cleared. And despite the intense work of the Comité, shops remain in front of the al-Salihiyya *madrassa* even today. But the Comité was able to rid this area of the city of its striped painting on buildings, a practice many scholars believe began in the early sixteenth century with the advent of Ottoman rule. The despised *badigonne* of Comité reports referred to the painted alternating striping that appeared on the old buildings throughout the city, e.g., on the complex of al-Qala'un in the accompanying photograph (FIGURE 2.9). Nevertheless, despite the work of the Comité, striped, painted buildings were the acceptable symbol of the buildings of medieval Cairo in world exhibitions well into the twentieth century.

As the Comité worked for authenticity along medieval Cairo's central spine, the organizers of the Columbian Exposition worked for authenticity in Chicago. Four plans for the street of Cairo were offered to the Exposition committee including one from the managers (Raphael Levy and Isaac Ben-Yacar) of the earlier Paris display. Eventually, however, the fair's committee awarded the concession to build the exhibit to Mr. Pangalo of Cairo and Henry I. Cobb of Chicago. Max Hertz drew the sketches and used his position in Cairo to enable a level of authenticity not attained in the representation of the medieval city in the Paris Exposition.[30]

The official photograph of the Street in Cairo from the Chicago Exposition shows the *sabil-kuttab* of 'Abd al-Rahman Katkhuda (1744) (FIGURE 2.10). Pangalo and Hertz promised the fair's committee an authentic street. And, while the committee members of the Columbian Exposition were more interested in real people, and processions and markets, more to the point here is the fact that Pangalo and Hertz supplied "authentic" windows, metal gratings, and some of the tile work for the *sabil-kuttab* in the Chicago Exposition by removing them from that building and others in Cairo. The audience intended to appreciate the authenticity of these buildings was international and it could have done so in Cairo. It is thus ironic that authenticity required relocating these elements halfway around the world.

Figure 2.9. Facade of the Sultan al-Qala'un complex
(Source: Undated photograph)

Figure 2.10. "Street in Cairo," Chicago Exposition of 1867
(Source: Herald, 1891)

This authentic street in Chicago shaped the actual street in Cairo in other visible ways. Note the uniform size of the *mashrabiyya* windows on the buildings in the "Street of Cairo" at the Columbian Exposition. Compare this with any early drawing or photograph of the facades of buildings displaying *mashrabiyya* windows in nineteenth-century Cairo. In the nineteenth century, and presumably before, windows in the same building were irregular in size, and *mashrabiyya* patterns varied too. Thus, after the Columbian Exposition, restorers of the Comité brought back to medieval, Islamic Cairo the mistaken reality of a street facade in which window sizes and patterns were uniform.

The Chicago Columbian Exposition offered the world more than a simple visual spectacle. The Exposition publications disciplined the eye. They, like other texts before them, trained the eye to perceive in installations what was not there. Newspaper accounts tell us that people experienced the "narrowness of Cairo's medieval Arab streets," when, in fact, all the streets of all the national installations at the Columbian Exposition were the same width. How easy it is to discipline the eye, and how complex the means by which some of us are able to see medieval Cairo in one image, and contemporary Cairo in another (REFER TO FIGURES 2.1 & 2.2).

NOTES

1. Within the last ten years this area has come to be called Historic Cairo.

2. Initially called Mohammadan Cairo, the term used here, Islamic, only became dominant in about 1910.

3. As a result of the whole process of which this essay is an overview, minority communities moved. The restoration/conservation processes as a whole conserved only the buildings used for Muslim communal practices. Buildings of minority communities such as churches and synagogues, schools and orphanages were not part of the program.

4. The sources for this period are copious. See especially T. Mitchell, *Colonising Egypt* (Berkeley: University of California Press, 1991); K. Fahmy, *All the Pasha's Men: Mehmed Ali, His Army and the Making of Modern Egypt* (Cambridge: Cambridge University Press, 1997); A. Marsot, *Egypt in the Reign of Muhammad Ali* (Cambridge: Cambridge University Press, 1984); A. Goldschmidt, *Biographical Dictionary of Modern Egypt* (Boulder, Colorado: Lynne Rienner, 2000); and D. Reid, *Whose Pharoahs?* (Berkeley: University of California Press, 2002).

5. Studies on countries in the Middle East that were colonized include Z. Celik, *Urban Forms and Colonial Confrontations* (Berkeley: University of California Press, 1998); R. Benjamin, *Orientalist Aesthetics: Art, Colonialism and French North Africa 1880–1930* (Berkeley: University of California Press, 2003); N. Abu El-Haj, *Facts on the Ground: Archaeological Practice and Territorial Self-Fashioning in Israeli Society* (Chicago: University of Chicago Press, 2001); and D. Prochaska, *Making Algeria French: Colonialism in Bône 1870–1920* (Cambridge: Cambridge University Press, 1990). Turkey stands as the example of a territory not col-

onized.   Studies include S. Bozdogan, *Modernism and Nation Building: Turkish Architectural Culture in the Early Republic* (Seattle: University of Washington Press, 2001); Z. Celik, *The Remaking of Istanbul* (Seattle: University of Washington Press, 1986); W. Shaw, *Possessors and Possessed Museums, Archaeology, and the Visualization of History in the Late Ottoman Empire* (Berkeley: University of California Press, 2003); and F. Choay, *The Invention of the Historic Monument*, trans. by Lauren M. O'Connell (Cambridge: Cambridge University Press, 2001).

6. M. Pelizzari, ed., *Traces of India: Photography, Architecture, and the Politics of Representation 1850–1900* (New Haven: Yale Center for British Art, 2003). The various contributors to this book discuss British practices in India, providing the bases from which we can understand the replication of these practices in Egypt.

7. This institute was created in Cairo and was patterned after the Institute de France. A new publication of its proceedings has been issued. J. Goby, *Premier Institute d'Égypte. Restitution des comptes rendus des séances, Institut de France, Memories de l'Academie, nouvelle serie*, tome VII (Paris: Boccard, 1987).

8. For example, M. Herz, *Catalogue raisonne des monuments exposes dans le Musee national de l'art arabe, precede d'un apercu de l'histoire de l'architecture et des arts industriels en Égypte* (Cairo: Imprimerie de l'Institut Français d'Archéologie Orientale, 1906); G. Wiet, *Catalogue generale du Musee arabe du Caire; lampes et bouteilles en verre emaille* (Cairo: Imprimerie de l'Institut français d'archéologie orientale, 1929); and G. Wiet, *Album du Musee du Caire* (Cairo: Imprimerie de l'Institut français d'archéologie orientale, 1930).

9. D. Gregory, "Scripting Egypt: Orientalism and the Cultures of Travel," in J. Duncan and D. Gregory, eds., *Writes of Passage: Reading Travel Writing* (New York: Routledge, 1999). Interesting statistics about tourists can be found in the appendix tables of Reid, *Whose Pharoahs?*

10. R. Chafee, "The Teaching of Architecture at the École des Beaux-Arts," in A. Drexler, ed., *The Architecture of the École des Beaux-Arts* (New York: Museum of Modern Art, 1977), p. 63; L. Hart, "Exploiting the Classical Past: Student Restoration Drawings from the French and American Academies in Rome," *Architronic*, Vol.2, No.3; and B. Smith, *European Vision and the South Pacific* (New Haven: Yale University Press, 1986). Smith argues that the training of the artist and of the draughtsman influenced each other in such circumstances.

11. Published in 22 volumes, (Paris: Imprimerie Imperiale 1809–28). There was also a second edition of 26 volumes (Paris: C.L.F. Panckouke, 1821–30).

12. A. Mubarak, *al-Khitat al-Tawfiqiyya al-Jadida*, 20 vols. (Cairo: Bulaq Press, 1888–89). Of course, of all Egypt's cities, only Cairo is considered modern. Alexandria, for example, is seen as part of Antiquity.

13. This metaphor is used fruitfully in C. Boyer, *The City of Collective Memory* (Cambridge, Mass.: MIT Press 1996), pp. 204–91.

14. 'Ali Pasha Mubarak was trained in France and wrote engineering papers. projects. In these he did use images.

15. For example, P. d'Avennes, *L'Art Arabe d'apres les Monuments du kaire depuis le Viie siecle jusqu'à la fin du XVIIIe*, 3 vols. (Paris: J. Savoy & cie., 1877). Reprinted and translated in English as *Arab Art as seen through the Monuments of Cairo from the 7th century to the 18th* (London:

Al Saqi Books, 1983). In their North African colonies, the French academic discourses distinguished between Arab and Berber art and architecture. In Algeria, to link Arab architecture to Europe rather than to the rest of the "Arab" world, the French recategorized such buildings calling them "Moorish." See N. Oulebsir, *Les Usages du patrimoine, monuments, musees et politique coloniale en Algerie (1830–1930)* (Paris: Maison des Sciences de l'Homme 2002).

16. This terminology began in the historical and art historical writing about buildings in India. In specific, see J. Fergusson, *The Illustrated Handbook of Architecture* (London: J. Murray, 1855). In this and his many other works that published and categorized buildings in India, religion was a basic categorization.

17. In discussing the styles for the building of Heliopolis, for example, Garo Balian, a prominent Armenian architect in Cairo, wrote about the properties of Arab style in his *Egypt and Arab Architecture* (Cairo: n.p., 1916). Personal communication from N. Hampikian.

18. The *Description* was not the first study of Cairo by a European that had used maps and illustrations. J.B. d'Anville, *Memoire sur l'égypte anciennne et moderne* (Paris: n.p., 1766). This historical geography, however, was produced without d'Anville ever leaving Paris. He produced the maps and depictions as well as the written commentary as a result of meticulous research in written texts. He mined these written sources that were separated by decades, even centuries, to depict an almost timeless past.

19. For a comparison of the displays of Egypt and the Ottoman Empire see Z. Celik, *Displaying the Orient* (Berkeley: University of California Press, 1992).

20. E. Viollet-le-Duc, *Dictionnaire raisonne de l'architecture francaise du XIe au XVIe siecle* (Paris: Morel, 1868). His ideas were well known and part of an international discourse involving Ruskin and others, all of whom had varying opinions. What is at issue is how important Viollet-le-Duc's ideas were for Cairo, at least in the initial years.

21. Celik, *Displaying the Orient*, pp. 32–35.

22. Its first publication was in 1836, and the fifth revised edition, called the "definitive" edition by Jason Thompson, was reproduced by him in full in 2000 by American University in Cairo Press. E. W. Lane, *Description of Egypt*, edited by Jason Thompson, (Cairo: American University in Cairo Press, 2000).

23. "All to begin: Egypt will be here," *Daily News*, May 23, 1881.

24. Auguste Mariette, *Description du parc Egyptian: L'Égypte a l'Exposition universelle de 1867* (Paris: n.p., 1867).

25. P. Nora, *Realms of Memory: The Construction of the French Past, Vol. 1, Conflicts and Divisions* (New York: Columbia University Press, 1996); J. Le Goff and P. Nora, eds., *Faire de l'histoire*, Vol. II (Paris: Gallimard, 1974); and Choay, *The Invention of the Historic Monument*.

26. Khedive 'Abbas opened this building on December 28, 1903.

27. Although Max Herz first mentioned this to the Comité in 1897 (see *Exercise* for that year), it really didn't come into being until around 1910–12.

28. Objects from ethnic or religious groups not represented by a museum—such as the Armenian or Jewish communities—are occasionally found in the Arab museum.

29. Comité de Conservation des Monuments de l'Art Arabe, *Exercise*. The process of these meetings took place over many years, and the discussions and decisions are documented. These discussions are well indexed. Plans, both executed and non-executed, are harder to come by, but can be found in various records. A general overview of the process can be found in A. El-Habashi and N. Warner, "Recording the Monuments of Cairo: An Introduction and Overview," *Annales islamologiques* 32 (1998), pp. 81–99.

30. "Egypt's Exhibit at the Fair," *Herald*, February 8, 1891; "Cairo at the Big Fair," August 19, 1891; *Herald*, August 22, 1891; and almost daily thereafter.

3

The Medieval Link: Maqrizi's *Khitat* and Modern Narratives of Cairo

Nasser Rabbat

A certain aura of cosmocentricity has pervaded most writing on the history of Egypt since long before the advent of nationalism as we know it, with its passionate and largely imaginary construction of a particular heritage for a specific people in a circumscribed land. From as early as Pharaonic times, Egyptians are believed to have possessed a conception of their homeland that has emphasized its distinct character, its single source of wealth (the Nile), and fixed natural boundaries formed by deserts to the east and west, obstructive cataracts in the Nile to the south, and the Mediterranean to the north. So solid was this notion that it outlasted the ancient Egyptian kingdom, and lived on even when Egypt became part of larger empires with their cultural and political centers elsewhere. It is even seen as permeating the religious and artistic expressions and outlook of the most culturally distinct of Egypt's invaders, such as the Macedonian Ptolemies and Romans, after they had been in Egypt for some time. And it later attached itself to Christianity when the new religion crossed into Egypt from Palestine in the second century C.E. to produce the Coptic Church, with its particular rites and ceremonies that go back to the deepest Ancient Egyptian roots.

This particularist Egyptian cultural tendency was, of course, dampened after the seventh century C.E. by the universalist message of Islam, the coming of Arabs as the new masters of the country, and the emergence of Arabic as the language of the southern and eastern Mediterranean. But it never died out. It stayed near the surface throughout the first three centuries Hegira to burst out again in medieval times as a result of a number of historical and geopolitical developments. Chief among them were the establishment of the Fatimid Caliphate, which created in Egypt a new state independent of Abbasid Baghdad, and, later, the founding of the Mamluk military empire, with its center firmly entrenched in Cairo and its boundaries extending to the Upper Euphrates, Anatolia, and Hijaz.[1]

THE *KHITAT* GENRE AND THE WORK OF AL-MAQRIZI

Nowhere has the sense of particularity been more clearly expressed in the literary sources than in the historical genre of *khitat*. *Khitat* (sg. *khitta*), also the traditional Arabic name for the planned urban quarter, especially in the early Islamic period, designates books which we would today call topographical/historical studies of cities.[2] They traditionally reported on a city's monuments, neighborhoods, and streets—in short, its architecture and urban history. Within this framework, buildings appear mostly as landmarks examined in their urban contexts, with their patrons, cost, circumstances of construction, and historical significance weighed. *Khitat* books were a peculiar offshoot of the more literal *kutub al-mudun* (books of cities), which appeared in the late ninth and early tenth centuries, at a time when various Islamic capitals such as Baghdad, Wasit, Isfahan, Damascus, and Fustat had accumulated a long civic history and developed their own identities and pride of place.

Although the use of the term *khitat* in an urban context was not restricted to Egypt, the *khitat* literary genre was almost exclusively Egyptian. Indeed, during medieval times, examples of *khitat* elsewhere were so few and far between that they never constituted a noticeable literary tradition outside Egypt. And although a few *khitat* compendia did appear in other Arabic countries in the twentieth century, probably under the influence of the Egyptian revival of the genre in the nineteenth century, they were isolated efforts that may better be understood as providing a transition between the medieval *kutub al-mudun* and the modern geographical treatises.[3] Only in Egypt did the titles of a whole series of books, spanning the entire medieval period from the tenth to the end of the fifteenth century and beyond, carry the term *khitat* and deal with topographical, historical, and urban issues. Some of these treated the whole country. Most, however, concentrated on one city: first, al-Fustat, the economic capital well into the thirteenth century; then al-Qahira (Cairo), two miles to the north of al-Fustat, and royal capital of the Fatimids before the two cities were joined under Salah al-Din al-Ayyubi in the late twelfth century.[4]

The *khitat* genre reached its zenith in the middle of the fifteenth century with the appearance of Taqiyy al-Din al-Maqrizi's outstanding *al Mawa'iz wa-l-I'tibar bi-Dhikr al-Khitat wa-l-Athar*, which offers the most elaborate and spirited testimony we have of Cairo's urban history.[5] Compiled over a quarter century (between 1417 and 1439/40, two years before its author's death), this encyclopedic work describes with loving care each and every street and important structure in Cairo (and to a lesser degree other Egyptian cities) and records the known history of everything connected with them.[6] It also expands the scope and reworks the method, underlying conception, and aim of the *khitat* genre itself. In fact, it could fairly be said that the entire scholarly construction of a discernible special genre of *khitat* in Arabic literature rests solely on this one work. Despite many imitators in the late medieval period, no comparable study of Cairo in Arabic was to be undertaken until the late nineteenth century, when a national Egyptian school of history arose.[7]

Al-Maqrizi's *khitat* had lofty pedagogical goals, albeit ones that are conceived and articulated from within the epistemological framework of a medieval Muslim scholar. Its text is annalistic in scope, morally critical in tone, and inherently teleological in its conclusions. Its style is literary and legalistic, reflecting the educational and professional background of its author. The book opens with a geographical survey of Egypt. It then turns to a summary of Egypt's pre-Islamic history. The urban history section begins with a succinct review of the major Egyptian cities, with only two cities receiving more than a cursory treatment—Alexandria and al-Fayyum. Al-Maqrizi then quickly moves to Cairo, first reviewing the site's ancient history, and then examining the first appearance of a city, al-Fustat, on the site of the ancient Roman fort of Babylon, and its growth and ruin. Next, he analyzes the founding of al-Qahira as the center of the self-consciously religious Fatimid Caliphate in the tenth-eleventh century. And he then spends the entire second half of the first volume describing the many spectacular structures and the order and decorum the Fatimids established in Cairo, and in Egypt in general.

The book's second volume is taken up by an extensive typological survey of Cairo as the capital of the Mamluk state in the thirteenth, fourteenth, and early-fifteenth centuries—by which time al-Maqrizi was mainly recording his own observations and impressions. The city's quarters, streets, squares, famous mansions, *hammams*, *khans*, *rab's* (apartment buildings), markets, *hukrs* (urban zones), bridges, ponds, hippodromes, citadels, mosques, madrasas, hospitals, *khanqahs*, shrines, and *zawiyas*, cemeteries and mausolea, and synagogues and churches are arranged in this order, and are each recorded, dated, and described. Woven into this typological narrative are biographical notices on the Ayyubid and Mamluk sultans and other patrons of the city's monuments, in addition to copious entries on its wonders and religious merits, the ceremonies observed by its various religious groups, and the sectarian history of Islam.

THE INTELLECTUAL CONTOURS OF AL-MAQRIZI'S *KHITAT*

In his introduction, al-Maqrizi explicitly divulges the impulse that led him to write his book. Like his predecessors, he explains how he was drawn to the topic because of his filial attachment to his country, his city, and even his neighborhood—Harat al-Burjuwan, a venerable *hara* in the heart of Fatimid al-Qahira. But al-Maqrizi is more emphatic about his feelings than any of his predecessors, and even many of his successors. To him, Cairo is "the place of my birth, the playground of my mates, the nexus of my society and clan, the home to my family and public, the bosom where I acquired my wings, and the niche I seek and yearn to."[8] Similar pronouncements are dispersed throughout the book in rhyming passages and revealing anecdotes. They are so ardent and so surprising for his time that they pose a challenge to the conventional opinion that full-fledged patriotic feelings would have to wait a couple of centuries and a few major revolutions to truly find their expressions in literature.

Al-Maqrizi also asserts that he has set out to record and describe the streets and monuments of Cairo before their imminent destruction, which he pessimistically anticipates, and which he bitterly blames on the neglect, rapacity, and corruption of the Mamluk rulers of his time.[9] His anxiety, melancholy, and moral indignation at the Mamluks may have contributed to the book's melancholic tone and its meticulous attention to architectural, topographic, and historical details which would normally have gone unnoticed. A heightened sense of loss imbues him with an urgent desire to capture cherished memories—both his own and those of the denizens of Cairo—before they slip away with the disappearance of the places and buildings to which they are attached. He is, in fact, trying to create through his words what Pierre Nora has termed a *lieu de mémoire* ("realm of memory"), because his Cairo, under attack from urban decay, recurrent plagues, and Mamluk greed, is threatened with no longer being the *milieu de mémoire* (environment of memory).[10]

Another influence on al-Maqrizi's method and scope was the sociohistorical theory of his revered teacher, the great Ibn Khaldun. The overarching cycle of the rise and fall of dynasties that formed the basis of Ibn Khaldun's hermeneutical framework for explaining historical processes seems to have informed al-Maqrizi's thinking and the structuring of his *khitat*, albeit in a roundabout way.[11] In particular, he seems to have subsumed the Khaldunian structure as a way of molding the vast amount of historical, topographic, and architectural material he had collected over the years into a general discourse on the urban and architectural history of Cairo.[12] To that end, he seems to have devised an analogous cycle of prosperity and urban expansion followed by decay and urban contraction to frame his exposition of the fate of Cairo under its successive ruling dynasties. The political fortune of each dynasty or family is plotted against the fluctuations of the urban and architectural prosperity of Cairo during the same time in a way that echoes the cyclical Khaldunian view of human history.[13]

The narrative culminates in the depiction of the irrevocable ruin of the city and the country under al-Maqrizi's contemporary sultans, especially the ill-fated Faraj ibn Barquq (1399–1412, with a short interruption), al-Mu'ayyad Shaykh, and al-Ashraf Barsbay, who is repeatedly blamed for the sorry state of the city and the sultanate.[14] To al-Maqrizi, the Mamluks of his age were no longer the deserving leaders their Bahri predecessors had once been, skillfully and thoughtfully managing a great empire and fighting for the cause of Islam. His deep chagrin translated into breaking all measures of caution and consideration in reporting their failings,

especially after he withdrew from public life around 1413 in despair of ever recon-
ciling his moral indignation with his professional ambitions. From that date on, he
unleashed his unmitigated antagonism towards the Mamluks to the point that—as
noted by Ibn Taghri-Birdi—he left no room for reconciliation or rapprochement.[15]
In a passage that best illustrates his understanding of the importance of the
Khaldunian notion of 'asabíyya (solidarity) in maintaining political power and social
stability, he analyzes the degradation of the Mamluk recruiting system in the Burji
period and connects it to the general decline of the sultanate. He concludes these
observations by dubbing his contemporary Mamluks "more lustful than monkeys,
more ravenous than rats, and more harmful than wolves."[16]

In the Khitat's plotting of the recursive fluctuations of Cairo's size and prosperity, architecture plays a crucial role. It represents the visual, palpable, and
measurable signifier of every stage in the historical cycle. Buildings, streets, neighborhoods, and the entire city are described meticulously by al-Maqrizi not only
because they embodied the longed-for and clearly idealized past, but also because
their own particular micro-histories collectively narrated the history of Cairo, and
Egypt in general, under its various rulers. Al-Maqrizi, under the combined effect
of his love of his city, his desperation at its obvious signs of decay, and the adapt-
able theoretical framework he absorbed from his teacher, produced a singular
book within his own historiographical tradition.

Certainly, no other Mamluk historian managed to adapt the Khaldunian
method to his subject, or to capture the intensity of feelings displayed in al-
Maqrizi's text. Nor was any other historian creative enough to juxtapose the pedagogical and moral aims with the topographical and architectural descriptions.
Top historians such as Ibn Taghri-Birdi, Ibn Hajar al-'Asqalani, al-Sakhawi, and
even Ibn Khaldun himself sought their moral lessons in the actions of kings and
holy men; al-Maqrizi located his in the marks of these actions on the face of the
city, on its khitat and monuments. Other Mamluk khitat authors, such as Ibn 'Abd
al-Zahir, Abu Hamid al-Qudsi, and al-Suyuti, composed their books to preserve
the actual memory of quarters and buildings. They drew up dispassionate inven-
tories of haras, streets, and buildings. But they did not use their lists to advance a
larger agenda—i.e., condemning Mamluk rapacity and advocating a return to the
true Islamic ruling system, which formed a critical program on the part of al-
Maqrizi. Their compilations were in fact limited to brief treatises that either
copied or summarized sections of al-Maqrizi's Khitat and commented on and
added updated information to them, with no underlying historical awareness.[17]
In contrast, al-Maqrizi's Khitat comes across not just as an invaluable historical
source but also, and perhaps more powerfully, as an overtly emotional and partic-
ularistic urban history laced with political innuendoes, sociocultural proclamations, and an intense filial affinity with the city and the country. It actually anticipates—though in a less self-conscious way—the problems Alois Riegl and other

fin-de-siècle archaeologists encountered as they tried to "historicize" the city by reconstituting as wholes the fragments of its spaces and structures.[18]

THE EMPIRICIST TRADITION

For all the above reasons, al-Maqrizi's *Khitat* stood unrivaled for well over 400 years, a scholarly feat that would not be contested until the appearance of the monumental *Description de l'Égypte* at the end of the eighteenth century.

The *Description*, however, cannot be considered a sequel to the literary *khitat* tradition of medieval Egypt—although al-Maqrizi's *Khitat* constituted one of its principal sources. Rather, it was a majestic herald of another intellectual tradition, one that would come to dominate the modern study of history: the empirical compilation of visual and textual evidence, archival research, and analysis. Following the model of Diderot's and D'Alembert's *Encyclopédie*, the *Description de l'Égypte* was the cumulative effort of more than 150 scientists, scholars, engineers, and students recruited by Napoléon to accompany his expedition to Egypt (1798–1801). They systematically collected, studied, classified, and graphically represented everything known and knowable about Egypt—its geography and topography, its flora and fauna, its Pharaonic and Islamic patrimony, as well as its contemporary conditions. After many difficulties the product of their labor was published in Paris between 1809 and 1828 in nine volumes of text and fourteen grand volumes of illustrations.[19]

A catalogue raisonné of prodigious proportions that formed the basis of the modern understanding of Egypt, the *Description de l'Égypte* was a paradigmatic Enlightenment project—both in its methods and epistemological principles of exhaustive coverage and scientific accuracy, as well as in its conjectures, biases, and goals. It brought back a sufficiently exhaustive and scientifically ordered body of knowledge about Ancient Egypt that helped establish and justify its foundational place in the history of Western civilization as we know it today. Conversely, it reinforced a prejudiced and negative impression of the conditions of contemporary Egypt, and the whole "Orient" by extension, and presented nineteenth-century Europe with rationalized pretexts for intervention there on the eve of its grand colonial project.[20]

In Egypt itself, the immediate successor to the *Description de l'Égypte's* precise method of recording architecture was the work of a French architect from Marseille, Pascal-Xavier Coste (1787–1879). Between 1817 and 1827, Coste worked for Muhammad 'Ali Pasha, the semi-independent ruler of Egypt, first as the designer and supervisor of large engineering projects, and later as an architect of palaces and commemorative structures. After his return to France, Coste published an impressive compendium, *L'Architecture Arabe ou Monuments du Kaire mesurés et dessinés de 1818 à 1826*, which, as the title indicates, focused exclusively on a selection of the Islamic monuments of Cairo. The book is conceived and presented in the grand tradition of the Ecole des Beaux Arts, where Coste was trained. Every example is depicted in plans, sections, elevations, interior and exterior perspectives, and what used to be called "analytiques"—that is, various details rendered in different scales and formats, and accompanied by short, descriptive text.

A concise historical introduction also summed up Coste's knowledge of the Islamic architecture of Egypt and contextualized the architecture of the "Arabs" in general in relation to medieval Western architecture. Despite its limited coverage, the book offered the first visually comprehensive and typologically codified analysis of Cairene architecture.[21] It also visually consecrated the notion of an endogamous Egyptian architectural tradition, first established by the *Description*'s practical focus on Egypt to the exclusion of its surrounding cultural milieu. Coste, in fact, was the first to describe and order a basic vocabulary for a Cairene Mamluk style, which he considered the most representative of the architectures of Cairo. He even managed to test his style in two unbuilt mosques he designed for Muhammad 'Ali in Cairo and Alexandria.

After Coste's study, several books on Cairo's architecture were published in the nineteenth and early-twentieth centuries. But none was as exhaustive architecturally or as speculative analytically. One study, Martin S. Briggs's *Muhammadan Architecture in Egypt and Palestine*, published in 1924, did, however, stand out for its conscious attempt to explore the links between the architecture of Cairo and the Syro-Palestinian cities which were historically and culturally close to it, like Jerusalem, Damascus, and Aleppo.[22]

THE WORK OF MUBARAK AND CRESWELL

The first modern Egyptian work on the urban history of Cairo, and to a lesser extent the rest of Egypt, is the celebrated yet controversial massive compendium, *al-Khitat al-Tawfiqiyya al-Jadida*, published in twenty volumes in 1888–89 by 'Ali Pasha Mubarak (1823–93). Mubarak was one of the paragons of the modernization process in nineteenth-century Egypt—which, after its firm institution under Muhammad 'Ali, was somewhat chaotically precipitated to insolvency by the extravagance of his grandson Khedive Isma'il (r. 1863–79). Mubarak, who served in various cabinet posts, was heavily involved in the planning of Cairo and the piercing of new straight avenues through its dense medieval fabric in the 1870s. He was an unabashed Westernizer and modernizer who loudly exclaimed that the old, at least in terms of city layout, had to give way to the new.[23]

But despite his modern outlook, his professional training in France as an engineer, and his reliance on statistics to gauge the expansion of the city, his *khitat* compendium depended more on the medieval Egyptian tradition than on the modern European empirical one. Most remarkably, it had no illustrations whatsoever, although Mubarak was known to have studied drafting and used it in his planning work. Instead *al-Khitat al-Tawfiqíyya* relied heavily on textual descriptions whose language was reminiscent of medieval *khítat* tracts. This seems to have been more a function of the book's composition than the difficulty of printing figures in Egypt when it was published. Nor did the absence of figures seem to be an attempt on the part of Mubarak to respond to the expectations of his presumed audience, most of whom would have had a similar background to his, i.e., a Western education. The main reason seems rather to lie in the strong grip of an intellectual paradigm, al-Maqrizi's *Khitat*, on Mubarak's conceptualization of his own book. *Al-Khitat al-Tawfiqíyya al-Jadída* was indeed consciously modeled and named after al-Maqrizi's *Khitat*, and relied heavily on al-Maqrizi's data for its discussion of medieval Cairo. It even reflected al-Maqrizi's idiosyncrasies and prejudices and closely followed his organizational scheme, while adding sections on the urban developments in Cairo and Egypt between the fifteenth and nineteenth centuries. Mubarak, however, focused on the modernization of Cairo—in which he himself played a major role under two patrons, Khedive Isma'il and Khedive Tawfiq (the monarch to whom the book is dedicated). But despite the rather laudatory passages celebrating the two khedives and the idea of modernization, Mubarak's text lacks the intensity and passion of al-Maqrizi's hermeneutic, mantra-like theme of using architecture as a sociopolitical commentary, or as a tool to illuminate the memories of bygone eras and their venerable historical figures.[24]

Then came the most comprehensive and most architecturally accurate study of Cairo's architecture, and the lifetime work of an English technical draftsman turned historian, K.A.C. Creswell. Diligent and dogged, Creswell single-handedly measured, photographed, researched, and drew all known Cairene monuments up to 1311, and published them in two heavy volumes which, with their two predecessors on early Muslim architecture, established the field of Islamic architecture on solid, definite grounds.[25] Creswell's systematic technique of documentation and thorough measurement was bolstered by his extensive perusal of the textual sources in search of any reference to the building under study. Naturally, al-Maqrizi's *Khitat* was one of his primary sources, and he quoted it verbatim countless times—but only as a purveyor of information that needs to be checked against empirical research and never as an interpretive or discursive argument.

This strictly positivistic approach was perfect for the formal evaluation of buildings, and has been adopted by several scholars since (most notably by Jacques Revault and Michael Meinecke) with spectacular results.[26] But in his drive for methodical rigor and quantitative accuracy, and his refusal to learn Arabic—which was symptomatic of his disdain for the contemporary culture whose historical architecture he was so passionately studying—Creswell overlooked or misread many subtleties. Thus, although his plans and architectural descriptions still furnish the basis for any serious study of early Islamic or Egyptian architecture, his sweeping and deterministic proclamations have since been superseded by more empathetic scholarship. Furthermore, Creswell's uncritical acceptance of established linear architectural chronology and the magnitude and obsessive focus of his documentation have indirectly furnished a number of scholarly motives for later arguments of an endogenic and seemingly insular Egyptian architectural tradition. This is even the impression one gets out of Creswell's own text, despite his fanatic preoccupation with "architectural origins," precedents, and formal analogy between buildings, regardless of their geographical or cultural connection.[27]

CONTEMPORARY EGYPTIAN SCHOLARSHIP

Thus, it is to be expected that the work of the Egyptian historians who came after Creswell would exude an air of self-centeredness and particularism. Laboring in a nationalistic atmosphere in which the cultural identity of Egypt was hotly debated, these historians were greatly affected by three authoritative and exclusivist scholarly approaches that demarcated their field of inquiry—one disciplinary, and two internal to their Egyptian context.

The first approach was the peculiar historiography of the study of Islamic history in the West that we have come to call Orientalism, and its various peregrinations both in the West and in the Islamic world. Orientalism, as Edward Said observed, formed a discursive and intricate network of scholarly and cultural conventions that used, produced, and controlled knowledge about the Islamic world. But its scope also reflected the dominant paradigm of traditional Western scholarship—which affirmed a self-conscious and historically evolving character for the West from Classical origins to its triumphant culmination in modern times, while consigning other areas of study to marginal places in its ordered chronology.[28] This epistemological framework, which depended on imperial postures rather than historical facts or scholarly reflections, called for comprehensive studies confined within clearly proscribed and exclusive time, space, and culture.[29] Lacking theoretical positions of their own, the Egyptian historians who came to the discipline at the height of the anti-colonial struggle fell into the trap of its dichotomous substratum, despite their vehement rejection of its premises and conclusions.[30] They ended up structuring and categorizing the history of "their" architecture or "their" cities, and of "their" culture in general, from an exclusive and ultimately narrowly defined national, religious, or cultural perspective.[31]

The exclusive Orientalist construct was flavored by the two locally grown and influential particularist scholarly currents: the long tradition of *khitat* exemplified by al-Maqrizi's powerful work and Mubarak's updating of it; and the idio-syncratic but authoritative Creswellian paradigm, which was also Egyptocentric, but probably for reasons stemming from its Orientalist models. Most modern Egyptian histories of Cairo reflect this mixed intellectual lineage in varying combinations, but the legacy of al-Maqrizi's *Khitat* is the most powerfully felt. It defines their parameters, dominates their discourse, and permeates their lan-guage. This is so not only because of the expansive scope of al-Maqrizi's *Khitat*—being the largest and most complete repository of topographic and historical information on medieval Cairo—but also, and perhaps more importantly, because of al-Maqrizi's ardent passion and filial affinity with his city. Many modern Egyptian historians reproduce these feelings not only for their histori-cal significance but also (ignoring anachronism) as exemplary patriotic procla-mations from a "true Egyptian citizen."[32] Furthermore, al-Maqrizi's *Khitat* offers modern historians an ideologically and historically sanctioned framework for their own nationalistically driven studies. Ideologically, al-Maqrizi can be con-sidered a model national historian—before the damning colonial influence, as it were—and therefore a positive example to follow. Historically, the Egyptocentric framework of his *Khitat* legitimizes similarly particularist treat-ment in modern studies, which can be observed in the little emphasis external factors receive in their analysis of the formation and development of Cairo's architecture and urban forms.[33]

Some of the studies are so influenced by the framework and introverted focus of al-Maqrizi's *Khitat* that they come across as essentially modern renditions of it, with a visually oriented outlook and architecturally precise verbal descrip-tions. This is the case, for instance, of the book written by Hasan 'Abdel-Wahab, *Tarikh al-Masajid al-Athariyya allati salla fiha faridhat al-jum'a hadret sahib al-jalala al-malik al-salih Farouq al-Awwal*; and that of Su'ad Maher, *Masajid Misr wa Awliya'uha al-Salihun*.[34] 'Abdel-Wahab's book, as the title indicates, deals with the distinguished mosques of Cairo and Alexandria in which King Farouq prayed up to 1946. This may be seen as an already circumscribed criterion without the superimposition of al-Maqrizi's framework. And, in fact, it is. But a careful examination of the entries on the individual mosques shows how much they owe to al-Maqrizi's method of weaving the history of the structure with that of its time and with anecdotal biog-raphies of its patrons, users, and builders (when they are known). This method insures the primacy of a vertical historical investigation in constructing any build-ing's architectural history, rather than a horizontal and synchronic approach, which might extend beyond the immediate context of the building and of the city itself to other comparable buildings. Su'ad Maher's book deals with Islamic reli-gious structures all over Egypt, and as such, her framework is closer to that of al-Maqrizi than 'Abdel-Wahab. But like 'Abdel-Wahab, and ultimately like al-Maqrizi, her investigation is more diachronic than synchronic on all scales, from the single edifice to the architectural type. And, like the two other authors, its self-centeredness is literally built into its structure, language, and scope.[35]

Other modern Egyptian historians of Cairo's architecture and urbanism are synchronic in their approaches. Their gaze encompasses a broad, comparative terrain, and their analysis establishes links with architectural traditions around the Mediterranean and other Islamic regions outside Egypt. Although they still depend on the *khitat's* data and syntax, their works diverge from the chronological or diachronic order of *khitat*-inspired studies and adopt one of two more inclusive methods. The first is the typologically structured survey—its most successful representative being Ahmad Fikri's three-volume book on Cairene religious architecture, *Masajid al-Qahira wa Madarisuha*.[36] The second is architectural history written as a continuous historical narrative—whose examples include the works of Creswell's collaborator, Farid Shafe'i (who at times engaged in challenging the conceptions of his former tutor), and the works of 'Abd al-Rahman Zaki, Ahmad 'Abd al-Razzaq Ahmad, and Amal al-'Umari.[37] For all these nationalist historians, the primary role of al-Maqrizi's *Khitat* was to provide the powerful medieval pivot in a continuous, Cairo-centric urban history which unfolds over time with minimal interaction with the outside world, and which is suffused with self-conscious patriotism.

AL-MAQRIZI'S INFLUENCE ON EGYPTIAN LITERATURE

But al-Maqrizi's impact is not limited to influencing modern Egyptian historical writing—an influence that, after all, comes most naturally with the territory. He also plays a potent role in modern Egyptian fiction, albeit in a more circumscribed way. His figure and lifework inspired some of the most intensely particularist and deeply patriotic recent works, which range from historical novels, to fictional autobiographies, to narratives based on time travel. He appears in some of them as an authoritative and erudite character: guiding, commenting, and correcting mistakes in history and attribution of events and buildings. He seems, however, to have achieved the transformation from history to historical fiction without losing any of the attributes that attracted Mustafa Ziyada and other Egyptian historians to him in the first place. In fiction as in scholarship, it was his "Egyptianness" and "patriotism" that were rhapsodized as true and cogent emotions, even before the terms were meaningful as identity framers.

The novelist Gamal al-Ghitani, for instance, wrote his own literary *khitat* (*Khitat al-Ghitani*, 1980), in which he follows his predecessor in recording the details of his beloved city, Cairo, for fear of its disappearance – but this time under the double threat of heedless modern development and omnivorous capitalist greed.[38] Ghitani's *khitat*, though thinly fictionalized, draws on the same range of feelings as his model. First is an intense filial identification with Cairo, constricted in al-Ghitani's case to what is left of the old Cairo of the Fatimids, where he himself roams in modern days in search of inspiration and solace. Second is the anxiety the entire 1973 generation felt at the rapid changes in Egypt's image, outlook, and commitment to its venerated Arabic and Islamic heritage following the *infitah* (the economic, political, and ultimately cultural opening to the West instituted by President Anwar al-Sadat in 1976). And, as it turns out, his attempt to find refuge in the symbols of native architectural ingenuity and affinity with the land—exemplified by the beloved old Islamic Cairo, especially in its more popular sections of al-Gamaliyya and al-Hussein—is a reaction not so different from that of al-Maqrizi. It is probably even consciously modeled after it, for the same reason that more prosaic architectural and urban historians modeled their writing after al-Maqrizi's *Khitat*. Al-Maqrizi provides the only authentic and extensive link with all that is antediluvian Grand Cairo (al-Qahira)—that is, the City Victorious before it was reduced to an Ottoman provincial capital and ultimately transmogrified into the modern, run-down, and identityless metropolis.[39]

Al-Ghitani, as a narrator, is associated primarily with the styles of Ibn Iyas, the late Mamluk chronicler of the end of the sultanate, and Ibn 'Arabi, perhaps the greatest mystic of medieval Islam. Al-Ghitani uses Ibn Iyas to great effect in many of his other famous works, especially in *al-Zayni Barakat* (1971).[40] Ibn 'Arabi's profound and cryptic style inspires al-Ghitani's prose in his trilogy *al-Tajaliyyat* (*The Apparitions*, 1983–87). This last is a thinly fictionalized autobiography in which Ibn 'Arabi himself appears as the spiritual and fantastic guide of the narrator.[41] But al-Ghitani's fascination with al-Maqrizi's persona led him to develop his own brand of fictonalized architectural/topographic writing to address emotional and reflexive issues, occasioned most probably by his recent brush with death after a critical heart surgery. This is clearly how his novel *Safr al-Bunyan* (*The Book of Building*) is conceptualized and arranged. From Pharaonic Egypt to modern-day Cairo, this collection of transcendental moments in the urban history of the country uses builders, buildings, and architectural elements to weave together his introspective reflections on time, life, eternity, belonging, and remembrance.[42] Al-Maqrizi, the archetypical lover of Cairo in the eyes of contemporary Egyptians, would have greatly approved of this lyrical evolution in topographical/historical writing.

Perhaps the most extraordinary demonstration of al-Maqrizi's enduring status as the true narrator of Cairo's trials and tribulations, however, comes from the most ambitious Arabic time-travel novel: Khayri Shalabi's *Rihalat al-Turshaji al-Halwaji* (*The Voyages of the Pickle- and Sweet-Vendor*).[43] This farcical, ironic, and ultimately pessimistic tale deals irreverently yet lovingly with Cairo's historical experience, and in that sense corresponds to Frederic Jameson's notion of the "national allegory."[44] In it, the narrator, Ibn Shalabi (i.e., the author himself), is uncontrollably tossed through time, but without ever leaving the circumscribed space of Islamic Cairo. The ostensible aim of this is to get to the table of the Fatimid Caliph, al-Mu'izz li-Din Allah, where Ibn Shalabi is invited to celebrate the first Ramadan after the founding of the new capital of al-Qahira. But the deeper intention of this spatially confined narrative of time travel is to conscript the entire Egyptian history in order to construct a transhistorical Egyptian character of bonhomie, openness, and tolerance. The reconfirmation of this time-honored character is desperately needed to counter the otherwise bleak observation, repeatedly made by the author, that contemporary Egypt is falling prey to fanaticism, dogmatism, and chaos.[45]

In his time travel, Ibn Shalabi encounters a number of apparently more informed fellow time travelers, such as the medieval historians Ibn 'Abd al-Hakam and Ibn Taghri-Birdi, the Orientalist Stanley Lane-Poole, the Nobel-laureate novelist Naguib Mahfuz, and al-Maqrizi himself. These famous figures are obviously selected for the purpose of guiding the protagonist in his flipping through time. But they also provide him with the historical authority necessary to anchor his various encounters in their proper and recognizable historical contexts. And they all are the right choices for the purpose.

But what is important here is how al-Maqrizi, in particular, is presented among this group. Whereas all others are made to tell the protagonist about some historical event or figure, al-Maqrizi is distinguished as the recorder and transmitter of Cairo's urban and topographic history. Throughout the novel, he is portrayed in a respecting and adoring way as the meticulous researcher always preoccupied with the correct information regardless of the circumstances. Thus, when Ibn Shalabi first encounters him, al-Maqrizi, an old man with the mien of a 'alim, is surrounded by soldiers shoving him around. But he is nonetheless busy recording the changes in the topography around him. Even when Ibn Shalabi half-heartedly asks him if he needs any help, al-Maqrizi asks only for more information about the spot upon which they were standing, saying "I have recorded every foot that has stepped on this spot over the time I know, but I will appreciate any revision."[46]

In another instance, al-Maqrizi shows his vast knowledge by describing to the narrator the layout of the Fatimid Palace and its transformation in the Mamluk period. This passage is lifted verbatim from the *Khitat* and put to use in the novel to allow Ibn Shalabi to find his way in space to the dinner table of al-Mu'izz. When Ibn Shalabi explains to al-Maqrizi what happened to the site of the *funduq* of al-Khalili after his time (the modern-day Khan al-Khalili), al-Maqrizi exclaims, "Nothing has remained but the name. O *Misr* [colloquial for Egypt but also Cairo], how many names has your memory retained."[47]

AL-MAQRIZI'S ENDURING LEGACY

This brief sentence epitomizes in a few words how al-Maqrizi, as the author of the most extensive and heartfelt *khitat* book, has become lodged in modern

Egyptian consciousness as the true keeper of Cairo's history across the ages. He is the one who saved the names of places, long after the places themselves and their contemporary records were gone. And he is the one who preserved the descriptions of these places and the stories of their names as they unfolded over time. To the identity narratives of our nationalist age, both historical and fictional, he thus provides two indispensable and interconnected mainstays: the history of the place, and the history of the people who occupied this place (at least until his death in the middle of the fifteenth century). As such, his *Khitat* has become the most important repository of Cairo's medieval heritage—in its most expansive sense as defined by David Lowenthal as total historical narrative and total material history—when most of the true material history (i.e., buildings and streets and objects), has effectively disappeared.[48]

This is probably also why most modern Egyptian historians cannot escape al-Maqrizi's hold on the history of Cairo. To do so would be tantamount to denying Cairo's particular and distinct heritage. Such a stand is impossible to imagine in the current nationalist atmosphere, an atmosphere in which the late Tahsin Bashir, one of Egypt's foremost diplomats, could exclaim with deadpan seriousness: "Egypt is the only nation-state in the region; the others are tribes with flags."[49]

NOTES

1. The idea that Egypt had a specific character and was a clearly defined entity has been the theme of many nationalist historical and analytical studies, especially in the 1990s. The pioneering study remains J. Hamdan, *Shakhsiyyat Misr, Dirasa fi 'Abqariyyat al-Makan*, 4 vols. (Cairo: 'Alam al-Kutub, 1980–84), passim. See also N.A. Fu'ad, *Shakhsiyat Misr* (Cairo: al-Hay'a al-Misriyya al-'Amma lil-Kitab, 1968, rprt. 1978); M.N. Galal and M. Mutawalli, *Hawiyat Misr* (Cairo: al-Hay'a al-Misriyya al-'Amma lil-Kitab, 1997); M.N. Galal, *Dynamics of the Egyptian National Identity* (Lahore: Sang-e-Meel, 1998); R. Habib, *al-Shakhsiyya al-Misriyya: al-tatawwur al-nafsi fi khamsin qarnan* (Cairo: Markaz al-Mahrusa lil-Buhuth wa-al-Tadrib wa-al-Nashr, 1997); M. Hanna, *al-A'mida al-sab'a lil-shakhsiyya al-Misriyya* (Cairo: Dar al-Hilal, 1990), translated as *The Seven Pillars of the Egyptian Identity* (Cairo: General Egyptian Book Organization, 1994); A-L.M. Khalifah and S.J. Radwan, *al-Shakhsiyya al-Misriyya: al-malamih wa-al-ab'ad: dirasah sikulujiyyah* (Cairo: Dar Gharib, 1998); and T. Radwan and F. Radwan, *Ab'ad al-Shakhsiyya al-Misriyya: bayna al-madi wa-al-hadir* (Cairo: al-Hay'a al-Misriyya al-'Amma lil-Kitab, 1999). A recent study, A. 'Ashur and S.S. 'Ashur, *al-Watan al-Umm: Dirarsa fi al-Thaqafa al-Qawmiyya al-Misriyya, Ta'sis Tarikhi* (Cairo: n.p., 1999), proposes a new historical interpretation to the political development of Egypt, and takes the cosmocentric argument to its logical end by seeing the history of the country from 332 B.C. to 1952 C.E. as basically a long period of occupation and acculturation of Egypt by "foreigners"—including the Arabs, which is a hot topic nowadays. To appreciate the

growing nationalistic tendency, see how the views on Ibn Khaldun of M.I. 'Abd al-Razzaq, one of Egypt's foremost medieval historians, have changed from his "Manhaj al-Mu'arrikh Ibn Taghri-Birdi fi Kitabihi al-Nujum al-Zahira" in *al-Mu'arrikh Ibn Taghri Birdi: Jamal al-Din Abu al-Mahasin Yusuf, 813–874 H.* (Cairo: al-Hay'a al-Misriyya al-'Amma lil-Kitab, 1974), pp. 109–22, esp. pp. 109–11; to his *Nihayat usturat nazariyat Ibn Khaldun: muqtabasa min rasa'il Ikhwan al-Safa* (al-Mansura: Amer lil-Tiba'a wa-al-Nashr, 1996).

2. C. Cahen, "Khitat," *Encyclopedia of Islam, 2nd edition*, Vol. 5, p. 22; and J. Crabbs, *The Writing of History in Nineteenth-Century Egypt* (Detroit: Wayne State University Press, 1984), pp. 115–19.

3. The most noteworthy of which is M. Kurd'ali, *Khitat al-Sham*, 6 vols. (Damascus: Matba'at al-Taraqi, 1927).

4. For a discussion of the medieval Egyptian *khitat* books, see N. Rabbat, "Maqrizi's *Khitat*: An Egyptian *Lieu de Mémoire*" in D. Behrens-Abouseif, ed., *The Cairo Heritage: Papers in Honor of Layla Ali Ibrahim* (Cairo: American University in Cairo Press, 2001), pp. 17–30.

5. Most modern Egyptian historians of Cairo rely heavily on al-Maqrizi's data, and many even adopt his methods and reflect his cosmocentric attitude by considering the city's architectural history an autonomous development. See N. Rabbat, "Writing the History of Islamic Architecture in Cairo," *Design Book Review* 31 (Winter 1994), pp. 48–51.

6. M.A. 'Inan, *Misr al-Islamiyya wa Tarikh al-Khitat al-Misriyya* (Cairo: al-Hay'a al-Misriyya al-'Amma lil-Kitab, 1969), pp. 52–54. Also see N. Rabbat, "Who Was al-Maqrizi? A Biographical Sketch," *Mamluk Studies Review* 7, no. 2 (2003), pp. 1–19.

7. For a review of the first modern Egyptian encyclopedist historians, see Crabbs, *The Writing of History*, pp. 166–209.

8. Al-Maqrizi, *al-Mawa'iz wal-I'tibar fi Dhikr al-Khitat wal-Athar*, 2 Vols. (Cairo: Bulaq Press, 1854), Vol. 1, pp. 2–3. See also Vol. 1, pp. 365–72 for a collection of diatribes against and panegyrics to Cairo.

9. Al-Maqrizi, *Khitat*, Vol. 1, pp. 2–3 and Vol. 2, pp. 95–96, and 214. Though he declares in his introduction that he will present the reasons for the deterioration and destruction of Egypt in the seventh section of his book, al-Maqrizi never does—aside from the laments dispersed throughout his text—get down to this task. See 'Inan, *Misr al Islamiyya*, p. 50; A.F. Sayyid, ed., *Musawwadat kitab al-Mawa'iz wa-al-I'tibar fi dhikr al-khitat wa-al-athar* (London: Mu'assasat al-Furqan lil-Turath al-Islami, 1995), pp. 65–66; and S.A. 'Ashur, "Adwa' Jadidah 'ala al-Mu'arrikh Ahmad ibn 'Ali al-Maqrizi wa-Kitabatihi," *'Alam al-Fikr* 14, no. 2 (1983), pp. 453–98.

10. See P. Nora, "Between Memory and History: Les Lieux de mémoire," *Representations* 26 (Spring 1989), pp. 7–25. The article forms the theoretical introduction to his collaborative project on the national memory of France, published in seven volumes as *Les Lieux de memoire*; Vol. 1, translated by A. Goldhammer under the title *Realms of Memory: Rethinking the French Past* (New York: Columbia University Press, 1996).

11. The influence of Ibn Khaldun's interpretive framework is evident in a number of short thematic books by al-Maqrizi, such as his treatise on the calamity of the early fif-

teenth century, *Ighathat al-Umma bi-Kashf al-Ghamma*; and his analysis of the rivalry between the Umayyads and the Abbasids, *al-Niza' wal-Takhasum fima bayn Bani Ummaya wa-Bani Hashim.* See M.M. Ziyada, "Tarikh Hayat al-Maqrizi," in *Dirasat 'an al-Maqrizi, Majmu'at Abhath,* (Cairo: al-Hay'a al-Misriyya al-'Amma li-l-Ta'lif wa-l-Nashr, 1971), pp. 13–22; and A. Allouche, *Mamluk Economics: A Study and Translation of al-Maqrizi's Ighathat al-Ummah bi-Kashf al-Ghummah* (Salt Lake City: University of Utah Press, 1994), pp. 4–7.

12. I have found only one explicit reference to Ibn Khaldun's historical theory in al-Maqrizi's *Khitat* (Vol. 2, p. 190), which actually suggests that he was thoroughly familiar with the *Muqaddima.* Another mention in al-Maqrizi's biography of Ibn Khaldun straight-forwardly states that the *Muqaddima* "unveils the cause of events and informs on the essence of things." See M. al-Jalili, "Tarjamat Ibn Khaldun li-l-Maqrizi," *Majallat al-Majma' al-'Ilmi al-'Iraqi* 13 (1965), pp. 215–42, citation on p. 235.

13. The most clearly structured cycles are those of Tulunid al-Qata'i and Fatimid Cairo. See al-Maqrizi, *Khitat*, Vol. 1, pp. 313–26 and 360–65 respectively.

14. Examples in al-Maqrizi, *Khitat*, Vol. 1, p. 60, 101, 110–11, 128, 184, 227, 265, 305, 361, 365, 372–73, 405; and Vol. 2: p. 52, 98, 105, 119, 120, 132–38, 214, 223, 232, 241, 280, 283, 296, and 311.

15. This is where Ibn Taghri-Birdi's repeated remarks on al-Maqrizi's hostility toward Barsbay gain their full meaning. See Ibn Taghri-Birdi, *al-Nujum al-Zahira fi-Muluk Misr wa-l-Qahira,* 15 vols. (Cairo: Dar al-Kutub, 1930–56); particularly Vol. 14, pp. 200–1, 245, 310–11; and Vol. 15, pp. 109–10.

16. Al-Maqrizi, *Khitat*, Vol. 2, p. 214. See also Ibn Taghri-Birdi, *al-Nujum*, Vol. 7, pp. 328–29, where he deplores the changes in the Mamluk army structure from the time of Qalawun and describes the Mamluks of his time as "holding their buttocks in the water and their nose in the sky" (meaning that they were both impotent and arrogant). There is a tendency among the Burji historians to idealize the Bahri period, but as David Ayalon ("Harb," *Encyclopedia of Islam, 2nd edition,* Vol. 3, p. 189) remarks, "this tendency is by no means without foundation." For a more complete analysis of al-Maqrizi's attitudes toward the Mamluks see N. Rabbat, "al-Madina wa al-Tarikh wa al-Sultah: al-Maqrizi wa Kitabuhu al-Ra'id *al-Mawa'iz wa al-I'tibar bi Dhikr al-Khitat wa al-Athar,*" *Annales Islamologiques* 35 (2001), pp. 77–100. See also, S. Massoud, "al-Maqrizi as a Historian of the Reign of Barquq," *Mamluk Studies Review* 7, no. 2 (2003), pp. 119–36.

17. Surveyed by A.F. Sayyid, "Introduction," in *Musawwadat kitab al-Maqrizi,* pp. 24–27.

18. See the succinct review of the romantic approach in A. Grafton, "Introduction: Notes from Underground on Cultural Transmission," in A. Grafton and A. Blair, eds., *The Transmission of Culture in Early Modern Europe* (Philadelphia: University of Pennsylvania Press, 1990), pp. 1–7. For the archaeological dilemma in reconstructing cultural history, see E. Naginski, "Riegl, Archaeology, and the Periodization of Culture," *Res: Anthropology and Aesthetics* 40 (Autumn 2001), pp. 115–32. Another example of a similar influence, this one of Ibn Khaldun on Arnold Toynbee, is discussed in R. Irwin, "Toynbee and Ibn Khaldun," *Middle Eastern Studies* 33, no. 3 (July 1997), pp. 461–79.

19. There exist two editions of the *Description de l'Égypte*. The first is the édition Imprimerie Nationale (1809–28), the second is the édition dite Panckoucke, 26 octavo volumes of text and 12 folio volumes of illustrations (Paris, 1821–29). For a review of the *Description*'s history, see the introduction by Charles Coulston Gillispie, in C.C. Gillispie and M. Dewachter, eds., *Monuments of Egypt: The Napoleonic Edition: The Complete Archaeological Plates from la Description de l'Égypte* (Princeton: Princeton University Press, 1987), pp. 1–29.

20. For critical reviews of the scope and impact of the *Description de l'Égypte*, see A. Louca, "La renaissance égyptienne et les limites de l'œuvre de Bonaparte," *Cahiers d'histoire égyptienne* 7 (1955), pp. 1–20; H. Laurens, *Les origines intellectuelles de l'expedition d'Égypte: l'orientalisme islamisant en France (1698–1798)* (Istanbul: Isis, 1987); and D. Prochaska, "Art of Colonialism, Colonialism of Art: The Description de l'Égypte," *L'esprit créateur* 34 (1994), pp. 69–91.

21. P. Coste, *Architecture Arabe ou Monuments du Kaire mésurés et dessinés de 1818 à 1826* (Paris: Firmin-Didot, 1839). Coste's work has begun to receive critical attention recently. See the articles collected in D. Armogathe and S. Leprun, *Pascal Coste ou l'architecture cosmopolite* (Paris: Éditions l'Harmattan, 1990); and N. Rabbat, "The Formation of the Neo-Mamluk Style in Modern Egypt," in M. Pollak, ed., *The Education of the Architect: Historiography, Urbanism and the Growth of Architectural Knowledge. Essays Presented to Stanford Anderson on His Sixty-Second Birthday* (Cambridge, MA: MIT Press, 1997), pp. 363–86. See also *Pascal Coste, toutes les Égypte* (Marseille: Parenthèses, 1998), published on the occasion of an exhibition organized by the Bibliothèque municipale de Marseille June 17–September 30, 1998, as part of the national observance "France-Égypte, horizons partagés."

22. M.S. Briggs, *Muhammadan Architecture in Egypt and Palestine* (New York: Da Capo Press, 1924, rprt. 1974).

23. For a review of Mubarak's career and the incongruity between his modernizing stance and political conservatism, see Nezar AlSayyad's chapter in this volume.

24. A. Mubarak, *al-Khitat al-Tawfiqiyya al-Jadida*, 20 vols. (Cairo: Bulaq, 1888–89); see especially Vol. 1, pp. 65–77. Also see Crabbs, *Writing of History*, pp. 114–19, where Mubarak is rightly dubbed an encyclopedist, perhaps in reference to his medieval predecessors, al-'Umari and al-Qalqashandi. A systematic study of the frame and purpose of Mubarak's *Khitat* is S. Fliedner, *Ali Mubarak und seine Hitat: kommentierte Übersetzung der Autobiographie und Werkbesprechung* (Berlin: K. Schwarz, 1990).

25. K.A.C. Creswell, *Early Muslim Architecture*, 2 vols. (Oxford: Clarendon, 2nd edition, 1969); and *Muslim Architecture of Egypt*, 2 vols. (Oxford: Oxford University Press, 1959). A recent volume of *Muqarnas*—Vol. 8 (1991)—was devoted to Creswell and his legacy.

26. Jacques Revault produced or supervised at least a dozen books on Islamic residential architecture in several Arab capitals—Tunis, Fez, Cairo, and Algiers—with detailed measured drawings of the houses, their plans, sections, elevations, and ornaments. Michael Mienecke's *opus magnum* was his exhaustive *Die Mamlukische Architektur in Ägypten und Syrien (648 1250 bis 923 1517)*, 2 vols. (Glückstadt: Verlag J. J. Augustin GMBH, 1992), in which he reproduced plans of most Mamluk structures in the same scale in addition to all the primary and secondary sources references related to them.

27. See the analysis of J.M. Rogers, "Architectural History as Literature: Creswell's Reading and Methods," *Muqarnas* 8 (1991), pp. 45–54.

28. The most graphic illustration of this dichotomy in architecture is Banister Fletcher's "Tree of Architecture," which very clearly assigns to non-Western architectural traditions, called non-historical styles, dead-end branches while preserving the trunk and growing branches to Western or historical styles. The Tree occupied the frontispiece of the first sixteen editions of the book, *A History of Architecture on the Comparative Method for the Student, Craftsman, and Amateur*, published between 1896 and 1961. For a critical discussion of Fletcher's structure, see, G. Nalbantoglu, "Toward Postcolonial Openings: Rereading Sir Banister Fletcher's *History of Architecture*," *Assemblage* 35 (1998), pp. 6–17.

29. G. Fowden, *Empire to Commonwealth: Consequences of Monotheism in Late Antiquity* (Princeton: Princeton University Press, 1993), p. 9, picked up on the same point by asserting that "There are roads out of antiquity that do not lead to the Renaissance." His book offers a historical reconceptualization of the Antiquity to Islam continuum that challenges previous frameworks.

30. This is the subject of several recent studies in Egypt, cf., M.K.H. Ahmad, *Athar al-fikr al-istishraqi fi al-mujtama'at al-Islamiyya* (Cairo: 'Ayn lil-Dirasat wa-al-Buhuth al-Insaniyya wa-al-Ijtima'iyya, 1997); and A. Shaykh, *Hiwar al-istishraq: min naqd al-istishraq ila naqd al-istighrab* (Cairo: al-Markaz al-'Arabi lil-Dirasat al-Gharbiyya, 1999).

31. The paradoxical psychological and epistemological consequences of cleansing a national culture of all possible colonial corruption have been insightfully analyzed by Frantz Fanon in "On National Culture," *The Wretched of the Earth*, (trans. Constance C. Farrington) (New York: Grove Press, 1963), pp. 167–99.

32. A tone of suprahistorical intellectual fellowship with al-Maqrizi emanates from the collection of studies in M.M. Ziyada et al., *Dirasat 'an al-Maqrizi,* where al-Maqrizi is repeatedly called a "true Egyptian citizen," and a "patriot." The same kind of feeling must have influenced the choice of Salah 'Issa's book title *Hawamish al-Maqrizi, Hikayat min Misr (The Margins of al-Maqrizi, Stories from Egypt)*, 2 collections (Cairo: Dar al-Qahira, 1983). The book is a collection of populist essays in which history and sociology are rhetorically conscripted to advance an ardent nationalistic message. For the author, al-Maqrizi's name seems to have presented a model of both a historian and a nationalist to whom he can relate.

33. This becomes more apparent when modern Egyptian studies are compared to modern Western studies that broke with the cosmocentric archetype to posit instead a framework of regional exchange. This is the case most noticeably of M. Meinecke, *Die Mamlukische Architektur in Agypten und Syrien.*

34. H. 'Abdel-Wahab, *Tarikh al-Masajid al-Athariyya allati salla fiha faridhat al-jum'a hadret sahib al-jalala al-malik al-salih Farouq al-Awwal* (Cairo: Dar al-Kutub, 1946; rprt. 1994); and S. Maher, *Masajid Misr wa Awliya'uha al-Salihun,* 3 vols. (Cairo: al-Hay'a al-Misriyya al-'Amma li-l-Ta'lif wa-l-Nashr, 1971). An earlier French survey of Cairo's mosques may have supplied another frame of reference to these books: L. Hautecœur and G. Wiet, *Les mosquées du Caire*, 2 vols. (Paris: Ernest Leroux, 1932).

35. A recent example of the persistence of the endogenous Maqrizian model, which might have been admirable in a pre-nationalist fifteenth-century treatise, but not in this late-twentieth-century survey is H.M. Nuwaysir, *al-'Imara al-Islamiyya fi-Misr: 'Asr al-Ayyubiyyin wa-l Mamalik* (Cairo: Maktabat Zahra' al-Sharq, 1996). See my review of this book in *Mamluk Studies Review* 5 (2001), pp. 205–8.

36. A. Fikri, *Masajid al-Qahira wa Madarisaha*, 3 vols. (Cairo: Dar al-Ma'arif, 1962–69).

37. F. Shafe'i, *al-'Imara al-'Arabiyya fi Misr al-Islamiyya, 'Asr al-Wulat* (Cairo: al-Hay'a al-Misriyya al-'Amma li-l-Ta'lif wa-l-Nashr, 1970); and *al-'Imara al-'Arabiyya al-Islamiyya, Madiha wa-Hadiraha wa-Mustaqbalaha* (Riyadh: Jami'at al-Malik Sa'ud, 1982). See also A.R. Zaki, *al-Qahira, Tarikhaha wa-Atharaha* (Cairo: al-Hay'a al-Misriyya al-'Amma li-l-Ta'lif wa-l-Nashr, 1966); *Mawsu'at Madinat al-Qahira fi Alf 'Am* (Cairo: Maktabat al-Anjlo al-Misriyya, 1969); A.A. Ahmad, *Tarikh wa Athar Misr al-Islamiyya* (Cairo: Dar al-Fikr al-'Arabi, 1977; rprt. 1993); and A. al-'Umari and A. Tayish, *al-'Imara fi Misr al-Islamiyya: (al-asrayn al-Fatimi wa-al-Ayyubi)* (Cairo: Maktabat al-Safa wa-al-Marwa, 1996).

38. G. al-Ghitani, *al-A'mal al-Kamila, al-mujallad 4* (Cairo: al-Hay'a al-Misriyya al-'Amma lil-Kitab, 2nd edition, 1990).

39. Al-Ghitani also wrote several lyrical studies on Islamic Cairo, cf., *Malamih al-Qahirah fi 1000 sanah* (Cairo: Dar al-Hilal, 1983); *Qahiriyat: Asbilat al-Qahirah* (Cairo: Maktabat Madbuli, 1984); and *The Cairo of Naguib Mahfouz* (Cairo: The American University in Cairo Press, 1999), photographs by B. Le Va, text by G. al-Ghitani, foreword by N. Mahfouz. See also the analysis of S. Mehrez, *Egyptian Writers between History and Fiction: Essays on Naguib Mahfouz, Sonallah Ibrahim, and Gamal al-Ghitani* (Cairo: American University in Cairo Press, 1994).

40. G. al-Ghitani, *al-Zayni Barakat: Riwayah* (Damascus: Wizarat al-Thaqafah wa-al-Irshad al-Qawmi, 1st edition, 1974). English edition is *Zayni Barakat*, trans. F. Abdel Wahab, (London: Viking, 1988).

41. G. al-Ghitani, *Kitab al-tajalliyat* (Cairo: Dar al-Mustaqbal al-Arabi, 1983).

42. G. al-Ghitani, *Sifr al-Bunyan* (al-Qahirah: Dar al-Hilal, 1997). See my analysis of the architectural metaphor in his writing in "Dala'il al-'Imran fi-Asfar al-Bunyan: al-'Imara fi Kitabat Gamal al-Ghitani," *al-Hilal* 107, no. 1 (January 1999), pp. 152–59.

43. K. Shalabi, *Rihlat al-Turshaji al-Halwaji* (Cairo: Akhbar al-Yawm, 1983).

44. F. Jameson, "Third World Literature in the Age of Multinational Capitalism," *Social Text* 15 (1986), pp. 65–88.

45. See the analysis of M. Cooperson, "Remembering the Future: Arabic Time-Travel Literature," *Edebiyat* 8 (1998), pp. 171–89, esp. pp. 179–84.

46. K. Shalabi, *Rihalat al-Turshaji al-Halwaji* (Cairo: Madbuli, 1991), p. 9.

47. Shalabi, *Rihalat al-Turshaji al-Halwaji*, pp. 20–22, the citation is from p. 21.

48. See D. Lowenthal, *Possessed by the Past: The Heritage Crusade and the Spoils of History* (London: Viking, 1997), pp. 127–72.

49. C. Glass in *Tribes with Flags: A Dangerous Passage Through the Chaos of the Middle East* (New York: Atlantic Monthly Press, 1990), p. 3, explains that he borrowed the title "tribes with flags" from Bashir.

4

'Ali Mubarak's Cairo: Between the Testimony of *'Alamuddin* and the Imaginary of the *Khitat*

Nezar AlSayyad

Nineteenth-century writings about Egypt and Cairo are abundant. In the European literature, Egypt was often characterized by two adjectives, "Egyptian" and "Arab," with a third, "modern," reserved mainly for the new section of its capital, Cairo. Scholarly writings in Arabic portrayed Egypt as an awakening nation whose capital was a cosmopolitan center with rich practices of daily life and numerous buildings from earlier dynasties.[1]

Irene Bierman and others have argued that by the end of the century, a "medieval" Cairo—whose manners and customs had to be recorded and cataloged—was born into existence, mainly as a result of English and French concerns. Indeed, the work of the Comité de Conservation des Monuments de L'Art Arab (often referred to as the Comité) was central to this project of "making Cairo medieval," as the title of this book puts it.

Although the central character of our story, 'Ali Pasha Mubarak, was for a time a member of this Comité, the Egyptian perspective that emerges from his positions seems to suggest a different project. Borrowing from Boyer, Bierman recognizes this when she tells us that 'Ali Mubarak's Cairo was a "city of sites," or places where social interaction and collective memory were at work, and not a "city of sights" scripted as an itinerary of spectacles, as Derek Gregory's work demonstrates.[2]

Of course, we can all agree, as Timothy Mitchell has demonstrated, that these changes in Egypt were part of a larger application of disciplinary knowledge.[3] We can also agree that such transformations were not unique to Cairo, as other older cities like London, Paris, and Delhi (or parts of them) were also recognized or fabricated as medieval.[4] The only question that remains unanswered relates to the role that the native population, particularly the Egyptian elite, may have played in this project.

'Ali Mubarak steps in as the ideal figure in this regard. He was an Egyptian who climbed the administrative ranks, occupied major ministerial posts for more than thirty years, studied and traveled in France, and wrote prolifically, producing a number of works ranging from a lesser known novel to the most encyclopedic history of Cairo and Egypt in the late nineteenth century. No other figure during this time seems to have encompassed these various dimensions.

Although modern historians are generally split on the writings of 'Ali Mubarak, particularly his *Khitat al-tawfiqiyya al-jadida*, as a source for the history of modern Egypt, all inevitably rely on him in telling their stories. Some, like Anwar Abdel-Malek, claim that Mubarak initiated no real school of historical writing.[5] Gabriel Baer, who wrote a very detailed article on this topic in the late 1960s, concludes that the *Khitat* is only important in "the field of social history."[6] "Neither in content nor in form can (the) *Khitat* really be considered a history," Jack Crabbs tells us.[7] But these critics' main charge is a methodological one, that the work is a derivative, inaccurate, superficial narrative encased in the annalistic mold of the traditional medieval format.[8] Other authors, like Gamal el-Din el-Shayyal, whose book *The History of Egyptian Historiography in the 19th Century* remains a classic, at least in Egypt, disagree with this characterization.[9] El-Shayyal argues that the works of Mubarak, and that of Tahtawi before him, "created a historical consciousness which led Egyptians to be interested in history, generally, and in the history of Egypt in various stages in particular."[10] He further argues that this understanding of Egyptian civilization as one continuous entity kindled a new patriotic and national spirit.[11]

If, as a historian, Mubarak is looked upon with some suspicion, as a political personality, he is equally controversial. The conservative nature of the political positions he advocated in the service of the khedival system and his seemingly patriotic but anti-revolutionary stances have made it difficult for Egyptian historians to fully embrace him or categorically dismiss him as a national figure.

But Mubarak was also a novelist of sorts, for he wrote *'Alamuddin*, a work of fiction that has recently received some attention. Although it was arguably the first modern Egyptian novel, it has largely been ignored in Arabic literary circles. It has also been dismissed as pseudo-fictional travel writing in the old tradition of *Abad al-Rihalat*, or as "simply no more than moralizing which may be understood as indirect criticism of the rulers."[12]

It is not my intention here to fundamentally challenge or attempt to reverse any of these assertions. I will not make the case that *Khitat* is a reliable history or that *'Alamuddin* is a significant novel. Indeed, I do not believe that any history can be reliable or any novel can be significant simply on its own merit. It is the context that makes it so. I will also not defend 'Ali Mubarak against the charge of being a simple-minded bureaucrat principally concerned with the maintenance of his own position.

Instead, I will attempt to use his somewhat lively novel *'Alamuddīn* to interrogate his static historical text, *al-Khitat*. Although I cannot provide a deeper analysis in this chapter because of space constraints, I will try to shed light on how Egyptians of the new Westernized upper classes viewed their own environment and constructed an Egypt and a Cairo to suit their newfound identity. The intent of my interrogation is to discover 'Ali Mubarak's idiom, or his processes of constructing meaning. By idiom I not only mean what is being said, but how it is said, and in what context. In the words of the feminist historian Joan Scott:

> The emphasis on how suggests a study of processes, not of origins, of multiple rather than single causes, of rhetoric or discourse rather than ideology or consciousness. It does not abandon attention to structures and institutions, but it does insist that we need to understand what these organizations mean in order to understand how they work.[13]

Toward this goal, I have divided this chapter into three sections. In sections one and two, I will present a biographical sketch of 'Ali Mubarak, the man, from the perspective of Egypt of the nineteenth century. I will examine his role in the making of modern Egypt and Cairo, and I will discuss both *'Alamuddīn* and the *Khitat* within a temporal and cultural context. In the last section, I will select a few common subjects from both works which I believe reveal Mubarak's true significance as an intellectual of a transnational inclination who used the West to interrogate the East, and vice versa—and who did so well before such practices became common.

MUBARAK, *'ALAMUDDIN*, AND MID-NINETEENTH CENTURY EGYPT

'Ali Mubarak was born around 1823 in Birinbal al-Jadida, a small village in the Egyptian Delta. A detailed account of his life and government service may be found in the twenty-three autobiographical pages which he placed under the coverage of this village in the *Khitat*. Although born into a family of Shaikhs who enjoyed social standing and minor privileges but no wealth, Mubarak seems to have had a tough childhood. At the *kuttab*, he explains, he was often beaten by his Quranic teacher. Before the age of ten, he started to work as a scribe for several clerks, and again he tells us that he was mistreated and sometimes not paid. In particular, he relates an incident where he was put in jail for having withheld his salary's worth from some money he was asked to collect for this boss, the clerk. But Mubarak's scripting skills served him well, and he was released when a black-skinned government policeman, a *ma'mour* by the name of Anbar Effendi, needed

a scribe to do his books. This encounter seems to have been a formative experience for Mubarak. He comments on the fact that no Abyssinian could have
reached such a powerful position had he not gone to a *madrasa*, or school.

It was at this time that Mubarak recognized the importance of formal, nonre-
ligious education in achieving upward social mobility. At the age of eleven, against
the wishes of his father, who did everything to dissuade him from doing so,
Mubarak joined a nearby *maktab*, a small primary school. The following year, again
against his father's wishes, he applied and was selected to attend the secondary
school of Qasr-al-'Ayni in Cairo—whose military training did not seem to suit him.
However, when that school was dismantled, he was transferred to another Abu
Za'abal school, where he tells us that he initially failed the subject of *handasa*, or
geometry, before he put his mind to it and excelled in it and other subjects.

His outstanding performance landed him a place in the Muhandiskanah, or
the School of Engineering, in 1830. And after graduating in 1844, he was chosen
to attend the educational mission in Paris. As fortune would have it, the mission
also included several of Muhammad 'Ali's children and grandchildren, including
Isma'il, who would later became khedive. Mubarak tells us that his decision to
join the mission, and continue as a student instead of accepting a job with a good
salary, was influenced by his desire to "increase his stature and honor," a matter
which again turned out to be formative in his later career. Indeed, the mission was
his ticket to higher ranks on the social ladder.

In Paris, he tells us that he was first unsuccessful in his work because he had
not learned French in advance. He talks about staying up all night studying
French from children's books. The reports sent to Cairo by Mubarak's French
instructors show him as stubborn and undisciplined, but also as intelligent and
industrious, possessing a "logical" mind.[14]

After spending another year in the Metz school for artillery and military
engineers, Mubarak returned to Cairo around 1849 when the mission was
recalled by the new Egyptian ruler, 'Abbas Pasha. Sometime during that year,
Mubarak returned to his village after fourteen years of absence to see his family,
and he spoke passionately of how his mother fainted when he suddenly arrived.

"One might almost say that 'Ali Mubarak was brought up by the state," suggests Janet Abu Lughod; and on his return, he had a debt to pay.[15] Under 'Abbas,
Mubarak started his governmental career. Yet, despite having acquired new qual-
ifications, the Egypt Mubarak returned to still required that he enlist the media-
tion of a relative or a friend to gain the attention of the authorities. It was Prince
Ahmad, his buddy from his Paris days, who intervened on his behalf. With
Ahmad's backing, Mubarak was appointed to a variety of positions in the khedival entourage. Most notably, he seems to have been put in charge of examinations
and budgeting in a government which was in the process of shrinking the educational and administrative system. But this was also a time when new projects like

the road between Cairo and Suez and the railroad between Cairo and Alexandria were being initiated. And Mubarak seems to have fared well under 'Abbas, who once threatened that he would make Mubarak wear *fallahín* clothes and live austerely if he ever displeased him. Eventually, 'Abbas promoted him to *amíralay*, or colonel, granted him 300 acres of land, and gave him the title of *bek*.

When Said became khedive in 1854, after 'Abbas' assassination, he disposed of all who worked for 'Abbas. Under these conditions it was normal that Mubarak fall out of favor. He was sent to perform services as a military engineer with the Egyptian garrison in Crimea, and later in Anatolia and Trabzon, where he tells us he learned Turkish during several months spent in Istanbul. He also comments that although he was homesick, it was worthwhile to encounter and learn about people and places he did not know existed.[16] However, on his return to Egypt this time, he received no recognition, and simply had to toil in low-ranking positions as an official in the Ministry of Interior, the Chamber of Commerce, and as a resident engineer in Upper Egypt. Toward the end of Said's reign, with the help of some friends, Mubarak entered the contract building business and purchased a house in the Isma'ilya quarter on Darb al-Jamamiz. This house would become his principal place of business for more than twenty years.

Although there is some disagreement on the exact dates, it is likely that 'Ali Mubarak wrote his novel *'Alamuddín* during this period of his career, after Said had dismissed him from serious government service.[17] However, although the book was checked and revised for publication in the mid-1870s, it was not published until 1882 in Alexandria.

'Alamuddín is the story of an Azhari Shaikh, who is hired by an English linguist to help him edit the Arabic lexicon, *Lisan al-'Arab*. The Shaikh agrees to accompany the Englishman to Europe to continue the work. Although reluctant at first, the Shaikh agrees, and embarks on a journey with his son, young Burhanuddin, which takes them and the Englishman to Paris, after first passing through Tanta, Alexandria, and Marseilles. On board the boat, the son befriends James, another Englishman and a former sailor. Once in Paris, the four characters engage in discussions as they visit the different places of the city.

Written as a mixture of prose and rhymes, the four-volume (1400-page) book is divided into 125 chapters called *musamarat*, or vignettes, which consist of informal conversations between two or three of the characters. The titles of the chapters usually designate events (marriage, travel), activities (going to the theater or the café), places (Tanta, Marseilles), or subjects (navigation, education). In the introduction to the book, Mubarak reveals that his principal purpose was educational. In fact, he had used the term *musamarat* in an earlier book about Arabic grammar.[18] In his introduction to *'Alamuddín*, Mubarak tells us:

I found that the souls of human beings prefer stories and anecdotes and not
the pure arts and sciences. . . . So I envision this as a book with much wisdom
and benefit told in the form of a simple *Hikaya* or story containing the most
comprehensive knowledge of arts, sciences, industry, and nature. . . . I have
expanded the encounters and the comparisons between the condition of man
in the past and the present, and between the here and there to awaken the
readers' mind and sharpen his vision to be able to critique events and balance
between good and evil and useful and harmful to gain an understanding of the
differences between the Eastern and the European conditions. . . . I have used
the two fictional characters, the Shaikh and the Englishman in a travelogue format so that the reader can move along with them like an entertained traveler.[19]

In one of the vignettes, the group arrives at a hotel, and the Shaikh and his
son are amazed by its service; in a second, the Shaikh expresses his reservations
about the mixing of men and women in public places; in a third, Burhanuddin
goes to the theater and is astonished at its being a forum for the subtle critique of
the governmental authorities; and in a fourth, the group become *flaneurs* as they sit
in an elegant glass-windowed café decorated by mirrors. In each of these cases, a
contrast with the equivalent conditions in the East is presented: where hotels are
untidy and smelly, cafes are dirty and noisy, and theatrical performances are lacking in any fine taste. The ideas of the book must have been formulated from
Mubarak's own journey and trip to France (1844–49), which bears a striking
resemblance to the temporal and geographic coverage in the novel.

Some have argued that *'Alamuddin* is a novel with autobiographical foundations,
where the character of the Shaikh is assumed to be Rifa'a al-Tahtawi, and
Burhanuddin to be Mubarak himself.[20] Others have suggested that the character
of the Englishman in the novel was inspired by the Orientalist Edward William
Lane, whom Mubarak seems to have admired. Indeed, we find in the *Khitat* the
account of Shaikh Ibrahim al-Dasouqi's relationship with Lane, their friendship,
and their collaboration on transcribing lexicographical material.[21] In fact, Dasouqi
copied all of Taj-al-'Arus for Lane, who took it with him to England, where it is still
part of the collection of the British Library.[22] Thus, it is quite possible that the relationship between Dasouqi and Lane inspired the basis of Mubarak's novel.

Mubarak must have been aware of all these possible references. He labors to
distinguish his work from that of Rifa'a's (although I have to mention here that
fourteen of his 125 vignettes have similar or identical titles to those of Rifa'a's forty-
five chapters). In the novel, Shaikh 'Alamuddin comments while in Paris: "Rifa'a
bey was full of praise for Paris and its people . . . but it seems he did not scratch
beyond the surface appearance or try to uncover her veil . . . he remained a wan-
derer in its peripheries, not a singer of its song. In any case, everything he has commented on has changed in the last thirty years."[23] Similarly, Mubarak also insists on

denying a connection between the characters of his novel and any real ones. In the introduction to the novel he invokes the Arabic term "Hayan Ibn Bayan" to remind us that these are fictional characters. But even if we exclude Lane and Rifa'a as possible references, there is no doubt that the characters of 'Alamuddin and his son Burhanuddin encapsulate the contradictions between Mubarak and his father, which he himself highlights in his autobiography. The intellectual hunger and curiosity of the son is always tempered and subdued by the more religiously conservative and often disinterested father. It is perhaps possible that Mubarak endowed both the father and son in his novel with all of the conflicting experiences he may have encountered himself in his five years in France.

In contrasting himself to Rifa'a, 'Ali Mubarak was not only going to inform the East about the achievements of the West, as Rifa'a did, but also, as Wadad al-Qadi put it, he "was going to put the East in a direct situation of actual confrontation with the West, so that the East before the West knows its proper place in world civilization."[24]

It is interesting to note that all of Mubarak's Eastern characters have names that convey religiosity ('Alamuddin, landmark of faith; Burhanuddin, proof of faith; and the wife Taqiya, faithful). It is as if Mubarak, through his characters, is talking about the entire East, whose identity is derived from its faith. In the novel, the two Englishmen—one of whom is never given a proper name—are always portrayed as knowledgeable even about the East, while both 'Alamuddin and Burhanuddin are ignorant even of knowledge about Egypt. For example, on the Pyramids, the Shaikh seems only to know "what Muslim tradition has to say about them."[25]

The East, 'Ali Mubarak implies, knows little about itself, and nothing else; while the West knows all about itself and much about the East. "What is worse," as Wadad al-Qadi puts it, is "that the East is unaware of its inferior position, (while) the West is aware of its superiority and the inferiority of the East."[26]

It is interesting that Mubarak chose his Western hero as an Englishman, not a Frenchman. Some have explained this by the fact that the English, at the time the novel was written, were not enemies of the Egyptians, and had never fought them.[27] But this also may have been the reason why Mubarak, having sat on the book for twenty years or more, decided to publish it in the same year as the British colonization of Egypt. It is further ironic that the book was being printed in Alexandria around the same time that the city was under siege by the British navy. One may even argue that publishing it at that time, with its inclusion of such a positive portrayal of the character of the Englishman, amounted to a subtle endorsement by Mubarak of the looming British occupation.

We have little knowledge of how influential the book was when it was published, but we certainly know that 'Ali Mubarak, who was later to become Minister of Education and Public Works during a very significant period in Egyptian history, was a thoroughly Westernized "'Alamuddin."[28]

MUBARAK, THE *KHITAT*, AND CAIRO OF THE LATE NINETEENTH CENTURY

Mubarak, the Westernizer, finally got his chance. This happened when Isma'il, the khedive, who would later declare "my country is no longer part of Africa, for we are now a part of Europe," became Egypt's ruler in 1863.[29] Isma'il had known Mubarak twenty years earlier during the Paris mission, and he immediately called him back to government service, first as a supervisor of the barrages and then as inspector and commissioner in various government offices. Egypt during this time was reopening to the West. It sent its first educational mission to Europe in thirteen years, the railways underwent major expansion, and a postal service and a water company were established. However, Mubarak does not seem to have played any role in these projects. Instead, in 1867, he tells us that he was sent on a forty-five day mission to Paris by the khedive on what he calls a "financial matter." But he ended up also looking at the latest school books and inspecting the city's sewer system, expressing great admiration for it. It is unlikely that Mubarak accompanied Isma'il to the Paris exposition. While the exposition opened in June and Isma'il was among the attending guests, Mubarak mentions in his autobiography that his trip took place around October of that year.

We know that the following year, around April 1868, Mubarak was Nazir, or Minister, of both Public Works and Education.[30] In the ensuing fourteen years, Mubarak saw his portfolio enlarged and reduced several times to include the railways and the Diwan al-Awqaf, or Charitable Endowments. Every time he would fall out of favor with the khedive, he would be gradually removed from his multiple positions, only to return a few months later with new assignments.

It is significant to note here that even when the khedive's son, Prince Husain Kamel, was appointed to head all of Mubarak's different ministries, Mubarak was still retained as his deputy (1873–75), and later as his consultant (1875–77) for public works. And in 1879 he was returned again as Minister of Public Works under the new Khedive Tawfiq for a period of almost two years. Overall, Mubarak was the main figure in Public Works in Egypt for fourteen of the first eighteen years, after the department was established as a cabinet-level ministry. This meant he was no doubt the chief planner and architect of Cairo during its transformation before the twentieth century.

Abdel Rahman al-Rafi'i considers the period between 1868 and 1872 as the "golden age of Mubarak."[31] Indeed, that is when Mubarak was first appointed to his position as Minister of Public Works and given the title of Pasha. Isma'il commissioned Mubarak with three major tasks: supervising the execution of the Isma'ilya quarter; redeveloping the older vacant lands leading to Azbakiyya; and drawing up a master plan for the whole city, including the old city, along the lines of Hausmann's Paris. As Janet Abu Lughod has shown in her classic book on

Cairo, Mubarak delivered on all three fronts, though to differing degrees of completion.[32] Gas street lighting, which had started a few years earlier, was now in full swing; cast-iron water pipes were being rapidly installed; and the Opera House, the Dar al-Kuttub, and the Dar al-Ulum were built. Bold new thoroughfares like Shari' 'Abdel Aziz were built. Breaking into the medieval city was a process which had already begun, when al-Muski Street was expanded by taking the Rue Nueve, or al-Sikka al-Jadida, all the way to the east. It culminated with the carving out of the two-kilometer Muhammad 'Ali Boulevard, which connected the old city to Azbakiyya, and which required the demolition of more than 700 dwellings, baths, shops, and mosques. New palaces like those in Giza, Jazira, and Abdin were built, and new bridges at Qasr al-Nil and al-Nil al-'Amay were completed. Mubarak had a hand in each and every one of these projects. Before he took over, Cairo had only three squares, or *maydans*; by the time he was done, it had sixteen.

When Egypt fell into hard times because of its debt problems, Mubarak was a member of the government that accepted the dictates of the European powers to depose Isma'il as khedive. But at the first signs of serious revolutionary activity during the time of Urabi, Mubarak withdrew from any significant political engagement.[33] He was clearly not supportive of the "popular" uprising, siding often with the new Khedive Tawfiq, whom he considered "fair minded," against what he considered were the excesses of the officers' movement.[34] It is significant that after the British occupation of Alexandria in July 1882, Mubarak was invited by Urabi to attend a meeting in the Interior Ministry in Cairo to discuss the state of the country after the loss in the war. The attendees agreed to send a delegation to Khedive Tawfiq in Alexandria, asking him to return to Cairo and support efforts to continue the war. Mubarak was chosen to lead the delegation. But on his arrival in Alexandria, and upon failing to achieve his objective, Mubarak switched sides and joined the khedive. In fact, he seems not to have returned to Cairo until later in the year, possibly accompanying the khedive—who only returned when British forces occupied the city.[35] (This was the period in which *'Alamuddin* was likely published in Alexandria). And, it is this particular position which allowed many figures in the national movement, like Abdullah al-Nadim, to brand Mubarak a *kha'in*, or an outright traitor.[36]

In any case, Mubarak stayed out of politics from 1884–88, and during that period he seems to have spent much of his time in his home village, Birinbal.[37] It was probably during this time that he wrote his twenty-volume *al-Khitat al-tawfiqiyya al-Jadida*, an enormous opus of a little less than two million words—although some like Gabriel Baer argue unconvincingly that the statistics he used may push the writing back to the mid-1870s, or a decade earlier.[38] It is possible, if not likely, that Mubarak did start gathering data for the book around that time. Indeed, the various sources of the book, which include *waqffiyat* (or official *waqf* deeds), title and property records, travelers accounts, and other Arabic and European written sources, must have required him to keep a well-developed cataloging system. While it is difficult to judge how much of the work was Mubarak's own, he stated openly that he depended on others and enlisted the work of various scholars, and concentrated on revising and editing what he did not write.[39]

Since *khitat* literature had been popular in Egypt and other parts of the Arab world, it was not surprising for Mubarak to model his work after it. Indeed, in the first page of the introduction, he tells of the difficulty that anyone using the great work of the medieval historian al-Maqrizi, *al-Mawaz wa al'Atabar fi Dhikr al-Khitat wa al-athar*, would encounter in attempting to locate any historical building in a city that had undergone such major transformation in the preceding four centuries. His *Khitat* was supposed to remedy this problem. Like al-Maqrizi, his text was peppered with extensive biographies that resemble the medieval *tabaqat*. Similarly, his book starts with a review of the various historical periods. He, in fact, devotes all of volume I to his assesment of the Fatimids, the Ayyubids, the Mamluks, and the Ottomans.

The structure is similar in all of the segments. The city is divided into elements, and between the coverage of each element and the next, a section dealing with an event or person is sandwiched. In each segment, he invokes the comments of an outsider or traveler (Khusraw, Ibn Radhwan, etc.), and the text is divided equally between buildings and spaces on the one hand, and personalities and events on the other. It is in a sense a history of a dynasty through the chronology of what it built. He starts the book by telling us:

Cairo, city of al-Mu'izz and seat of the present Khedival government, has been often mentioned in books of geography and history and biography, and its buildings and gardens have been delineated. It is however no longer the way it once was. We have found no one among the sons of Egypt who can interpret for us these changes or instruct us in understanding the country's notable monuments. We look upon these works but do not know the circumstances of their creation, we wander through them but do not know who made them. . . . How many of the mounds that were once towering buildings, the ravines that were once splendid gardens, the tombs that lie hidden among the narrow lanes and the shrines scattered about in the open country, which the common people are wont to misidentify. . . . How many the mosques which are ascribed to men who did not build them, and (structures) to persons who had not even seen them. . . . But it is our duty to know these things, for it is not fitting for us to remain in ignorance of our country or to neglect the monuments of our ancestors. They are a moral lesson to the reflective mind, a memorial to the thoughtful soul. . . . For what our ancestors have left behind stirs in us the desire to follow in their footsteps, and to produce for our times what they produced for theirs.[40]

Although Mubarak is quite restrained, he does not, as Crabbs has argued, refrain from personal commentary.[41] He tells us, for example, that the Caliph al-'Adhad has a name with no meaning, and that the Caliph al-Fa'az, whose name meant "the triumphant," does not.[42] In reporting the incident surrounding Caliph Al-Aziz's attempt to dismantle some pyramids in search of treasures, Mubarak's language becomes sarcastic.[43] His assessment is that while in power, the Fatimids' ability to control the destiny of their caliphate created the natural conditions for buildings and activities to thrive.[44] He was not as generous toward the Ayubbids. He tells us that when the Fatimid dynasty fell it was replaced by the Ayubbids, and that the new conditions were colored by the habits of the new governing power, as was the case in his day.[45] He proceeds with other dynasties, insisting that he will always measure its present in relationship to its past.[46] The next five volumes are devoted to Cairo, while the seventh volume deals with Alexandria. The remaining volumes cover the rest of Egypt, with the last three dedicated to general issues ranging from the Nile, to the Suez Canal, to coinage and currency.

He starts the section on Cairo by slowly building through his narrative a full map of the city.[47] He first introduces the concept of sea level, and invokes the different flood levels that the city had experienced in recent history. Having established this horizontal plane, he then outlines the main streets of the city and the structures that they lie on. It is a method that allows the reader to mentally construct the topography of the city in relationship to specified coordinates—akin to building a three-dimensional physical model with only the important landmarks.

Anyone who could ever have characterized 'Ali Mubarak's work as aspatial need only read this section thoroughly to change his/her mind. But having declared 'Ali Mubarak not guilty of this charge, I cannot find him equally innocent of the charge of being avisual. Although he was a skilled draftsman who drew and used maps, he failed to include a single illustration or diagram in the *Khitat*. One can only speculate that Mubarak felt that his audience did not need, or would not have understood, such a medium.

In commenting on the architecture of his time, Mubarak does not hesitate to endorse the new *rumi* (foreign) building style, although he simplistically attributes its popularity to its being "handsome, cheaper, and better fitting."[48] He goes on to say that "the elevations of houses built in the new style have decorations and follow a regular building code unlike those of the old days that did not allow one to distinguish between house and tomb."[49]

The Cairo of Mubarak's *Khitat* was still described in terms of its eight districts (*athman*), classified since the time of the French expedition, in addition to Bulaq and Misr al-Qaddima. Mubarak lets us know that he would have liked to have indicated the exact boundaries of each district, but he refers those who want to know more to the relevant municipal offices.[50] It was a city that had 264 mosques, 294 tombs, 18 Tekkyas, 26,000 houses, 12,000 shops, 500 Rabas, 600 courts, 3,000 shacks, 16 hotels, 5 hospitals, 55 bathhouses, 44 pharmacies, and 20 water fountains.[51]

It was a city with 349 important streets that measured 82 kilometers and a number of smaller ones that measured more than 100 kilometers. It had 150,000 linear meters of cast-iron water pipe and 2,800 gas light posts. It covered an area of about 2,900 *feddans*, of which the old city constituted more than two-thirds. It housed a population of 374,838 people, of whom foreigners constituted 22,422, or around 5 percent (the majority being French, Italian, and Greek). These people lived in 31,632 dwellings, with an average of eleven persons/dwelling. It was a city that had many entertainment places. And while it had more than 1,000 cafes, it also had more than 500 bars and liquor stores (many of which were in Azbakiyya).

Although evidence to the contrary existed all around him, the Cairo of Mubarak's *Khitat* was not a divided one. The contrast between the areas where most of the foreigners lived and those where the majority of Cairenes lived had become, as many travelers of this time observed, a clear one. But Mubarak did not see it, or at least did not care to comment on it. Indeed, his public-works projects were about removing these distinctions by subjugating the old to the new. It followed, in turn, that his textual project had to focus on the old—to document it, without the need to contrast it to what was to overcome it.

Although Mubarak's role in the reshaping of Cairo cannot be made more specific, there is little doubt that his hand was heavy. After the excess of the Muhammad 'Ali Boulevard project, the approach changed at the end of the 1870s from an obsession with regular shapes to a more relaxed geometry, and from an ideal plan that ignored site particularities to one that allowed for compromise and dialogue.[52] This change was a product of what Asfour calls the "demystification of knowledge," a process of modifying the Hausmannian model so that a new one, more sensitive to the requirements of local culture, could emerge from it.

But 'Ali Pasha Mubarak remained unrepentant. While the Comité, which had recently been formed, was busy drawing up a list of 800 buildings to be preserved, the Tanzim, which was still under Mubarak's control in his last year at Public Works, was busy implementing demolitions. When the committee protested to Mubarak, he responded aggressively that beside these ancient monuments there had once stood places of execution. He went on to declare: "We no longer wish to preserve such memories. . . . We want to destroy them as the French destroyed the Bastille."[53]

But if Mubarak was not a preservationist as an administrator, he indeed was one as a writer. But his was only a symbolic preservation project, for he simultaneously realized the importance of both documenting the city, and initiating its transformation. His was the preservation of an imagined environment on its last gasp, a discursively constructed city divorced from the imperatives of his own actions.

'ALAMUDDIN AND THE *KHITAT* IN A TRANSNATIONAL CONTEXT

It should have become clear by now that to truly understand 'Ali Mubarak's positions and actions, it is necessary to concurrently employ *'Alamuddin* and the *Khitat*. If when reading the *Khitat* we have the impression that we are faced with a relic from an older literary tradition, with *'Alamuddin* we have certainly entered a more modern world.[54] And if in the *Khitat* Mubarak wanted to be descriptive and informative, in *'Alamuddin* he wanted to be instructive, and for this, expressing critical judgement was mandatory.[55] To use *'Alamuddin* to interrogate the *Khitat*, for the purposes of this chapter, I will only take two short subjects which are common in both works: the postal service and the railways.

In the *Khitat*, we are only told about the importance of the postal service. For example, we are told that in 1872 the service delivered more than two million packages, and we are made to recognize that securing communication through the service was necessary for the state to perform its functions.[56] And that is that! In *'Alamuddin* we learn a lot more—not from 'Alamuddin but from the Englishman who explains to the Shaikh how and when the collection from the boxes happens and how the parcels are transported. We learn of the postal servants who deliver mail based on a street map. We are also told, however, that in Cairo, people don't know the mail service or use it, and that mailmen have no street map or street guide, but they have to ask around. The Shaikh goes on to confess that while in Cairo, he thought about writing to his father, but he never used the postal service because it always required using surrogate names and connections to guarantee delivery. Without all of this detail, the postal service in the *Khitat* remains empty and contextless.

The case of the railways is even more revealing. In the *Khitat* we are told about 2,112 kilometers of railway lines which in 1871 transported more than seventy million passengers. We learn of the improvements 'Ali Mubarak brought to the service in terms of workshops for fixing the train cars, a new pricing system, and levels of service which improved passenger comfort and made the railways competitive.[57]

Compared to the eight pages on the railways in the *Khitat*, we get forty-four in *'Alamuddin*, and we learn a fuller story. We are told about how trains work, and we learn the history of both the steam engine and the railways in England and France. Then, when the Englishman asks 'Alamuddin about the introduction of the railways to Egypt, the Shaikh expresses his astonishment at the question and confesses his ignorance. He goes on to comment that the average Egyptian (Easterner) is not interested in those things, nor in how trains function. Instead, he seems only curious about the price of the ticket that would take him to his destination. We learn of 'Alamuddin's desire to see the trains used more creatively in Egypt. He particularly suggests that they can be employed to transport human

and animal excrement from the city to the fields where it can be used as fertiliz-
er. But knowing of the limitations in Egypt, he goes on to say that "for everything
there is an appropriate time and for every time, an appropriate condition. The
time will come when such things will happen (in Egypt), for nothing can happen
at once, but it must come gradually."[58]

CONCLUDING THOUGHTS

So where does this all leave us? It is clear from the *Khitat* that Mubarak's
approach to history, as evidenced by his reliance on numbers and statistics, was
colored by the positivist mood which dominated the nineteenth century.[59] In
Alamuddin every serious vignette is a discussion of historical change. Europeans,
Muslims, trade, cities, buildings are all placed in the context of progress and
decline.[60] Mubarak believed in progress and the possibility of change. Fictional
writing, which employed the conversational format in *Alamuddin*, gave him the
freedom to explore the notion of human beings as makers of history and con-
trollers of their own destinies. Thus, the fictional narrative is loaded with social
commentary that makes *Alamuddin* a factual testimony on Egypt of its time.

But 'Ali Mubarak, the planner, was a Westernized Westernizer who does not
seem to have had any doubts whatsoever about his course of action.[61] His *Khitat*
therefore reflected his desire to document an environment that he appreciated
for it past achievements, but one whose time he felt was over.

'Ali Mubarak was an Egyptian, and was proud of it. He was not one of those
foreign consultants imported by the khedive from abroad. His cause "was no less
than the transformation of his country." Speaking in moral terms, he held that
"Egyptians had somehow to be taught the necessity of subordinating their private
interests to a common good, a belief that underlies his persistent effort to instill
the idea of loyalty to an Egyptian *watan* (homeland or nation)."[62] Mubarak tells us
that sometimes a people have to be told what to do. He reminds us that when
Muhammad 'Ali introduced Indian cotton to Egypt, people only planted it under
great protest. And although they initially considered it oppressive, they all soon
converted to it when they realized the tremendous value and economic benefit
that would befall them.[63]

This was the kind of *watan* he wanted to see, and it was different from the one
in which he lived. Thus, in the *Khitat*, after describing the architectural features of
al-Azhar, Mubarak goes on to describe its scholars and students as ignorant, dirty,
and undignified.[64] In *Alamuddin*, the Shaikh makes the causes of illness among the
Azharis quite clear by reflecting upon his own experience. He says:

When I became a student in al-Azhar, I found the movement (of its members) very minimal. They sit for long periods reading and they have no time for entertainment. For the sake of attaining knowledge, I did like them, and was static all the time, although I knew that was a bad habit, especially for one's health, for the floor was cold and the covers on it thin. . . . I even got used to sleeping in my place. . . . This way, I developed all kinds of ailments.[65]

This was the static East that Mubarak was on a mission to eradicate.

In both *'Alamuddîn* and the *Khitat*, Mubarak seems to demonstrate, albeit to differing levels, some critical awareness of the idea of a socially constructed knowledge of the "other," from another time or another place. His project can be considered more transnational than comparative because, although preliminary, it is based on the recognition that what goes on over here is always shaped in terms of what goes on over there.[66]

In looking at the Parisian context, and in accepting the mediations and the translations of the Englishman, Mubarak also took a geopolitical position. He was not trying to adopt these ideas, or directly apply them to the Egyptian context; he was smarter than that! Mubarak knew that these concepts had to be reworked within national paradigms of meaning and action. This was a process of translation in which slippages of meaning were often deliberate, a process in which the certainties of home as *watan*, and of the other as the generic West, confronted one another in constant interrogation.

Among the characters that participated in reshaping the city in the nineteenth century, Mubarak stands out as different. It may be ironic, but it is not surprising, that the man who was in charge of managing the city's transformation for the longest time, the man who also wrote the most elaborate account of the city during the nineteenth century, was not indeed a contributor to the project of "making the city medieval." He may have been in fact one of its principal, and principled antagonists—and a declared one at that! It is my conviction that Mubarak's contribution to reinventing Cairo as an authentic Islamic city entering the modern world was only one of words, not deeds. These are the words found in both the testimony of his *'Alamuddîn*, and the imaginary of his *Khitat*.

NOTES

1. I. Bierman, "The Time and Space of Medieval Cairo," Unpublished paper, Misr Group (1997), p. 1.
2. Bierman, "The Time and Space of Medieval Cairo."
3. T. Mitchell, *Colonising Egypt* (Cambridge: Cambridge University Press, 1988).
4. Bierman, "The Time and Space of Medieval Cairo," p. 2.

5. As cited in J. Crabbs, *The Writing of History in Nineteenth-Century Egypt: A Study in National Transformation* (Cairo: American University in Cairo Press, 1984), p. 128.

6. G. Baer, "'Ali Mubarak's Khitat as a Source for the History of Modern Egypt" in P.M. Holt, ed., *Political and Social Change in Modern Egypt* (London: Oxford University Press, 1968), p. 27.

7. Crabbs, *The Writing of History*, p. 118.

8. M.J. Reimer, "Contradiction and Consciousness in 'Ali Mubarak's Description of Al-Azhar" *Journal of Middle East Studies* 29 (1997), p. 53.

9. G. el-Shayyal, *A History of Egyptian Historiography in the Nineteenth Century* (Alexandria: University of Alexandria, 1962).

10. El-Shayyal, *A History of Egyptian Historiography*, p. 108.

11. As cited in Reimer, "Contradiction and Consciousness," p. 65.

12. P. Starkey, "Some Egyptian Travellers in Europe" in P. Starkey and J. Starkey, eds., *Travellers in Egypt* (New York: I.B. Tauris, 1998), p. 283; and Baer, "'Ali Mubarak's Khitat," p. 24.

13. J.W. Scott, *Gender and the Politics of History* (New York: Columbia University Press, 1988), p. 32.

14. As cited in R.F. Hunter, *Egypt under the Khedives, 1805–1879* (Pittsburgh: University of Pennsylvania Press, 1984), p. 127.

15. J. Abu Lughod, *Cairo: 1001 Years of the City Victorious* (Princeton: Princeton University Press, 1971), p. 105.

16. A. Mubarak, *Al-khitat al-Tawfiqiyya al-Jadida li-Misr al-Qahirah wa Muduniha wa Biladiha al-Qadima wa al-Shahira*, Vol. 9 (Cairo: Bulaq Press, 1887–89), p. 45.

17. M. Amara, *'Ali Mubarak: Mu'warkh wa Muhandas al-Umran* (Cairo: Dar al-Shorouk, 1988), pp. 116–20. Evidence of this may also be found in vignette #119 in *'Alamuddin* which gives cotton statistics of 1858; vignette #109 which talks about the difference between his description of Paris and that in al-Tahtawi thirty years earlier in 1826–31; and in the introduction which refers to the copy editor, Abdalallah Fikry, who held the position of Wakil in the Ministry of Education in 1879.

18. Cited as *Kitab Tariq al-Hija* in B.F. Musallam, "The Modern Vision of 'Ali Mubarak" in R.B. Serjeant, ed., *The Islamic City* (Paris: UNESCO, 1980), p. 191.

19. A. Mubarak, *'Alamuddin*, Vol. 1 (Alexandria: Mahrousa Press, 1882), p. 3.

20. Amara, *'Ali Mubarak*, p. 80.

21. Mubarak, *Al-khitat*, Vol. 11, p. 10.

22. G. Roper, "Texts from Nineteenth Century Egypt: The Role of E.W. Lane" in Starkey and Starkey, eds., *Travellers in Egypt*, p. 248.

23. Mubarak, *'Alamuddin*, Vol. 4, p. 1334, as cited in Musallam, "The Modern Vision of 'Ali Mubarak."

24. W. Al-Qadi, "East and West in 'Ali Mubarak's 'Alamuddin," in M.R. Buheiry, ed., *Intellectual Life in the Arab East, 1890–1939* (Beirut: American University of Beirut, 1996), p. 25.

25. Ibid., p. 28.

26. Al-Qadi, "East and West," p. 29.

27. Ibid., p. 34.

28. Ibid., p. 37.

29. A. Al Rafi'i, *Asr Ismail*, Vol. 3 (Cairo: Al-Ma'araf, 1932), p. 94, cited in M. Serageldin, "Urbanization and Social Change in a Foreign Dominated Economy, Cairo 1805–1930," unpublished Ph.D dissertation, Harvard University (1972), p. 115.

30. A. Sami, *Taquim al-Nil*, Vol. 3, No. 2 (Cairo: Al-Matba'al-Amiriya, 1916), p. 695.

31. Al-Rafi'i, *Asr Ismail*, p. 232.

32. Abu Lughod, *Cairo*, p. 105.

33. Crabbs, *The Writing of History*, p. 113.

34. Ibid., p. 113.

35. A. Shafiq, *Musakarati*, Vol. 1 (Cairo: Al-Hai'a al-Misriya, 1934); and Al-Rafi'i, *Asr Ismail*, Vol. 1, p. 242.

36. As cited in Crabbs, *The Writing of History*, p. 113.

37. Amara, *'Ali Mubarak*, p. 112.

38. Baer, "'Ali Mubarak's Khitat," p. 14.

39. As cited in Crabbs, *The Writing of History*, p. 116. In this paper, I cannot do justice to the *Khitat* as a major text, and I will assume adequate knowledge of it by the readers.

40. As translated by Reimer, "Contradiction and Consciousness," p. 60.

41. Crabbs, *The Writing of History*, p. 119.

42. Mubarak, *Al-khitat*, Vol. 1, p. 18.

43. Ibid., p. 24.

44. Ibid., p. 22.

45. Ibid., p. 27.

46. Ibid., p. 50.

47. Ibid., Vol. 2, p. 80.

48. Ibid., Vol. 1, p. 85.

49. Ibid., p. 86.

50. Ibid., Vol. 2, p. 83.

51. Ibid., Vol. 1, pp. 94–97.

52. K. Asfour, "The Domestication of Knowledge: Cairo at the Turn of the Century," *Muqarnas* 18 (1998), p. 129.

53. As cited in J. Berque, *Egypt: Imperialism and Revolution* (trans. J. Stewart) (London: Faber and Faber, 1972), p. 92.

54. Starkey, "Some Egyptian Travellers in Europe," p. 284.

55. Al-Qadi, "East and West," p. 25.

56. Mubarak, *Al-khitat*, Vol. 7, p. 86.

57. Ibid., pp. 87–92.

58. Mubarak, *'Alamuddin*, Vol. 1, pp. 89 and 130.

59. N. Najib, *Rihlat Alam al-Din* (Beirut: Dar Al-Kma, 1981), p. 88.

60. Musallam, "The Modern Vision of 'Ali Mubarak," p. 196.

61. Musallam, "The Modern Vision of 'Ali Mubarak," p. 193.

62. Hunter, *Egypt under the Khedives*, pp. 137–38.

63. Mubarak, *'Alamuddin*, Vol. 4, p. 1445.

64. Mubarak, *Al-khitat*, Vol. 4, p. 29, as cited in Reimer, "Contradiction and Consciousness," p. 68.

65. Mubarak, *'Alamuddin*, Vol. 4, p. 1181, as cited in Al-Qadi, "East and West," pp. 30–31.

66. I. Grewal, *Home and Harem: Nation, Gender, Empire, and the Cultures of Travel* (Durham, NC: Duke University Press, 1996), p. 17; and G. Spivak, *The Post-Colonial Critic* (New York: Routledge, 1990).

PART II

REPRESENTING AND NARRATING

5

Performing Cairo: Orientalism and the City of the Arabian Nights

Derek Gregory

> Cities and narratives have at least one thing in common: they are both desire-
> producing machines. . . . These two trajectories can be said to cross when
> the object of desire becomes, precisely, desire for the narrativized city, for its
> fictional images.[1]

This essay is about the ways in which the city of Cairo was "narrativized"—or,
more prosaically, ordered as a story—by European and American travelers and
tourists during the nineteenth century.[2] These were, of course, neither the only
people nor the only terms through which the city was made intelligible. There
were other imaginative geographies in play, and these were neither self-enclosed
nor self-sufficient constructions. It is certainly not part of my purpose to privilege these narratives, therefore, which were fictions in the original sense of *fictio*:
"something made." But for this very reason they had a substantial reality. What
visitors "made" of Cairo (or any other city) was rendered not only through their
accounts but also through their actions, and we need to know much more about
these spatial stories and how they worked. As Michel de Certeau has reminded
us, "every story is a travel story"—what he calls a "spatial practice"; and these nar-
rations at once produce "geographies of actions" and drift into "the common-
places of an order."[3]

My focus here is on the stories that made up the *Thousand and One Nights*, or the
Arabian Nights Entertainments. As Robert Irwin has noted, these stories were narrated "for the most part by people in the cities about people in the cities for people
in the cities," but in the course of the nineteenth century the *mythos* of the *Nights*
was inscribed in one city in particular: Cairo.[4] This was more than a genealogical
claim; not only were the *Nights* supposed to have been staged in medieval Cairo,

they were also held to capture the essence of the city in the nineteenth century. Many actors were involved in the staging of Cairo as the city of the *Arabian Nights*, but here I consider one of the central players in this Orientalist repertory theater—not only actor but also director and stage manager—the British Orientalist Edward William Lane.

In 1819, Lane, then just eighteen years of age, abandoned plans to study at Cambridge and moved to London to work with his older brother, an accomplished engraver and lithographer. In 1820 Belzoni's published account of his "operations and recent discoveries in Egypt and Nubia" excited considerable public interest, and the following year an exhibition of the artifacts he had brought back to England opened at the Egyptian Hall in Piccadilly and attracted large crowds. Caught up in the whirlwind of Egyptomania, Lane began to read about Egypt and to learn Arabic. Then, when he contracted a chronic respiratory disease that ruled out any hope of a career in the fume-filled workshops of the engraving industry, he decided to travel to the land that had completely captured his imagination.

This is no exaggeration; Lane's desire to know Egypt was intense. In September 1825, as he approached the port of Alexandria for the first time, he said that he "felt like an Eastern bridegroom, about to lift up the veil of his bride, and to see for the first time, the features which were to charm, or disappoint, or disgust him."[5] This first visit lasted for three years. Lane rented a house in Cairo, staying there on and off for fifteen months or so, and made two long voyages up the Nile into Nubia. All the while he made extensive notes and sketches that provided the basis for his *Description of Egypt*, a masterwork which nonetheless remained unpublished during his lifetime.[6]

Lane's second visit took place between 1833 and 1835, and he used his renewed residence in Cairo to compose his celebrated account of the manners and customs of the modern Egyptians, which was published in two volumes in 1836.[7] It was in the preface to that book that Lane first recorded his admiration for the *Arabian Nights*:

> There is one work . . . which presents most admirable pictures of the manners
> and customs of the Arabs, and particularly those of the Egyptians; it is "*The
> Thousand and One Nights; or Arabian Nights' Entertainments*." If the English reader
> had possessed a close translation of it with sufficient illustrative notes, I might
> almost have spared myself the labour of the present undertaking.[8]

In fact, Lane referred to the *Arabian Nights* throughout *Modern Egyptians* and repeatedly declared his confidence in its "faithful pictures." He completed his own translation of the stories two years later. This was originally published in serial form between 1838 and 1840—the episodic structure of the *Arabian Nights* made the stories ideal for serialization—and then in three bound volumes between 1839 and 1841. In order to understand Lane's pivotal role in staging Cairo as the city of the *Arabian Nights* it is necessary to understand the relations between these two central texts.

CHOREOGRAPHIES OF CAIRO

Despite its general title, *Modern Egyptians* focused on Cairo, which Lane saw as the epitome of what he called "the Arab city."

> In every point of view, *Masr* (or Cairo) must be regarded as the first Arab city of our age; and the manners and customs of its inhabitants are particularly interesting. . . . There is no other place in which we can obtain so complete a knowledge of the most civilised classes of the Arabs.[9]

In this book Lane made Cairo visible not so much as a *produced space* of topographies, streets, and buildings as a *performed space* of costumes, gestures, and movements. This is so important that I need to take time to establish the distinction. In his draft of the *Description of Egypt* Lane had provided a map of Cairo based on the map produced by the French army of occupation, and he had included detailed sketches and annotated views of particular districts and descriptions of individual buildings.[10] In contrast, *Modern Egyptians* contained no map; indeed, it provided only the briefest of physical descriptions of the city—and that as mere "Introduction," not as a chapter. In addition, only a handful of its 130 illustrations showed mosques, streets, or houses, none of which were identified by name or location.[11] In their place, Lane offered exquisitely detailed renderings—in word and image—of costume and ornamentation, of bodily postures and sequences of movement. He began by describing the sumptuary distinctions between different social orders, and then immediately set these costumed figures in motion. Lane provided elaborate renditions of ritual ablutions and sequential "postures of prayer" (FIGURE 5.1). He furnished detailed accounts of modes of salutation, eating, and bathing, in which he paid close attention to the precise placement and movement of the body; he described modes of physical punishment through the dispositions of the body, and the different postures adopted for playing different musical instruments.[12] Lane followed groups of people as they moved through the city in circumcision parades, bridal processions, religious celebrations, and funerals. And at every step he recorded the order of precedence, pace, accoutrements, and ritual ejaculations (FIGURE 5.2).[13] When Lane described the public shows put on by dancers, "serpent-charmers and performers of legerdemain," jugglers, rope-dancers, farce-players, and storytellers, he drew elaborate word-pictures of their gestures, sleights-of-hand, and bodily movements.[14]

Figure 5.1. Postures of prayer
(Source: E.W. Lane, Manners and Customs of the Modern Egyptians*)*

Even when Lane addressed the realm of fantasy, superstition, and mysticism, his accounts of spirits—*ginn, efreets,* and *ghools*—and holy men (*welees*) were acutely physical. He described how the *ginn* were supposed to inhabit "rivers, ruined houses, wells, baths, ovens, and even the latrina." According to Lane's informants, these spirits flew across the landscape "in a whirlwind of sand or dust," and they could assume the shapes of cats, dogs, "and other brute animals." If they were disturbed, they perched on the roofs of houses and threw stones onto the streets below. Some *welees* wandered the city "perfectly naked," Lane noted, eating "a mixture of chopped straw and broken glass, and attract[ing] observation by a variety of absurd actions," while others subjected themselves to "austerities" and even physical abuse. "At the present time there is living in Cairo a *welee* who has placed an iron collar round his neck, and chained himself to a wall of his chamber," Lane reported, "and it is said that he has been in this state more than thirty years." One of the most holy of these men, the Kutb, was supposed to be able to transport himself in an instant from Mecca to Cairo; one of his favored stations was the gate of Bab Zuwayla, where believers would drive nails into the door to cure a headache or wedge extracted teeth into a crevice to prevent toothache. Lane recorded in meticulous detail attempts to ward off "the Evil Eye" by, for example, burning alum and feeding its fetishized shape to a black dog, or by dissolving passages from the Koran in water and drinking the liquid. Among other practices, Lane described attempts to cure ophthalmia by removing dried mud from one bank of the Nile to the other, or by washing in water from the trough at Rumayla where the bodies of decapitated criminals were cleansed.[15]

Figure 5.2. Bridal Procession
(Source: E.W. Lane, Manners and Customs of the Modern Egyptians*)*

Lane's descriptions amounted to an intensely physical *anatomy* of the day-to-day practices of ordinary Egyptians. For the most part these details were conveyed through sets of exacting stage directions, but on occasion he sought to draw the reader into the *mise-en-scène*.

One episode that was often remarked by his readers involved Lane's attendance at a performance by "the Magician." Lane had been instructed to prepare a concoction of frankincense and coriander seed. He then describes in his customary detail how the magician placed this in a chafing dish and set it alight; how written invocations were cast into the flames; and how the magician drew a "magic square" on the palm of a young boy (which Lane reproduced to accompany his text) and poured ink into the center of the square to create a "magic mirror" through which the boy was supposed to be able to peer into "the invisible world." Lane then writes how the magician asked him if he "wished the boy to see any person who was absent or dead." When Lane called for Lord Nelson, "of whom the boy had evidently never heard," he was astonished to hear the boy describe him as indeed he would appear in a mirror: "a man, dressed in a black suit of European clothes; the man has lost his left arm." The boy's description was "faultless," Lane writes; and his next request was met with similar success. But, thereafter, the boy represented each subsequent figure "as appearing less distinct than the preceding one, as if his sight were gradually becoming dim."

By the end of the performance, Lane confesses that he is "completely puzzled," "unable to discover any clue by which to penetrate the mystery." There can be no doubt about Lane's fascination; his prose shifts from anatomy to narrative, a movement that simultaneously mirrors his own involvement and draws the reader into the vortex with him. Even when Lane struggles to recover his analytical voice, he picks through a series of possible explanations only to discard each of them in turn. And yet his unease is also palpable: aware of his momentary loss of perspective, he hopes the reader "will not allow the above account to induce in his mind any degree of scepticism with respect to other portions of this work." Only in a later edition did Lane add a footnote to report that he had since witnessed two further performances "which were absolute failures." It is as though, having teetered on the perimeter of enchantment, Lane is relieved finally to revert to his own space of modern reason.[16]

A second incident is even more telling. Lane has already described the different orders of dervishes (religious fraternities) and subjected their costumes and devotional exercises to his usual impassionate dissection.[17] But then he decides to conduct the reader to one of their ritual performances. His narrative begins with him in Turkish dress, making his way to the mosque of al-Hosayn, "the most sacred of all the mosques in Cairo." It is early afternoon, and as he moves through the crowded streets he is accosted by a succession of dancing-girls, water-carriers, and children clamoring for alms. At the mosque he leaves his shoes at the door and threads his way barefoot into its vast interior. There is a confusion of noises, men and women calling to each other, and children crying. Some of the youngest had urinated on the floor, and since it was impracticable to perform the usual ablutions, it is not many minutes before Lane's feet are "almost black, with the dust upon which I had trodden, and with that from other persons' feet which had trodden upon mine." "The heat too was very oppressive," he continues, "like that of a vapour-bath, but more heavy." The physical sensations that Lane evokes—the noise, the dust, the crush of the crowd, the soaring humidity—transport him to the edge of sensuality, and his passage into the heart (and heat) of the festival is laced with a barely contained *frisson* of desire:

It is commonly said, by the people of Cairo, that no man goes to the mosque
of the Hasaneyn on the day of 'Ashorà but for the sake of the women; that is,
to be jostled among them; and this jostling he may indeed enjoy to the utmost
of his desire, as I experienced in this pressing forward to witness the principal
ceremonies which contribute with the sanctity of the day to attract such
swarms of people. . . . I was so compressed in the midst of four women, that,
for some minutes, I could not move in any direction; and was pressed so hard
against one young woman, face to face, that, but for her veil, our cheeks had
been almost in contact: from her panting, it seemed that the situation was not
quite easy to her; though a smile, expressed at the same time by her large black
eyes, showed that it was amusing: she could not, however, bear it long; for
soon she cried out, "My eye! Do not squeeze me so violently."[18]

Eventually, Lane forces his way through the throng until he reaches the place
where the dervishes are to perform their *zikr*. "But in getting thither," he notes, "I
had almost lost my sword, and the hanging sleeves of my jacket; some person's
dress had caught the guard of the sword, and had nearly drawn the blade from the
scabbard before I could get hold of the hilt. Like all around me, I was in a pro-
fuse perspiration." Before the *zikr* can begin, the dervishes drive back the crowd
to clear a space. "But as no stick was raised at me," Lane explains, "I did not retire
so far as I ought to have done; and before I was aware of what the [dervishes]
were about to do, forty of them with extended arms and joined hands, had
formed a large ring in which I found myself enclosed." Lane now breaks the circle and passes "outside the ring"; and as he does so, he immediately regains the
customary, detached position from which he describes the performance in his
standard analytical style. But he has already evoked an acutely physical, sensual
space which he has both literally and figuratively penetrated, and through which
he has permitted the reader a glimpse of the event from the inside.[19]

These summary observations permit two general conclusions. First, all the
way through *Modern Egyptians*—in all of Lane's accounts of bodies in motion, of the
materiality of everyday beliefs, of the physicality of public festivals—his descriptions are embedded in particular places. But rather than enumerate these as so
many sites in a general topography, he evokes them through the practices that take
place within them. The overall effect of *Modern Egyptians* is thus to stage Cairo as
an immense, intricate choreography—corporeal, fantastic, and seductive—whose
spaces are continuously and elaborately *performed*.[20]

Ostensibly, of course, the performances are those of Lane's "modern
Egyptians." But, secondly, it is important not to lose sight of Lane's *own* practices
and engagements, and in particular the way in which his desire for the Orient
draws him into the *mise-en-scène* so that he too is performing the spaces of the city.
He not only records the corporeality and physicality of the "manners and customs"

he observes, but he also registers his immersion in them through his *own* body. Thus, even as he struggles to turn the city into an object of knowledge, to maintain his distance, and to impose his own discipline of detail, Cairo nonetheless appears in Lane's text as a space in which corporeality, fantasy, and desire collide.[21]

Many travelers took Lane's *Modern Egyptians* to Egypt with them, and it became a *vade mecum* for European and American tourists for the rest of the century and beyond. The first edition was sold out in a fortnight; 6,500 copies of the second edition were sold in short order. It was on virtually every list of books travelers were recommended to read, and travel writers and guidebooks routinely parroted Lane's observations and pirated his illustrations. "I have taken the greater part of these observations from Mr. Lane's invaluable work," Warburton confessed, "the highest authority." Others were reduced to awed silence. "So perfect an account of the Arabian population of Cairo is to be found in Mr. Lane's *Modern Egypt[ians]*," wrote Robert Curzon, "that there is little left to say on that subject." Still others regretted that Lane was not accompanying them in person. To Curtis the cries of the street-sellers were "Babel jargon"; but "had erudite Mr Lane accompanied us, Mr Lane, the Eastern Englishman, who has given us so many golden glimpses into the silence and mystery of Oriental life," then "we should have understood those cries."[22]

Later guidebooks did not so much supplant as proliferate the rumor of Cairo offered by *Modern Egyptians*. Murray's *Handbook* (to take only the most prominent example) detailed a series of architectural sights—the Pyramids, the tombs of the Caliphs and the Mamluks, the principal mosques, the palace and gardens at Shubra, and the Citadel—and most tourists seem to have dutifully followed its exacting instructions. But Murray also emphasized the "Oriental character" of Cairo that would inevitably recall "the impressions [the traveler] received on reading the *Arabian Nights*," and drew his own readers' attention to "the accurate work of Mr. Lane" in rendering "the mode of living" in this singularly interesting city.[23] It was this side of Cairo that increasingly claimed the attention of tourists. Many of them shared Lane's taste for the corporeal, which often turned into a predilection for the grotesque and the bizarre: visits to the bodies exhibited in the slave market, the Lunatic Asylum, and the hospital were *de rigueur* until the 1840s. Most remained at a greater remove, however, content to rehearse Lane's sketches in their own journals, and effortlessly transposing the "moving panoramic displays of human beings" in the streets and bazaars into a parade of different ethnographic "types."[24]

Emboldened by Lane's example, there was little that they considered properly concealed from their gaze. Middle-class distinctions between the public and private, commonplace in Europe, literally had no place in their appropriations of Cairo. They desperately wanted to know—to know by *seeing*—what went on behind the closed doors and the latticed balconies of the houses they passed.

"Domestic manners and customs, the interiors of houses, and the common habits of the higher classes in everyday life among the Orientals have an unspeakable interest to Europeans," Smith explained, which "is undoubtedly heightened in no inconsiderable degree by the reserve with which they have thought fit to envelop their home life."[25] Inquisitive tourists set aside not only their own proprieties about the private sphere but also the still more elaborately gendered visual codes through which the spaces of the *hara* and the household were regulated in an Islamic city. While men had to accept that access to the harem was denied to them, that did nothing to stop speculation (quite the reverse); and many thought nothing of straying from the well-defined tourist routes into local neighborhoods where they found, like Bayle St. John, that "in retired places it is sometimes not too discreet to push too far into the labyrinth of gloomy blind alleys formed by these quarters."

> I was once, in my prowlings about in search of the picturesque, shut in by the porter, who walked off with the key. Energetic expostulation procured us an exit at last, without any disagreeable consequence, except the delay; but we were very nearly mobbed by a crowd of women returning from the market, whom we found collected outside.[26]

St. John was seemingly quite oblivious of the visual codes that his casual sightseeing had transgressed.

Tourists had no hesitation in entering the mosques to observe (on occasion, even to draw) Cairenes at prayer. In the early decades of the nineteenth century, foreigners were obliged to wear Turkish dress to gain admission. But as late as 1842 Lane's sister managed to visit the mosque of al-Hosayn, one of the most sacred in the city, through just such an imposture.[27]

In 1849 Florence Nightingale found that gaining entrance to those where admission was less restricted was still a performance: "You must have a *firman* [written permission], and a Pacha's *janissary* [escort], and pistols, and whips, and I don't know what to visit them." But to be able to watch the observances was an invaluable experience. Nightingale repeatedly described Islam as a "sensual" religion, by which she seems to have had in mind the way in which a faith without the icons and images that were so central to Christianity was literally embodied in the postures and dispositions assumed by its adherents. For this very reason she doubted that Europeans would ever be able to grasp its "mixture of sensuous enthusiasm and purity of idea." Nightingale described wandering through the vast, silent spaces of the mosques to watch the "prostrate men with their faces to the ground." "It is the religion of the *Arabian Nights*," she declared, "the most dreamy, the most fantastic, the most airy and yet sensuous religion." Later she visited the al-Azhar mosque, the primary seat of Islamic learning in Egypt. Its outer court was "crowded with people, sitting, standing, praying, talking"; beyond, in the portico, she found circles of men "intently listening, or writing, or learning by heart" from the Koran. "That was the most Oriental sight I ever saw," she told her family, "those lecturing *ulama*, those silent circles sitting on the ground: no need of desks or benches; each had his little plate to write on upon his knee, his ink-horn in his girdle, each sat cross-legged on the mat."[28]

It would be possible to follow more tourists through Cairo, peering with them over Lane's shoulder as they gazed at sight after sight—wedding processions, funerals, festivals, and more—but the point is surely clear enough. As Lane's imaginative geography was repeated with variations from text to text, so a repertoire gradually emerged whose iterations simultaneously conjured and confirmed Cairo as a performed space: a city of bodies in motion. The Countess Hahn-Hahn was not alone in finding that "the busy throng of men in the streets, stunning the ear and dazzling the eye, [is] yet altogether so essential a part of the whole scene, that you find no attraction in the more quiet and unfrequented parts of the city." Martineau confessed that "the mere spectacle of the streets" became "more bewitching every day." Clot Bey thought that it was precisely the singular motion of "the gaily coloured crowd" between its flights of houses, along the streets that snaked through them and beneath the minarets that towered above them, that made Cairo "a real city of the *Thousand and One Nights*." And Moritz Busch was quite explicit. "To many," he wrote, "the life and bustle of the streets of the city will be more interesting than the city itself, reminding them of the 'Arabian tales.'"[29]

SPACES OF FANTASY

All of this laid the foundation for the figuration of Cairo as the city of the *Arabian Nights*. The nucleus of the *Nights* (in Arabic, *Alf Layla wa-Layla*, or *The Thousand and One Nights*) appeared in Arabic in the ninth century. But the tales have multiple origins—Indian and Persian as well as Arabic—and they were far from stable in either their oral or their textual forms. The European reception of the tales was itself highly mediated: "Because the *Nights* was textually uncertain, fragmentary, contradictory, and, probably most of all, Arabic, Europeans treated it with a freedom unconstrained by post-medieval perceptions of textual rights."[30] Some of the individual stories contained within the *Nights* were known to Europeans—at least in outline—as early as the fifteenth century, but they were first translated as a corpus by Antoine Galland, whose *Mille et une nuits: contes Arabes* was published in twelve volumes between 1704 and 1717. Galland's edition was loosely based on a fourteenth-century manuscript version of the tales that he had bought in Istanbul, but he also incorporated an extraordinarily diverse range of other sources, oral as well as written. His was an artistic reworking, in which he both excised from and elaborated on his originals. In doing so, Galland enhanced the magical tonalities of the tales; but his preface also drew attention to the insights they offered into the manners and customs of their subjects, and he added glosses to the text to explain cultural usages that would be unfamiliar to his French audience.[31]

This double emphasis on the fantastic and the factual was retained when Galland's early volumes were translated into English as *The Arabian Nights Entertainments* between 1706 and 1708. This anonymous Grub Street version captured the imagination of its audience too; already in its third edition by 1715, it was reprinted many times and spawned a fashion for "Oriental tales" that endured well into the nineteenth century. In 1811 Jonathan Scott produced a more literary but still immensely popular English translation; he had intended to translate directly from the Arabic, but produced what was, for the most part, a new translation of Galland. These adaptations were all celebrated for their fantasy, but the *Nights* also continued to be advertised as a text,

> . . . where the customs of the Orientals and the ceremonies of their religion were better traced than in the tales of the travelers. . . . All Orientals, Persians, Tartars and Indians . . . appear just as they are from sovereigns to people of the lowest condition. *Thus the reader will have the pleasure of seeing them and hearing them without taking the trouble of travelling to see them in their own countries.*[32]

By the close of the eighteenth century, and certainly by the early nineteenth century, cultivated European audiences appear to have accepted that the tales were authentic, and that it was possible to derive a virtual experience of "the Orient" through reading the *Arabian Nights*.

However, when Lane offered his translation from the Arabic in the late 1830s, he argued that Galland had "excessively perverted" the specificity of the original, and sacrificed what he took to be its most remarkable quality—namely, "its minute accuracy with respect to those peculiarities which distinguish the Arabs from every other nation, not only of the West, but also of the East." "Deceived by the vague nature of Galland's version," he complained, "travellers in Persia, Turkey and India have often fancied that the *Arabian Tales* describe the particular manners of the natives of the countries." Lane was adamant that they did not. "It is in Arabian countries," he insisted, "and especially in Egypt, that we see the people, the dresses and the buildings which [they] describe." Even when the tales made direct reference to Baghdad or Damascus, Lane claimed that their real locus was Cairo. "Cairo is the city in which Arabian manners now exist in the most refined state," he declared, "and such I believe to have been the case when the present work was composed."[33] In his own translation, Lane declared that "all the complete copies (printed and manuscript) of which I have any knowledge describe Cairo far more minutely and accurately than any other place."[34] Although there were several regional variants of the *Nights*, Lane's edition was primarily based on an Egyptian manuscript that had been published by Muhammad 'Ali's state printing press at Bulaq in 1835 and which provided a specifically Cairene version of them.[35] Lane emphasized the embeddedness of his source text in Cairo, and went out of his way to enhance those connections in two mutually reinforcing ways.

In the first place, Lane traded on his own experience—his ethnographic presence—to trump Galland's bookish knowledge and to confirm the locus of the *Nights*. The root of the Frenchman's inadequacy, according to Lane, was that "his acquaintance with Arab manners and customs was insufficient to preserve him always from errors of the grossest description." By contrast, Lane derived a superior authority from his extended visits to Egypt.

> I consider myself possessed of the chief qualifications for the proper accomplishment of my present undertaking, from my having lived several years in Cairo, associating almost exclusively with Arabs, speaking their language, conforming to their general habits with the most scrupulous exactitude, and [being] received into their society on terms of perfect equality.[36]

In the second place, no doubt influenced by his experience in his brother's workshop, Lane was keenly aware of the power of the visual, and he was particularly concerned to ensure the fidelity of the engravings that accompanied his translation.

> [T]o insure their accuracy, to the utmost of my ability, I have supplied the artist with modern dresses, and with other requisite materials. Thus he has been enabled to make his designs agree more nearly with the costumes &c. of the times which the tales generally illustrate.[37]

Providing his artist, William Harvey, with "modern dresses"—contemporary Egyptian costume—served to set "the times which the tales generally illustrate" in a perpetual present, and this setting was enhanced by the attention Lane paid to the scenography itself. Through his friend Robert Hay, he secured access for Harvey to "a very accurate and very beautiful collection of drawings of a great number of the finest specimens of Arabian architecture in and around Cairo executed by M. Pascal Coste."[38] In places he identified the precise location of the building shown in the illustration (FIGURE 5.3).

Lane furnished the text with copious "illustrative notes," whose ethnographic and lexicographic weight was more than sufficient for most readers. These drew on the empirical observations he had made for *Modern Egyptians*, and so they

Figure 5.3. Bab Zuwayla, Cairo
(Source: E.W. Lane, The Thousand and
One Nights: The Arabian Nights'
Entertainments*)*

embedded the tales still more firmly in contemporary Egypt, and gave them still
more solidity and substance. But even more importantly, these annotations
enforced a strategically vital distinction between observer and observed. In the
original, the individual tales were framed by the story of Sheherazade artfully
telling a different tale each night to forestall her death at the hands of her husband. But in his own presentation of the *Arabian Nights* Lane effectively removed
Sheherazade to the margins and substituted his own narrative commentary as the
master-frame. His annotated scaffolding constructed a vantage point where his
readers could perch, and from which the text itself could become "a means for
talking to Europeans about the people who made and heard the tales."[39] This was
a profoundly colonizing gesture. Reading the text became not merely an entertainment but an occasion to observe "the other"—in fact, to constitute the other
as other. As one critic has remarked:

> Lane's notes appear more and more oppressive as one reads on; no arbitrary
> detail is left hermetic—each is pinned down, like an ill-fated butterfly, by Lane's
> imperturbable attestations. Repeatedly, the course of the narrative is stayed to

accommodate Lane's parallel and dictatorial [commentary]; the text for him is pretext, the translation a mere vessel for his counterpart deliberations.[40]

Neither did Lane leave the original untouched. His translation was an expurgated version, to the evident relief of his nephew. "'*Arabian Nights*' is not a prurient book," Lane-Poole insisted, "but in the original it often frankly describes things we do not talk about, and it was inevitable that it must be carefully cleansed of such details if it were to be placed in everyone's hands."[41] Lane's edition sanitized the imaginative geography of Cairo—his was a version of the *Arabian Nights* suitable for the English middle-class drawing room—but this was plainly part of its popular appeal. In erasing the coarse and the carnivalesque, which seem to have been precisely what captivated its Cairene audience, Lane domesticated the *Arabian Nights* for his own domestic audience.

The impression that these stories provided the reader with access to contemporary Cairo depended upon the close connections that Lane established between *Modern Egyptians* and the *Arabian Nights*.[42] His nephew rehearsed Lane's sense of the connective imperative between the two when he described the *Arabian Nights* as an "indispensable supplement" to *Modern Egyptians*. He also captured the conflation of fantasy and fidelity achieved by this rhetoric of supplementarity when he introduced a new edition of Lane's translation of the tales. "The fashion of travelling in the East," he wrote, "has not a little added to the desire for a standard and annotated edition of a work, unique in those lands of genii and adventure, in its remarkable portrayal of Eastern character, life, and when closely translated, idiom." The sutures holding Lane-Poole's sentence together are instructive: "a land of genii" captured in a "remarkable portrayal" of the manners and customs of modern Egyptians. As Lane said himself of the *Arabian Nights*: "Its chief *value* consists in the fullness and fidelity with which it describes the character, manners, and customs of the Arabs, though its *enchantment* is doubtless mainly owing to other qualities."[43]

It was not only English and American readers who were under its spell. Although Ampère thought Lane too severe toward Galland, he had high praise both for Lane's translation—"the first correct version"—and for the illustrations that accompanied it, which "reproduced very faithfully a costume, a group, a street corner, such as one encounters with every step one takes in Cairo."[44] The *Arabian Nights* were invoked over and over again in an interpretative spiral where, following Lane's lead, Cairo was identified as the setting for the tales; their imagery was used to validate the continued "authenticity" of daily life in the city; and the city was thereby confirmed as the setting for the tales.[45] The citationary structure sustained by repetition from one text to another anticipated, organized, and verified the scene. Thus Warburton enthused at his approach to Cairo because it was thronged with "a masquerading-looking crowd" that contained "all the *dramatis personae* of the *Arabian Nights*"; Hahn-Hahn delighted in the way in which the city "continually reminds us of scenes in the *Thousand and One Nights*"; and Bartlett marveled at the way in which the city of Saladin and the *Arabian Nights*, "creations which once so fanciful and visionary, seem[ed] to kindle into life as we gaze upon every object that surrounds us."[46] In a passage whose imagery was repeated time and time again, Curtis wrote that he saw on the Bulaq road "all the pageantry of Oriental romance quietly donkeying in to Cairo."

> It was a fair festal evening. The whole world was masquerading, and so well that it seemed reality.

> 'Abon Hassan sat at the city gate, and I saw Haroun Al-Rashid quietly coming up in the disguise of a Moussoul merchant. I could not but wink at Abon, for I knew him so long ago in the *Arabian Nights*. But he rather stared than saluted, as friends may, in a masquerade. There was Sinbad the porter too, hurrying to Sinbad the sailor. I turned and watched his form fade in the twilight, yet I doubt if he reached Bagdad in time for the eighth history.[47]

Descriptions like these could be multiplied endlessly; and they were. Tourists filled page after page of their journals with the stock characters of the *Arabian Nights*, and Curtis's account became so hackneyed that it was satirized later in the century.[48] But I don't think that these figurations ought to be dismissed as mere whimsy, literary flourishes, and embellishments. The "reality-effect" of Cairo as the city of the *Arabian Nights* was achieved by something more than reading the city *through* the text of the *Arabian Nights*; it was also achieved by reading the city as the text of the *Arabian Nights*. Cairo was to be turned into a book written by insiders, and for this very reason it was widely supposed to give its readers access to an everyday world—at once ordinary and extraordinary—that would otherwise have remained hidden from view. As Lane-Poole explained,

> The *Nights* were written for the people, for the audience who gathered in the coffee-shops to listen to the professional reciter, for the large uneducated middle class of Cairo. This is what constitutes their special merit in the eyes of the student of medieval Egypt. The doings of kings and emirs we learn from the detailed pages of Makrizy and many other scholarly writers: it is from the *Thousand and One Nights* that we gain our insight into the life of the people—a life divided from that of the great by a gulf over which the Oriental historian rarely leaps.[49]

And yet, at the same time, the ability to *read* this book was made the prerogative of the outsider. In *Modern Egyptians* Lane had noted that public recitations of the tales were rare in Cairo because written copies were scarce: "When a complete copy of 'The Thousand and One Nights' is found, the price demanded for it is too great for a reciter to have it in his power to pay."[50] Readers of Lane's translation were thus privileged to hold the text in their hands. More than this, however, Lane turned reading the tales into a form of sightseeing by his forceful reversal of their structure. For Arab audiences the material world that the *Nights* described was mere background to the narrative, incidental to its main purpose. But Lane's textual scaffolding maneuvered this to the foreground so that it became an end in itself—what Sallis has called "an object of the voyeur's voyage."[51] To call this voyeurism is not, I think, to overstate the case. In the original framing, Sheherazade's storytelling is a stratagem. In spinning out her stories night after night she tricks her husband into postponing her death; and in this sense she outwits, even deceives, her male audience. But in substituting his *own* annotated narrative as the master-frame, Lane reasserts a power that was at once Orientalist *and* masculinist: through his persistent, probing commentary, "the Orient" was to be made transparent, its secrets laid bare, and its deceptions revealed.

By these means, the power to read—to *make* Cairo make sense—was conferred upon the observer. This was true both for the reader as traveler, and, conversely, the traveler as reader. Under Lane's tutelage, with him as cicerone, the *Arabian Nights* made it possible to peer into the lifeworlds of ordinary people, to turn their domestic lives and their material culture into exhibits, and thereby to glimpse the marvelous in the mundane. While Lane succeeded in reaffirming the virtuality of the *Arabian Nights*, as also claimed for Galland's original translation—triumphantly redeeming the possibility of "visiting" Cairo by reading the text—his canonical achievement was to ensure that the mobilization of this imaginative geography, the proliferation of its rumor of Cairo, was active, practical, and thoroughly *reciprocal*. Pückler-Muskau put this very well when he described how he "roamed for many hours about the streets of the interminable city, and it always seemed to me as if I were reading the '*Arabian Nights*'; or, rather, as if their gay scenes were placed in living pictures before me."[52] If to read the *Arabian Nights* was to wander the streets of Cairo, then in Ampère's view "to wander the streets of Cairo was to re-read the *Thousand and One Nights*."[53] Curtis thought it perfectly impossible to concoct an account of Cairo "without a dash of the *Arabian Nights*," precisely because it was impossible to confine the "poetry" of what he called "that airy arabesque" within the covers of a book. The characters of the *Arabian Nights*, he wrote, continually "step forward into the prose of experience." Poetry was thus turned into prose, the marvelous into the mundane: or, as he put it in artful elision, the conjunction between the *Arabian Nights* and Cairo meant that, in this city at least, "the romance of travel is real."[54]

SPACINGS

By these various means, the space of the text and the space of the city were constantly being folded into one another. In doing so, it was not only space but also time that was pleated. While he was in Cairo in 1843, Gérard de Nerval wrote to his father that he "wanted to see each place only after having made myself sufficiently aware of it from books *and memories*."[55] "Memories"—yet this was his first visit to Cairo; those "memories" derived, in large measure, from reading the *Arabian Nights*. It has already been suggested that the *Arabian Nights* came between Nerval and the city to such an extent that Cairo lost its presence: that in his *Voyage en Orient* "the subject's inauguration into the field of desire always passes through the 'defiles' of signifiers that are purely textual."[56] Maybe so; but Lane's writings opened up an altogether different passage, in which Cairo was made vividly and magically *present* in the constant performance of folds *between* city and text.

It was through the movements of travelers in these folds between city and text that Cairo was "re-cognized" as a *lieu de mémoire*. I say "text," but—as I have emphasized—these images of Cairo were equally derived from words and the illustrations that accompanied them: this was a thoroughly *graphical* imagination in both senses of the term. One visitor expressed

> . . . the strong feeling that we were living in the midst of scenes so familiar to us in childhood from that favourite book, the *Arabian Nights Entertainments*, but never realised till now. . . . [N]one of us probably imagined how graphic were those descriptions, how true to the life many of the details therein recorded. But now, as we rode among the bazaars of Cairo, and watched the habits and manners of the people, it is wonderful how that old, highly-prized volume, the delight of our childhood, was always recurring to our thoughts.[57]

Another explained that his wife, busy obtaining the stores for their voyage up the Nile in 1869, spent her time "riding donkey-back about the crowded streets, and recognising everywhere the scenes she had lived amongst, both in the letterpress and illustrations of her *Arabian Nights*."[58] These repeated acts of re-cognition transposed medieval Cairo into the modern, activating the flow of its everyday practices within a continuous historical present.

These recollection-images need to be located within a culture of travel—not confined within the pages of a book or the shelves of a library—because it was through such dispersed, open locations that their rumors of Cairo entered into the *performance* of the city. They were not only reproduced through the iterations of citationary structures, those constant borrowings from one text to another; neither were their performative capacities ceded to the inhabitants of the city alone. Just as Lane's rendering of Cairo was accomplished through his own performances, so too did the staging of Cairo as a space of fantasy within this Orientalist culture of travel depend, centrally, upon *tourists'* performances—"readings" of the city—that were at once textual-visual practices *and* so many activations of "bodily knowledge."[59]

Indeed, tourists not only shared Lane's interest in the body; their *own* performances were profoundly corporeal. The ways in which they made their way around the city and comported themselves when seeing the "sights" turned on a series of bodily protocols that provided the physical grid within which their visual practices took place (and, for that matter, took *possession* of place). "Donkey riding is universal," Taylor remarked, and "no one thinks of going beyond the Frank quarter on foot." Careering through the streets on these "long-eared cabs," the tourist gaze was acutely physical. "There is no use in attempting to guide the donkey," Taylor advised, "for he won't be guided. The driver shouts behind; and you are dashed at full speed into a confusion of other donkeys, camels, horses, carts, water-carriers and footmen." The whirlwind of people and animals, buildings, and bazaars meant that it was only possible to "judge the rapidity of your progress," so Mrs. Damer said, "by seeing how fast you lose sight of succeeding objects." Tourists were thus "borne onward by the irresistible stream, through the labyrinths of bazaars, in which everything appears like a confused dream," and through these spaces-in-motion—*through* them in every sense of the word— Cairo was visualized as a vivid, flickering, "flitting phantasmagoria," its viewers continuously presented with "the ever-shifting scenes of [a] living kaleidoscope" that seemed to open out before them "at every turn."[60]

This was a gaze that engaged all the senses—it was a *haptic* not a purely optical appropriation of the city—and for this very reason it was shot through with anxiety: it was not always easy to secure the detachment that opticality could confer upon the viewer. Emma Roberts recalled how, "mounted upon donkeys, we pushed our way through a dense throng, thrusting aside loaded camels, which scarcely allowed us room to pass, and coming into the closest contact with all sorts of people." Disconcerted, she confessed that "the perusal of Mr. Lane's book had given me a very vivid idea of the interior of the city, [but] *I was scarcely prepared to mingle thus intimately with its busy multitude.*"[61]

Within this culture of travel it was necessary to be able to gaze upon other (extraordinary) bodies while protecting one's own person from closer encounters. When Busch recommended that tourists observe the "great masquerade" of the streets from a hotel window, he was, therefore, enunciating a general rule. To see Cairo as a magic theater, to bring off such a fantastic staging of the city, it was necessary for travelers to be *in* but not *of* the masquerade, to maintain a strategic distance between their own bodies and those of the inhabitants: all the while observing, recognizing, and judging. Shepheard's Hotel was "the central point from which the show could best be seen by an outside observer," recalled the American consul. Gazing out over the gaily-colored crowd parading round the

Azbakiyya, its guests "had an 'Arabian Nights' Entertainment' improvised for them always, without care and without cost."[62] And, he might have added, without contact. Paine was also delighted that her hotel faced the Azbakiyya, "a situation that furnished its inmates with endless amusement."

> It stood upon the principal new street, facing the large public gardens, so that . . . there was always passing beneath our windows some picturesque group or festive scene that kept us ever on the alert.

> We were desirous of losing none of the peculiarities of the country, and the startling sound of the cracking whip, giving notice of the approach of some display, allowed us no repose.[63]

In this way, moving between the view from the window or the terrace and the encounter in the street and the bazaar, Europeans and Americans arrogated to themselves the characteristically—and I would say *crucially*—Orientalist power to enter and leave the space of their fantasy, the spectral theater, "the Orient" itself, at will. When Nerval enumerated what he called "places of refuge from Oriental life"—the hotels around the Azbakiyya, the Frank theater, Castignol's pharmacy, and the post office where he collected his mail and heard European news—and wrote to his father that these constituted "almost Europe in an entire quarter of the city"—he was mapping a vital choreography of containment.[64] In much the same way, one can sense William Thackeray's bemused pleasure at "finding England here in a French hotel [the Hotel d'Orient] kept by an Italian at the city of Grand Cairo in Africa," and hear Norman Macleod's evident relief on his return from sightseeing to find that "once in the hotel, we are again in Europe."[65]

The "virtual" order of Lane's *Arabian Nights*—the *va-et-vient* between note and text, between commentary and narrative, between reason and fantasy—was thus replicated in a "physical" ordering of Cairo put in place by the performance of an endlessly repeated movement between "the same" and "the other," between the hotel and the street:

text	narrative	fantasy	other	street	city
note	commentary	reason	same	hotel	text

If there was nothing outside this text, it was not a text bounded by margins and boards. The folds between city-text and text-city activated not only a *graphical* imagination, therefore, but also a *geo*-graphical imagination in which an Orientalist Cairo was continuously, elaborately performed as a series of *spacings*. Lane did not, of course, invent these distinctions or the orderings that were (re)produced through them. But, as I hope to have shown, he was instrumental in orchestrating their performance in—and *of*—Cairo.

NOTES

1. C. Prendergast, *Paris and the Nineteenth Century* (Oxford, Blackwell, 1992), p. 28.

2. The distinction between "tourist" and "traveler" reappears in European and American cultures of travel throughout the nineteenth century, but this class-laden terminology conceals important identities between the two figures. See J. Buzard, *The Beaten Track: European Tourism, Literature and the Ways to "Culture" 1800–1918* (Oxford: Oxford University Press, 1993). In this essay I use "tourist" as a generic signifier to mark anyone traveling primarily under the sign of pleasure. It was this that puzzled most inhabitants of Egypt for much of the century. Arab cultures of travel understood the movement of pilgrims, ambassadors, and envoys; merchants, soldiers, and sailors; slaves and forced laborers. But the cognitive accommodation of tourists was much more difficult.

3. M. de Certeau, *The Practice of Everyday Life* (Berkeley: University of California Press, 1984), pp. 115–16.

4. R. Irwin, *The Arabian Nights: A Companion* (London: Allen Lane, 1994), p. 121.

5. E.W. Lane, "Draft of Description of Egypt," Bodleian Library, University of Oxford: MS. Eng. Misc. d. 234, ff. 5-5v. For Lane's biography, see L. Ahmed, *Edward William Lane: A Study of His Life and Works and of British Ideas of the Middle East in the Nineteenth Century* (London: Longman, 1978).

6. Some of Lane's notes and drafts were incorporated into his sister's account of her residence in Cairo with him during his third visit to Egypt. See S. Lane-Poole, *The Englishwoman in Egypt: Letters from Cairo* (London: Charles Knight, 1844; rprt. Cairo: American University in Cairo Press, 2003). Part of Lane's original manuscript of the "Description of Egypt," revised by his nephew, was published as E.W. Lane, *Cairo Fifty Years Ago* (London: John Murray, 1896). But a complete edition was only published very recently: E.W. Lane, *Description of Egypt*, edited by J. Thompson (Cairo: American University in Cairo Press, 2000).

7. E.W. Lane, *An Account of the Manners and Customs of the Modern Egyptians Written in Egypt During the Years 1833–1835* (London: Charles Knight, 1836)—hereafter referred to simply as *Modern Egyptians*. The book went through numerous printings and four editions before its fifth, definitive edition was published by John Murray in 1860. All my references are to the most recent reprint of this edition (Cairo: American University in Cairo Press, 2003). Lane's third and final period of residence in Egypt was between 1842–49, which he devoted to gathering materials for his *Arabic-English Lexicon*, published in 1863–93.

8. Lane, *Modern Egyptians*, p. xxiv (note).

9. Lane, *Modern Egyptians*, p. 25.

10. Lane, *Description of Egypt*, pp. 71–97 and figure 14. The map was included in a second draft of the manuscript, but was not referred to in the final draft.

11. Stanley Lane-Poole noted as a "singular omission" that "although the larger part of the 'Modern Egyptians' refers to the inhabitants of the capital, where Lane spent many years, the book contains no description of Cairo itself." See Lane, *Cairo Fifty Years Ago*, p. v.

12. Lane, *Modern Egyptians*, pp. 61, 68–71, 76–79, 84–90, 122–23, 142–51, 199–202, 337–43, and 356–68.

13. Lane, *Modern Egyptians*, pp. 58–59, 157–74, and 511–28.

14. Lane, *Modern Egyptians*, pp. 377–93.

15. Lane, *Modern Egyptians*, pp. 394–99, 401–3, and 415–25.

16. Lane, *Modern Egyptians*, pp. 268–75. That reversion was completed by the account Lane furnished for this sister's book of letters from Cairo, where he attributed the magician's "successes" to leading questions put to him by his interlocutor, and claimed that he had been "deceived." See Lane-Poole, *The Englishwoman in Egypt*, Vol. II, pp. 163–70.

17. Lane, *Modern Egyptians*, pp. 240–46.

18. Lane, *Modern Egyptians*, pp. 430–31.

19. Lane, *Modern Egyptians*, p. 432. Similar movements between inside and outside, between participation and observation, recur throughout Lane's accounts of public festivals.

20. Here there is a close parallel between Lane and the French novelist Gérard de Nerval, whose fictionalized account of his own *Voyage en Orient* between January and May 1843 transforms Cairo into a theater: see C. Aubaude, *Le voyage en Égypte de Gérard de Nerval* (Paris: Éd. Kimé, 1997) p. 11. More specifically, Nerval renders the space of Cairo not primarily "as a landscape to be reproduced [in his text] but as a place of actions and movements." See I. Daunais, *L'art de la mesure, ou l'invention de l'espace dans les récits d'Orient (XIXe siècle)* (Paris: Presses Universitaires de Vincennes, 1996), p. 166. The parallel is not altogether accidental. Nerval consulted Lane's *Modern Egyptians* in Paris, made a rough-and-ready translation of the English text on his return, and relied on several of Lane's descriptions for his own composition (which was first published in serial form between 1844 and 1847). See J. Carré, *Voyageurs et écrivains français en Égypte* (Cairo: Institut Français d'Archéologie Orientale, 1956), pp. 34–36; and Aubade, *Le voyage en Égypte de Gérard de Nerval*, pp. 49 and 56.

21. For this tripartite way of characterizing "performed" space I am indebted to Gillian Rose. See G. Rose, "Performing Space," in D. Massey, J. Allen, and P. Sarre, eds., *Human Geography Today* (Cambridge, UK: Polity Press, 1999), pp. 247–59. In describing *Modern Egyptians* in these spatializing terms I depart from E. Said, *Orientalism* (New York: Pantheon Books, 1978), pp. 159–64. Said emphasizes the temporality of Lane's narrative as it traces the life cycle of the ordinary Egyptian from birth through marriage to death. I don't, of course, deny this temporalizing arc; Lane himself recognized that he had followed the Egyptian "from the period of infancy to the tomb" (see Lane, *Modern Egyptians*, p. 528). But I do think that Lane's other, unambiguously *spatial* story had a greater impact on Orientalist cultures of travel. I should also note that Said sees an "unyielding bridle of discipline and detachment" enforcing a "cold distance from Egyptian life" in Lane's narrative, and (partly in consequence) claims that Lane repressed his own sexual desire. This reading has met with astringent criticism from John Rodenbeck. See J. Rodenbeck, "Edward Said and Edward William Lane," in P. Starkey and J. Starkey, eds., *Travellers in Egypt* (London and New York: I.B. Tauris, 1998), pp. 233–43. As I hope to have made

clear, I think it more accurate to read Lane as oscillating *between* detachment and desire. And it is this very oscillation—with all its precarious openings for the disruption of routine scriptings and established cultures of travel—that marks the sense of performance I invoke here as distinctively different from conventional accounts of tourism as (rote) performance.

22. E. Warburton, *The Crescent and the Cross: Romance and Realities of Eastern Travel* (London: Colburn, 1844), p. 59n; R. Curzon, *Visits to Monasteries in the Levant* (London: John Murray, 1849), p. 99; and G.W. Curtis, *Nile Notes of a Howadjii* (New York: Harper, 1856), p. 4.

23. I.G. Wilkinson, *Handbook for Travellers to Egypt* (London: John Murray, 1858), pp. 125–26. I follow the convention of describing the *Handbook* as "Murray," but as I have explained above, the author of these early editions was I.G. Wilkinson. In addition to noticing Lane's writings, he also praised the drawings of Pascal Coste, Robert Hay, John Frederick Lewis, and David Roberts: p. 126.

24. J.V.C. Smith, *A Pilgrimage to Egypt* (Boston: Gould and Lincoln, 1852), p. 65.

25. A.C. Smith, *The Attractions of the Nile and its Banks* (London: John Murray, 1968), p. 72.

26. Bayle St. John, *Village Life in Egypt*, Vol. I (London: Chapman and Hall, 1852), pp. 118–19.

27. Lane-Poole, *The Englishwoman in Egypt*, Vol. I, pp. 156–65.

28. F. Nightingale, *Letters from Egypt 1849–1850* (London: Barrie and Jenkins, 1987; first edition 1854), pp. 188–99.

29. I. Hahn-Hahn, *Letters of a German Countess during her Travels in Turkey, Egypt, the Holy Land, Syria and Nubia in 1843–4*, Vol. III (London: Henry Colburn, 1845), p. 45; H. Martineau, *Eastern Life, Present and Past* (Philadelphia: Lea and Blanchard, 1848), p. 244; A.B. Clot Bey, *Aperçu general sur l'Égypte* (Bruxelles: Meline, Cans, 1840), pp. 284–85; and M. Busch, *Guide for Travellers in Egypt* (London: Trübner, 1858), pp. 44–45.

30. E. Sallis, *Sheherazade Through the Looking Glass: The Metamorphosis of the Thousand and One Nights* (Richmond, UK: Curzon Press, 1999), p. 44. See also S. Nadaff, *Arabesque: Narrative Structure and the Aesthetics of Repetition in the 1001 Nights* (Evanston: Northwestern University Press, 1991), pp. 3–4, who notes that the *Arabian Nights* "has no fixed or privileged textual identity," and that its genealogy speaks "both of the difficult metamorphosis from oral to written text and, perhaps even more eloquently, of the forced translation from East to West."

31. The base manuscript that Galland used was the earliest extant manuscript of any size; it is usually attributed to the Syrian series of texts. See Sallis, *Sheherazade Through the Looking Glass*, pp. 29–33. Galland also relied on Hanna Diab, a Christian Arab from Aleppo, who dictated additional stories to him from memory. It was Galland who incorporated the stories of Sindbad into the *Arabian Nights*, which originally formed a separate Persian cycle of tales. It was also Galland who introduced European audiences to Aladdin and Ali Baba: neither of these stories appears in any Arabic manuscript before Galland composed his version. See R. Hawari, "Antoine Galland's translation of the *Arabian Nights*," *Revue de la littérature compare* 54 (1980), pp. 154–64; and Irwin, *The Arabian Nights*, pp. 15–18. By 1793 Galland's version was already in its eighteenth edition, and it remained popular with

French audiences until the very end of the nineteenth century, when a new—and controversial—translation appeared by Joseph Charles Mardrus (1899–1904).

32. F. Moussau-Mahmoud, "English Travellers and the Arabian Nights," in P. Caracciolo, ed., *The Arabian Nights in English Literature: Studies in the Reception of the Thousand and One Nights into English Culture* (New York: St Martin's Press, 1988), pp. 95–110, quotation from p. 95.

33. E.S. Poole, ed., *The Thousand and One Nights: The Arabian Nights' Entertainments*, Vol. 1, trans. E.W. Lane (London: Chatto and Windus, 1883), pp. ix–x. This revised edition was prepared by Lane's nephew. Lane's original translation was issued in serial form between 1838 and 1840—the episodic structure of the *Nights* made the stories ideal for serialization—and then in three bound volumes between 1839 and 1841.

34. Poole, *The Thousand and One Nights*, Vol. III, p. 680.

35. It did so by excluding "much of the material from the Syrian and Iraqi recensions." See G. Roper, "Texts from Nineteenth-Century Egypt: The Role of E.W. Lane," in Starkey and Starkey, eds., *Travellers in Egypt*, pp. 244–54, quotation from p. 247.

36. Poole, *The Thousand and One Nights*, Vol. 1, pp. ix–x.

37. Ibid, Vol. 1, p. xxi.

38. Ibid, Vol. 1, p. xxi. Many of Coste's drawings were completed as studies for his aborted design of the Mosque of Muhammad 'Ali. Coste had sold his drawings to Hay shortly before he left Egypt, on the understanding that they would be published in England, but the project came to nothing (despite Lane's offer to supervise the engraving). See M. Darby, *The Islamic Perspective: An Aspect of British Architecture and Design in the Nineteenth Century* (London: Leighton House Gallery, 1983), p. 31; and M. Volait, "Les monuments de l'architecture arabe" in D. Jacobi, ed., *Pascal Coste, Toutes les Égypte* (Marseille: Parenthèses: Bibliothèque municipale de Marseille, 1998), pp. 97–130, especially pp. 114–15. Seventy of the plates were finally published in France as P. Coste, *Architecture Arabe ou Monuments du Kaire* (Paris: Firmin Didot, 1839).

39. Sallis, *Sheherazade Through the Looking Glass*, pp. 51–53, and 72.

40. R. Kabbani, *Imperial Fictions: Europe's Myths of Orient* (London: Pandora, 1994), p. 44.

41. Poole, *The Thousand and One Nights*, Vol. 1, p. xxii.

42. Lane's readers were well aware of the connections. "All this is well documented in Mr Lane's Book of the Modern Egyptians," wrote one American afficionado, "and pictured in his fine edition of the Illustrated Arabian Nights." See "An American," *Journal of a Voyage up the Nile* (Buffalo: Phinney, 1851), p. 21.

43. Poole, *The Thousand and One Nights*, Vol. 1, p. xviii; and Vol. III, p. 686 (original emphasis).

44. J.J. Ampère, *Voyage en Égypte et en Nubie* (Paris: Lévy, 1868), p. 183.

45. One commentator suggests that not only did it become "part of the task of the travellers to verify the authenticity of the *Nights* and relate them to what they saw," but "*their experiences were quoted in new editions of the Nights.*" See Moussau-Mahmoud, "English Travellers and the Arabian Nights," quotations from pp. 95 and 97 (my emphasis).

46. Warburton, *The Crescent and the Cross*, p. 31; Hahn-Hahn, *Letters of a German Countess*, Vol. III, p. 43; and W.H. Bartlett, *The Nile Boat, or Glimpses of the Land of Egypt* (London: Hall and Virtue, 1849), p. 46.

47. Curtis, *Nile Notes of a Howadjii*, pp. 2–3. Haroun al-Rashid was Caliph of Baghdad between 788 and 809.

48. The humorist Moberly Bell repeated Curtis's description to his travelling companion, Georges Montbard, as though it were his own:

> The words sounded familiar to him. "There's something like that in an American book," he said. "Good heavens! You've read it then! Why, I sat up all last night learning pages on purpose to please you; and there's lots more of it. . . ."

See C.F.M. Moberly Bell, *From Pharaoh to Fellah* (London: Wells Gardner, Darton, 1888), pp. 14–15. The primary object of Bell's satire were the tourists who repeated these familiar descriptions to one another, or diligently passed them off in their notebooks as their own; but in making his jest, Bell also testified to the extraordinary tenacity of these borrowings from one text to another, which is the point I seek to sharpen here.

49. S. Lane-Poole, *The Story of Cairo* (London: J.M. Dent & Co., 1924; first edition, 1902), p. 262.

50. Lane, *Modern Egyptians*, p. 415.

51. Sallis, *Sheherazade Through the Looking Glass*, pp. 11–12.

52. H. Pückler-Muskau, *Egypt under Mehemet Ali*, Vol. I (London: H. Colburn, 1845), p. 143.

53. Ampère, *Voyage en Égypte et en Nubie*, p. 182.

54. Curtis, *Nile Notes of a Howadjii*, p. 7.

55. G. de Nerval, *Oeuvres* (Paris: Gallimard, 1974), p. 925 (my emphasis), letter dated March 18, 1843.

56. A. Behdad, *Belated Travelers: Orientalism in the Age of Colonial Dissolution* (Durham: Duke University Press, 1994), pp. 26–27. I. Daunais, *L'art de la mesure, ou l'invention de l'espace dans les récits d'Orient (XIXe siècle)* (Paris: Presses Universitaires de Vincennes, 1996), p. 172, makes a similar claim: "Nerval does not have before him dream and reality but their mutual effacement one by the other."

57. Smith, *The Attractions of the Nile*, p. 50.

58. F. Eden, *The Nile Without a Dragoman* (London: King, 1871), p. 52.

59. P. Bourdieu, "Bodily Knowledge," in his *Pascalian Meditations* (Stanford: Stanford University Press, 2000), pp. 128–63.

60. B. Taylor, *A Journey to Central Africa, or Life and Landscapes from Egypt to the Negro Kingdoms of the White Nile* (New York: Putnam, 1854), pp. 37–38; G.L. Dawson Damer, *Diary of a Tour in Greece, Turkey, Egypt and the Holy Land*, Vol. II (London: Henry Colburn, 1842), p. 146; J. Clayton, *Letters from the Nile* (London: Bosworth, 1854), p. 104; Bartlett, *The Nile Boat*, p. 55; and Smith, *The Attractions of the Nile*, pp. 46–47.

61. E. Roberts, *Notes of an Overland Journey through France and Egypt to Bombay* (London: W.H. Allen, 1841), p. 116 (my emphasis).

62. Busch, *Guide for Travellers in Egypt*, p. 45; and E. de Léon, *Thirty Years of My Life on Three Continents* (London: Ward and Downey, 1890), pp. 157 and 162. Léon was recalling Shepheard's in 1856. There were, of course, limits to this *cordon sanitaire*, even in hotels. In J. Miesse, *A Journey to Egypt and Palestine in the Year 1855* (Chilicothe: Scioto Gazette, 1859), p. 102, Miesse confessed that he "did not notice on the first day that with the exception of the first steward and the cooks, the whole array of servants in our hotel were natives. There were a great many of them—and their numbers made up for the deficiencies occasioned by their laziness and other unfitness for such a place. . . . The host told me that, besides boarding, these native servants get no remuneration for their services."

63. C. Paine, *Tent and Harem: Notes of an Oriental Trip* (New York: Appleton, 1859), pp. 88–89.

64. G. de Nerval, *Voyage en Orient* (Paris: C. Levy, 1884), pp. 170–71; de Nerval, *Oeuvres*, p. 931; letter dated May 2, 1843.

65. W.M. Thackeray, *Notes of a Journey from Cornhill to Grand Cairo* (rprt. Heathfield, UK: Cockbird Press, 1991), p. 132; and N. Macleod, *Eastward* (London: Strahan, 1866), p. 27. There were differences between tourists from different countries, but what is striking about all these observations is their common appeal to Europe.

6

Nineteenth-Century Images of Cairo: From the Real to the Interpretative

Caroline Williams

It is from the nineteenth-century Western artists—French, English, Italian, American, and Austrian—that we have our first and continuing images of Cairo; and it was to the places and culture of the city's medieval core that they were drawn. This chapter focuses on chronological development: on how nineteenth-century images of Cairo began as visual descriptions of the city's physical aspects (1820–60) and ended as an interpretation of its Islamic culture and a portrayal of its inhabitants (1860–1900).

Many factors account for the transition from "description" to "interpretation." The development of the camera and the mass production of photographs played key roles in the change. Art dealers, between 1850 and 1880, in both France and England, transformed the art market from one in which aristocratic patrons bought the paintings of dead masters to one in which the new class of manufacturers and merchants bought art by living painters. Genre subjects became popular, as travel to Egypt became easier and authors wrote about its Islamic culture. Artists, who found working on the spot difficult and trying, painted their compositions in their studios from artifacts they had collected in Egypt and from photographs and prints that were increasingly available. Artists were influenced, consciously or unconsciously, by what other artists painted, and by how the Islamic world was displayed in the great World's Fairs of the second half of the nineteenth century. Among the artists there were interactive linkages, and among the images there were intertextual weavings.

Encapsulating the change from descriptive to interpretative are two images of the portal of the Madrasa of Sultan Hasan. In the first, from the *Description de l'Égypte* (1803), the portal is shown as an architectural element of the exterior facade (FIGURE 6.1); in the last, "Le Tribut," painted in 1898 by Ludwig Deutsch,

Figure 6.1. Facade of the Madrasa of Sultan Hasan, *Description de l'Égypte*, 1810, lithograph
(Source: Courtesy of the Rare Books Library, the American University in Cairo)

except for two identifying roundels, the portal forms a fake background for gor-geously costumed Orientals (FIGURE 6.13).[1]

TOPOGRAPHICAL DESCRIPTION: 1820–1860

The period of discovery and description, for the European artist, began in the 1820s. It was in 1822 that the last volume of the *Description de l'Égypte* was pub-lished, and it was here that the first group images of Cairo were printed. These twenty tomes of scholarly descriptions and visual information that made up the *Description* were produced from 1810 to 1822 to exalt and justify Napoleon's 1798 expedition to Egypt.[2] The fifty-eight plates included in the section entitled "L'État Moderne," were the first images to give visual, descriptive information about the buildings and people of Cairo. The sites chosen were those which were familiar to the occupying French: the port of Bulaq, the grand residences of

Azbakiyya, the lake of Birkat al-Fil, the houses sequestered for the work of the French Institute, the Citadel, and the North Walls. The Aqueduct and the Nilometer, as historical survivors, were also subjects. Only three mosques were included: Ibn Tulun, the most venerable; al-Hakim, adjacent to the North Wall; and the Madrasa of Sultan Hasan below the Citadel, which in seven plates was the most extensively "described."[3] This thoroughness of depiction—a view of the back, the main facade (FIGURE 6.1), the interior courtyard, the *qibla* wall, details of columns, ablutions fountain, *mihrab* and *minbar*, as well as elevations and a plan—would point the way for future representations.

There are people in these scenes—sailing in boats on the Azbakiyya Lake, transacting business, leading camels, standing about—but they are stiffly posed, and are scattered about the page primarily for scale. Indeed, as represented in the *Description*, the living inhabitants of Egypt were confined to the categories of "Arts and Trades," in which they were shown in explanatory roles (for example, raising water, baking bread, and weaving), and as models and types in "Costumes and Portraits." In conveying information about an unfamiliar country, these images were prephotographic, descriptive, and documentary. However, for the first group of European artists to come to Egypt, the plates in the *Description* became both a model and a challenge against which to measure their own work, since many felt they could do a better job of visual description.

The first "followers" in this category came as explorers, scholars, architects, and engineers. Many of them came at the invitation of Muhammad 'Ali Pasha, who actively solicited their help in modernizing Egypt. Among those who gave Cairo early visual substance, four names are prominent: Pascal Coste, Robert Hay, Edward William Lane, and David Roberts.[4] Their volumes were published between 1836 and 1849, and the connection between them is tangible.

EARLY PRACTITIONERS

Pascal Coste (1787–1879) was the earliest "discoverer" of Cairo. His connection with the *Description* was a direct one, for it was Edme-François Jomard, editor of "L'État Moderne," who recommended Coste to Muhammad 'Ali.[5] Coste was an architect by profession, but he initially came to Egypt in 1817 to set up a saltpeter factory. Afterwards, however, he successfully oversaw many diverse projects (a telegraph connection between Alexandria and Cairo; the digging of an important network of canals; the first local School for Engineers; the building of Muhammad 'Ali's Shubra palace in Cairo). In the process he became one of the Pasha's most trusted counselors. For seven of the nine years he was in Egypt, Coste was 'Ali's chief architect; and as such he was commissioned to design two mosques: one in Alexandria, and one for the Citadel in Cairo. Coste was also given a *firman*, or official permission, to visit all the principal mosques in Cairo so that he could make detailed drawings of the local architecture—interiors, as well as exteriors. His book, *Architecture Arabe ou Monuments du Kaire: Mesurés et Desinnés de 1818 à 1825*, was based on these studies and appeared in 1837–39.[6]

Coste's volume of architectural drawings was the first systematic and detailed study of Cairo's Islamic architecture. As an architect, he was one of the first Europeans to appreciate the fact that "Cairo was the only city, in the whole Orient, which still possessed a collection of Arab monuments of all periods, that is from the seventh to the eighteenth centuries."[7] His sixty-four plates depicted a wide variety of monuments (mosques, commercial depots, houses, public fountains, and aqueducts) and settings (a barbershop, a Bedouin encampment, and a garden at Shubra). Coste drew elevations, details of ornament, outside facades, inner courtyards, and plans. Careful observation and meticulous draftsmanship make the plates in this volume some of the most valuable documents that remain of early-nineteenth-century Cairo.

One notable view is that in Plate LXI showing the complex of the Amir Khayrbak, with the Rab' of Ibrahim Agha Mustahfizan on the opposite side of the road—as it once stood, but is now no more. An engaging human touch in this plate is provided by a group of harem ladies on an outing, riding on donkeys behind their handsomely mounted custodian. The ladies are swaddled in black *milayas*, or overwraps, and peer out through white face veils, while grooms hold each of them in place on her precarious perch. Another important view is that in Plate LII. It shows the *Sabil-kuttab* of Ibrahim Bey al-Kabir, once a magnificent monument to a powerful self-made member of the Ottoman militia, but now a derelict wreck. Coste also provided several illustrations of the houses on either side of the Khalij, or main canal, of Cairo, which was filled in 1898 to accommodate a tramline. The current restoration of arches around the courtyard of the Mosque of Mu'ayyad Shaykh is based on the view in Plate XXX.[8]

The human figures that form part of Coste's compositions are engaged in activities appropriate to the scene: praying, rowing, leading camels, tending stalls, and walking and riding along streets. They are convincingly engaged, but their numbers are sparse, and they are included largely to provide a human scale. Coste was primarily concerned with the architecture; his intent, as he wrote in the book's preface, was to make known to Europe the "Arab" monuments and architecture in Cairo (FIGURE 6.2).

In 1827 a bite from a yellow scorpion necessitated medical treatment, and Coste left Egypt. Before he departed, however, he sold his architectural drawings to Robert Hay. A scholar-enthusiast from Scotland, Hay (1799–1863) came to Egypt to "discover" and "record" its Pharaonic past; but it is for his *Illustrations of Cairo*, drawn between 1829–30 (but not published until November 1840) that he is primarily known.[9] Hay lacked financial sense, and his volume did not sell well, but it was remarkable for the new interest in contemporary Cairo and Islamic urbanism it portrayed. The volume contains thirty lithographic plates, mostly the

Figure 6.2. Facade of the Mosque of Sultan al-Mu'ayyad Shaykh, Pascal Coste, 1822, lithograph
(Source: Courtesy of the Rare Books Library, the American University in Cairo)

work of Owen Browne Carter, an architectural draftsman from Winchester.[10] Hay was interested in the "picturesque," and it was a monument's context that was more important to him than its architectural details. Thus, instead of two separate views of the main gates in Cairo's North Wall, and a focus on them as architectural structures as previously depicted in both the *Description* and by Coste, Owen Carter shows them together as part of a larger urban setting.

Views of the port of Bulaq, Birkat al-Fil, and the Aqueduct are also present, but in each case the scene has been expanded to show the Nile and its traffic in large and small varieties, as well as the people along the shores, waiting, fishing, tending animals, and fetching water. The Bayn al-Qasrayn area is shown twice. One view looks north, with the fourteenth-century complex of Sultan Barquq on the left and the contemporary fountain and school of Isma'il Pasha on the right. By showing both monuments Hay emphasized Cairo's architectural span and wealth.[11] The second view looks south, with the minaret of the complex of Sultan Qalawun in the distance.[12] In this scene the monument seems but a pretext for the lively wedding procession in the foreground. Likewise, in the view of Bab Zuwayla one sees not the

Figure 6.3. "A Street in Cairo near the Bab al-Khark," Owen B. Carter, 1828, lithograph
(Source: R. Hay, Illustrations of Cairo; *Courtesy of the Rare Books Library, the American University in Cairo)*

gate, but the minarets of the Mosque of Mu'ayyad Shaykh towering above the street whose central figure is a laden camel moving past open shopfronts.[13]

Another plate, "A Street in Cairo near the Bab al-Khark" (FIGURE 6.3), illustrates the overhanging *mashrabíya*, or wooden lattice windows, of the private residences, but also shows a scene from daily life.[14] Here, ladies, enveloped in wraps and veils, but more naturalistically deposed than in Coste's image, process down the street on donkeys behind a harem attendant, while a merchant on the *mastaba*, the bench in front of his stall, transacts business. In the accompanying commentary, Hay points out, "since these drawings were made the *mastabas* have in many parts been pulled down."

Another drawing in Hay's book, of the Khan al-Khalili (still a popular shopping area), shows the overall arrangement and activity of the bazaar area.[15] Among the people traversing the stall-lined alleys under the canopied beams are a mother with a small child sitting on her shoulder, a young boy carrying a tray of coffee cups to provide welcoming refreshments to customers, and a water carrier with his goat's hide full of water to damp down the dust.

For certain Cairo vistas and structures, these plates are the only surviving visual records today. One of these structures is the fourteenth-century Qasr al-

Ablaq, or Great Audience Hall, built on the Citadel, which was destroyed in 1837 to clear the way for Muhammad 'Ali's mosque.[16] Owen Carter showed the building from the outside, but the description under the plate fits the interior view drawn in the *Description*:

> The walls were well constructed and ornamented with kufic inscriptions in
> gigantic characters . . . in the corners . . . elaborate pendants of woodwork,
> formed of numerous small tiers . . . descended from the roof, and thirty-two
> large and beautiful columns of red granite were still standing unroofed amidst
> the ruins, . . . until removed by Muhammad 'Ali.[17]

The Birkat al-Fil, the Elephant Lake, with its pavilions, villas, and mansions, also only survives in Hay's book, since it was later filled in by Muhammad 'Ali and his dynasty.[18] Hay's interest in the Cairene context today gives his illustrations a documentary urgency, and makes them part of the historical record.

Hay dedicated the book to Edward William Lane (1801–76), his friend and agent. As an intermediary and an author, Lane played an important role in the development of the nineteenth-century portrait of Cairo. Lane was also the connecting link between Hay and Coste. Before Hay left for Scotland after his first expedition to Egypt in March of 1828 he bought all of Coste's original drawings on the stipulation that Hay would publish them by the end of 1830.[19] Lane later became the middleman in the correspondence between the two men; and eventually, after Hay procrastinated, Coste published his own book based on copies of his own drawings. Meanwhile, Lane urged Hay to publish his own views on the basis that "most of the views in the great 'Description de l'Égypte' are extremely inaccurate."[20] Finally, having decided not to include any of Coste's work in his own book, Hay lent the whole volume of drawings to Lane, who used both the drawings he had done himself in Cairo and those by Coste in preparing the illustrations for his own book on Egypt.[21]

Lane's book, *An Account of the Manners and Customs of the Modern Egyptians*, provided authoritative visual and textual information on Cairo not only to his own circle of friends, but to subsequent generations of artists as well.[22] Lane collected the material for his account between 1825 and 1835, just before the "galloping" changes introduced by Muhammad 'Ali and his successors committed Egypt to an irrevocable process of Westernizing modernization. A classic description of Cairo as a medieval city untouched by Western influences, first published in December 1836, it became an invaluable information tool and *aide mémoire* for a generation of subsequent visitors to the city. Lane was also an artist of accuracy and skill, and his textual illustrations highlighted and pinpointed his verbal descriptions.[23] In fact, many of Lane's people appear in the Hay *Illustrations*. For example, Lane's man modeling the striped *jíbbah* (over-robe) and his water carrier appear in Hay's "Fountain of Toosoon Pasha," while Lane's mounted lady has been transposed to Hay's "A Street in Cairo."[24]   In Hay's "Mosque of el-Barmaweeyeh," the leader of the circumcision parade is derived from Lane's barber's servant who holds up the *heml*, or wooden case.[25]

THE WORK OF DAVID ROBERTS

   Of the early documentary images of Egypt, the most familiar, however, are those of David Roberts (1796–1864). An associate of the Royal Academy, Roberts was the first professional artist to come to Egypt, and he visited with the specific purpose of returning to England with a publishable portfolio of images.[26] Born in Scotland, Roberts started his professional life painting theatrical sets and panoramas, which taught him to paint architectural and topographical views quickly and accurately. He was familiar with the *Description*, and his intent was to make corrections in its views. "I am the first British artist who has been here, and there is much in the French work that conveys no idea of these splendid remains," he wrote.[27] Roberts had also read all the publications that had appeared to date on Egypt, and for Cairo that included Lane's *Modern Egyptians*.[28] He was the last and the best of the prephotographic topographical artists. He returned to England in July 1839 with what he boasted was "one of the richest and most interesting folios that ever left the East." Indeed, his drawings, published in the mid-1840s, were a summation of the art produced during this documentary period of the early nineteenth century.[29]

   Roberts was forty-two years old when he arrived in the Middle East in August 1838, a visit he acknowledged as "the central episode of my artistic life." He spent seven weeks in Cairo, sketching the Islamic monuments as part of the urban landscape. Twenty-seven, or one-fourth, of the lithographs contained in the volume dedicated to Egypt were of Cairo's monuments and people. In his *Journal*, Roberts recorded both his buoyant enthusiasm and the furious pace he set for himself as he tackled his subject. On December 29 [1839] he wrote: "Made *two* drawings, one of the street leading to the lunatic asylum, and another of the same street opposite. They are glorious subjects."[30] Here he refers to the heart of medieval Cairo, the area known as Bayn al-Qasrayn. In fact, Roberts's view of the "Lunatic Asylum" [the Maristan of Sultan Qalawun] is the very same view drawn by Owen Carter for Robert Hay and called "Beyn-el-Kasreyn." Hay's scene features a wedding procession, whereas Roberts covers the street with a dense grouping of people, animals, and merchants, illustrating an observation about Cairo by the medieval traveler Ibn Battuta: "[her streets] surge as the waves of the sea with her throngs of folk . . ." (FIGURE 6.4).[31]

   Roberts's second view, "The Bazaar of the Coppersmiths," shows a corner of the portal of the Madrasa of the Sultan Barsbay, long since destroyed in the cutting of a new road. On December 31 he wrote: "Made one drawing today of the prin-

**Figure 6.4. "Mosque El Mooristan
(Bayn al-Qasrayn),"** David Roberts,
1838, lithograph
*(Source: Courtesy of the Rare Books
Library, the American University in Cairo)*

cipal bazaar [of the Silk Mercers], the finest I have done in Cairo . . . a city that sur-
passes all that an artist can conceive. I shall not lose an hour while in it to cull its
beauties" (FIGURE 6.5). Roberts's view of the Ghuriya, as the area is known,
improves on the earlier view in Hay's volume.[32] Roberts includes merchants in the
foreground, but the real star of the lithograph is the complex of Sultan al-Ghuri.
Two-thirds of the plate is taken up by the architecture of the buildings, highlighting their scale, high portals, overhanging roofs, and elevated entrances.

   However, as his *Journal* also makes plain, this was not easy work: "No one in
looking over my sketches will even think of the pain and trouble I have had to
contend with in collecting them." He wrote of "the crowded streets"; "of the
filthy and impertinent mob who jostle and stare at me"; "of the need of guards to
keep back the crowd"; "of a half-sucked orange thrown from a window above me";
"of the risk of being squeezed to a mummy by the loaded camels"; "of a mid-
January sun so hot I could hardly sit out the day"; "of wind and dust"; and "of constant diarrhea." Although he received a special dispensation from Muhammad

Figure 6.5. "Bazaar of the Silk Mercers," David Roberts, 1838, lithograph
(Source: Courtesy of the Rare Books Library, the American University in Cairo)

'Ali, the Pasha of Egypt, to draw in mosques, he wrote: "I must espouse the Turkish dress, . . . and divest myself of my whiskers. This is too bad, but . . . my object can be accomplished in no other way."[33]

Roberts did not include views of the Port of Bulaq, or Azbakiyya—more contemporary areas. His prime interest was the more traditional and (to him) more exotic areas of the city's medieval nucleus such as the monuments along Mu'izz li Din Allah, the main ceremonial artery from north to south gates, and the area around the Citadel.[34] Several of his scenes were drawn in the interior of mosques (Sultan Hasan, al-Ghuri, and Mu'ayyad Shaykh), where he depicted men in the proper attitudes of worship. His views improved pictorially on those of Hay, and he also extended his views geographically to include the cemeteries that flanked the city to the east. Although he did not know the monuments there well enough to identify them individually—they are labeled either "Tombs of the Caliphs," or "Tombs of the Memlooks"—he captured the ambiance of magnificent memorial monuments in desolate settings.

Roberts also made several panoramic views that expanded the cityscape away from the single monument. For "Cairo from the Gate of Citzenib [Sayyida

Zaynab in the Southern Cemetery]" he climbed a hill to obtain a vista looking toward the Madrasa of Sultan Hasan and the Citadel on the horizon. In "Cairo looking West" his vantage point was the medieval rubbish tips outside the Ayyubid walls, looking southeast towards the Madrasa of Sultan Hasan with the Pyramids of Giza in the distance.

Five of Roberts's scenes of Cairo concentrate on people engaged in various typical activities, rather than on the architectural settings: the letter writer, dancing girls, the slave market, the coffee shop, and the Nile ferry to Giza. In addition, his street views are peopled with all the traffic of a preindustrial community: women on donkeys, men on camels, boys carrying water, women with children, and merchants conversing, smoking, and dealing. These scenes capture some of Cairo's civic activities, and as portraits of a stream of life they breathe atmosphere into the city's past. In hindsight, Roberts left the single best visual record of the medieval Cairene cityscape.[35] For the Victorians, an intensely curious and avid public, his exquisitely beautiful and intricately detailed scenes described a city they could not see for themselves. For today's audiences, he preserved monuments and urban contexts that have either disappeared or stand only in skeletal form.

THE COMING OF PHOTOGRAPHY

David Roberts's departure from the Mediterranean in July 1839 coincided with the birth of photography, a new medium of reproduction. In August 1839, the daguerreotype was perfected. In November 1839, the first image in Africa produced by mechanical means was made—an image of Muhammad 'Ali's Harem in Alexandria. Thus, from the start, Egypt and photography were linked.[36] The technical advances in this new medium were so rapid that by 1849, when the final volume of Roberts's views appeared, John Ruskin wrote: "Roberts brought home records of which the value is now forgotten in the perfect detail of photography."[37]

The wet-plate collodion process, which produced not only a sharp image but also enabled photos to be mass-produced, brought to an end the first period of topographical description of Egypt. One of the earliest and best practitioners of this process, and a preeminent early travel photographer, was Francis Frith.[38] In 1856 Frith set sail for Egypt. In the next three years, he made three trips to Egypt and Palestine, where he worked for a total of twenty-four months. As both entrepreneur and artist, Frith combined the contemporary British enthusiasm for the photographic image with an increasing Victorian fascination with Egypt and the Holy Land. The photographic views he brought back immediately established his reputation as Britain's first great photographer-publisher. Frith was familiar with the painted images of the area, especially those of Roberts, and Roberts's success undoubtedly stimulated Frith's entrepreneurial and artistic ambitions.[39] A new edition of Roberts's multiple volumes, *The Holy Land, Syria, Idumea, Arabia, Egypt and Nubia*, for which the plates were reproduced photographically, had appeared in

1855–56, before Frith set sail for the Middle East. Under his own photograph of the fallen colossus at the Ramesseum in Thebes, Frith wrote: "David Roberts, in his splendid work, has bestowed upon it a very respectable and recognizable profile; but my picture shows that the face is so mutilated as scarcely to leave a feature traceable. . . ."[40] Frith wrote elsewhere: "A truthful record is of more value than the most elaborately beautiful picture."[41] Frith often photographed the same scene that Roberts had drawn, as much because it was an important monument as to correct the artistic record. For example, under his view of the statues of Memnon, he wrote: "As regards the shattered condition of these statues, I have only to refer to the Photograph, which will again, I fear, contradict some of the representations of previous artists."[42]

Frith was a superb craftsman and a man of great stamina. His commentary provides an insight into the skill, resource, patience, and speed required to produce at most six pictures a day in the newly developed wet-plate collodion process. Frith described the logistical burden of "cumbrous loads of apparatus," which could weigh up to one hundred and twenty pounds, and in the field had to be transported by animate energy. Often a goodly part of each photo opportunity was spent packing and unpacking the equipment. Furthermore, in composing a photograph, Frith had to work with the scene as it was; he could not add the picturesque, or eliminate the awkward. Because of the cumbrous nature of his equipment he also could not photograph in busy streets or bazaars. In a city full of the bustle and curiosity or people, he wrote: "my camera was surrounded by scores of idlers, and innumerable half-naked children."[43] Finally, because of long exposure times, even in bright sunlight and broad daylight, moving people could not be part of the composition. This limited his point of view and his subject matter. However, with the camera, Frith was able to capture complicated compositions with speed and accuracy. In his photograph of the sixteenth-century Mosque of Amir Akhor, for example, every leaf of the arabesque design on the dome is clear, and every word of the Quranic inscription below is legible (FIGURE 6.6).[44] Frith writes of an encounter with a French artist: "When, in a few minutes I had possessed myself of more accuracy than his labor of perhaps days would yield, he exclaimed: 'Ah mousieur! que vous êtes vite, vite. . . .'"[45]

By 1860 photographers were producing a documentary record which was quick, accurate, and eliminated the need for the topographical artist. But the mid-nineteenth-century camera could not record the interaction of groups of people, dimly lit settings, or color. Frith himself bemoaned this limitation: "Did but the sun paint *in colour* upon our bits of magic glass, what a delightful series of pictures would eastern costume furnish."[46]

The camera could capture the "real," but it could not convey ambiance or atmosphere. The pairing of two contemporary verbal descriptions and images of Cairo make this point. The first was by Mrs. Sophia Poole, Edward Lane's sister.

Figure 6.6. "The Mosque of Emeer Akhor," Francis Frith, 1860, photograph
(Source: Courtesy of the Rare Books Library, the American University in Cairo)

When she accompanied her brother back to Egypt in 1842, she wrote: "... the first impression received on entering this celebrated city [Cairo], is, that it has the appearance of having been deserted for perhaps a century, and suddenly re-peopled by persons who had been unable, from poverty or some other cause, to repair it, and clear away the antiquated cobwebs."[47] The crumbling, patched vista of these words is well captured photographically in Frith's "View of Boolaq."[48] The second verbal description was that of William Makepeace Thackeray in 1844: "How to describe the beauty of the streets to you!—the fantastic splendour; the delightful accidents of light and shade; ... the brilliancy of the crowd; the interminable vast bazaars with their barbaric splendour!... I never saw such a variety of architecture, of life, of picturesqueness, of brilliant colour, and light and shade."[49] William James Müller's "The Carpet Bazaar at Cairo" aptly visualizes this verbal description.[50]

Obviously, Cairo was both places: the static, stark, literal image of decaying physical forms in Frith's photograph; and the color, the spontaneity, and variety of the people in Müller's painting.

CULTURAL INTERPRETATION, 1860–1900

Between 1860 and 1900 foreign artists took up the challenges of color, texture, light, and movement that the nineteenth-century camera could not record, as they focused on ethnographic genre scenes: how people looked, what they wore, and how they went about their daily lives.

THE WORK OF JOHN FREDRICK LEWIS

John Frederick Lewis (1805–76) was a British artist who belonged to this interpretative group.[51] He lived in Cairo between November 1841 and May 1851, which gave him an opportunity to paint from a direct experience that few other artists had. However, practically all of his work was produced in England from 1851–76. While in England, Lewis relied on the more than 600 sketches he had drawn in Cairo, on his memories, and on the artifacts and objects he had collected during his stay in Egypt, all of which affected the way he presented his material. No other Orientalist artist seems to have been quite so conflicted by the dilemma Lewis felt: How to present the culture and context of a place of which he had once been so happily a part to the Victorian audience with whom he now lived?

Lewis had lived in Egypt at a time when its cultures, Pharaonic and Islamic, were being described for the first time. Edward William Lane, for contemporary Egyptian society, and Sir John Gardner Wilkinson for the ancient world, had just published volumes explaining their "manners and customs."[52] Lewis had known Lane, who had returned to Cairo during 1842–49 to work on his Arabic lexicon, and Wilkinson, who was in Egypt from 1841–50 to gather information for the *Handbook for Travellers in Egypt* that he was writing for John Murray.[53] The need for such a book was further evidence of Egypt's increasing appeal as a travel destination, since advances in railroad and steamship locomotion had made Egypt a part of the Grand Tour.[54] William Thackeray, on an Eastern Tour, described his visit with Lewis in 1844.[55] James William Wild, an architect, also visited Lewis, and drew the main reception room in Lewis's house in the Azbakiyya quarter of Cairo.[56] Lewis thus knew the men who were discovering, commenting upon, and interpreting a new country and its cultures. This was a view he took back with him to England but which, once at home, became affected by new influences.

Lewis had been absent from Britain for almost fourteen years, and he returned in 1851 to a changed country.[57] The success and wonders of the Industrial Revolution were celebrated that year in the Great Exhibition. Meanwhile, in the art world, there were new patrons, new themes, new dealers. The newly rich industrial barons of the Midland cities bought genre paintings, those that showed the scenes of everyday life, preferring them to the complicated or erudite iconography of the old masters. Art critics like John Ruskin evaluated paintings for them, and art dealers like Ernest Gambart held exhibitions and promoted individual artists.[58]

Figure 6.7. "Cairo from the East," Francis Frith, 1860, photograph
(Source: Courtesy of the Rare Books Library, the American University in Cairo)

Lewis, as a painter, became part of the Victorian art world. And in 1858 he resigned both his membership and the presidency of the Old Watercolour Society to paint in oil. As a medium, oils were more lucrative than watercolors, and they also provided a means for him to gain membership in the Royal Academy, an important venue to artistic success. He was elected an associate member in 1859 and a full member in 1865.[59]

Under the presidency of Charles Lock Eastlake (1850–65), the Royal Academy displayed a strong interest in modern life and in moral genre narratives. Illustrative of this trend were the works of William Frith and August Leopold Egg. In "Derby Day" (1858) and "The Railroad Station" (1862), Frith painted with unusual realism and meticulous detail, basing his human types on photographic studies. Meanwhile, Egg's famous triptych "Past and Present" depicted the downfall of an adulterous wife. Lewis also knew the work of the Pre-Rafaelite Brotherhood (Williams Holman Hunt, J. Everett Millais, Thomas Woolner) who painted subjects topical of modern life, often with social or moral dimensions. It was in this setting of a new rugged class of buyers, and the appeal of meticulously realistic and moralizing subjects, that Lewis produced his genre paintings of Cairo.

Catering both to the taste and values of the increasingly affluent British middle class, Lewis concentrated on two aspects of Islamic society: the bazaar and the harem. In "The Street and Mosque of the Ghooreyah" (FIGURE 6.8), Lewis set

Figure 6.8. "The Street and Mosque of the Ghooreyah," J.F. Lewis, 1876, watercolor
(Source: Wherabouts unknown)

his scene in the same area that Roberts, and before him Hay, had set his "Bazaar of the Silk Mercers" (see FIGURE 6.5).[60] However, Lewis uses the architectural context only to frame the action taking place in the street—which for him, with its people, was the most interesting element of the composition. Lewis's actors illustrate two aspects of commercial life in Cairo: the role of the *saraff*, money-changer, who certified the value of the many coins in circulation; and of the *dallal*, the middleman broker between seller and buyer. They appear often in Lewis's bazaar paintings. Lewis cited Edward Lane as an explanatory source on the *dallal*.[61] He was also indebted to Lane for other images and reminders. For example, Lane's illustration "A Party at Dinner or Supper," in which two servants, one with a fly whisk and the other with a water bottle, serve three men seated around a low tray/table, helped Lewis compose his "A Midday Meal." Meanwhile, Thackeray's description of Lewis's house in Cairo served Lewis as the model for "The Hosh (Courtyard) of the House of the Coptic Patriarch, Cairo."[62]

"The Hhareem" is a rare picture Lewis painted while in Egypt.[63] In terms of theme it was his most overtly Orientalist, and its style set the tone for his other harem scenes. A young Bey, seated on a divan, watches intently as the chief eunuch unrobes a newly acquired young Abyssinian. The Bey's wives also witness the proceedings. Lewis sent the painting back to the Old Watercolour Society,

Figure 6.9. "An Intercepted Correspondence," J.F. Lewis, 1869, oil on panel
(Source: Wherabouts unknown)

where it was exhibited to critical applause. Twenty years later, in 1869, Lewis painted "An Intercepted Correspondence," which in setting was similar to "The Hhareem" (FIGURE 6.9).[64] But this time it was an old Bey who sits on the divan, and before whom stands a *duenna* who has caught a young inmate with a message-laden bouquet of flowers.[65]

In this painting, and in others such as "Life in the Harem—Cairo" (1858) and "The Reception" (1873), Lewis faithfully reproduced the intricate patterns and beautiful settings of a Cairene house of the Ottoman period.[66] In this regard, Lewis's compositions remain the most sumptuously explicit and most comprehensively documented of any Orientalist painter. He also used the living spaces of the upperclass of the Ottoman world to show a style of life similar to that of the middleclass in Victorian Britain. For example, in both societies, women were identified with home, and were seen as its chief ornament. In this female domain, the ladies—healthy, attractive, and elegantly dressed—lived lives according to similar cultural dictates. Thus, in Cairo as in London, there was a male world and a female world, each with its own spaces, duties, and prerogatives; and in these worlds, men and women were connected by the human realities of age and sex, and women were trophies of male wealth and power.[67] Lewis set his paintings in Cairo, but the themes were those that a Victorian businessman could understand

and appreciate, and the opulent, textured compositions were ones that his Victorian wife could hang on her walls.

In his depiction of the anecdotal and the illustrative aspects of human relations, and the colorful and varied contexts in which they took place, John Fredrick Lewis focused on material that the genre artists who followed him to Egypt took up. For example, Lewis's domestic paintings had a great effect on Frank Dillon, a younger contemporary who made several trips to Cairo between 1854 and 1874. As an Orientalist painter, Dillon was unusual for his almost exclusive concentration on interior scenes. In "The House of Shaykh Sadat," Dillon carefully—although not with Lewis's technical virtuosity and sensibility—renders the exotic details: the wooden lattice windows, the carved cupboard, the blue and white Ottoman tiles, the rich fabrics, the peacock feather fan, the fly whisk, and the incense burning in a silver stand on the mother-of-pearl inlaid table.[68] This was undoubtedly drawn from reality. Walter Tyndale, an artist who was in Cairo in 1895, wrote of the same house: "It was my good fortune to have been introduced to the late Sheykh . . . and I was allowed to paint there as much as I pleased. No house more recalls to my mind the pictures of Lewis."[69]

Lewis's influence as an interactive link in the Orientalist genre extended beyond his British contemporaries. For example, in 1852 Lewis painted "The Arab Scribe" (FIGURE 6.10).[70] The subject here, an old man using his literacy as a skill, was a popular one. David Roberts, in 1838, had painted "The Letter Writer—Cairo" as a record of what he saw: a simple one-on-one depiction of a young woman sitting demurely next to the turbaned shaykh who writes down her words. And a few years later, in 1841, Sir David Wilkie painted "The Turkish Letter Writer," showing two young women leaning toward an old man, seemingly engaged in the writing process.[71] Wilkie was a friend of Lewis, and Lewis's "Scribe" was an elaboration of Wilkie's drawing. In it, Lewis adopted the participatory nature of the process, but he painted one companion as a white mistress and the other as a black servant, a contrast of race and station that would influence subsequent Orientalist imagery.

JEAN-LÉON GÉRÔME AND HIS STUDENTS

In 1855, four of Lewis's paintings were exhibited at the Exposition Universelle in Paris, among them "The Hhareem" and "The Arab Scribe." Jean-Léon Gérôme (1824–1908), a young French artist who was beginning his career, undoubtedly saw Lewis's paintings and was influenced by them.[72] Gérôme was another major interpretive artist in this second period of Cairene Orientalist art. In Gérôme's vignettes of daily life, which concentrated on colorful costumes and on the light and textures of a new and exotic world, there is a direct continuation of Lewis's style, but also a change of emphasis. Gérôme's scenes, seemingly authentic stage pieces, become more and more draped with imaginative interpre-

Figure 6.10. "The Arab Scribe," J.F. Lewis, 1852, watercolor
(Source: Wherabouts unknown)

tation, and the reality becomes more elusive. His output of almost 250 canvases, a third of his work, made him one of the most prolific Orientalist artists. He made six trips to Egypt from 1856 to 1880, returning with studies and sketches, artifacts and costumes, photographs and ideas for paintings that he finished in his studio in Paris, not in Cairo.

As recorded by Roberts, painting "live" in the streets of Cairo was not pleasant. Frederick Goodall, a British artist and contemporary of Gérôme's, who spent eight months in Cairo from September 1858 to April 1859, expanded on Roberts's experiences:

> At last I began painting in the streets of Cairo . . . the authorities made arrangements for me to have a soldier to guard me—it was not safe without. Sometimes, however, he would fall asleep; and when he did so on one occasion a ragged fanatic old wretch took up a big stone with the intention of hurling it at my head. This I avoided by jumping up suddenly from my seat. . . .

> On another occasion, when I was sketching, a police-officer, a Turk—thinking to make himself exceedingly useful to me, scattered the crowd, driving them away and beating them with his *courbash* made of hippopotamus hide. This always made them angry at me!

Figure 6.11. "Arnaut Smoking,"
Jean-Léon Gérôme, 1865, oil on panel
(Source: Wherabouts unknown)

But what I feared even more than stones and insults was the silent tread of the camels, for there was no pavement and the drivers did not warn me.[73]

For realistic objects and costumes in his paintings, Gérôme relied on the many artifacts in his own collection.[74] He also made use of those in the collection of his brother-in-law, Albert Goupil, who was among the earliest and most important nineteenth-century collectors of Islamic art, and who displayed his objects in elaborately furnished "Islamic" rooms.[75] These rooms were full of car-pets, banners, curtains, metalware, arms, *narghile* (water pipes), panels of inlaid wood, and even whole sections of *mashrabíya* windows.

Many of Gérôme's paintings are portraits of "types," such as the *bazí-bazouk* and the *arnaut* (Albanian militia) (FIGURE 6.11), and the dancing girl. With an artifact or architectural detail to verify the setting, models were posed in appropriate cos-tumes and painted in the studio. Some of the items, such as the green and white *jíbbah*, the pink shirt, the Mamluk helmet, and Gérôme's pet whippet dogs, made multiple appearances in his paintings. For some scenes he used photographs. Francis Frith's photograph "Cairo from the East" (1860) (FIGURE 6.7) provided the urban setting for Gérôme's "The Muezzin's Call to Prayer" (1880) (FIGURE 6.12).[76]   And Henri Bechard's photograph "Intérieur de la Mosquée d'Amrou" (1870) provided the urban setting for "Prayer in the Mosque of 'Amr" (1872).[77] The backdrop for Gérôme's painting "General Bonaparte in Cairo" (1863) is based on a photograph by James Robertson and Beato, "Tombs of the Mamelukes below the Citadel" (1856).[78] Illustrations in books provided other sources. "The Rose or Love Token" (1887) was undoubtedly inspired by Prisse d'Avennes's "Zawiya of 'Abd al-Rahman Katkhuda" (1879).[79] Gérôme also used Lane's book. Thus, the main figure in his "The Guard of the Harem" (1859) stands beside a door that is the exact replica of Lane's "Door of a Private House in Cairo."[80]

Sometimes, because the culture was imperfectly understood, there were errors in these images. In "Prayer in the Mosque of 'Amr," Gérôme filled the setting with splendidly dressed worshippers.   However, the half-naked madman would not have been part of the congregation. In "Prayer on the Rooftops of Cairo" (1865) he drew men at prayer in various poses, but they are facing north rather than southeast, the true *qibla* in Cairo.[81] In "The Rose or Love Token," Gérôme did not realize that a *zawiya* was where Muslim mystics lived, and that the balcony he copied so carefully from Prisse d'Avennes's book was for the call to prayer, not for improbable flirtations.

Perhaps these were inadvertent mistakes, but in other cases "reality" was sacrificed for appeal. Frederic-Auguste Bartholdi, the sculptor, was a close friend of Gérôme. He was also a photographer and the author of *Au Yemen en 1856*. In "Cairene Horse Dealer" (1867) Gérôme deliberately transposed the ornate demiswan console supporting the *mashrabiya* window from Bartholdi's photograph of the architecture of al-Mukha (a port in Yemen).[82] This kind of falsification of detail for effect was later picked up by other Orientalist artists in depicting Cairo.[83]

Whether inadvertent or deliberate, these errors of fact were intended to create mood and atmosphere. Although Gérôme's paintings were based on the reality of what he had seen, because they were improvised in his studio, he felt free to interpret or add to his original observations and impressions. Gérôme was fascinated by the genuineness of Islamic prayer. In "The Muezzin's Call to Prayer" (see FIGURE 6.12), Gérôme depicts the scene as it impressed him: the small figure of the *muezzin* in the upper balcony of a minaret making the call that floats down over the neighborhood below. But like an experienced raconteur, he edited, interpreted, and embroidered the details of his story to serve his purpose. Thus, in the painting he has rearranged the components of the real scene, changing the minaret and doubling the dome of the sixteenth-century Mosque of Khayrbak, so it appears both as monument and as detail.[84]

Gérôme often repeated scenes: the *muezzin* in the minaret, individuals at prayer, and women in the bath. This thematic repetition leads to another aspect of Gérôme's work. Gérôme was not only an artist, but an entrepreneur, and in this guise he was helped by Adolphe Goupil, the influential art publisher and

Figure 6.12. "The Muezzin's Call to Prayer," Jean-Léon Gérôme, oil on canvas
(Source: Wherabouts unknown)

dealer. Goupil's firm, excelling in the production of fine but inexpensive photogravure prints of modern painters, brought art publishing into the industrial age. For more than forty years Gérôme had a double bond with Goupil: as artist and son-in-law.[85] Goupil marketed what Gérôme produced: 122 of Gérôme's paintings reproduced in 370 different editions, and 337 sold and resold through his galleries in Europe and New York.[86] Goupil also worked with Ernest Gambart, the prime art dealer in London, to sell the works of living French artists in America. By 1880 many of America's wealthiest magnates owned Gérôme's paintings.

Jean-Léon Gérôme was not only the most renowned and successful French Orientalist painter, with wide appeal to a variety of patrons, but he was also a popular teacher. In the forty years in which he was *chef d'atelier* at the École des Beaux-Arts in Paris, it is calculated he taught 2,000 students. He exerted an enormous influence on this new generation of artists, many of whom became Orientalist painters themselves.[87] Many of his students also followed their teacher's example in using accurately rendered details to authenticate otherwise imagined situations. This creation of managed tableaux also echoed the way that Islamic society was displayed in the great

World's Fairs of the second half of the nineteenth century. These "universal" exhibitions—in London, 1851; in Paris, 1867, 1878, 1889, and 1900; in Vienna, 1873; and in Chicago, 1893—offered idealized platforms for encapsulated vignettes of Islamic culture. Selected portions of the Ottoman, Egyptian, and North African worlds were presented through artifacts and architecture as exotic spectacles and enticing events for the stay-at-home travelers who wandered through them in the millions.[88]

One of Gérôme's students was Ludwig Deutsch (1855–1935), an Austrian by birth, and a Frenchman by residence. As a painter he is representative of the late-nineteenth-century artists who used Cairo as an incidental backdrop for anecdotal arrangements of various "types." One of his best-known paintings is an arrangement he titled "The Scribe."[89] The man sits on a wooden lattice bench, positioned beside a precisely rendered door of the Ottoman period. He gazes contemplatively skyward. Pen, paper, and inkwell are at hand as he waits for a customer. Deutsch's presentation continues the interest in the topic, but it offers none of Roberts's descriptive quality or Lewis's anecdotal possibilities. In concentrating on the nonnarrative but visually interesting elements of textiles and architectural details, Deutsch also created an assembly line of paintings, repeating the setting, while using different actors and activities to create a semblance of variety.[90]

Deutsch traveled to Cairo several times in the 1890s, where he made sketches and bought artifacts, but most of his paintings were executed in his studio in Paris. He painted the fanciful "Le Tribut" in Paris in 1898 (FIGURE 6.13).[91] Here, the artist has placed the tribute bearers, the scene's focus, in front of a suggested Islamic palace. In reality, however, the backdrop is the entrance porch of the Madrasa of Sultan Hasan, to which has been added a panel of Turkish tiles. The Nubian guard standing at the door has a real function in this painting, but in other paintings guards exist simply as an excuse to paint the exotic costumes and weapons Deutsch had collected in the East.[92] The precision of the architectural details (the roundel, the interlace borders) make it likely that Deutsch actually visited the Madrasa of Sultan Hasan. But by the 1870s and 1880s commercial photographs in the form of studio portraits and architectural shots were readily available to serve as visual aids.[93] The real setting can be identified, but Deutsch has minimized it in the interests of his imaginary cultural narrative.

CONCLUSION

In sum, therefore, Orientalist images and cultural projections changed over the century. The topographical artists—Hay and Roberts—documented and recorded the external environment of a new culture. In a period that culminated with the invention of photography, they drew essentially what they saw.

In the next period, the genre artists provided cultural interpretation. John Frederick Lewis moved the scene to the bazaar and domestic settings, and in his

Figure 6.13. "Le Tribut," Ludwig Deutsch, 1898, oil on panel
(Source: The Najd Collection; Courtesy of the Mathaf Gallery, London)

visual anecdotes, he tried to provide a sympathetic understanding between two cultures. For his part, Jean-Léon Gérôme also attempted to give cultural validity to what he painted, but he also responded to market demand. His patrons were the new commercial elite, who perceived in the Orient an escape from the drab world of European industrialism and the dull conventions of bourgeois domesticity. Later, Gérôme's students capitalized on the fantasies of these patrons, and provided them not with true depictions of the Other, but with fanciful escapes and colorful wall hangings.

Cumulatively, the production of these artists has documentary and atmospheric value. Since the beginning of the 1800s the Cairene cityscape has changed enormously, and these images, however interpreted, are the only surviving representations of a setting that once was. Today, in 2004, the old city of Cairo is on the threshold of a new architectural/urban presentation. The images that survive from the nineteenth century, both descriptive and interpretative, therefore, become cherished and nostalgic evocations.

NOTES

1. *Description de l'Égypte* (Köln: Benedikt Taschen, 1994), "L'Etat Moderne," Vol. 1, Plate 38; and R. Benjamin, ed., *Orientalism: Delacroix to Klee* (Sydney: The Art Gallery of New South Wales, 1997), Plate 55, p. 114.

2. *Description*, "L'Etat Moderne," Vol. 1, Plates 15–72 in the 1994 Taschen edition "a paperback containing reduced versions of all the plates." The plates of the first two volumes of "L'État Moderne" were published in 1810, while a second edition of the whole work appeared in 1820–29. For its comprehensive bibliography, see J. Rodenbeck, "An Orientalist Monument Reconsidered," in J. Thompson, ed., *Egyptian Encounters* (Cairo: The American University in Cairo Press, 2002), pp. 90–132.

3. "L'Etat Moderne," Vol. 1, Plates 32–38.

4. Not included in this group is Achille Constant Theodore Emile Prisse D'Avennes (1807–79)—artist, cartographer, traveler, adventurer, eccentric, plunderer, Orientalist, and scholar, whose documentary interest in the monuments of Cairo did not occur until the 1860s. In 1829, at the age of twenty-two, a veteran of the war for Greek independence, and just out of art school, he went to Egypt, where he took service with Muhammad 'Ali as a civil and hydrographic engineer and topographer. During this time he became fluent in Arabic, embraced Islam, and lived as an Egyptian. After seven years he resigned from his jobs to become a professional traveler, artist, and looter of Pharaonic antiquities. In 1857, after a period in France, D'Avennes returned to Egypt, at which time he discovered the Islamic monuments of Cairo, and began the compilation of drawings, paper casts, daguerreotypes, sketches, photographs, and notes which were the source material for *L'Art Arabe d'après les Monuments du Kaire Depuis le XVIIeme Siècle Jusqu'à la fin du XVIIeme* (Paris: A. Morel et Cie, 1869–77).

5. P. Coste, *Mémoires d'un Artiste: Notes et Souvenirs de Voyages (1817–1877)* (Marseille: Cayer et Cie, 1878), pp. 8–10.

6. Coste's book is based on copies of his drawings, since he had sold the originals to Robert Hay (see below in text) before he left Egypt in 1827. The original drawings were bought by Rodney Searight in 1977 and are now in the Searight collection in the Victoria and Albert Museum, London. For an account of this transaction, see S. Tillett, *Egypt Itself: The Career of Robert Hay, Esquire of Linplum and Nunraw, 1799–1863* (London: SD Books, 1984), pp. 43–45, 84–85, 92, and 108.

7. Coste, *Mémoires d'un Artiste*, p. 125 (my translation).

8. The following plates are reproduced in A. Raymond, *The Glory of Cairo: An Illustrated History* (Paris: Editio-Editions Citadelles & Mazenod, 2000): "View of Bab al-Futuh," Plate 91; "Façade of Mosque of Mu'ayyad Shaykh," Plate 221; "View of Prayer Hall of Qaytbay," Plate 273; "View of Summer Houses on the Khalig," Plate 323; "Wakala of Dhulfiqar Katkhuda," Plate 336; "Barber's Shop," Plate 340; "Sabil of Sultan Mahmud," Plate 371; "Sabil-kuttab of Ibrahim Katkhuda," Plate 372; and "View of Summer House on the Khalig," Plate 377.

9. Tillett, *Egypt Itself; Dictionary of National Biography* (Oxford: Oxford University Press,

2000) new edition; and T.G.H. James, *Egypt Revealed: Artist-Travellers in an Antique Land* (London: The Folio Society, 1997), pp. 130–55. See also R. Hay, *Illustrations of Cairo* (London: Tilt & Bogue, 1840).

10. Hay, *Illustrations*. Six drawings are by Hay himself: The Aqueduct, Island of el-Rodah, El-Geezeh, Joseph's Hall, and Boolak, Part 1 and 2.

11. Hay, *Illustrations*, Plate 9.

12. Hay, *Illustrations*, Plate 15.

13. Hay, *Illustrations*, Plate 13.

14. Hay, *Illustrations*, Plate 17.

15. Hay, *Illustrations*, Plate 24.

16. Hay, *Illustrations*, Plate 20.

17. *Description de l'Égypte*, "L'Etat Moderne," Vol.1, Plate 70.

18. Hay, *Illustrations*, Plate 21.

19. In Coste, *Mémoires*, Vol. I, p. 44, there is the following paragraph: "An English tourist, whose name I no longer remember, came to see the drawings I had made of the Arab monuments. I sold them to him for 12,000 francs. I had retained copies." This might seem dismissive about something that preoccupied Lane so much, but Coste was writing fifty years after the fact, so a certain amount of bottom-line sparseness is perhaps understandable.

20. As quoted in Tillett, *Egypt Itself*, p. 85. Lane's original manuscript was entitled *Description of Egypt*, a direct reference to the French *Description*. See E.W. Lane, *Description of Egypt*, edited and introduced by J. Thompson (Cairo: The American University in Cairo Press, 2000); and J. Thompson, "Edward William Lane's 'Description of Egypt,'" *International Journal of Middle East Studies*, Vol. 28, 1996, pp. 656–83.

21. Tillett, *Egypt Itself*, p. 84; and M. Darby, *The Islamic Perspective* (London: The World of Islam Festival Trust, 1983), pp. 31 and 81.

22. E.W. Lane, *An Account of The Manners and Customs of the Modern Egyptians* (London: John Murray, 1836). I have used the edition of 1963 (London: Everyman, 1963).

23. Lane was a great-nephew of Thomas Gainsborough. See J. Thompson, "Edward William Lane as an Artist," *Gainsborough's House Review*, 1993/94, pp. 33–42.

24. Lane, *Modern Egyptians*, pp. 31 and 328; and Hay, *Illustrations*, Plate 30. Also see Lane, *Modern Egyptians*, p. 197; and Hay, *Illustrations*, Plate 17.

25. Lane, *Modern Egyptians*, p. 59; and Hay, *Illustrations*, Plate 20.

26. His own interest was certainly sparked by a visit to Spain and Morocco (October 1832–October 1833), which resulted in *Picturesque Sketches from Spain* in 1837, and from his work redrawing sketches done on the spot by amateur artists for Finden's *Landscape Illustrations of the Bible* (London: John Murray, 1836).

27. J. Ballantine, *The Life of David Roberts, R.A.* (Edinburgh: Adam and Charles Black, 1866) p. 102; and D. Roberts, "Eastern Journal," unpublished transcript by C. Bicknell, 2 volumes, National Library of Scotland, December 20, 1838.

28. In Roberts, "Eastern Journal," January 8, 1839, he notes about the Mahmal procession: "for a more particular account see Lane."

29. D. Roberts, *Egypt and Nubia* (London: F.G. Moon, 1846–49), Vol. 3; H. Guiterman and B. Llewellyn (compilers), *David Roberts*, exhibition catalog (London: Barbican Art Gallery, 1986). Reproduced in Raymond, *The Glory of Cairo*, "The Bazaar of the Silk Mercers," Plate 166; "Grand Mosque of Sultan Hasan from the Great Square of Rumayla," Plate 228; "Sultan Hasan, Interior Courtyard," Plate 234; and "The Citadel," end pages.

30. Roberts, "Eastern Journal."

31. *The Travels of Ibn Battuta*, trans. H.A.R. Gibb (Cambridge: Hakluyt Society at the University Press, 1958), Vol. 2, p. 45.

32. Roberts, *Egypt and Nubia*, Vol. 3, Plate 96; and Hay, *Illustrations*, Plate 4.

33. Roberts, "Eastern Journal," January 1–31, 1839.

34. For a geographical grouping, see C. Williams, *The Islamic Monuments of Cairo: The Practical Guide* (Cairo: American University in Cairo Press, 2002).

35. In fact, by overexploitation as note cards, calendars, prints, and postcards, they have become cliché views of medieval Cairo.

36. Taken by the daguerreotypist Frederic Goupil-Fesquet, accompanied by the artist Horace Vernet, on the first photographic expedition to the Orient. Joseph-Philibert Girault de Prangey was another photographer who traveled to Egypt in 1842. He was a reclusive man who died without heirs, and his photographs were not discovered until 1952. See Christie's, *Important Daguerreotypes by Joseph-Philibert Girault de Prangey from the Archive of the Artist*, auction catalogue, London, May 20, 2003, pp. 44–60.

37. J.R. Abbey, *Travel in Aquatint and Lithography 1700–1860* (London: Dawsons of Pall Mall, 1972), Vol. 2, p. 341.

38. *Francis Frith: Photographs of Egypt and the Holy Land*, Introduction by C. Williams (Cairo: American University in Cairo Press, 1999); and *Egypt and the Holy Land in Historic Photographs: 77 Views by Francis Frith*, Introduction and Bibliography by J. van Haaften (New York: Dover, 1980).

39. About Philae, Frith writes: "This is one of the few views which a photograph can render without, perhaps, greatly detracting from its artistic fame. Everybody has sketched it; many clever artists have painted it; Murray has engraved it for his 'Guide.'" Also see F. Frith, *Lower Egypt, Thebes and the Pyramids* (London: William Mackenzie, 1862), "The Approach to Philae." Frith also mentions Lewis and Goodall by name.

40. Frith, *Egypt and Palestine Photographed and Described by Francis Frith* (London: J.S. Virtue, 1860), "Osiride Pillars."

41. F. Frith, *Sinai and Palestine* (London: W. Mackenzie, 1862), "Jerusalem from Mt. Scopus."

42. Frith, *Egypt and Palestine Photographed and Described by Francis Frith*, "The Colossi of Memnon."

43. Frith, *Egypt and Palestine Photographed and Described by Francis Frith*, "View at Girgeh."

44. Frith, *Egypt, Sinai and Jerusalem*, "The Mosque of Emeer Akhor."

45. Frith, *Lower Egypt, Thebes and the Pyramids*, "Osiride Pillar at Medinet-Haboo."

46. Frith, *Egypt and Palestine Photographed and Described by Francis Frith*, "Portrait: Turkish Summer Costume."

47. S. Lane-Poole, *The Englishwoman in Egypt: Letters from Cairo. Written during a Residence there in 1842, 3 & 4*, 3 volumes (London: C. Knight, 1844–46), p. 42.

48. F. Frith, *Egypt, Sinai and Palestine, Supplementary Volume* (London: W. Mackenzie, 1862).

49. W.M. Thackeray, *Notes of a Journey from Cornhill to Grand Cairo*, New Introduction by S. Searight, Illustrations compiled by B. Llewellyn (Heathfield: Cockbird Press, 1991), p. 141.

50. Reproduced in M. Stevens, ed., *The Orientalists: Delacroix to Matisse* (Washington, D.C.: National Gallery of Art, 1984), Plate 103, p. 71.

51. He was a contemporary and friend of David Roberts, had traveled to Spain in 1833–34, and was attracted to the Middle East by his work as a re-draw artist for Coke-Smyth's *Illustrations of Constantinople* published in 1836. See Stevens, *The Orientalists*, pp. 181–86; C. Williams, "John Frederick Lewis: 'Reflections of Reality,'" *Muqarnas: An Annual on the Visual Culture of the Islamic World* (Leiden: Brill, 2001), Vol. 18, pp. 227–43; and B. Llewellyn, "Eastern Light," *FMR Magazine*, No. 3, 1984, pp. 131–53.

52. J.G. Wilkinson, *Manners and Customs of the Ancient Egyptians* (London: John Murray, 1847).

53. In fact, Wilkinson mentions Lewis in the *Handbook* as an artist living in Cairo. See also J. Thompson, *Sir Gardner Wilkinson and His Circle* (Austin: University of Texas Press, 1992), pp. 167–72.

54. S. Searight, *The British in the Middle East* (New York: Atheneum, 1970).

55. William Thackeray found Lewis living like a well-to-do Turk in a rented house in the Azbakiyya quarter. See Thackeray, *Cornhill to Grand Cairo*, pp. 142–45.

56. Wild was the brother-in-law of Owen Jones and a friend of Joseph Bonomi, one of Robert Hay's main Egyptological artists. Wild had come to Egypt in 1842 on an expedition sent out by the King of Prussia under Dr. Lepsius. After 1845 Wild stayed on in Cairo to study Arab domestic architecture and the mosques, for which, like Roberts, he wore native dress to enter. Among Wild's sketchbooks, now at the Victoria and Albert Museum (E 3763–1938), is a drawing of the main reception room in Lewis's house. It is reproduced in Darby, *The Islamic Perspective*, p. 46. This is the very room that Lewis used in the painting "The Reception" (1873).

57. Aspects of these changes are described in the novels *Coningsby* and *Sybil* by Benjamin Disraeli, and *The Way We Live Now* by Anthony Trollope. See B. Disraeli, *Coningsby* (London: Dent, 1963); and *Sybil* (London: Oxford University Press, 1926). Also A. Trollope, *The Way We Live Now* (London: Chapman and Hall, 1874–75).

58. J. Maas, *Gambart: Prince of the Victorian Art World* (London: Barrie & Jenkins, 1975). See in passing, S. Mitchell, *Victorian Britain: An Encyclopedia* (London: Garland Publishing Inc., 1988).

59. When he was elected as an associate member, David Roberts wrote him a congratulatory letter. When David Roberts died, it was his place that Lewis filled at the Royal Academy. See M. Lewis, *John Frederick Lewis, R.A. 1805–1876* (Leigh-on-Sea: The Tithe House, 1978), p. 31.

60. "The Street and Mosque of the Ghooreyah" (1876), ex-Forbes Collection, illustrated in Thackeray, *Cornhill to Grand Cairo*, p. 136.

61. For other works that feature the Ghuriya area, see Lewis, *John Frederick Lewis*, cata-

logue items 515–17, 626, and 627. And for the *dallal*, see catalogue items 603, 618, and 691. For the description of a *dallal's* function, see Lane, *Modern Egyptians*, p. 324.

62. Lane's illustration "A Party at Dinner or Supper" appears in Lane, *Modern Egyptians*, p. 149. "A Midday Meal" (1875) is illustrated in Thackeray, *Cornhill to Grand Cairo*, p. 145. "The Hosh (Courtyard) of the House of the Coptic Patriarch, Cairo" (1864) is illustrated in Thackeray, *Cornhill to Grand Cairo*, p. 143, and described on pp. 143–44.

63. Reproduced in Thackeray, *Cornhill to Grand Cairo*, p. 146; and in Benjamin, *Orientalism*, pp. 19–81.

64. Reproduced in Stevens, *The Orientalists*, p. 50; and in Sotheby's, *Important Orientalist Paintings from the Collection of Coral Petroleum*, New York, May 22, 1985, Plate 11.

65. For a further analysis of this painting, see Williams, "John Frederick Lewis," in *Muqarnas*, pp. 231–38, note 50.

66. "Life in the Harem—Cairo" (1858) and "The Reception," (1873) are reproduced in Llewellyn, "Eastern Light," Plate 4 and Plate 1.

67. For Cairo, see Lane, *Modern Egyptians*. For London, see Mitchell, *Victorian Britain*; and G. Saunders, *Public and Private: Women's Lives in Nineteenth Century Art*, exhibition catalogue, April 9–September 14, 1997, Prints, Drawings, and Paintings Department, Victoria and Albert Museum, London.

68. Reproduced in E. Atil, C. Newton, and S. Searight, *Voyages and Visions: Nineteenth-Century European Images of the Middle East from the Victoria and Albert Museum* (Seattle: University of Washington Press, 1995), p. 105.

69. W. Tyndale, *Below the Cataracts* (Philadelphia: J.B. Lippincott Co., 1907), p. 56.

70. Reproduced in Llewellyn, "Eastern Light," Plate 9.

71. Stevens, *The Orientalists*, Plate 121.

72. Jean-Léon Gérôme's own "Age of Augustus" was on exhibit also. The most comprehensive work on Jean-Léon Gérôme is G. Ackerman, *The Life and Work of Jean-Léon Gérôme, with a Catalogue Raisonné* (London: Sotheby's, 1986); and C. Williams, "Jean-Léon Gérôme: A Case Study of an Orientalist Painter," in S.J. Webber and M. Lynd, eds., *Fantasy or Ethnography? Irony and Collusion in Subaltern Representation*, Ohio State University Papers in Comparative Studies 8 (Columbus, Ohio: 1993–94), pp. 117–48.

73. F. Goodall, *The Reminiscences of Frederick Goodall, R.A.* (London: Walter Scott Publishing Co., 1902), pp. 87–88.

74. "Gerome Photographed in his Studio" (1890), in *Jean-Léon Gérôme: Sa vie, son oeuvre* (Paris: ACR Poche Couleur, 1997), p. 9. See also the photograph by Auguste Giraudon, "Jean-Léon Gérôme" in Christie's, *The Paris Salon*, New York, February 11, 1997, p. 48. He had 173 costumes. See Ackerman, *The Life and Work of Jean-Léon Gérôme*, p. 158.

75. H. Lavoix, "La Collection Albert Goupil," *Gazette des Beaux-Arts*, Vol. 32, 1885, pp. 287–307. Albert Goupil's "Islamic Room" (1888) is illustrated in G.D. Lowry, *A Jeweler's Eye: Islamic Arts of the Book from the Vever Collection* (Washington, D.C.: Smithsonian Institute, 1988). "Albert Goupil's Oriental Room" is illustrated in *Gerome & Goupil: Art and Enterprise*, exhibition catalog. New York, Dahesh Museum of Art, 2001, p. 18.

76. F. Frith, *Cairo, Sinai, Jerusalem, and the Pyramids of Egypt: A Series of Sixty Photographic Views by Francis Frith, With Descriptions by Mrs. Poole and Reginald Stuart Poole* (London: W. Mackenzie, 1861); and Stevens, *The Orientalists*, Plate 36, p. 62.

77. Benjamin, *Orientalism*, Plate 125 on p. 198; and Stevens, *The Orientalists*, Plate 32, p. 65.

78. Stevens, *The Orientalists*, Plate 30, p. 87; and photograph by Robertson and Beato, "Mamluke Tombs," salted paper print, c. 1856, in D. Bull and D. Lorimer, *Up the Nile: A Photographic Excursion: Egypt 1839–1898* (New York: Clarkson Potter, 1979), p. 24.

79. P. d'Avennes, *L'Art Arabe d'après les Monuments du Kaire*, Plate 37, illustrated in Raymond, *The Glory of Cairo*, Plate 340, p. 296; and "The Love Token," Arnot Art Museum, Elmira, New York, illustrated in G. Ackerman and R. Ettinghausen, *Jean-Léon Gérôme*, exhibition catalog, Dayton Art Institute, 1972, p. 20.

80. Wallace Collection, London; and Lane, *Modern Egyptians*, p. 7.

81. Perhaps also inspired by Lane's drawings in *Modern Egyptians*, pp. 78–79.

82. For "Cairene Horse Dealer" (1867), see *Gérôme & Goupil*, p. 81; and for Bartholdi photograph see *Au Yemen en 1856, Photographies et Dessins d'Auguste Bartholdi* (Colmar: Musée Bartholdi, 1994), pp. 84–85.

83. For the pastiche composition of Gérôme's "The Snake Charmer," see Williams, "Jean-Léon Gérôme," p. 137 and n. 77.

84. Stevens, *The Orientalists*, Plate 36, p. 62; and Williams, "Jean-Léon Gérôme," p. 126.

85. In January 1863, Gérôme married Marie Goupil.

86. *Gérôme & Goupil*, pp. 150–62.

87. Frederick Bridgman, Edwin Lord Weeks, Albert Aublet, Alberto Pasini, Hamdi Osman, and Lecomte de Nouÿ.

88. Z. Celik, *Displaying the Orient: Architecture of Islam at Nineteenth-Century World's Fairs* (Berkeley: University of California Press, 1992).

89. "The Scribe" (1906), reproduced in Stevens, *The Orientalists*, Plate 19, p. 74.

90. "The Scribe" (1904), reproduced in Benjamin, *Orientalism*, p. 115; and "The Scribe" (1911), reproduced in Mackenzie, *Orientalism*, Plate IV. The 1904, 1906, and 1911 versions are identical in composition, but differ in details. The Dahesh Museum in New York owns an undated oil sketch (LOTLON 112) featuring the same doorway, tiles, furniture, and books, but the scribe is black and has no pen, paper, or inkwell. "The Furniture Maker" (1900), reproduced in Thornton, *Orientalists*, p. 212, shows a similar composition but with different details; and "Outside Moorish Coffee Shop" (1903), with similar bench, man, and panel of Ottoman tiles.

91. Benjamin, *Orientalism*, p. 114.

92. See Nubian guards of 1883, 1893, 1895, 1902, and 1907.

93. D'Avennes, *L'Art Arabe d'après les Monuments du Kaire*, Plate 11, illustrated in Raymond, *The Glory of Cairo*, Plate 233. See also Bull and Lorimer, *Up the Nile*. A photograph of a groom, c. 1870, with foot forward clasping his riding stick, stands in a similar way to many of Deutsch's guards, p. 15. A photograph by H. Béchard, c. 1875, shows a niche in the portal of the Madrasa of Sultan Hasan, p. 22.

7

The Museum of What You Shall Have Been

Donald Preziosi

The Parisian Universal Exposition of 1900 was organized spatially in such a man-ner that the pavilions or "palaces" built to house the products of the two major French colonies of Algeria and Tunisia were situated between the Trocadero Palace on the right bank of the Seine and the Eiffel Tower on the left bank. Looking north from the elevated eye of the tower toward the Trocadero across the river, you would see these colonial buildings embraced by the two arms of the Trocadero's "neo-Islamic" facade. From here, France's North African colonies—indeed, all of them—would appear to occupy a place within the nurturing and protective arms of the French nation, whose own identity would appear to be fig-ured as assimilative, and thus supportive of, the peoples and products that were contained and exhibited in and by these colonial edifices.

Taking up the view from the opposite direction, looking south from the Trocadero toward the exposition ground across the river, there was a markedly dif-ferent morphology. The entire fairground was dominated by the Eiffel Tower, that gigantic technological feat of modern French engineering. Like a colossus (or a colossal figure of the sublime) dwarfing all the colonial edifices, its four great piers were grounded among the massed buildings of France's colonial possessions, as well as other European and American nations. Appearing to have been built on top of these buildings, the tower, one might say, put things (back) in a proper perspective.[1]

THE POINT OF ART HISTORY

The extraordinary tableaux described above—a veritable two-way mirror—is a clear and poignant emblem both of the imaginary logic of nationalism (and its imperialist correlates) and of the rhetorical carpentry and museological stage-craft of art historical practice.[2] Consider the following: From a Eurocentric point of view, art history has been constru[ct]ed as a universal empirical science, systematically discovering, classifying, analyzing, and interpreting specimens of what is thereby naturalized as a universal human phenomenon. This is the ("natural") artisanry or art of all peoples, samples of which are all arranged relative to each other both in museum space and in the more extensive, encyclopedic, and totalizing space-time of art historicism—that distillation and dynamically expanding refraction of universal exposition. All specimens in this vast archive sit as delegates or representatives (that is, as representations) in a congress of imaginary equals, as the myriad of manifestations making up a universal world history of art. To each is allotted a plot and display space, a platform, or a vitrine.

And yet if you shift your stance just a bit—say by taking up a position among the objects and histories of non-European (or, in recent disciplinary jargon, "non-Western") art—it becomes apparent that this virtual museum has a narrative structure, direction, and point. All its imaginary spaces lead to the modernity of a European present, which constitutes the apex or observation point, the vitrine within which all else is visible. Europe, in short, *is* the museum space within which non-European specimens become specimens, and where their (reformatted) visibility is rendered legible (the "media").

European aesthetic principles—in the guise of a reinvented generic modern or neoclassicism, or "universal principles of good design,"[3] as promulgated by Ruskin in Oxford and his disciple and friend Charles Eliot Norton at Harvard[4]—constituted the self-designated unmarked center, or Cartesian zero point or degree zero, around which the entire virtual art historicist edifice circulates, on the wings of which all things may be plotted, ranked, and organized in their differential particularities. There can of course be no "outside" to all this: all different objects are ranked as primitive, exotic, charming, or fascinating distortions of a central classical (European) canon or standard—the unmarked (and seemingly unclassed, ungendered, etc.) point or site toward which all others may be imagined as aspiring. A veritable Eiffel Tower, if you will.

What would be afforded pragmatically by this archive was the systematic assembly or recollection of artifacts now destined to be constru[ct]ed as material evidence for the elaboration of a universalist language of description and classification: the operating vocabulary of art history. Even the most radically disjunctive differences could be reduced to differential and time-factored qualitative manifestations of some panhuman capacity, some collective human essence or soul. In other words, differences could be reduced to the single dimension of different (but ultimately commensurate) approaches to artistic form (the Inuit, the Greek, the Welsh, etc.). Each work could be construed as approximating, as attempting to approach, the ideal, canonical, or standard. The theoretical and ideological justification for a practice that came to be called "art criticism" is thus born in an instant, occluding, while still instantiating, the magic realisms of exchange value.[5]

In short, the hypothesis of art as a universal human phenomenon has clearly been essential to an entire enterprise of commensurability, intertranslatability, and (Eurocentrist) hegemony. Artisanry in the broadest and fullest sense of "design" is positioned—and here, of course, archaeology and anthropology have their say—as one of the defining characteristics of humanness. The most skilled works of art shall be the widest windows onto the human soul, affording the deepest insights into the mentality of the maker, and thus the most clearly refracted insights into humanness as such. The art of art history is thus simultaneously the instrument of a universalist Enlightenment vision and a means for fabricating qualitative distinctions between individuals and societies.

You may well ask: How could this astonishing ideological legerdemain have survived for so long?

Consider again that essential to the articulation and justification of art history as a systematic and universal human science in the nineteenth century was the construction of an indefinitely extendable archive, potentially coterminous (as it has since, in practice, become) with the "material (or 'visual') culture" of all human groups.[6] Within this vast imaginary museographical artifact or edifice (every slide or photo library as an *ars memorativa*)—of which all museums are fragments or part objects—every possible object of attention might then find its fixed and proper place and address relative to all the rest. Every item might thereby be sited (and cited) as referencing or indexing another or others on multiple horizons (metonymic, metaphoric, or anaphoric) of useful association. The set of objects displayed in any exhibition (as with the system of classification of slide collections) is sustained by the willed fiction that they somehow constitute a coherent "representational" universe, as signs or surrogates of their (individual, national, racial, gendered, etc.) authors.[7]

The pragmatic and immediately beneficial use or function of art history in its origins was the fabrication of a past that could effectively be placed under systematic observation for use in staging and politically transforming the present. Common to the practices of museography and museology was a concern with spectacle, stagecraft, and dramaturgy; with the locating of what could be framed as distinctive and exemplary objects such that their relations among themselves and to their original circumstances of production and reception could be vividly imagined and materially envisioned in a cogent and useful manner—useful above all to the production of certain modes of civic subjectivity and responsibility. The problematics of historical causality, evidence, demonstration, and proof constituted the rhetorical scaffolding of this matrix or network of social and epistemological technologies.

Needless to say, much of this was made feasible by the invention of photography—indeed, art history is in a real sense the child of photography, which has been equally enabling of the discipline's fraternal nineteenth-century siblings, anthropology and ethnography. It was photography that made it possible not only for professional art historians but for whole populations to think art historically in a sustained and systematic fashion, thereby setting in motion the stage machinery of an orderly and systematic university discipline.

Photography also, and most crucially, made it possible to envision objects of art as signs. The impact of photography on determining the future course of art historical theory and practice was as fundamental as Marconi's invention of the wireless radio sixty years later was in envisioning the basic concept of arbitrariness in language—which, as linguists of the 1890s rapidly saw, paved the way for a new synthesis of the key concepts of modern linguistics.

THE FRAMING OF EGYPT

As we have seen, a clear and primary motivation for this massive archival labor was the assembly of material evidence justifying the construction of historical narratives of social, cultural, national, racial, or ethnic origins; identity; evolution; and progressive development. The professional art historian was an essential instrument for scripting and giving voice to that archive, providing its potential users, both lay and professional, with secure and well-illuminated access routes into and through it. Museology itself became a key art of this House of Historicist Memory, evolving as it did as a paradigmatic instrument for the *instituting of* archivable events. To understand these processes the most complete information we have comes from the Middle East in the late nineteenth century—in particular, from Egypt.

In nineteenth-century Cairo, Egyptians appeared while Europeans looked. The colonialist exhibitionary order and its supportive modes of representation (in which objects are signs of some abstract system of meanings and values, whose reality is in turn made manifest in material things and peoples) not only came to constitute the stagecraft of museums and the disciplinary practices of imperial capitalism, hygiene, and education, but it also came to provide the paradigm for the massive rebuilding of cities throughout the Middle East and North Africa during the nineteenth and early twentieth centuries. In this new urban order, several features were common to European colonialist enterprises everywhere, and most especially characteristic of French and British colonialism in Egypt. Most importantly, sharp distinctions were made between a modern, Western quarter and a native or indigenous Arab "old" city, these being endowed with clearly opposed aesthetic and ethical values. The Western town framed was the obverse of the native city. In the words of Henri Pieron in 1911,

[the older city] must be preserved to show to future generations what the former city of the Caliphs was like, before there was built alongside it an important cosmopolitan colony completely separate from the native quarter. . . .
There are two Cairos, the modern, infinitely the more attractive one, and the
old, which seems destined to prolong its agony and not to revive, being unable
to struggle against progress and its inevitable consequences. One is the Cairo
of artists, the other of hygienists and modernists.[8]

Although the colonial order seemed to exclude the older native city of Cairo
(Al-Qahira), in reality it included it by defining itself in a direct and indispensa-
bly obverse relationship to it. Echoing similar observations by Frantz Fanon,
Timothy Mitchell has noted:

The argument that the native town must remain "Oriental" did not mean preserving it *against* the impact of the colonial order. The Oriental was a creation
of that order, and was needed for such an order to exist. Both economically
and in a larger sense, the colonial order depended upon *at once creating and excluding its own opposite.*[9]

This dependence on the old city for maintaining the modern identity of the
new town made the old city paradoxically essential and integral to the modern
city's own identity as modern: its invisible core reality. Part of this ordering of
itself extends, in short, throughout the fabric of the indigenous town. This is
especially clear in the particular work of the Comité de Conservation des
Monuments de l'Art Arab (Committee for the Conservation of Monuments of
Arab Art), founded in 1882 and composed of European and Egyptian art historians, archaeologists, architects, and urbanists.

What has become clear in recent years is the extraordinary extent to which
the Comité's encyclopedic "restoration" projects were as often as not creations
designed to fashion an "old" city in the European image of the picturesque Cairo
mentioned by Pieron: a Cairo familiar to the millions of visitors to the many *expositions universelles* in Paris and elsewhere throughout the second half of the nineteenth century that re-created romantic slices of a Cairo street, or that, behind
the facade of a national pavilion, created a confusing labyrinth of picturesquely
winding alleys.

In fact, it was the construction of the modern Western quarter of Cairo, with
its high rents and prices, that increasingly drove native Cairenes eastward into
what was becoming the old city, thus increasing its disorder and poverty, and creating acute overpopulation and congestion beyond any real hope of economically and politically effective amelioration. The Comité's "restorations" of many
prominent and obscure buildings in the old city were designed in no small meas-

ure to create what can only justly be termed a theme-parked facade of structures visible down the eastern ends of the new boulevards and squares of the Western city, beckoning the European visitor toward an exoticized past. The Comité accomplished literally thousands of such "restorations" throughout the city, "re"-creating a "medieval" past in conformity to European fantasies. It may be added that this dyadic or dualistic urban morphology materially replicated the masculinist geographic discourse recently articulated by geographers such as Steve Pile, in which there is an often violent opposition between the desire for "critical distance" and separation from objects and people, and the desire to get "under the skin" of the Other.[10]

The modern quarter, with its gridded streets, squares, an opera house (built for the premiere of *Aida*, itself commissioned in an international musical competition—lost by Wagner and won by Verdi—to celebrate the opening of the Suez Canal), streetcars, telegraph and railway stations, cafes and restaurants, was all about transparency and visibility—the lack of any panoptic or panoramic viewpoints in the old city having been a source of great and continuing frustration for tourists and foreigners for decades (a frustration, in short, that was itself obviously essential to maintaining and sustaining European curiosities and desires). In fact, the new town visually enframed a medieval past—thereby imposing upon Islam a distinctly Eurocentric chronology—embodied in an old city increasingly morphed as a kind of living urban museum: an embodiment of the European framing, or frame-up, of Islamic culture as merely a bridge between the West's own antiquity and its modernity—which, after all, was the ultimate point of Orientalism as such.

Such reframings were underway elsewhere in the eastern Mediterranean of nineteenth century—as, for example, in Greece, where the new nation-state reframed Ottoman Islamic culture as but a foreign interlude between a purely Hellenic antiquity and its anticipated more purely Hellenic modernity. And such reframings continued well into the second half of the twentieth century, when the Jewish colonization of Palestine entailed the symbolic and literal erasure of a millennium and a half of Arab Muslim and Christian culture to materially juxtapose and sew together the archaeological traces of a Judaic antiquity with Israeli modernity.[11]

For the Egyptian colonial system to function properly and efficiently, it required a powerful investment in reframing the past of the country on many fronts. This entailed above all the reorganization of the city itself, as just mentioned, as the simulacrum of a (European) exhibition, an urban space representing Egypt's present and past in juxtaposition. Essential to this exhibitionary order was a series of archival and taxonomic institutions with homologous functions in different media and at different scales—hospitals, prisons, schools, zoos, legal codes, army and police barracks, stock exchanges, a university and a system of primary and secondary education—and, of course, museums.

THE MUSEUMS OF EGYPT

In a previous article I quoted from an 1868 essay by the linguist Michel Breal, who wrote that, in standing before a picture:

> Our eyes think they perceive contrasts of light and shade, on a canvas lit all
> over by the same light. They see depths, where everything is on the same
> plane. If we approach a few steps, the lines we thought we recognized break
> up and disappear, and in place of differently illuminated objects we find only
> layers of color congealed on the canvas and trails of brightly colored dots, adja-
> cent to one another but not joined up. But as soon as we step back again, our
> sight, yielding to long habit, blends the colors, distributes the light, puts the
> features together again, and recognizes the work of the artist.[12]

In the modern enterprise of art historicism, the masses of objects in a museum or exhibition came to be understood as analogous to the gobs of color and the
abstract dots and dashes described by Michel Breal on a painted canvas. Only if the
viewer takes up a proper perspective and distance may these bits and pieces be seen
as joining up to create the image, the figure, the physiognomy of the character or
mentality of a person, people, or period. I have previously demonstrated the optical illusion of the Ames Room in connection with my discussion of the Crystal
Palace of 1851.[13] It is precisely this pursuit of such a perspectival position that constitutes the modern discipline of art history as a politics of the gaze, an instrumental technology for fabricating genealogies of value, character, race, spirit, or mentality through the mediating fictions of style, intention, authorship, and reflection.

The museum was the place within which the dramaturgy of the nation's origins and evolution would be staged in the most encyclopedic and synoptic manner, and also in the most dense and minute detail, at the level of the juxtaposition
of the individual citizen-subject with individual object-relics staged so as to be
read as representing moments in the evolving spirit, mentality, will, and mind of
the nation. Each such staged and framed fetish object was indeed an object lesson, and a powerfully evocative sign to be consumed by native and foreign viewers—both in the masses of original and authentic artifacts archived in institutional spaces, and in the millions of replicas with which the country of Egypt (and
the city of Cairo, in particular) came increasingly to be saturated, as it continues
today to be awash in masses of tourist garbage.

Just as the reorganized city of Cairo was arranged in such a way as to reveal
or represent the abstract object behind the name "Egypt," that idealist or virtual
entity knowable through its material embodiments, and legible to those possessing expert knowledge, so too did the history of that object become knowable in
the chronological choreographies of landscape, cityscape, and museum space.

The museums were organized in such a way that their contents were arranged to reveal a preexisting evolutionary journey, adventure, or plan—each object staged as a sign, and each sign a link in a vast archival consignment system in which all the elements might articulate a synchronic slice (or a diachronic moment) of Egypt. The museum, in short, was what I recently referred to as a pantographic instrument for projecting that larger abstraction, "Egypt," up from its relics and minutiae. The museum gallery was (and indeed still remains) one of those spaces within the envelope of urban space where all the confusion of time and history are banished in favor of legibility and narrative and causal sense.

However, there was a problem peculiar to Egypt: to European eyes there was more than one historical Egypt—an original, Pharaonic civilization with its own 4,000-year history; a Greco-Roman civilization just less than 1,000 years long and succeeding and overlapping and partially assimilating the first; a Christian (Coptic) culture, now itself 2,000 years old (Egypt being the first officially Christian country, and the language of the Coptic Church being the modern descendant of the ancient indigenous language of the country), partly coterminous with the Greco-Roman, and tracing its ethnic roots to the older Pharaonic society; and an Islamic civilization, introduced by Arab speakers from the Arabian peninsula, and now itself 1,400 years old. Egypt, in short, was historically a multiethnic and polyglot country, the home to not insignificant numbers of various different peoples—Greeks, Armenians, Jews, Italians, Turks, and, over the past 500 years, other European or Levantine communities, in the two major cities of Cairo and Alexandria.

The colonialist solution to representing this complex social and cultural amalgam, this heterogeneity, as it was perceived by Europeans, was arrived at beginning in the 1880s, largely by the art historians and connoisseurs of the Comité, and realized over the following quarter century. It entailed the formation of four different museum institutions housing the artworks and material culture of the Pharaonic, Greco-Roman, Coptic Christian, and Arab Islamic facets of, or stages in, the modernizing nation's history.

In effect, what the Comité accomplished was to resolve perceived contradictions by crafting narrative fantasy based on evolution and chronology, whose logic was that of hindsight and of the future anterior, grounded in an image of what the country shall have been for what it was imagined to be in the process of becoming—namely, a modern nation-state among a family of distinct nations all modeled on those of Europe (in particular France and England), and positioned as client states on the margins of the central European imperial heartland.

In Egypt, this colonialist/Orientalist enterprise began with Napoleon's invasion of the country at the beginning of the nineteenth century and was emblematized quite poignantly in the frontispiece of the great Napoleonic publication during the first couple of decades of the century (the *Description de l'Égypte*), which presented a view of the country literally as a bird's-eye look down the Nile from north to south, where famous monuments were repositioned with later ones at the front and older ones toward the back. In short, the entire country was reformatted as a scholarly or tourist itinerary, a journey back through time.[14]

What the Comité accomplished in the last quarter of the nineteenth century was to actually reformat the country as such an itinerary; a European walk through time from the present to the past. Central to this task was the founding of museums specifically organized around then current ideologies of race, ethnicity, and historical evolution. The first museum to be founded was dedicated to the history of ancient Pharaonic Egypt—what a recent television ad referred to as "the oldest and most important civilization in history" (and if you subscribe to their ancient Egypt book club, you will receive monthly a "genuine replica" of a stone antiquity). This is a museum still bearing the name "the Egyptian Museum," although it originally housed artifacts of *all* periods and cultures. It was founded under French patronage quite early—in 1835—near the great Giza pyramids. The museum has a complex history because it immediately outgrew its accommodations, thanks to the exponential growth of archaeological activity—official and amateur—in Egypt during the nineteenth century. It was soon rebuilt, and in 1845 it was moved to a larger building. In 1863 it was relocated on the east bank of the Nile (in the neighborhood of Bulaq, in a former post office) and, after returning to the west bank and a brief sojourn in a Giza palace, was refounded in 1900 in its present neoclassical institutional form (as shown here) and reopened in 1902 on one of the modern city's immense central squares (Midan al-Tahrir). Tahrir itself at the time was bounded on its west and south by the barracks of the British military. The chief dedicatory inscriptions over the doorway of the building were in Latin—a language, it might be added, that at best might be legible to about one-thousandth of one percent of the population of Cairo, then or now.

The museum's location gave it pride of place among all the cultural institutions of the new city, in a neighborhood of major government ministries and foreign embassies. By its designation as *the* Egyptian Museum, the institution commanded an indigenous national authenticity, distinctiveness, and originality, in comparison to which the cultural institutions and museums dedicated to other facets of the country's immensely long history—the Greco-Roman, the Christian, and the Muslim—were in effect marginalized as somehow less authentic. In being given urban centrality, the pharaonic past of the country constituted that in which the modern West was primarily (and indeed, still today, virtually exclusively) interested.

From the year of its founding in 1882, the Comité also undertook the massive project of separating out the artistic monuments of different ethnic and religious communities and dedicating itself to "exchanging" artifacts of "distinct aesthetic categories" ("des objets *purement* musulmans contre les objets *purement* coptes") so as to quite explicitly "relieve the confusion" of visitors.

This resulted in the virtually simultaneous foundation of separate ethnically marked museums in the 1890s: the Museum of Arab Art in 1893 (today the Islamic Museum), originally formed by the Comité as a collection in 1883 in (what at the time was) the ruined mosque of Al Hakim in the old city; the Coptic Museum, created in 1895 in the Christian quarter of the city; and the Greco-Roman Museum, founded in 1892 in the Mediterranean city of Alexandria (the Greek and Roman capital of Egypt), and referred to in twentieth-century guidebooks as the "link" between the Egyptian and Coptic Museums in Cairo. In other words, the ideal tourist visitor was urged to visit the history of Egypt from its earlier to later periods by visiting museums in the chronological order of their contents. You started at the Egyptian Museum in Tahrir Square, then took the train to Alexandria to the Greco-Roman Museum, returning to Cairo and the Coptic Museum, ending up in the Museum of Islamic Art. Each museum (apart from the classicizing Egyptian Museum building) was built in a style echoing or evoking the culture and period of its contents.

A VISION OF ORDER

Cairo's museums thus helped create a sense of the urban landscape as a phantasmatic topography itself, as well as a disciplinary order: a simulacrum of the very international exhibitions and expositions that were representing the country in Britain, France, Germany, and America. Perhaps the most famous of these was the "Street of Cairo" exhibition at the Columbian Exposition on the Midway in Chicago. Here, an entire street in the old city was recreated and organized with its striking juxtaposition of the new city and the old. Echoing the mid-century Crystal Palace in London, it featured locals dressed as Egyptian natives.[15] Each day a mock native wedding procession, a musical concert, and other events presented as typical of Egyptian culture were staged. What is interesting about the Chicago "Street of Cairo" was that the facades of buildings were not imitations but actual facades bought up from householders in the old city of Cairo and transported and mounted at the exposition.

This interplay of urban redevelopment in Cairo and international expositions also went in the other direction, as when later in the century the government of Cairo (through the Comité) commissioned French artisans in Paris to supply glass mosque lamps to replace old ones. The replacements were crafted according to stylistic criteria dictated by the Comité itself. The new modern city featured long, broad boulevards, which the mid-century ruler of Egypt, Muhammed 'Ali, commissioned after viewing the work of Hausmann in Paris.

These new arteries were cut through the labyrinth of old streets to the west of what was becoming the old city, and they intersected at squares or roundabouts (*rond-points*), on which came to be sited major governmental institutions and ministries, as well as hotels. Several major Hausmannesque boulevards were also cut through the old city, and the headquarters of the police and the major city prison were placed on the boundary between the old and new quarters.

The Museum of Arab Art was situated in this liminal zone between the old city and the new, facing east and the old quarter, across a new boulevard (formerly a canal) from the police headquarters, on a new major intersection. The Coptic Museum was situated in the old Coptic Christian quarter to the south, adjacent to several ancient churches, and near the remains of the Roman settlement of Babylon, a town that was the immediate precursor to the first Arab colony in the region, Fustat (641 A.D.). The city of Cairo (Al-Qahira, "the conqueror," referring to the planet Mars) was founded in 969 A.D. immediately to the north of Fustat by a new group of rulers from North Africa known as the Fatimids. The southernmost Coptic quarter, prior both to the settlement of Fustat and to that founded later by the Fatimids (Al-Qahira), was now the *older* old quarter (i.e., premodern, pre-Islamic [pre-"medieval"], and postancient) and was also, during both Roman and Arab times, the chief Jewish quarter; and today the principal synagogue in the area, the Ben Ezra Synagogue near the Coptic Museum and the place where the important *geniza* documents were found, still survives in a kind of museological half-life.

These museums had as their primary function the representation of the country's history and the reformatting of its complex (and, to European eyes, confusingly miscegenated and hybrid) identity as an evolutionary narrative, a succession of stages leading inexorably to the presentness and modernity of the new Westernized nation-state. This new Egypt was in the process of becoming a nation-state controlled by European-educated native elites—both Muslim and Christian—endowed with cultural, financial, and technological aspirations, partnered with their European mentors and advisers, and tied more and more tightly to the global economies of the British and French empires. All of this entailed an empowering of certain portions of the population as the subjects of representation (primarily the Westernized Christian and Muslim elites), and others (the non-Westernized indigenous populations of various religious and ethnic affiliations) as objects of their representation.

Essential to this Orientalist enterprise was the solicitation of the support of indigenous elites in this disciplinary project of representation. In the case of Egypt, this took place through a specific linkage of aesthetics and ethics, within a hierarchical system of values linking together subjects and their objects (and vice versa). It was the writings of the French social theorist and historian Gustave Le Bon—one of the most widely read writers in Egypt during the last quarter of the nineteenth century—that played a key role. Essentially, Le Bon argued (in his book *Lois psychologiques de l'evolution des peuples*, which had run through twelve editions by the turn of the century in French, English, and Arabic) that

> what most differentiates Europeans from Orientals is that only the former possess an elite of superior men. . . . [This small phalanx of eminent men found among a highly civilized people] constitutes the *true incarnation of the forces of a race*. To it is due the progress realised in the sciences, the arts, in industry, in a word in all the branches of a civilization.[16]

The statement could have been written by Hegel, who similarly, half a century earlier, wrote of a small group of leading thinkers in each country as embodying the same characteristics, as guiding a people artistically and culturally because in them was distilled the nation's genius most purely. So much ethnographic research in the latter half of the nineteenth century seemed to demonstrate that the "less-civilized" peoples of the world were egalitarian in social organization. From this followed the conclusion that modern progress should be understood as a movement toward increasing *inequality*—which may help explain the enormous popularity of Le Bon's theories among European ruling classes and indigenous Egyptian elites.

Echoes of the sentiments of Le Bon permeated the *proces-verbales* of the weekly meetings of the Comité in Cairo in their ongoing discussions about the proper disposition of the hundreds of thousands of artifacts and monuments being unearthed and circulated among the newly founded Cairo museums. These discussions invariably centered on the worth or value of objects destined for display, and there was a clear (and unanimously shared) attitude toward the role of the Cairo museums in exhibiting only the best works of art—by which was specifically meant those works that the members of the Comité regarded as the "truest" representations and the most authentic effects of a people's spirit or mind. All the rest were to be sold, given away as souvenirs to foreign dignitaries, or simply discarded. The museums, in fact, contained sales rooms precisely for such a purpose, to aid the ongoing refinement of the collection so that it might encompass only the most aesthetically worthy objects. A process of the refinement of objects was not inconsistent with the culling and marginalizing of inferior subjects and subject peoples. These practices effectively ceased by the end of the 1940s.

PRESERVING THE WORLD FOR ITS OWN GOOD

I have previously written of how at mid-century the Crystal Palace powerfully put all of this in the proper scale and perspective for all to see. In so doing, this supreme taxonomic and comparative instrument was arguably the first fully realized modernist institution. The Crystal Palace was in fact the historical realization and the implicit ideal, the ur-form and *Gesamtkunstwerk*, of what Cairo (and other colonial institutions, notably in India) echoed and played out as the century progressed.

I'd now like to look at another solution to the formatting of ethnicity, progress, evolution, artistic development, and cognitive specificity, in this case right within the nineteenth-century imperial heartland. I'd like us to consider the Pitt-Rivers Museum and the work of its founder, Lieutenant General Augustus Henry Lane Fox. Born in 1827, Fox died in 1900, but not before assuming the name Pitt-Rivers as a requirement of his succession to the Rivers property—the 25,000-acre Cranborne Chase—on the borders of Wiltshire and Dorsetshire at the death of the sixth Lord Rivers in 1880. Pitt-Rivers was fifty-three at the time. His museum was founded in 1884 to promote his views on cultural evolution as an index of racial, social, and cognitive differences among peoples. His views achieved their first major synthesis in a book he published in 1875 called *The Evolution of Culture*, which reflected the opinion, common at the time, that so-called savage or primitive races were surviving relics of the early history of the human species, and that they bore a relationship to the peoples of modern Europe—and in particular the upper classes of Victorian England—that was complementary to the relationship of different species in biological evolution.[17] The varying degrees of development in artifacts and implements that Pitt-Rivers collected from all over the world bore for him a direct relationship both to cultural development and to the relative capacities of different peoples to achieve progress toward civilization.

Believing essentially that the savage was "doomed" and "morally and mentally an unfit instrument for the spread of civilization" (and in his view not unlike the British lower classes, as well as all non-Protestant Europeans), Pitt-Rivers saw it as his mission to preserve these "relics" of barbarism so as to educate his contemporaries in the ways in which the progressive stages of human development could properly be identified. His collection was installed in 1874 in a branch of the South Kensington Museum in Bethnal Green—itself a reflection of that museum's mission to educate East Londoners—in a building that now houses the Bethnal Green Museum of Childhood, itself yet another structural descendant of the great Crystal Palace.

It moved to larger quarters in South Kensington in 1878, and eventually (in 1884) Pitt-Rivers bequeathed his collection to Oxford with the stipulation that the university build an appropriate building for it and appoint someone to lecture in it. The university added an annex to the Oxford Museum of Natural History to house Pitt-Rivers's collection, and it appointed its first lecturer in anthropology, Edward Burnet Tylor, and a young Trinity College research student named Henry Balfour as the collection's curator. The present museum opened in 1891.

For nearly fifty years Balfour was in charge of the museum, and its subsequent state—and the vastly increased size of its holdings—owed as much to Balfour's vision as to Pitt-Rivers's original intentions.

But let's return to that original vision. Pitt-Rivers's aim was to display the hierarchy of human cognitive development he had laid out in 1875 in his study of human cultural evolution as a direct index of both cognitive advancement and the cognitive capacity of different peoples and races to achieve civilization. What resulted in his museum was a kind of treasure house of obsolete technologies (and, by implication, obsolete peoples and cultures), grouped together typologically, according to the type of instrument, object, or function—travel by water, objects of religious veneration, burial customs, screwdrivers and doorknobs, weapons of many different types, and so forth. The overall aim was to arrange in exhibitionary space evolutionary development from the simple to the complex. The driving force in this cultural "survival of the fittest" was the human "struggle for mastery with brute creation," as Pitt-Rivers put it.

As he wrote in 1874, in an essay on the principles of classification, "progress is like a game of dominoes . . . all that we know is that the fundamental rule of the game is *sequence*."[18] This was a view curiously and coincidentally echoed in the work of the writer and traveler in Egypt W.J. Loftie, who in his 1879 book *A Ride in Egypt* praised the Egyptian Museum in Cairo (then in a small building in Bulaq) because of its concerted effort to arrange its objects in strict developmental sequence of style and complexity.[19] What Loftie also commented on, in addition to saying that it was "hopeless for us to expect the British Museum to be so enlightened" (as to arrange its collection so logically), was that the curator of the Egyptian Museum, the archaeologist Mariette, was able to thereby cope with the widely recognized "scandal" of Egyptian art history—namely, that the farther back in time one traced Egyptian art, the better was its quality (according to criteria based on a classical Greek canon).

In concluding, the point I wish to make here is that what is *absent* from the Pitt-Rivers Museum is in fact its determining principle or canon—namely, the contemporary world outside the museum that informs the art and artifice of the modern European world. Europe was the brain of the earth's body, in contrast to which everything and everyone else was anterior. To leave Europe was in fact to enter the past—the past of what we shall have been for what we were in the process of becoming, to evoke Lacan.[20] Europe was the horizon of the present, that toward which all these sad little superseded societies, cultures, and peoples might be imagined to aspire, but which in the end went the way of the dodo. A Europe, in short, whose burden, whose *mission civilatrice*, was to curate and preserve the rest of the world for its own good. Pitt-Rivers quite seriously believed that a half century from his own death, all traces of savagery and primitive society and customs would have disappeared from the face of the earth.

The phantasmatic Cairo bequeathed us by the Comité should come as no surprise. Our own sense of this astonishing museum is of course quite different, and I will use a quotation from an article about the museum published in *Smithsonian* magazine about a decade and a half ago to illustrate this.

> The General's single-minded determination to substantiate his racist theory is from an era long past. Today's Pitt-Rivers speaks to the collective creativity of people everywhere, to the wealth and range of concepts that various cultures have to offer. Finding better ways to do things has been, needless to say, very different in the Arctic, the desert, and the jungle, but the end result is a communality of invention the world over, invention that has been amended and improved, and succeeded by newer and better, generation by generation.[21]

You may well ask whether being happy campers in a globalized, multiculturalist reservation or theme park is an improvement upon Pitt-Rivers's vision, or on the ethnocentrist sectarianism—which at first glance seems like the antithesis of Pitt-Rivers's mission—promoted in Cairo by the Comité at the same time.

NOTES

This chapter first appeared as "The Museum of What You Shall Have Been" in D. Preziosi, *Brain of the Earth's Body: Arts, Museums, and the Phantasms of Modernity* (Minneapolis: University of Minnesota Press, 2003).

1. I owe this image to a fine paper by Zeynip Celik, "'Islamic' Architecture in French Colonial Discourse," presented at the 1996 UCLA Levi Della Vida Conference, Los Angeles, May 11, 1996. See Z. Celik, *Displaying the Orient: Architecture of Islam at Nineteenth-Century Worlds Fairs* (Berkeley: University of California Press, 1992), esp. pp. 70–71, 90–91. The images referred to are reproduced on pp. 90–91, originally having been published in the exposition's official guidebook of 1900, *Exposition universelle internationale de 1900, vues photographiques* (Paris. Exposition universelle, 1900). On the sublime, see J. Derrida, "The Colossal," part 4 of "Parergon," in his *The Truth in Painting*, trans. G. Bennington and I. McLeod (Chicago: University of Chicago Press, 1987), pp. 119–47.

2. On individuals as/on exhibit, see T. Mitchell, *Colonising Egypt* (Cairo: American University in Cairo Press, 1988); and M. Armstrong, "'A Jumble of Foreignness': The Sublime Musayums of Nineteenth-Century Fairs and Expositions," *Cultural Critique*, No. 23, Winter 1992–93, pp. 199–250. In the latter is a fascinating discussion of the exhibition of a living Turk.

3. Which can be discovered or unearthed in the "best" of, say, the carvings of the Inuit peoples, or in Aboriginal bark paintings, and can be marketed as such: as "classic" examples of a (native) genre. The marketing itself constitutes a mode of canonizing and classicizing of the "typical," which characteristically feeds back on the contemporary production of marketable typical (i.e., classical) examples of a (reified) genre.

4. On Charles Eliot Norton and the founding of a Ruskinian Department of Fine Arts at Harvard, see D. Preziosi, *Rethinking Art History: Meditations on a Coy Science* (New Haven: Yale University Press, 1989).

5. See T. Keenan, "The Point Is to (Ex)Change It: Reading Capital, Rhetorically," in E. Apter and W. Pietz, eds., *Fetishism as Cultural Discourse* (Ithaca: Cornell University Press, 1993), pp. 152–85; and W. Pietz, "Fetishism and Materialism: The Limits of Theory in Marx," in Apter and Pietz, eds., *Fetishism as Cultural Discourse*, pp. 119–51.

6. On the question of the archive, see M. Foucault, *The Archaeology of Knowledge*, trans. A.M. Sheridan Smith (New York: Pantheon Books, 1972), esp. part 3, "The Statement and the Archive," pp. 79–131. Also see J. Derrida, "Archive Fever: A Freudian Impression," *Diacritics*, Vol. 25, No. 2, Summer 1995, pp. 9–63; and *Archive Fever: A Freudian Impression*, trans. E. Prenowitz (Chicago: University of Chicago Press, 1996).

7. On which see E. Donato, "Flaubert and the Quest for Fiction," in *The Script of Decadence* (New York: Columbia University Press, 1993), p. 64; and H. Sussman, "Death and the Critics: Eugenio Donato's *Script of Decadence*," *Diacritics*, Vol. 25, No. 3, Fall 1995, pp. 74–87. On collection as narration, see M. Bal, "Telling Objects: A Narrative Perspective on Collecting," in J. Elsner and R. Cardinal, *The Cultures of Collecting* (London: Reaktion Books, 1994), pp. 97–115.

8. H. Pieron, "Le Caire: Son esthetique dans la ville arabe et dans la ville moderne," *L'Egypte contemporain*, No. 5, January 1911, p. 512.

9. Mitchell, *Colonising Egypt*.

10. See S. Pile, *The Body and the City: Psychoanalysis, Space, and Subjectivity* (New York: Routledge, 1996).

11. Illustrated, for example, in the Skirball Museum in Los Angeles with an exhibition made up of an "archaeological dig," which enables children to uncover imitations of ancient Jewish artifacts suspended in an ahistorical and ethnically cleansed sandbox of time.

12. M. Breal, *Melanges de Mythologie et de linguistique* (Paris: Hachette, 1887), p. 321.

13. D. Preziosi, *The Brain of the Earth's Body: Art, Museums, and the Phantasms of Modernity* (Minneapolis, Minn.: University of Minnesota Press, 2003), p. 111–12.

14. Recently reissued in a facsimile edition of plates, *Description de l'Égypte: Publiee par les ordres de Napoleon Bonaparte* (Cologne: Benedikt Taschen, 1994). The frontispiece is reproduced on p. 34, "Perspective de l'Égypte, d'Alexandrie à Philae."

15. See the discussion of the World's Columbian Exposition of 1893 in Chicago in Celik, *Displaying the Orient*, pp. 80–85.

16. G. Le Bon, *Lois psychologiques de l'evolution des peuples*, 12th ed. (Paris: Felix Alcan, 1916). English edition published as *The Psychology of Peoples* (New York: Macmillan, 1898).

17. P. Rivers, *The Evolution of Culture, and Other Essays by the Late Augustus Lane-Fox Pitt-Rivers*, edited by J.L. Myers, introduction by H. Balfour (Oxford: Clarendon Press, 1906).

18. Ibid, p. 19.

19. W.J. Loftie, *A Ride in Egypt, from Sioor to Luxor in 1879* (London: Macmillan, 1879).

20. J. Lacan, *Ecrits: A Selection*, trans. Alan Sheridan (New York: W.W. Norton, 1977).

21. J. Reader, "An Odd Collector's Odd Collections," *Smithsonian*, Vol. 18, No. 4, July 1987, p. 116.

PART III

DISCIPLINING AND MAKING

8

Nineteenth-Century Cairo:
A Dual City?

Heba Farouk Ahmed

> The Arab town must be preserved to show to future generations what the for-
> mer city of the Caliphs was like, before there was built alongside it an impor-
> tant cosmopolitan colony separate from the native quarter. . . . There are two
> Cairos, the modern . . . and the old. . . . One is Cairo of the artists, the other
> of hygienists and modernists.[1]

If tourists and travelers came to Cairo in the latter part of the nineteenth century
to see and experience one of the "two Cairos," what reasons did they give for
favoring one over the other? What were the criteria upon which they based their
selections? Old Cairo, New Cairo: where were these? How could one draw
boundaries between such different cities that knew so little of each other? Who
claimed ownership, and/or governed them? Who lived there?

These are but a few questions that come to mind when one reads about Cairo
in the nineteenth century. Outsiders at that time portrayed Egypt's capital as a
"dual city," using such conceptualizations as East/West, old/new, traditional/mod-
ern, and Oriental/Westernized. Indeed, foreigners and travelers seemed to need
such dualistic categories to understand Cairo's complex urban form. Yet, through
time, these impressions and representations have also become important historical
narratives, and today they are still prevalent in scholarship about the city.

It is not my intent here to revisit the "Orientalist discourse." However, it is
important to raise questions about the originality and significance of nineteenth-
century descriptions of Cairo's supposedly dual urban and cultural landscape. I
rather believe that Cairo in the nineteenth century continued to develop along
lines set earlier with the foundation of the Fatimid city. Was there ever an
Ayyubid Cairo that existed by itself independent of the Fatimid core? Was there

a Mamluk city that could be identified as separate from the tenth-century city? One still cannot categorize/generalize these terms and historical periods as representing a division and separation of the city. Why then apply terms like "old Cairo" and "new Cairo" to the city as it evolved during the nineteenth century?

Khedive Isma'il—Egypt's ruler from 1863 to 1879—succeeded in applying his "project of modernity" several years before his country came under foreign control in 1882.[2] However, based on written and visual evidence, as well as analysis of urban forms, I will argue here that scholars have largely misinterpreted his actions toward the city. Comparing descriptions of Cairo by foreign residents and travelers with those of native Egyptians, one sees how different their experiences of Cairo were. And even though Cairenes implemented Isma'il's "project of modernity," their vision and experience has largely been forgotten in favor of that history imposed by foreigners.

NINETEENTH-CENTURY VIEWS

To write the urban history of Cairo in the latter part of the nineteenth century involves deciphering the various layers of the city and the urban community that witnessed its transformation. This stage in the life of the city was certainly crucial, reflecting important changes in Egypt in general. But it is also possible to show how the so-called "two Cairos" that existed in the minds of many people in fact referred to a single, harmonious city that was passing through a period of profound expansion, restructuring, and regeneration.

Nevertheless, the view that nineteenth-century Cairo embodied two impossibly separate worlds is still with us today. Thus, in 1988, in *Lifting the Veil: British Society in Egypt*, this is how Anthony Sattin described his first encounter with Cairo:

> Our hotel was part of an international chain, a new concrete tower. . . . In London it had been suggested that this place combined the excitement of the East with the comforts of the West, but it had a lot to live up to. Baedeker's Handbook for 1929 called them [Cairo's hotels] excellent and smart. . . . [But] Cairo then was also just as famous for its visitors as for the hotels they frequented.[3]

Sattin's description goes on to present a view of Cairo in the 1980s that is remarkably similar to those of many nineteenth-century travelers. It was as if it was still that Baedeker guidebook—among the most popular in the nineteenth century—that Sattin relied on for information (FIGURE 8.1).[4]

> If this "certain element of romance" and the true sense of the East were present in our hotel, we failed to notice it as we checked in and went up in an air-

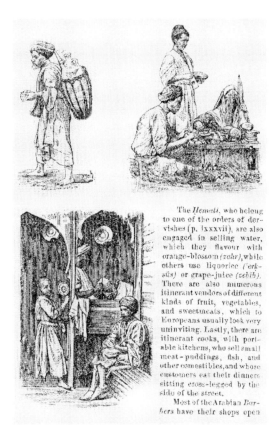

The *Hemali*, who belong to one of the orders of dervishes (p. lxxxvii), are also engaged in selling water, which they flavour with orange-blossom *(zehr)*, while others use liquorice *(erk-sûs)* or grape-juice *(zebîb)*. There are also numerous itinerant vendors of different kinds of fruit, vegetables, and sweetmeats, which to Europeans usually look very uninviting. Lastly, there are itinerant cooks, with portable kitchens, who sell small meat-puddings, fish, and other comestibles, and whose customers eat their dinners sitting cross-legged by the side of the street.

Most of the Arabian *Barbers* have their shops open

Figure 8.1. Baedeker's guidebook provided extensive information on the city as well as illustrations that portrayed Cairenes and their activities. Every aspect of the city and its life was covered in the book. *(Source: Karl Baedeker, 1898)*

conditioned elevator to the sound of mid-Atlantic musak. . . . Even being more than twenty floors up we were surrounded by the dark and noise and dust. . . . We did see some of that *imaginary city*.[5]

If not for the references to twentieth-century technology, as one reads *Lifting the Veil* one might easily imagine that Sattin was writing in the late nineteenth century. Either that, or he primed his consciousness before his visit with the same literary and visual sources as nineteenth-century travelers.

Works by Sattin and other contemporary intellectuals—both foreigners and Egyptians—show how persistent the "dual city" notion of Cairo has been.[6] But how did the city come to be represented this way? Were nineteenth-century tourists describing a city they were actually experiencing? Or were they fantasizing about, and constructing, an "imaginary" city? Could the books they read before arriving really have created expectations that allowed them to ignore the reality of what they eventually encountered?

For perspective, it is important to compare such foreign travelers' accounts to work by Cairenes themselves. A number of works in Arabic do show that Egyptians were aware of how their history was being written at the time and how they were being represented to the outside world. Duse Mohamed, for example, emphasized in his 1911 history of Egypt that his work was written from a native's point of view, and thus was an account "having authority."[7] He further explained that his aim was to reveal his native land through a statement of facts, since Europeans—in their own versions—typically used information imparted by natives to advance their own agendas. Egyptians, indeed, could gain by adopting certain traits of Western life and culture. But Mohamed also complained that Europeans who resided in Egypt in the late nineteenth century, or who simply spent time there, often assumed they could present an authoritative view, even when they paid little attention to the culture itself.

Looking back today we can clearly see how, as the nineteenth century progressed, the interests of European travelers began to turn away from Egypt's antiquities toward more contemporary concerns: the Egyptian landscape, street scenes in Cairo, and the manners and customs of the people. Moreover, artists, as well as writers, became concerned with the life of contemporary Egyptians (FIGURE 8.2).

Figure 8.2. The commodification of Egyptians. Interest in contemporary Cairenes and their everyday life—a new phenomenon in the nineteenth century.
(Source: Amelia Edwards, 1877)

The result was an enormous output of books, diaries, letters, illustrations, and lithographs that portray aspects of life in nineteenth-century Cairo.

One might note how at this time the West was beginning to divide the world into realms of "representation" and the "real." It may thus not be surprising to find narratives describing Cairo written as if their authors had just visited a World's Exposition. Indeed, many Europeans arrived in the Orient after seeing plans, pictures, and exhibitions at just such events. They came seeking the original. In search of some sense of the "authentic," real or not, "travelers wanted to immerse themselves in the Orient and touch with their fingers a strange civilization."[8] And, in the process, they produced their "own" manufactured versions of Cairo. Today, these sources are useful in helping uncover how the East was constructed by the West, but they are inadequate as a sole source of information on the city itself.

Of course, just as travelers experienced Cairo differently, so did their accounts vary. Some referred with pride to the development and modernization of the city as a result of the new Western presence; others disliked the changes, wanting to freeze the city in time and space to preserve a sense of the "exotic" East. Some were also extraordinarily dedicated to their self-appointed task. Among the best-known early European travel writers were Edward William Lane and David Roberts.[9] Both were inspired to visit Egypt after reading the mammoth Napoleonic *Description de l'Égypte*, and both declared their intent to correct its inaccuracies.

Upon his arrival to Egypt in 1825, Lane wrote:

> I felt like an Eastern bridegroom, about to lift the veil of his bride, and to see for the first time, the features, which were to charm, or disappoint, or disgust him. I was not visiting Egypt merely as a traveler, . . . but I was about to throw myself entirely among strangers; to adopt their language, their customs and their dress; and in associating almost exclusively with the natives, to prosecute the study of their literature.[10]

Lane eventually produced his own comprehensive work that included a description of Cairo's urban geography, its principal quarters, streets, and monuments. And although he never published it in its entirety, sections covering modern Egyptian society did appear as *Manners and Customs of the Modern Egyptians*.[11]

Lane and his contemporaries shared a common belief that "in every point of view, Egypt is an object of the highest interest, and is likely to become increasingly such."[12] But to illustrate their assertions, they appropriated whatever buildings and monuments they needed to create the right scenographic effects (FIGURE 8.3). Leila Ahmed has pointed out that some travelers even believed they were better able to construe the significance of native forms of behavior in Egypt than in countries that were less familiar to their *imagination*.[13] In this regard, many noted how pleasant it was to think of *The Arabian Nights* as they wandered the streets of Cairo, or donned native dress to visit the city's grand and famous mosques.

Figure 8.3. "An elaborate depiction" of Cairo capturing a distant view of the city without having to mingle with the population.
(Source: Edward W. Lane, 1936)

In a similar fashion, but from a different perspective, Rifa'ah al-Tahtawi—the prominent Egyptian writer and educator, born in the same year as Lane (1801)—wrote about an extended nineteenth-century trip to the West. Among other things, al-Tahtawi described the outdoor public spaces of Paris. Comparing them to the *maidans* (squares) of Cairo, he explained that although some were of the same width, they were far cleaner. Throughout his travel commentary, however, al-Tahtawi reminded readers that whatever he was presenting might be interpreted differently by natives. Nevertheless, he claimed, his accounts were not exaggerations; and to keep the reader on track, he alluded to both similarities and differences. In his description of Paris he wrote:

> Some of the advantages and signs of development that we see here is how they put the sewage system underground to supply the baths at different locations of the city with water from the river, and provide the various tanks. This is simple as compared to Egypt where there they fill up the tanks with water that was carried and transferred by camels. . . . There is a major difference between the taste of the water from the Seine and that from the Nile, if they purify that of the Nile before they use it, it would be better than any medicine.[14]

Al-Tahtawi has been portrayed in Arab literature as a tourist who meandered through a museum, fascinated by everything he saw, and who tried to record it all using more of an index (*dalil*), than a narrative format. Thus, he referred often to names and dates, and provided brief descriptions of many things, but not full details.[15] Characteristically, al-Tahtawi described French society as more scientific than Egyptian—as less reliant on inherited values, and more forward looking. But, despite the major changes taking place in French society, he never described Paris as a dual city, or as a combination of cities each embracing a different style. To him, there were no boundaries between its public/private spheres, or its cultural, social, and economic features.

Like European travelers to Cairo, al-Tahtawi also described many aspects of Paris's architecture, explaining how its buildings were impressive both in design and quality of construction. However, in his opinion, they were not rich enough, since they were not as decorated with marble as Cairene ones.[16] In general, unlike Europeans in Cairo, he kept comparing what he saw to what he had experienced back home. He never forgot his native city. He even wrote that if Misr (Cairo) could one day acquire the tools and skills of "modernity," it would become the leading city of the world.[17]

GUIDEBOOKS OR INSTRUCTION MANUALS?

> [M]ost modern travelers prepared for their journeys by reading the account of
> other travelers and noting the recommendations of the guidebooks. If this
> helped to reduce the anxiety of travel then it also aggravated . . . "the anxiety of
> travel-writing."[18]

Western travelers frequently showed off in regard to the number of guidebooks they read and the amount of knowledge they had about Egypt. Both *Murray's Handbook* and *Baedeker's Travel-guide* were popular, and travelers read them either at home or on their way to Egypt. However, in some cases they might also "abandon" their guidebooks and explore the city on their own. This was because guidebooks not only pointed to the major sites and monuments in the city, but *prescribed* ways to go about seeing them.

The recommendations of guidebooks were extremely influential in shaping travelers' experiences, and they subsequently influenced travelers' own reports of the city—in agreement, or in reaction. Thus, in *Egypt Painted and Described*, R. Talbot Kelly advised travelers: "If you want really to see Orientalism in Cairo, the best plan is to pick up an intelligent donkey-boy and comfortable animal, and explore for yourself without your Baedeker or dragoman."[19] He added that wandering about the streets was tiring, but it was the only way to understand the real Cairo.

Throughout the nineteenth century, Thomas Cook's company dominated the tourist industry in Egypt. Cook originally popularized travel there in 1860 by offering package tours from London and by running its own steamers up the Nile. The company also offered and promoted travel by preparing guidebooks. The 1897 edition of Cook's *Handbook*, described Cairo as

> . . . still the city of Arabian Nights, and all who are well up in those veracious chronicles will find themselves perpetually localizing the scenes and individualizing the characters of which Scheherazade chattered well and to such good purpose.[20]

Other guidebooks offered maps and plans of mosques, churches, pyramids, and other monuments. They appeared under such titles as *Egypt and How to See it; Cairo and its Environs*; and *How to See Cairo*. Like Cook's *Handbook*, they also referred to Cairo as the city of *The Arabian Nights*. Indeed, the stories of this enduringly popular work of fiction often became a point of reference for the "real" city tourists were encouraged to experience. Thus, Baedeker's described Cairo as follows:

> The street scenes presented by the city of the Khalifs afford an inexhaustible fund of amusement and delight, admirably illustrating the whole world of Oriental fiction, and producing an impression on the uninitiated denizen of the West. This Oriental life must be sought for in the old Arabian quarters, which are still inaccessible for carriages, in spite of the many new streets that have been constructed in Cairo of late years.[21]

The Baedeker guidebook advised travelers in search of Oriental scenes not to waste time on the city's modern quarters.[22] Most travelers did not come to Cairo seeking its modernity, but its "otherness." And the guidebooks complied, emphasizing an "exotic" Orient and leaving little space for travelers to see the real Cairo or gain an appreciation for its inhabitants' everyday lives.

Central to this imaginary were the stories of *The Arabian Nights*, which told of a fascinating, faraway people. According to *Murray's Guidebook*:

> The narrowness of the streets of Cairo, and their great irregularity, may strike an European as imperfections in a large city; but their Oriental character compensates for this objection, and of all Eastern towns none is so interesting in this respect as the Egyptian capital. Nor is this character confined to the bazaars, to the [mosques], or to the peculiarities of the exterior of the houses; the interiors of the same original Arab style, and no one can visit the harems and courts of the private dwellings of the Cairenes without calling the impressions received on reading the *Arabian Nights*.[23]

In the mid-nineteenth century *The Arabian Nights* were retranslated by Edward W. Lane, who added notes and illustrations that related the beliefs, cus-

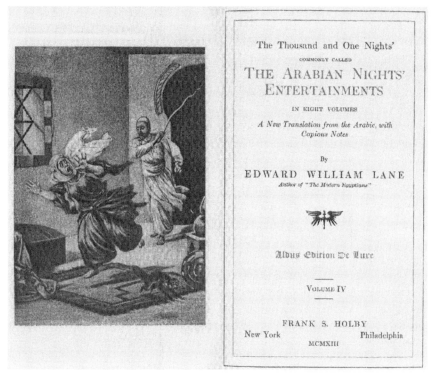

Figure 8.4. Edward W. Lane's translation of *The Arabian Nights*. Note how he also includes images that helped shape the readers' imagination. These images were not part of the original collection. *(Source: Edward W. Lane, 1913)*

toms, and society of the stories directly to Cairo (FIGURE 8.4).[24] Leila Ahmed has referred to these additions as "spectacularly novel in their brilliant and accurate illuminations of the scenes of the East."[25] Indeed, the combined effect was to "all but place the reality [of the stories] bodily before them [readers]." However, Robert Irwin, in tracing the decline in the grip of the stories on the English literary imagination, also pointed out that Lane's presentation of "fuller and more accurate knowledge [eventually] led to closing gates of imagination."[26]

Etchings and illustrations of Cairenes were also a key ingredient of guidebooks. But they placed European artists who produced them in a difficult position. According to Nicholas Warner, even if artists wanted to accurately represent life in the city, there was a better market in fulfilling the preconceived fantasy of "Eastern exoticism."[27] Representations of the city in different media eventually became as common as written accounts. William Thackeray noted the underlying logic:

There is a fortune to be made for painters in Cairo, and materials for a whole academy of them. I never saw such a variety of Architecture, of life, of picturesqueness, of brilliant color, and light and shade. There is a picture in every street, and at every bazaar stall.[28]

As tourism to Egypt increased, artists focused ever more closely on Cairo's medieval quarters. At the same time they hardly documented anything about Isma'il's "project of modernity"—as if to deny Cairo a future in their drive to proclaim, or even remake, its past. And the few who did seek out modernity in Cairo attributed its presence to European influence.

Just how this "culture of travel" affected the views of Cairo among Westerners, I believe, becomes fully evident when one reads the works of three writers: Stanley Lane-Poole, Lady Duff-Gordon, and Edwin De Leon. Among the vast array of literature produced by Westerners, their work stands out for several reasons. First, all three lived in Cairo for extensive periods rather than just passing through as tourists, or "birds of passage." Second, they all witnessed the transformations that resulted from Isma'il's effort to modernize the city, and each reacted differently. Third, they represented a diverse group: Lane-Poole held several quasi-official positions during the British occupation; Duff-Gordon was a private English citizen who came to Egypt to recover from tuberculosis;[29] and De Leon was American Consul-General in Cairo from 1854–60.

Lane-Poole began his career in Cairo by editing the monumental work of his uncle, Edward W. Lane, from the 1820/30s. Originally entitled "Description of Egypt" by Lane, Lane-Poole renamed it *Cairo: Fifty Years Ago* for publication. Mostly, Lane-Poole worked as a teacher, but his final position in Cairo was as a member of the Comité (Commission for the Preservation of Arab Monuments). He also wrote two books on the city—*Cairo: Sketches of its History, Monuments, and Social Life* (1898), and *The Story of Cairo* (1906)—as well as other books on Islam and the history of medieval Egypt.

Duff-Gordon's work consists of a group of letters she wrote between 1863 and 1865. She was not engaged in any official position, or in the political affairs of the country, and her letters were not intended for publication. But after her death in 1869, her mother, Sara Austin, had her correspondence published as *Letters From Egypt, 1863–65*. In a preface, Austin alluded to the fact that Duff-Gordon had written letters while she was sick, "far from all the resources which civilized society offers to the suffering body . . . above all, far from all the objects of the dearest affections." Austin had little information about Egypt and its people other than what was contained in the letters, but she noted Duff-Gordon's friendship with the Egyptians and the satisfaction that life there seemed to have provided her.

De Leon's book, *The Khedive's Egypt*, was published in 1878, after his consular appointment. It was important for its specific comparisons of Cairo before and after the period of modernization under Isma'il, and for the opinions it expressed about the changing city.

To better understand the biases of these Western observers and establish a clearer picture of the relationship between European visions of Egypt and the transformation of Cairo, however, it is important also to examine the works of three Egyptians: Rifa'ah al-Tahtawi, 'Ali Mubarak, and Muhammad al-Muwaylihi. They not only wrote about Cairo during the years of its transformation, but were themselves active in the "project of modernity" in administrative, political, or intellectual capacities. All three had also traveled to the West, and had written of it—as well as their subsequent perceptions of their own country in comparison.

As a group, the three produced works in the form of journals, newspaper articles, novels, and topographical studies. Their idea was to open the eyes of their countrymen to a larger world. Gamal al-Shayyal, an Egyptian historian, has argued that the works of al-Tahtawi and Mubarak, in particular, "created a historical consciousness which led Egyptians to be interested in history in general, and in the history of Egypt in various stages in particular."[30]

Of the three authors, al-Tahtawi is today described as an Egyptian equivalent of Edward W. Lane—however, al-Tahtawi wrote about Paris, not Cairo.[31] As already mentioned, in *Takhlis al-Ibriz fi talkhis Bariz*, he attempted to present a factual account of European/Parisian civilization: the geography of the place, the order of the cities, and the customs, clothes, and culture of its population.

'Ali Mubarak also spent a number of years in France in the 1840s and after his return held a series of administrative positions, including Minister of Public Works, Minister of Charitable Endowments, and Minister of Education. His writings included a novel, *'Alamuddin* (1882), and a major biographical/topographical work, *al-Khitat al-Tawfiqqiyah al-Jadidah* (1889), which covered the history and geography of Egyptian cities.[32] Mubarak's sources varied widely—from traditional Arabic accounts, to the writings of Europeans, to maps, and property records.

In a similar fashion, Muhammad al-Muwaylihi's *Hadith Isa Ibn Hisham*, written in 1898 portrayed aspects of Egyptian society in the nineteenth century, including the clash of East and West, Turk and Egyptian, town and country, and traditionalism and modernism in religion.[33] Roger Allen has explained that al-Muwaylihi's work is particularly important as a critique of middle- and upper-class society from a middle-class perspective, and it is a particularly accurate source for the social conditions of Egypt in the post-1882 period.[34]

ARABIAN NIGHTS NOSTALGIA: DUALITY OF DESIRE

Of the three European writers referred to in the last section, Lane-Poole's work was perhaps most wrapped in the fantasy of the Orient. Indeed, he referred to his experience of arriving in Cairo as "approaching a city which was still to all intents the city of *Arabian Nights*." Although he was aware of the origins of these famous stories in Persia, India, and Baghdad, he argued that it was in Cairo that the tales could at last be seen to take definite shape, as demonstrated by his uncle's translation. Lane-Poole began his own *Cairo: Sketches from its History, Monuments and Social Life* by reminding readers of this correlation. Thus, every step in the quarters of the Mohammedan city retold a story with a famous past:

> A few streets away from the European quarter, it is easy to dream that we are acting a part in the veracious histories of the Thousand and One Nights—which do, in fact, describe Cairo and its people as they were in the fourteenth century.[35]

For Lane-Poole, the older quarters of the city were nothing less than the actual stage against which stories had originally been written, and "in its very dilapidation the city helps the illusion." But it was this "illusion" that eventually also became the subject matter of his work, and which helped him establish Cairo as a "dual" city. Thus, when talking about "natives," he might refer to a particular Cairene as "the same man whom we saw keeping shop or taking his venture to sea in the faithful mirror of the *Arabian Nights*." Although he lived in the city for almost two decades, he never ceased to use the characters of *The Arabian Nights* to represent its inhabitants. A similar perspective seems to have pervaded the works of the Comité, for which he worked at the end of his career in Cairo.

Duff-Gordon's experience was more complex and ambiguous. She explained in her first letter, written from the Port of Leghorn, that she was looking forward to seeing the "beauty of Cairo." However, she explained that she did not think she would get much good out of life in an Eastern town, as "the dust is intolerable, and the stuffiness indoors very unwholesome." By her third letter, however, she had arrived in Egypt and referred to "Grand Cairo" as the place from which she was writing. She began by saying, "I write to you out of the real *Arabian Nights*. . . . Cairo is a golden existence, all sunshine and poetry, and I must add, all kindness and civility."[36] When describing a wedding she attended, she kept referring to the characters of *The Arabian Nights* as if she were part of one of the stories. Likewise, in writing of her visit to the bazaar, she repeatedly referred to "more Arabian Nights," as if the stories were the reality, and her trip the illusion.[37]

It was only after residing in Egypt for a few months that Duff-Gordon finally began to refer to the city as simply "Cairo"—except when she reported her dragoman Omar's references to "Misr al-Qahirah." It was during this part of her residence that she wrote:

> The more I see of the black slums of Cairo, the more in love I am with it.
> The dirtiest lane of Cairo is far sweeter than the best street of Paris. As to the

beauty of Cairo, *that* no words can describe: the oldest European towns are tame and regular in comparison . . . . Cairo is the Arabian Nights; there is a little Frankish varnish here and there, but the government, the people, are unchanged since that most faithful picture of manners was drawn.[38]

Throughout this period Duff-Gordon referred to the beauty of the city, but also to its dilapidated condition. In this regard she wrote that the days of its beauty were "numbered," since its mosques were falling into decay and its exquisite lattice windows were rotting away, only to be replaced by European glass. "Only the people and the government remain unchanged."[39]

Interestingly enough, however, by her nineteenth letter Duff-Gordon was referring to the city as "Misr-al-Qahirah," and only in parentheses as Cairo. The following summer she left for Marseilles. Then, when she returned, she hardly made any further reference to *The Arabian Nights*. Clearly, her point of reference had changed based on her firsthand experience. As she started to see through the myth, she also wanted to see the real and be part of its true experience. In one of her later letters, she even announced: "I have a black slave—yes, but a *real* one." It was as if by invoking the term "real" she was trying to show that she was aware of the tendency of other Europeans to see Egyptians as fictions.

Of the three writers, De Leon was the most taken by Isma'il's modern project. In his chapter "Old and New Cairo" he included a description of his approach to Cairo in 1869, and its unexpected transformation from the city he had visited twelve years earlier.[40]

It is on approaching the Cairo station that the great improvement of the city and its suburbs, becomes perceptible to the visitor who has been absent for years. He rubs his eyes, and almost distrusts his vision; for looking up the Shubra road which leads into Cairo, as well as outside the former limits of the city, where formerly stretched for miles fields under cultivation, he now sees, far as his eyes can reach, in every direction well-built and even palatial residences, surrounded by gardens, adding on new cities, for miles.[41]

De Leon continued by recounting how Cairo had formerly been surrounded by massive walls, and entered by a wide gate. Both of these had now disappeared, and instead broad boulevards opened an easy way into Cairo and out to the desert. Moreover, blocks of high buildings had replaced the "picturesque" old erections of mud and wood, providing further surprises for the returning visitor.

In their own ways, all three authors addressed the new appearance the city was taking on under Isma'il (FIGURE 8.5).[42] For the opening of the Suez Canal, Isma'il had wanted to present Cairo as a modern city, and he had developed areas like Azbakiyya, Isma'ilya, and al-Jazirah to accommodate a modern lifestyle. Of course,

Figure 8.5. Khedive Isma'il: The Father of Egyptian Modernity
(Source: Author's Collection)

not everything built during Isma'il's years was alien and Western, as had been described by many scholars. Nevertheless, Isma'il had been impressed and influenced by Paris and its architecture. For his part, Lane-Poole affirmed that a European urban vision, "inevitable, and in many ways most desirable," was behind the widespread destruction of mosques and historic buildings during those years. Such buildings impeded carriage traffic or stood in the way of the streets and squares. Lane-Poole believed that Isma'il and his successors planned these new public spaces with little or no regard for existing antiquities. But official documents in the Cairo National Archives challenge such a judgement. For every new street opened through Cairo's old urban fabric there was an accompanying plan and survey of buildings involved, and a study of how much compensation should be paid.

Lane-Poole dismissed the value of most of these changes to the more enduring qualities of the city:

> The limits of the modern additions are only too plain, but the street improvements of the reigning dynasty happily do not extend to the old Fatimy quarter, . . . the modern additions extend from the Ezbekiyya to the river, and consist of a number of parallel boulevards and *rondes places*, where ugly Western uniformity is partly redeemed by some cool verandahed villas and the grateful shade of trees.[43]

Not only did the buildings in these new quarters give a European impression, Lane-Poole explained, but half the people in the streets there wore European dress, modified in the case of native officials and others by the red fez and coat. Even the street lamps would have seemed familiar to visitors from his native isle. Nevertheless, he complained that,

> At Qasr al-Nil and all along the neighboring banks of the Nile, on the islands of Roda and Jazirah, at Giza, Abbasiyah, Shubra—everywhere rise the unsightly and ill-built palaces in which vice-regal extravagance and ostentation have found an outlet. Not one of these huge buildings is other than an eyesore. Not one is tastefully furnished. The Khedive's reception room at the Abdin Palace used to be a monument of the meretricious style, which rejoices in gold and crimson and pier glasses.[44]

From another standpoint, however, Duff-Gordon referred to the "progressive" native schemes of Isma'il—how he built and expanded the country's canal system to wrest fertile land from the desert; how he extended the railway, built bridges, made and paved roads. His "triumph," of course, was the Suez Canal, which was in the making for all the years she was in Egypt. However, Duff-Gordon also criticized the presence of Europeans in Cairo. And she startled many when she decided to travel to Luxor on a government steamer, in the company of Egyptians, rather than on "Cook's."

During this same period, al-Tahtawi was writing that "education" was the cornerstone of civilization, essential for all Egyptian citizens—male and female. His trip to Paris had in many regards shaped his succeeding intellectual career, and in his later writings he supported efforts to modernize Cairo. Not only did he address issues of education and science, but he discussed the role of the state in the betterment of society. He also helped guide many of the Egyptian students who followed in his footsteps and traveled abroad, emphasizing the importance of contact with Europe as a stimulus toward developing a more modern Arab civilization.[45] Al-Tahtawi should also be credited for making Arabic more prominent as a language, encouraging it as a replacement for Turkish, and calling for the printing and distribution of more Arabic books.

Al-Tahtawi's interest in "urban modernity" was also reflected in comments on changes that were yet to come in Cairo based on European influence. He wrote: "Those are the kings who want to be remembered, and their approach is building. For construction and building, if we elaborate, they do reflect on the richness of the place."[46] Thus, al-Tahtawi expressed a belief that the built environment was largely produced by political will. Only succeeding generations would be able to decipher the processes behind its making.

Similarly, 'Ali Mubarak wrote extensively about the new urban amenities—railroad, telegraph, postal service, opera house, theaters, and parks—that were being introduced in Egypt, and his belief that these aspects of "modernity" would not alienate existing urban culture or the Cairene population. This was not surprising, since Mubarak was active in bringing these changes. But, in contrast with al-Tahtawi, Mubarak explained that he not only favored informing the East about the achievements of the West, but " . . . put[ting] the East in a direct situation of actual confrontation with the West, so that the East before the West knows its proper place in world civilization."[47] As a result of such comments, some scholars have interpreted Mubarak's writings as obsessed with the need to eliminate Egyptian "backwardness." Yet Mubarak also painted a highly flattering picture of Egyptian character, stressing the natural kindness, patience, and perseverance of its people, as well as their readiness to accept new ideas. For Mubarak, the Egyptians' only real sin was that they were poor.[48]

Mubarak's descriptions of Cairo were at times extremely technocratic. For example, he explained how the city had been divided into eighths (*athman*) for administrative purposes (FIGURE 8.6). And he told how each eighth section was

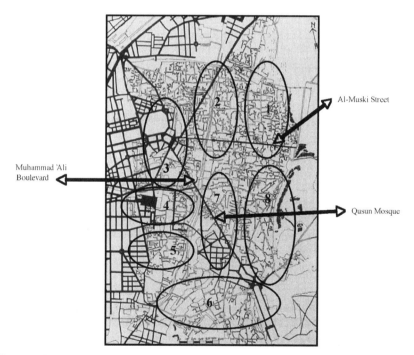

Figure 8.6. Map of Cairo showing the different administrative districts. 1) al-Gamaliyah, 2) Bab al-Shariyah, 3) Azbakiya, 4) Abdin, 5) Darb al-Gamamiz, 6) al-Khalifah, 7) Qusun, 8) al-Darb al-Ahmar Al-Muski Street connects the different areas of the city. Muhammad 'Ali Boulevard extends two kilometers from Maidan al-Ataba east of Azbakiya to the Citadel. Although the street intersected with Qusun Mosque, it hardly changed its spatial organization.
(Source: Drawn by author)

then divided into quarters to allow it to develop its own economic and social identity. But beyond such technical specificity Mubarak's *Khitat* also provided an important source for understanding the social, religious, and architectural dimensions of
life in nineteenth-century Egypt. In its introduction, Mubarak explained that

> In former times, descriptions of the city of Cairo, the seat of the khedivial gov-
> ernment, were abundant in books of *khitat* and in histories and biographies; its
> buildings and gardens were adequately described. But the city is now different
> from what it was then, due to the transformation of what had been the case in
> the time of the Fatimids who first mapped it out, through the changes of
> political regimes, sometimes it flourished and was brilliant, at other times it
> was weakened and fragile. Yet we have not found any one of us among the
> community of its children who would guide us through those transformations,
> instruct us in the causes of its changes, and point out their results. For we
> looked around the city, and we did not know its conditions; we roamed about
> its districts and did not know who had laid them down.[49]

Although Mubarak incorporated references to some European travelers'
writings in his own work, he was aware that European Orientalists were actively
engaged in appropriating Egypt—its cities, its history, and its monuments—for
themselves and their governments. Several scholars have argued that his *Khitat*
may thus be seen as a device to counteract European intellectual appropriation,
and document the nationalist claims of Egyptians.[50]

ESTABLISHING THE PHYSICAL DUALITY: A NEW DRESS

To make a clear distinction between tourists, foreigners, elites, and natives,
Lane-Poole explained how thousands of tourists, mounted on donkeys, explored
the native quarters every winter. But such people were "birds of passage," and not
inhabitants of the city. By contrast, foreigners who lived in "European Cairo" did
not ride donkeys, and were only reluctantly dragged to the bazaars when they had
visitors. He further explained that the "blessed conservatism" of the East had
maintained much of the old city in beautiful, ruinous, unprogressive order. In *The
Story of Cairo* he wrote, "[W]atch the throng pass by: the ungainly camels, laden
with brushwood or green fodder, which seem to threaten to sweep everything and
everybody out of the street."[51] After twenty years of living in the city he still
referred to the streets of Muslim Cairo (or his "Egyptian Cairo") as hardly
spoiled, and to a great degree still the city of *The Arabian Nights*.[52]
    In his first book, Lane-Poole had often referred to the changes that had
occurred during the previous fifty years, comparing the Cairo of his day to that of

his uncle. Yet considering all the changes in transportation and urban layout, he still criticized the city's streets as "dusty, rattling, and old-fashioned"—thus portraying his dissatisfaction with the new services introduced under Isma'il.[53] And those changes, which he later approved of, he attributed to the British occupation.

> We have given them public order and security, solvency without too heavy taxation, an efficient administration, even-handed justice, the means of higher education, and above all to every man his fair share of enriching Nile.[54]

For Lane-Poole, "order" was a European trait, which Cairo only came to reflect after being exposed to the West. Thus, despite all the reforms of Isma'il's "project of modernity," Egyptians only acquired literacy and urban amenities as a result of direct colonial rule. Indeed, he referred to these reforms as "the reforms of the Firengy [foreigners]."

Yet, Lane-Poole also questioned the purpose of new urban amenities:

> [T]hen all this fiddling with water and drains and streets; what is it all for? . . . [Having] put pipes and patent traps and other godless improvements into the mosques, will one's prayers be better than they were in the pleasant pervasive odor of the old fetid tanks? The streets are broader, no doubt, to let the Firengis roll by in their two horsed 'arabiyas and splash the Faithful with mud.[55]

"Modernity," it seemed, was good for the foreign residents of Cairo, but not for Cairenes themselves.

Throughout his work, Lane-Poole's described his "Two Cairos" as distinct in character, but only barely divided in space. "Egyptian Cairo" was that of the native quarters and bazaars. By contrast, "European Cairo" knew little of this medieval sister, even though there were many signs that it existed not far away. Al-Muski Street seemed to be the cutting fissure between the two (REFER TO FIGURE 8.6).

Unlike more casual visitors who reveled in the sensuous qualities of the difference, Lane-Poole believed the best way to appreciate the old city was to view it from a distance.

> It is in the bazaars that one feels most the shock of contact with the unfamiliar; but, in a less intimate yet deeply impressive way, to drink in the full inspiration of the Muslim city one must climb to the ramparts of the Citadel about sunset and slowly absorb the wonderful panorama that spreads below and around. . . . All in that wide range beneath the eye is of the East Eastern. . . . Here we realize Cairo for the first time as a city of the Middle Ages, and more than that, a city with an heritage from the dawn of history.[56]

In such writings, Lane-Poole cast Cairo as a museum, a picturesque display. However, to achieve this view from on high, "unhappily, . . . one usually passes along the most terribly defaced street in all Cairo." By this he was referring not to the narrow streets of the medieval quarters, but to Muhammad 'Ali Boulevard, which had been cut through them as part of Isma'il's modernization program.[57] But, of course, he reminded readers, this happened before "England took the reins of Egypt."

Foreigners living in Cairo thought differently about its medieval quarters. For example, in *Childhood in Egypt*, Anne Barber explained that although she, as a child, enjoyed going to the older parts of Cairo, her English nurse rejected the idea. Barber wrote: "Another walk would be fun if I could go up all the steps, but nurse says that fleas live up there. I picture the fleas in their tiny houses and wish I could see them."[58] Such a story tells much about how foreigners viewed the natives and their quarters, and subsequently enforced that vision.

By comparison, as Cairo's modernization progressed, European shops with their plate-glass windows became a common scene in Azbakiyya. And, according to Lane-Poole, travelers had to go some distance before they could find the picturesque cupboard-shop of the East, fetching for what they imagined. If those travelers desired, they could also "hear a French opera and see a French ballet in a theater exactly resembling those [they] left behind in London." Not only that, but they could go around, if they chose, "in as European a manner as through Switzerland."

Parts of this "European Cairo" were discussed by Duff-Gordon during her stay at Shepheard's Hotel—the central meeting place for expatriates in Cairo. Every day Omar, her dragoman, led her from the "Frank" quarter into an Egyptian "golden world" which assailed all her English senses. If her health had improved, Duff-Gordon might have been tempted to linger in Cairo indefinitely.

In his book, De Leon referred in detail to the disappearance of Azbakiyya—once the pride and the glory of the city and its people. Here, "picturesque" old Eastern buildings had been replaced by new stone ones, whose arcades were an imitation of those along Paris's Rue de Rivoli. Meanwhile, De Leon described the new Azbakiyya Park as a French or German tea garden under a French ornamental gardener: "partly on the trim Versailles model, partly in imitation of Bois de Boulogne, with its artificial lake with swans, and small mock-steamers for sailing over three feet of water."[59]

De Leon did not point to the separation of the two Cairos as sharply as Lane-Poole, but he did contrast his experiences in the different parts of Cairo. For example, on the opposite side of Azbakiyya, near al-Muski, the street of the Frank shops, he explained how the Arab population assembled nightly around favorite storytellers, who rehashed the "Thousand and One Nights." However, to him, this seemed like the "mirage of the desert."

Unlike Lane-Poole, De Leon described the "Isma'ilya quarter" as "entirely a new creation, . . . one of the prettiest portions of Cairo."[60] And he referred to how Isma'il had encouraged the construction of good houses for Europeanized residents,

and how he hoped to attract new residents from abroad by offering building lots free
to anyone who would build a house of a fixed value. There were also lots mapped
out in the rear of hotels, where there were no buildings, and "a new town of several
thousands of houses occupied the site,"[61] some of which were palatial.

Toward the end of his trip, after he had left Egypt and reached France, De
Leon explained that

> . . . before descending, you feel that your Oriental dream-life is finished, and
> that you are returning to matter-of-fact places and people, and less sunny skies.
> . . . As far behind us now in thought and feeling (though but a week has elapsed
> since we left our hospitable shores), as if centuries and the whole globe divided
> us, must Egypt now be to the returned pilgrim of our widely different civiliza-
> tion; but the memory of the land and of the people, like the subtle perfume
> which still scents the mummy-cloth after thousands of years, lingers and must
> ever abide with those who have visited and dwelt in the "Khedive's Egypt."[62]

Not only did De Leon give his impressions of the city, but he also prescribed
steps that should be taken to redeem and regenerate it. However, even with all
these changes and "improvements," he explained, Cairo's system of narrow streets
and the plans of its old Eastern buildings were perhaps better suited to the cli-
mate, the place, and the people. Thus, De Leon both praised and criticized Isma'il
for his "modernizing" efforts. He clearly feared losing the sense of the "authentic" Orient that was so popular among travelers.[63]

DUALITY THROUGH THE ACT OF PERCEPTION

Giving us a different perspective as to how Cairenes interpreted the changes
that were taking place in their Cairo is Muhammad al-Muwaylihi who wrote
about a former Pasha's visit to the Azbakiyyah garden.[64] The Pasha, who had
never seen anything like this before, could not help but admire the beautiful view
and splendor of the park that was in front of him. He asked in amazement,
"Which ruler in this land owns this land?"

> Isa Ibn Hisham, his companion, replied by explaining that "[i]t's public prop-
> erty. It doesn't belong to any single person. The government created it as
> part of public service facilities for all classes of people to stroll in."[65]

Al-Muwaylihi explains that the Pasha and Isa Ibn Hisham walked around the
various parts of the garden looking at the leafy trees, luxuriant branches, and pret-
ty flowers. Their conversation continued thus:

Pasha: "Why isn't this place thronged with people? Why aren't they walking around looking at the beautiful views and taking advantage of the shade? You've just been telling me that the government has opened it up to anyone passing by. So why are the only people I can see those foreigners over there? Has the government reserved this place for Westerners and banned Egyptians from using it? Up till now, I haven't noticed a single Egyptian since we came in."

Isa: "The government doesn't discriminate between one nationality and another. Egyptians, it seems, have grown accustomed to scorning spiritual pleasures and utterly disregard them. It's as though Egyptians have put themselves into some kind of prison."[66]

At this point, the Pasha seemed more puzzled and overwhelmed by the fact that Egyptians were absent from the park. He added,

"May the Creator and Maker be exalted! How is it that Egyptians have got into this habit of disregarding the enjoyment they can get from a blessing like this, by this I mean the observation and study of all kinds of things?"

Isa: "As far as I can see, the only reason for it is that Egyptians . . . can't be bothered to stimulate the innate feeling hidden deep inside them or to cultivate it through practice, meditation, and constant repetition. Foreigners, on the other hand, have devoted particular attention to this type of practice. They have also developed a passion for ancient relics. They compete with each other to acquire them and go to excessive lengths to keep them exclusively to themselves."[67]

This dialogue gives a sense of another type of encounter with "modern" Cairo, one involving only Egyptians. The dialogue also shows how Egyptians and foreigners often had different points of reference toward spatial settings—not only in terms of how they used these spaces, but how they appreciated them.

This work by al-Muwaylihi marked a new period in the development of modern Arabic literature. It is structured around a Minister of War (Ahmad Pasha al-Manakili) from the time of Muhammad 'Ali who is resurrected from his grave, and the narrator (Isa Ibn Hisham)—a contemporary Egyptian—who serves as his guide to Cairo as it is rapidly being transformed into a cosmopolitan metropolis.[68] Al-Muwaylihi used this narrative device to illustrate the extent of changes from the earlier condition of Cairo. And at one point he even has Isa decide he will allow the Pasha to remain unaware that a generation has passed since his death so that he can better compare the two eras.[69]

In another instance, when the Pasha asks Isa to take him to his house, Isa replies by saying that he has no idea where his house is. Feeling rather uncomfortable, the Pasha answers:

Tell me for Heaven's sake, which country are you from? You can't be an
Egyptian. There's no one in the whole country who doesn't know where my
house is. I'm Ahmad Pasha al-Manakili, the Egyptian Minister of War.

Isa Ibn Hisham replies:

Believe me Pasha, I'm Egyptian. The only reason why I don't know where
you live is that houses in Egypt are no longer known by the names of their
owners, but by the name of their street, lane, and number. If you would be so
kind as to tell me the street, name, and number of your house, I will go there
and bring you the things you've requested.

The Pasha, rather annoyed, answers:

It's clear to me that you're out of your mind, my dear author! Since when have
houses had numbers to be known by? What are they? Some kind of government legislation or army regulations?[70]

The Pasha clearly cannot comprehend the changes taking place in the city,
even when these seem quite normal to Isa. In the end, Pasha can only understand
these things as a form of regulation enforced by a government that does not
respect Egyptian culture. In this case it has ignored difference in status among the
population, allowing houses to be identified by street name and number rather
than the status of their residents.

The exchange is in fact based on a real occurrence in Cairo. In 1883 a committee was appointed to name the streets in all Cairene quarters and install plaques carrying their names.[71] As part of this effort, documents in the Cairo National Archive
indicate, the number of streets, alleyways, and *haras* were estimated to be 1,892, and
the number of plaques to identify them to be 6,778. These plaques were eventually
placed at the intersections of every *hara* and street, written in both Arabic and French.

Elsewhere in al-Muwaylihi's book, Isa explains that his aim is to inform the
Pasha how things have changed. This involves showing him places he has not
seen, telling him stories he has not heard, and explaining aspects of "modern history." In this manner Isa hopes to discover the Pasha's opinion of the present, and
learn which of the two periods is superior.

Likewise, al-Muwaylihi started most of the editions of *Hadith Isa* by writing,

It is a true picture dressed up in imaginary garb . . . which we have tried to use
to comment on the morals and conditions of present-day people, and to
describe the faults of various classes of people which should be avoided and
those qualities which should be maintained.[72]

But not all the judgements in al-Muwaylihi's book were unfavorable. For example, when the Pasha and Isa pass the Isma'ilya quarter and the Pasha is astonished to see the mansions, palaces, and villas there, he asks: "please tell me what place this gleaming paradise occupies in the city of Cairo?" Isa explains that Isma'il laid out the plans as part of a project to adorn the Nile valley. He tells the Pasha the area had been a barren wasteland during his time, but today it is where the wealthy people reside, where flowers grow, and exotic birds live. And he explains that foreigners also reside there.

Al-Muwaylihi's biography refers to the fact that he was writing for a cultured readership, and that he was fully aware of the literary merit of his work. In particular, his use of dialogue was a remarkably subtle way to portray the changes that were taking place in the city. Yet it is also clear from the dialogue that there were many differences between the way natives and foreigners viewed these.

In his sequel, *The Second Journey*, al-Muwaylihi turned to a portrayal of life in Paris, and alluded to the differences between East and West.[73] He pointed out the advantages and the disadvantages of the West, and advised his own people—those of the East—to learn from the West. But he also asked that in transferring such knowledge, they would choose only what applied to Egyptian culture and what would not cause harm to Egypt's people.

WHOSE CAIRO? / WHICH CAIRO?

As seen from the above encounters, the experience of Cairo varied considerably. It is not clear to which Cairo Lane-Poole belonged, or which one he admired. Although he praised "European Cairo" for pushing Egypt toward development, he criticized the form of what was emerging as a low-quality imitation of Europe. He also pointed out that Egyptians themselves were not sensitive enough to Arab monuments, and that they had needlessly demolished many in the process of modernizing the city.

Two major views dominate Lane-Poole's writings. First, Cairo was a "dual" city—part Egyptian and part European—although one might better refer to these as "The City of the Arabian Nights" and "The City for the Europeans," where the first reflected his desire to project his imagination on reality, and the second represented the unappealing reality of cities in his native land. Second, this duality had many facets: us and them; East and West; his uncle Edward W. Lane's Cairo and his Cairo. In the end, it was only through these dualities that Lane-Poole could visualize and comprehend the city. The reason was that he was not attempting to see the Cairo in front of him, but to create a sense of the Orient, instead.

Unlike Lane-Poole, Duff-Gordon was typical of another group of travelers, who came to Cairo with a preconceived idea, but did not waste time looking for what they only imagined. During her life, Duff-Gordon managed to change her point of reference and comprehend beyond her imagination. But it was only through experience, willingness, and desire that she was able to free herself from the "imaginary" and appreciate the "real."

As an anonymous reviewer said of the literature on Egypt in the mid-nineteenth century: "Were we to pile together the various works that have appeared of late years upon the subject of Egypt and Palestine, we might readily construct a monument rivaling in magnitude, if not in durability, some of those that still frown on the waters of the Nile."[74]

Many foreign writers alluded to the story of Cairo as that of *The Arabian Nights*. To many, this was the "original," and they portrayed nineteenth-century Cairo according to what they imagined and desired, rather than what they witnessed and experienced. But this tradition of travel writing resulted largely in the commodification of the city and its people for the European consumer of Orientalism.

It was a basic unfamiliarity with certain aspects of Cairo, and their replacement with an imaginary "blueprint," that made the city appear to many foreigners as a "dual city." At times the split was so extreme that Europeans even alluded to different areas/districts as different cities. Few contemporary scholars have questioned these accounts. As a result, most contemporary literature dealing with nineteenth-century Cairo has described the city in these very terms, just as travelers interpreted a "dual" representation out of a single culture.

But even in their sense of duality there were differences between writers such as Lane-Poole and De Leon. In large part this had to do with their points of reference. Lane-Poole based his work largely on a comparison with the Cairo of his uncle; De Leon based his work only on the Cairo he had known during his own lifetime. The sense of "duality" also stemmed from a relative sense of social status. Duff-Gordon made this point when she wrote that one must come to the East to understand absolute social equality. She clarified this by explaining that although there was little education in Egypt, there was no reason a donkey boy could not become a great man, as all Muslims are equal.

Representations often reveal more about the culture of their authors than the people and places portrayed. Whether in writing, painting, or photography, the work of Europeans on Cairo was tainted by a foreign looking glass. The vision of many travelers was shaped by a world of inherited legends, and many exerted more effort constructing and presenting an illusion than documenting and comprehending what was in front of them.

But by comparing foreigners' writings with those of native Egyptians one can see there was another Cairo behind these illusions. Under Isma'il's direction, a cultural renaissance was induced to express the vitality of Egypt as a powerful nation. And although not all Cairenes benefited equally from the changes it brought, it does not seem that they were alienated in the process.

In all the literature that has been produced on Cairo from a multiplicity of approaches, few scholars have considered Cairenes as participants in this native project of modernity—or considered their works as necessary sources. But as every story has different facets, these writings by Cairenes should be given as much respect as those of Europeans. As shown, the sharp distinction between an old and a new city was an image that appealed largely to outsiders. The social reality of the Cairene context was more complex than this simplistic assertion of East and West, old and new. Nevertheless the transformation of the city in the nineteenth century has come to be embodied in these terms. A more careful reading of Cairo's urban history would reveal the complexity of the process of urban development within the Egyptian project of modernity.

Cities are not meant to be frozen in time and space; when this happens, they only decay. Giving the city a facelift and developing new quarters to reflect a new age did not mean giving it a new identity. The "dual" city paradigm therefore was largely an *ethnocentric* platform that helped drive foreign travel writing in the nineteenth century. Unfortunately, it has continued to unduly influence scholarship today.

NOTES

1. H. Pieron, "Le Caire: Son esthétique dans la ville Arabe et dans le ville Moderne," *L'Égypte Contemporaine* 5 (January 1911), pp. 512.

2. For a detailed account of Khedive Isma'il's contributions refer to H.F. Ahmed, "Pre-Colonial Modernity: The State and the Making of Nineteenth Century Cairo's Urban Form," Ph.D. diss., University of California, Berkeley, 2001.

3. A. Sattin, *Lifting the Veil: British Society in Egypt 1768–1956* (London: J.M. Dent & Sons Ltd, 1988), pp. 178.

4. Karl Baedeker was a German book publisher who printed many guidebooks/travel handbooks. The series—which was published in German, French, and English—was composed of guidebooks to most European countries, the United States, Egypt, and several European cities. In these books, he indicated views of special interest, included maps, and designated "reliable" hotels.

5. Sattin, *Lifting the Veil*, pp. 177, my emphasis.

6. See books written by Egyptians like Husayn Kafafi. H. Kafafi, *Ismail wa Mashuqatuhu Misr* (Cairo: Dar al-Kutub, 1988).

7. D. Mohamed, *In the Land of The Pharaohs: A Short History of Egypt* (London: Stanley Paul & Co., 1911), pp. 3. As the book was written at the turn of the century, Mohammad explains that his father was an officer in the Egyptian army and a supporter of Ahmed Urabi; accordingly, he is writing from this nationalist standpoint. Another point worth mentioning here is that Mohamed explained that in many cases where the Europeans found the "modern" Egyptian difficult to understand, the difficulty had been produced by Europeans themselves.

8. T. Mitchell, *Colonising Egypt* (Cambridge: Cambridge University Press, 1988), pp. 26. Mitchell further explains that Europeans came to the Orient without realizing they had left the world-as-exhibition. They came looking for a reality, which had invariably already been seen in an exhibition.

9. There were several other works. Refer to G. Flaubert, *Flaubert in Egypt: A Sensibility on Tour*, trans. Francis Steegmuller (London: Bodley Head, 1972); J.L. Gêrome, *Le Fayoum, le Sinai et Pétra* (Paris: H. Plon, 1872); W.H. Bartlett, *The Nile Boat* (London: Hall and Virtue, 1849); R.T. Kelly, *Egypt Painted and Described* (London: Adam & Charles Black, 1904); and S. Lane-Poole, *The Englishwoman in Egypt: Letters from Cairo Written during a Residence there in 1845–46* (London: C. Knight, 1844).

10. E.W. Lane, "The Draft of the Description of Egypt," M.S. Eng. Misc. d. 234, as quoted in L. Ahmed, *Edward W. Lane, A Study of his Life and Works and of British Ideas of the Middle East in the Nineteenth Century* (London: Longman, 1978), pp. 1. Ahmed explains that for three full years before embarking for Egypt, Lane intensively prepared himself for his enterprise. During that time, he pursued the study of "Eastern things." He studied Arabic and Arabic grammar, and subscribed to the publications of the Egyptian Society.

11. This work by Lane is now a basic text for historians of the Arab world, and is deemed a classic, not only by Orientalists but also by anthropologists. Jason Thompson took on the task of publishing it in its original form. See E. W. Lane, *Description of Egypt*, edited by Jason Thompson (Cairo: American University of Cairo Press, 2000).

12. *Eclectic Review*, N.S. XVIII (November 1842), pp. 444.

13. Ahmed, *Edward W. Lane*, pp. 69.

14. R. al-Tahtawi, *Takhlis al-Ibriz fi Talkhis Bariz* (Cairo: Matba'at Bulaq, 1849), my translation.

15. N. Najib, *al-Rihlah ila la-Sharq wa al-Rihlah ila al-Gharb* (Bierut: Dar al-Kalimah lil Nashr, 1981), pp. 56.

16. Al-Tahtawi, *Takhlis al Ibriz*, pp. 244.

17. Al-Tahtawi, *Takhlis al Ibriz*, pp. 203.

18. J. Duncan and D. Gregory, eds., *Writes of Passage: Reading Travel Writing* (London: Routledge, 1999), pp. 7. Also see D. Porter, *Haunted Journeys: Desire and Transgression in European Travel Writing* (Princeton: Princeton University Press, 1991), pp. 12.

19. Kelly, *Egypt Painted and Described*, pp. 14.

20. *Cook's Tourists' Handbook for Egypt, the Nile and the Desert* (London: Thomas Cook & Son, 1898), pp. 101.

21. K. Baedeker, ed., *Egypt: Handbook for Travellers* (Leipsic: Karl Baedeker, fourth edition, 1898), pp. 33.

22. Baedeker, ed., *Egypt*, pp. 41.

23. I.G. Wilkinson, *A Handbook for Travellers in Egypt, Murray's Handbook* (London: John Murray, 1865), pp. 125.

24. Leila Ahmed explains that the notes provided by Lane were closely related to the text as they take their departure from a particular form or image in the text and it is that

form and image that they then define. The images were provided by William Harvey when he worked close to Lane, and Lane subjected each of his productions to careful examinations.

25. Ahmed, *Edward W. Lane*, pp. 145.

26. R. Irwin, *The Arabian Nights: A Companion* (London: Allen Lane, 1994), pp. 274.

27. N. Warner, *An Egyptian Panorama, Reports from the 19th Century British Press* (Cairo: Zeitouna Press, 1994), pp. xx.

28. W. Thackeray, *Notes of a Journey From Cornhill to Grand Cairo* (London: Chapman and Hall, 1846).

29. It is known that she did not find a cure. However, she fell in love with Egypt and stayed there until she died and was buried in Cairo in 1869.

30. G. al-Shayyal, *The History of Egyptian Historiography* (Alexandria: Alexandria University Press, 1962), pp. 108.

31. Najib, *al-Rihlah ila la-Sharq wa al-Rihlah ila al-Gharb*. The difference between Lane and al-Tahtawi is that al-Tahtawi continued to wear his Arab attire and dress during his entire stay in France, while Lane adopted the Turkish/Oriental dress once he arrived in Egypt. Najib further referred to the differences in their intention of writing, where al-Tahtawi wants the cities of Islam to look at the ways of modernization and development of societies, whereas Lane wants to portray those manners and customs before they change. For Lane, he was just after the changes, while al-Tahtawi was pointing at the differences in a comparative mode. Lane's main objective is to draw a picture of the lives of "Egyptians" before it is affected by Westernization as a result of Muhammad 'Ali's reforms.

32. *'Alamuddin* is a novel of an Azhari Shaykh who travels with an Englishman to Europe, and with whom he discussed in detail the positive and negative aspects of the two civilizations. The book's purpose was clearly educational, where Mubarak wrote about Egyptian history. It is structured around conversations between a Shaykh, his son, and a British Orientalist. I will not cover his writings in *'Alamuddin* as Nezar AlSayyad explains it in depth in another chapter of this book.

33. Al-Muwaylihi had been the director of the Waqf administration for four years, and was able to describe the corruption that pervaded it. Al-Muwaylihi uses Isa ibn Hisham, and the Pasha, along with the *umda* (mayor), and a playboy where he discusses a variety of institutions, social groups, and classes within Egyptian society. The chapters first appeared as articles in the paper *Misbah al-Sharq*. Roger Allen explains that *Misbah al-Sharq* was a paper which catered to the tastes and expectations of the cultured and well-read segments of Cairene society. See R. Allen, *A Period of Time: A Study and Translation of Hadith Isa Ibn Hisham bu Muhammad al-Muwaylihi* (Oxford, UK: Ithaca Press, 1992), pp. 20. Allen further explains that al-Muwaylihi describes Egyptian society in considerable detail by using a literary device whereby he depicts one character who is eager to see all aspects of contemporary Egyptian life, and a second who is prepared to take him on a conducted tour of Cairene society; curiosity, investigation, and commentary.

34. Allen, *A Period of Time*, pp. 69. Allen adds that al-Muwaylihi delved deep into the

faults of society and the institutions which represented it, and produced caricatures of public figures which were embarrassingly close to the real thing.

35. S. Lane-Poole, *Cairo: Sketches of its History, Monuments and Social Life* (London: J. S. Virtue, 1898), pp. 2.

36. Lady Duff-Gordon, *Letters from Egypt* (London: Macmillan and Co., 1865). In another part (pp. 80), Duff-Gordon wrote: "The real life and the real people are exactly as described in that most veracious of books, the 'Thousand and One Nights.' The tyranny is the same, the people are not altered; and very charming people they are." In another part (pp. 96), where she also referred to the *Arabian Nights,* she explained that she thought of her servant, Omar, as Badr-ed-Deen Hasan, another one of the characters of the stories.

37. Duff-Gordon made it clear in many sections of her letters that none of the people she ran into begged or asked for *baksheesh*. This is a point that was repeated over and over in many of the traveler accounts.

38. Duff-Gordon, *Letters from Egypt*, pp. 76–77.

39. In a later section, Duff-Gordon wrote that if she could afford it, she would have a sketch of a beloved old mosque of hers, "falling to decay," with three palm trees growing in the middle of it. She further added that she would have a full book as everything was exquisite, however, she was afraid that all of this might vanish soon.

40. E. De Leon, *The Khedive's Egypt* (New York: Harper & Brothers Publishers, 1878), pp. 20.

41. Ibid, pp. 49.

42. The volume of work produced on Khedive Isma'il's period is enormous, and the authors vary in their position and opinions about his contributions to Egypt.

43. Lane-Poole, *Cairo: Sketches of its History*, pp. 7.

44. Lane-Poole, *The Story of Cairo* (London: J.M. Dent & Sons, Ltd., 1902), pp. 27.

45. Prince Umar Tusun explained in his book *The Egyptian Missions in the Period of Muhammad 'Ali* that Jomard not only taught Egyptian subjects about the achievement of the West and introduced them to the different students, but also reminded them of their rich history and civilization. He advised them to continue on the same path because the future of Egypt lies in its history. He also told them to acquire as much knowledge as they could while in France, as France had helped Europe leap forward, and then to return to their country, and return those benefits, and reflect on the arts. He pointed out to them that Egypt—the country they represented—would thus retrieve its original characteristics through them, and that France that taught them would thus be returning its debt to the East on behalf of the entire West. *Al-Bi'that al-Ilmiyah fi Ahd Muhammad 'Ali, thuma fi ahdai Abbas al-Awal wa Said* (Alexandria: Matbaat Talai' al-Din, 1934), pp. 33–34.

46. Al-Tahtawi, *Takhlis al Ibriz*, pp. 207. It should be noted that he referred to advancement in society, as related to development and elaboration in its architecture and urban form.

47. W. Al-Qadi, "East and West in Ali Mubarak's Alamuddin," in M. Buheiry, ed., *Intellectual Life in the Arab East, 1890–1939* (Lebanon: American University of Beirut, 1996), pp. 28.

48. J.A. Crabbs, *The Writing of History in Nineteenth-Century Egypt, A Study in National Transformation* (Cairo: The American University in Cairo Press, 1984), pp. 114.

49. 'Ali Mubarak, *al-Khitat al-Tawfiqiyyah al-Jadidah*, Vol. 1 (Cairo: Bulaq Press, 1889), pp. 2. Mubarak used a variety of sources in writing his work: oral evidence; official documents, both published and unpublished; census records; trade reports; statistical collections; cadastral documents; title deeds for urban properties; *awqaf* documents; and records of the departments of Education and Public Works. He also relied heavily on the *Description de l'Égypte* for information on Cairo and other Egyptian cities.

50. See J. Berque, *Egypt: Imperialism and Revolution* (London: Faber, 1972); G. Baer, *Studies in the Social History of Modern Egypt* (Chicago: University of Chicago Press, 1969). Baer had pointed out that there are a number of errors in Mubarak's work. Some are misprints, others are errors in locating a place in relation to others, or in the distance between two places; however, he does not refer to these in his work.

51. Lane-Poole, *The Story of Cairo*, pp. 8.

52. *The Story of Cairo* was written in 1902, and published in 1906. At that time, Lane-Poole was a professor of Arabic at Trinity College, Dublin.

53. Lane-Poole, *Cairo: Sketches of its History*, pp. 283.

54. Lane-Poole, *The Story of Cairo*, pp. vii.

55. Ibid, pp. viii.

56. Ibid, pp. 6–31.

57. Muhammad 'Ali Boulevard linked the different quarters of Cairo, Azbakiyya, and the Citadel. Many scholars have described it as an example of "Hausmannization." But in "Pre-Colonial Modernity," I show it was constructed according to a different plan than that used to open up the boulevards of Paris.

58. A. Barber, *Childhood in Egypt* (London: Geoffrey Bles, 1968), p. 26.

59. De Leon, *The Khedive's Egypt*, p. 51.

60. Ibid.

61. Ibid.

62. Ibid.

63. In his description of the khedive and his achievements, De Leon alludes to the duality in his character too. He explained that the khedive lived in a fashion partly European, partly Eastern: "European as to *cuisine* and mode of taking his meals, the latter of which he does in company with the chief members of his household, his chamberlains, private secretaries."

64. Muhammad al-Muwaylihi's "Fitrah min al-Zamman" as translated in Allen, *A Period of Time*. *Hadith Isa Ibn Hisham* was first published in book form in 1907. Originally it appeared in article form in the newspaper *Misbah al-Sharq* over a number of years starting from 1898. In 1927, the author revised it for use as a textbook in secondary school. Later, it was regarded as a classic of modern Arabic literature. Abbas Khidr describes al-Muwaylihi's work as a "bridge" that looks both forward and backward. In A. Khidr, *al-Qissah al-Qasirah fi Misr* (Cairo: Dar al-Qawmiyyah, 1966), p. 53.

65. Allen, *A Period of Time*, p. 291.

66. Ibid, p. 291.

67. Ibid, p. 292.

68. P. Starkey, "Egyptian Travellers in Europe," in *Travellers in Egypt* (London: I.B. Tauris, 1998), pp. 280–86. Starkey explains that al-Muwaylihi's work serves both as a work of social criticism and as a "pivotal literary creation."

69. Allen, *A Period of Time*, p. 51.

70. This dialogue is based on Roger Allen's translations of al-Muwaylihi's work.

71. Cairo National Archive, (6/1) Maslahat al-Tanzim.

72. It is present in all the introductions of *Hadith Isa Ibn Hisham*, translated by Roger Allen.

73. Al-Muwaylihi dedicated two chapters of his *Second Journey* to discussing the innovations and the advancement of the West in constructing the Eiffel Tower and referred to it as the eighth wonder of the world.

74. M.R. Kalfatovic, *Nile Notes of a Howadji: A Bibliography of Travelers' Tales from Egypt, from the Earliest Time to 1918* (London: The Scarecrow Press, 1992), pp. ix.

9

Modernizing Cairo:
A Revisionist Narrative

Khaled Fahmy

On a spring morning in 1878 a child playing with his mates under Qasr al-Nil Bridge—which had only recently been constructed across the Nile in Cairo—noticed a stray dog sniffing closely at a semi-buried old rag. On unearthing it, the rag was discovered to contain human remains, and immediately the local police and health authorities were informed. Then, after the Qasr al-'Aini Hospital, the main hospital in Cairo, had conducted a forensic examination, it was concluded the rag contained the remains of either a stillborn female child or of a fetus. The uncertainty stemmed from the fact that the body was in an advanced stage of decomposition, and hence it was impossible to ascertain whether death had occurred before or after delivery.

After lengthy police investigations in the neighborhood, an eighteen-year-old woman called Fadl Wasi' confessed that it was she who had buried the body in this crude manner. She explained that she was originally from Jirja in the south; that she had gotten pregnant there by a soldier who had later deserted her to join his battalion in Cairo; that she had left the village after her pregnancy started to show; that she had arrived in Cairo in search of the father; and that she had given birth two months prematurely. After the local midwife who had helped Fadl had been fetched, and after questioning two men who had taken pity on her and who had given her refuge, the police decided not to press murder or manslaughter charges on Fadl and her "accomplices." It turned out that Fadl had endured a long and dangerous labor. She and one of the men who had helped her by pretending to be her husband had then decided not to register the newborn baby because they could not afford to pay the birth registration fees and because Fadl could not report the name of the real father. Police also discovered that soon after the baby's death, Fadl and her "husband" had faced a dilemma, for they could not report the death of someone who, as far as the authorities were concerned, was nonexistent. Accordingly, they had decided to bury the body without performing any rituals, and without informing the authorities.

In spite of the fact that there were no criminal charges brought against Fadl and her "husband," they were both found guilty of violating many ordinances regarding public health. Specifically, these included a requirement that all new-born babies be promptly registered, a corresponding requirement that all deaths be reported, and a ban on intra-mural burial. Accordingly, Fadl's case was forwarded to the Cairo Court of First Instance for a ruling.[1]

There are two reasons for choosing to open a chapter on nineteenth-century Cairo with the sad story of an unfortunate girl who lost her baby in what must have appeared an intimidating and even hostile city. The first is that it is a story that takes place *under*, and not *over*, Qasr al-Nil Bridge, and it thus helps introduce a main purpose of this chapter—that of offering a subaltern view of Cairo's modern history. In this regard, it is important to understand that this bridge, under which the body of Fadl's child was found, has featured prominently in the historiography of modern Cairo. Hastily built in 1869, together with many other constructions for the celebrations surrounding the inauguration of the Suez Canal, it was intended to be used by the illustrious French Empress Eugénie, for whom the Egyptian ruler, Khedive Isma'il, had reserved the newly constructed al-Jazira palace across the river.

Traditional historiography on this exciting period of Egypt's modern history has stressed how Isma'il's financial policies were ruinous to Egypt. And it has highlighted, as an example of these imprudent financial policies, the disastrous impact of the Suez Canal celebrations. Commenting on Isma'il's extravaganza, Marlowe, for example, has argued that even though what turned Europe against Isma'il and helped to depose him in 1879 was his insolvency and not his extravagance, his indebtedness could not have been helped by such ostentatious displays.[2] The story of the construction of Qasr al-Nil Bridge, therefore, although a mere anecdote in the larger story of Isma'il's extravaganza and of the modernization of Cairo, fits perfectly in this grand narrative of elites, power politics, colonialism, and nationalist struggle. Fadl Wasi"s story, on the other hand, provides an antidote to this elitist historiography, reminding us that equally, if not more profound stories were taking place under the bridge. And it suggests that no narrative of Cairo's modernization in the nineteenth century would be complete if it did not take people like Fadl into account.

The second reason for starting with this rather sad story is that it reflects an increasing concern in nineteenth-century Cairo about health and public hygiene. Another purpose of this essay therefore will be to stress how measures taken to improve Cairo's health conditions considerably affected its development during those years.

Historians of Cairo have long argued that the elegant, straight boulevards of Paris provided the inspiration for the engineers and town planners who modernized Cairo in the third quarter of the nineteenth century. And they have shown how the biases of the Comité de Conservation des Monuments de l'Art Arabe (the Comité) helped influence the architectural heritage of the city—and even alter its very shape. By contrast, concern about health conditions in the city, fear of epidemics, and incessant efforts to improve the level of public hygiene do not feature prominently, if at all, in these now familiar accounts of Cairo's modernization. Specifically, little is said about theories of miasmas, or "thick airs," which the majority of Egyptian administrators and health officials adhered to strongly and dogmatically.[3] According to this theory of disease etiology, vapors emanating from such sites as stagnant lakes, cemeteries, and rubbish mounds were thought to form a grave danger to the city's health conditions. And the strong measures eventually taken to eradicate sources of foul smell considerably affected the shape of the city.

By insisting that Paris was the model after which Cairo was refashioned, traditional accounts of how Cairo was modernized in the nineteenth century ignore this important dimension of change. However, by relying on documents housed in the Egyptian National Archives pertaining to public health and town planning, this chapter will offer an alternative version of Cairo's path to modernity.

TRADITIONAL ACCOUNTS OF THE MODERNIZATION OF CAIRO

Echoing Eurocentric tendencies within the larger historiography of Egypt, the story of modern Cairo is often seen as beginning with the brief period of the French occupation, 1798–1801, or with the subsequent, much longer, reign of Muhammad 'Ali (1805–1848).[4] Given the very short duration of their stay, however, the French are normally considered to have affected the shape of the city in only a minimal way. Specifically, they are seen as having introduced only two long-lasting innovations. One involved reorganization of the city's administrative districts and consolidation of the city's thirty-five *harat* (neighborhoods) into eight *athman* (or *arrondissements*). The other involved improvements in the city's street pattern—a change originally motivated by purely military reasons, but which left an enduring mark on the city.[5] With regard to Muhammad 'Ali's long reign, during which Egypt witnessed many ambitious and imaginative innovations, Abu-Lughod has likewise commented that it is perhaps ironic that during the forty-odd years he ruled Egypt, Cairo seems not to have changed much. Thus, even though Muhammad 'Ali is often dubbed the "founder of modern Egypt," he should rather go "down in the history of Cairo in the rather prosaic role of housekeeper. Cairo and its problems never seemed to have captured his imagination."[6]

His successor, 'Abbas I (r. 1848–1854), occupies an even more ignominious role in the annals of Cairo. Suspicious of European designs on his wealthy province, reputed to be a homosexual, and possessing a strange proclivity for Arabian horses and desert palaces, 'Abbas has attracted the wrath of historians as a mad pervert.[7] Moreover, Cairo is seen in his reign to have been neglected in favor of his strange, eerie palaces. Only two developments during his reign left their mark on the face of Cairo: one was the construction of a railway line linking Cairo to Alexandria; the other was the construction (to the north of the city) of Abbasiyya, a huge military compound which still bears his name.[8]

'Abbas's successor, Sa'id (r. 1854–1863), fares only slightly better. Cairo still does not seem to be of interest to him, and with the exception of the construction of few buildings (most notably the Qasr al-Nil Barracks, where the present Nile Hilton is located) and the Nuzhah Palace in Shubra, he does not seem to have been that concerned with the city. It is only with Isma'il (r. 1863–1879) that Cairo finally seems to receive the full attention of Egypt's ruler. Indeed, in the fifteen-odd years of his reign the city witnessed unprecedented transformation and expansion.

Isma'il first directed his attention to large infrastructural projects intended to supply Cairo with water and gas. As part of his early initiatives, in 1865 both the Cairo Water Company and the Cairo Gas Company were established. Water pipes were then extended to Azbakiyya, which was poised to become an important new center for the city once the large lake that had occupied it had been dried out. And soon thereafter a pumping station and newly laid conduits made it possible to distribute water to areas further away. In all, Isma'il's efforts are normally judged to have divided Cairo into two cities: an "Oriental" one lying to the east, with inward looking, clogged, and twisted alleyways and closed cul-de-sacs; and a "Western" one to the west with open squares, straight boulevards, and clean air.[9]

As significant as these early developments were, however, it is very common to date the rapid transformation that Cairo witnessed to an event that took place four years into Isma'il's reign. This was his visit to Paris to attend the Universal Exposition in 1867 and his inauguration of the Egyptian Pavilion there.[10] Having become familiar with Paris during his student years in the 1840s, Isma'il was impressed by what Baron Hausmann, Napoleon III's enterprising Prefect of the Seine, had accomplished. In particular, he envied Hausmann's successful street planning efforts, which had transformed the city's twisted, dank streets into wide and clean boulevards, crisscrossing at fixed intervals and giving rise to its famous *places* and roundabouts. Soon after returning from his trip, Isma'il embarked on a feverish round of construction activity with the aim of turning Cairo into a "Paris along the Nile," and giving it a facelift befitting the huge celebrations he had planned for the inauguration of the Suez Canal the following year.[11]

To help him transform Cairo, Isma'il relied on 'Ali Mubarak, an old friend from his student years in Paris. Mubarak is traditionally regarded as an impressively energetic official, one of Egypt's most remarkable men; more than anyone else, it is insisted, modern Cairo owes its shape to his diligent, imaginative efforts.

Born in a village in the Delta in 1823 (or 1824), he was sent to one of the newly established government schools, a move that eventually proved decisive in allowing him to rise from his *fellah* origins to a series of senior public posts. After being chosen to join a government-funded student mission to Paris in 1844, 'Ali Mubarak spent five years in that city learning French, engineering, and principles of administration. On his return to Egypt, he first assumed some menial posts, but after Isma'il's accession, he rose quickly, eventually serving as head of the prestigious departments of the Barrages; Railways and Communication; Public Instruction; Religious Endowments; and Public Works—sometimes heading two or even three of these departments simultaneously.[12]

Traditional accounts of Cairo's modernization also stress the fact that although the large entourage that accompanied Isma'il to Paris in 1867 did not officially include Mubarak, he too made an important visit to Paris that year.[13] The accounts point out that in October 1867, one month after being appointed Director of the Schools Department, Mubarak joined his patron on a visit to the Universal Exposition, in which the Egyptian pavilion was one of the most popular.[14] Officially, Isma'il is said to have sent Mubarak to Paris on a mission concerning finances. But it is also plausible that Isma'il summoned him there to urge him to emulate Hausmann in his "civilizing mission."

The trip that Isma'il and Mubarak made to Paris is normally thought to occupy a central position in the story of modern Cairo. Immediately after returning to Cairo, Mubarak was given the portfolio of Public Works and was entrusted with the daunting task of refashioning Cairo for the Suez celebrations in two years time. However, realizing that all of Cairo could not be "Parisianized" in such a short period, the khedive and his energetic public works minister decided to limit their immediate activities to Azbakiyya, which was becoming home to many of the city's elite.[15] But eventually, Isma'il entrusted Mubarak with three main tasks: developing Azbakiyya; executing a plan for the huge area that lay between the Nile and the western edge of the old city, which would be called Isma'ilya; and drawing up a master plan for the entire city. During 1868 and in a little over five months, Mubarak made sure that the first of these three tasks was accomplished: an Opera House was constructed; the squares of al-'Ataba al-Khadra, Opera, and al-Khazindar were consolidated; and the park at the center of the quarter was completely redesigned with the help of Barillet-Deschamp, the landscape engineer who had planned the Bois de Boulogne and the Champs de Mars in Paris.

Mubarak set out with equal diligence to undertake the second task entrusted to him, that of creating the new neighborhood of Isma'ilya. A grid pattern was chosen and, as in Paris, the roundabouts that resulted from the intersection of vertical, horizontal, and diagonal streets were deemed suitable sites for future statues of public figures.[16] Members of the Turkish-speaking ruling elite, as well as others, were granted plots of land at nominal prices there. And to prevent speculation, they were forbidden from selling their land before five years had elapsed. During this time, the government also reserved the right to retake the land if the new owners showed no signs of initiating construction. Finally, strict building codes were set down to ensure that the planned villas and mansions were European, not Oriental, in style.

Such developments were truly impressive. However, the third task entrusted to Mubarak, i.e., drawing up a master plan of the entire city, was slower to come by; and even slower was the attempt to open up the heart of the medieval city for modern transport. Indeed, a master plan for the city done in 1874 shows a series of main thoroughfares that were never executed. Of those that were built, Muhammad 'Ali Boulevard (linking Azbakiyya to the Citadel) took thirty years to be finished (1845–1875). And the construction of Muski Street (al-Sikka al-Gadida), whose idea originated in Napoleon's expedition, and which was also started in 1845, inched forward at such a slow pace that ten years later it extended only to al-Nahhasin, less than half way to the eastern desert.

The traditional account of the modernization of Cairo normally relies heavily on the descriptions given in Mubarak's own *Khitat*.[17] And in recent scholarship it has found its best expression in Janet Abu Lughod's magisterial 1970 study of Cairo, as well as in numerous Arabic publications.[18] Lately, however, many of the central points of this narrative have come under strong attack. Specifically, Jean-Luc Arnaud, in his impressively researched study *Le Caire, mise en place d'une ville moderne, 1867–1907*, has argued that the shape of Cairo owes less to Isma'il's visit to Paris in 1867 than to the bankruptcy of the Egyptian government in 1876 and the establishment of the *Caisse de la debte publique*, which assumed control over its finances.[19] Arnaud provides compelling evidence to show that from that moment onward many of Isma'il's grand projects were taken over by private companies and speculators, a fact to which he attributes the uneven development of the city and the lack of a coordinated urban policy.

Furthermore, Arnaud argues that very significant projects had already been undertaken before Isma'il's visit to Paris, challenging the supposed importance of this visit. But of more significance is Arnaud's reliance on the Watha'iq 'Asr Isma'il (Documents of Isma'il's Reign), a huge collection of mostly French documents housed in the Egyptian National Archives that has only rarely been consulted. Arnaud argues that these documents vividly illustrate Isma'il's relations with foreign companies, private investors, different branches of his administration, and key figures in charge of developing Cairo. Unlike 'Ali Mubarak's *Khitat*, which stresses the role played by the Ministry of Public Works (Nizarat al-Ashghal), Arnaud contends, the Watha'iq 'Asr Isma'il shed light on other departments that contributed significantly to the development of Cairo. Among them were the Water Company, which was initially entrusted with important street planning duties; the Roads Department (Maslahat al-Turuq), which was initially established within the

Governorate of Cairo (Muhafazat Misr), and which followed the jurisdiction of the Ministry of Interior and not of Public Works; and the Department of Public Parks (Maslahat al-Mutanazzahat). These documents also highlight the roles played by many individuals hitherto viewed as playing only minor roles. These include Nubar Pasha, head of the Ministry of Public Works before 'Ali Mubarak; Cordier, the head of the Water Company; and Grand Bey, head of the Roads Department. Relying on these documents, Arnaud has raised serious doubts about Mubarak's depiction of himself as mastermind of Cairo's development, and in so doing, he has presented a different picture of the city's development. Indeed, Arnaud specifically criticizes Mubarak for attributing to himself many of the accomplishments of Grand Bey.[20] And he argues that as far as modern Cairo is concerned, "Ali Mubarak plays not an insignificant role; his, however, was only a secondary one."[21]

As valid as many of Arnaud's critical points are, his account leaves many of the implicit assumptions of the old narrative unchallenged. For example, by arguing that it was Grand Bey and Cordier rather than 'Ali Mubarak who should be cred- ited for pioneering the design of a new street plan for the city, Arnaud makes an important correction to the record. But the question of what informed these attempts, regardless of who undertook them, remains unasked, let alone answered. Furthermore, while some of the public works that took place before 1867 are high- lighted, the centrality of Isma'il's visit to Paris is not effectively questioned, and consequently the Eurocentric implications of the "Paris-as-model" argument are left intact. Finally, while a challenge to the narrative presented in Mubarak's *Khitat* is long overdue, overlooking the Arabic documents housed in the Egyptian National Archives and stressing instead the French documents of Watha'iq 'Asr Isma'il can only produce a picture that privileges the role of foreign companies and private interests in shaping the city. The motivations that prompted Isma'il (and, it has to be stressed, previous governors of Egypt) to reform Cairo, and the princi- ples that guided them, can certainly be gleaned from the shape the city took and from an attempt to "read" the city, as it were, as the result of the logic of city plan- ners and engineers. But these motivations and principles are also more directly revealed in the copious correspondence, both in Arabic *and* French, of the many government agencies that together gave Cairo its modern shape.

In short, as welcome as Arnaud's critical take on the traditional narrative of Cairo's transformation is, a more complete account of the city's development in the nineteenth century, one based on the rich collection of the Egyptian National Archives, is still needed. As the following discussion will show, this involves the activities of many other government and municipal bodies. In addition to the Ministry of Public Works, these include the Streets Department, the Public Parks Department, and other less known government bodies such as the Engineering Unit (Qalam al-Handasa), the Quarantine Board (Jam'iyyat al-Korantina), and the City Planning Board (Jam'iyyat al-Tanzim). Furthermore, while it is important to identify who exactly was instrumental in shaping the form of modern Cairo, it is of no less importance to identify the logic that informed these efforts. So far the emphasis has been on aesthetic values and the desire by Khedive Isma'il and his officials to give a "modern" *look* to Cairo. But it is important also to question the supposed centrality of aesthetics, and ask if there were not other considerations in the minds of the city's planners.

Finally, any account of the development of Cairo in the nineteenth century will necessarily be incomplete if it fails to consider the manner in which its denizens reacted to and/or understood the rapid changes to their city, their neighborhoods, and, often enough, their own dwellings.

PRE-1867 MUNICIPAL PLANNING

Soon after his return from Paris, 'Ali Mubarak handed Isma'il an ambitious thirty-four-article plan to organize the street pattern and control the construction companies working in Cairo.[22] The aim was a thorough organization of the building activity within the city by dividing it into eight districts, starting with the core of the old city and ending with its most remote suburbs. The plan fell short of the minimum requirements for the city's development—namely, having "a sufficient budget and precise, intelligent [urban] legislation."[23] Nevertheless, it was hailed as a pioneering attempt to remedy Cairo's problems, given that it "at least identified the problem and, in so doing, suggested the beginning of a solution."[24]

Even though this plan was turned down by the khedive and was never implemented, it is revealing of the desire to overcome many of the administrative problems facing the city.[25] Among these were inadequate funds, an insufficient number of administrators, delay in adjudicating legal cases resulting from new city planning ordinances, and violations of Tanzim codes.[26] Drafted in 1868, the plan also gives credence to the argument that the Universal Exposition in Paris the previous year had "provided a model for the new city and stimulated the motivation for it."[27]

Nevertheless, it is an exaggeration to argue that this plan ushered in a new phase of state concern about street planning and construction activities in Cairo. Ample evidence exists that Egypt's rulers have always been concerned about the streets of Cairo, its buildings, and even its appearance. Raymond, for example, has shown that during the seventeenth century Ottoman governors paid considerable attention to cleaning rubbish mounds and clearing the Hakimi and Nasiri canals.[28] And Jabarti has mentioned the case of the early-eighteenth-century Ottoman governor of Egypt, Muhammad Pasha, who "ordered removing the awnings and [protruding] shops in order to widen the [public] roads and the markets. . . . He then ordered the leveling of the streets and removing earth . . . until the [buried] walls had been revealed."[29]

THE FIRST TANZIM COUNCIL, 1844

Earlier in the nineteenth century, contrary to Abu Lughod's claim that Pasha Muhammad 'Ali paid no attention to Cairo, there is compelling evidence that shows he supported ordinances aimed at improving his capital city. In late 1843/early 1844 a key institution was also founded to oversee the organization of the city. This was the famous Majlis Tanzim al-Mahrusa, or simply the Tanzim, which would later play a very significant role in such activities as street planning, issuing building and renovation permits, dealing with *waqfs*, and implementing and revising ordinances pertaining to public hygiene. Unlike the Majlis al-Urnatu, Alexandria's municipal council, established in 1834, the Tanzim has never been the subject of an independent study, even though it has often been referred to in secondary literature.[30] This may be due to the fact that it was never an independent council, but always part of a larger administrative body. Indeed, for its first twenty years it seems it was part of the Department of Education (Diwan al-Madaris).[31] Then in 1863 it fell under the jurisdiction of the Cairo Governorate (Muhafazat Misr), before finally becoming part of the Ministry of Public Works in 1866.

Despite its lack of financial and administrative independence, the Tanzim left a clear mark on Cairo not only after 1863, the year of Isma'il's ascension, but also during its first twenty years of existence.[32] As far as can be ascertained, the first decree related to this important municipal body was the inauguration decree issued in December 1843 by 'Abbas Pasha in his capacity as Governor of Cairo and addressed to the head of the Department of Education. In this decree, 'Abbas stipulated that the new council should take the Alexandria Urnatu council as a model, and should concern itself with beautifying Cairo and straightening its streets.[33] A short time later, the Tanzim council was formed and was presided over by Edhem Bey, head of the Department of Education. Its members included the Cairo Police Prefect (Ma'mur Zabtiyyat al-Mahrusa); Clot Bey, head of the Health Council; Hekeyan Bey, former head of the Engineering School; the Director of the Department of Public Buildings; Linant Afandi, the engineer in charge of al-Qanatir al-Khayriyya (the Nile Barrages); Mustafa Bahjat Afandi, head of the Engineering Unit within the Department of Education (Ra'is Qalam al-Handasa Bi Diwan al-Madaris); M. Duvigneau, member of the Health Council; and M. Lambert, head of the Engineering School.[34]

This council was to meet every Sunday morning to go through the many requests for building permits presented by the public.[35] One of its main criteria was to ensure that all new construction and renovation work would respect a straight street line. The Tanzim also frequently had to address the problem of *waqf* buildings, an issue it dealt with on a case-by-case basis.[36] Another duty of the council was to evaluate property that needed to be demolished in order to carve new streets.[37] Furthermore, the Tanzim was entrusted with a mammoth task of naming streets, numbering houses, and installing street signs.[38]

THE 1859 DECREE OF CAIRO STREET PLANNING

A number of decrees organizing Cairo's streets and aiming at easing the condition of its traffic predate 'Ali Mubarak's 1868 decree about building codes. The first of these was that issued by Majlis al-Khususi, the Privy Council, in 1859.[39] Its preamble mentions that an earlier draft had been prepared by Linant Bey, Chief Architect and head of the Architecture Unit (Sirr Muhandiss wa Nazir Qalm al-Handasa), the previous year which included many stipulations regarding organizing Cairo (Tanzim al-Mahrusa), widening its streets and alleyways, and easing its traffic.[40] That earlier draft, the preamble says, stipulated the payment of taxes on the city's carriages, on windows, and on protruding balconies. It also set pecuniary punishments in the form of fees for violations of building codes and traffic laws, and for obstructing free passage in streets and alleyways. However, when these stipulations were presented to the Ma'iyya (the khedive's cabinet), serious objections were raised to the idea of fines, and an alternative system of punishments was preferred (see below). As to the funds needed to compensate landlords for their confiscated property, the Ma'iyya suggested setting aside a fixed sum of 500 purses (*kisas*) to be spent annually for that purpose. Regarding other large city planning projects (such as opening new streets), no exact figure was set, but the Department of Interior (Diwan al-Dakhiliyya) was directed to prepare an estimate of the amount needed to buy property and complete construction of such projects. Once approved by the Ma'iyya, an order would be issued to the Finance Department (Diwan al-Maliyya) to release the monies needed.

With these general guidelines at hand, a committee composed of the directors of the departments of Awqaf, Interior, Finances, and Foreign Affairs was formed within the Privy Council and came up with a comprehensive decree of nine sections and a conclusion. This was eventually named the Decree of Street Planning (Qanun Tanzim al-Harat). In Section One it established a ten-member Tanzim committee (Mashurat al-Tanzim) headed by Linant Bey and including a chief architect (*mi'mar*), the Cairo police commissioner (*ma'mur al-zabtiyya*), a deputy of the Department of Health Inspection (*wakil mufattish al-sihha*), and an inspector of buildings (*mufattish al-tanzim*). This committee was entrusted mainly with the important task of widening and straightening existing streets, as well as planning new streets and *midans*. In Section Three the committee was authorized to use maps to be drawn by a special Cartography Unit (Firqat al-Rusumat) supervised by the committee, and to rely squarely on these maps in its street planning activities.

The Decree of Street Planning envisioned different types of streets with specific widths, and different regulations were to be applied on them. For example, it specified that all protrusions (*khargat*) needed to be elevated at least 4.5 meters above street level. For streets that were ten or eight meters wide, these *khargat* should not protrude more than one meter; for streets that were six meters wide, protrusions should not extend more than 0.75 of a meter; and for streets that were three or four meters wide, the protrusions should not extend more than 0.5 of a meter. Strict regulations were also set to prevent any obstruction of passage in the streets. Special attention was given to the rubble resulting from building and construction activities, and certain locations were specified as dumps for this rubble. Green grocers and fruit sellers were prevented from exhibiting their merchandise in the thoroughfares. And carpenters, barrel-makers (*barmilgiyya*), coppersmiths, marble cutters, "and every activity that may obstruct the main street" were prevented from obstructing traffic. Finally, an attempt was made to set speed limits for carriages on different kinds of streets, although these limits were necessarily imprecise (the decree refers to "medium speed" and "slow speed").

The decree also established an important "investigating unit" (*taftish al-tanzim*) which was headed by an "investigator" (*mufattish*), whose job was to check with a team of architects all buildings whose owners wanted to renovate, rebuild, or demolish them. He also had to pass through the streets to make sure that the different building codes and the Tanzim lines were strictly followed.

With regard to punishment, the decree ordered people who undertook construction activities beyond a street line to demolish these constructions if they had been undertaken without prior authorization by the Tanzim, and to do so at their own expense. Those who did not remove rubble resulting from construction activities were to be given a three-day grace period, after which they were to be punished by *ta'zir*—i.e., a *sharia*-stipulated corporal punishment varying according to the status of the person and his/her social standing.[41] The same punishment was stipulated for merchants of all kinds who did not remove their merchandise from public thoroughfares. Owners of coffeehouses were similarly punished if they put chairs and tables in the main street; however, they were given special dispensation during religious festivals (*mulids*), when pilgrims from rural areas swelled the city's population. In fact, *ta'zir* was the preferred punishment for most offenses, and, as already mentioned above, the decree was devoid of any pecuniary penalties.

Finally, the decree did not allow for compensation of property except after paying for its market value. This amount was to be established by experts chosen jointly by the landlord and the Tanzim. In the case of a landlord who wanted to build on a piece of land that he owned, he had to apply to the Tanzim for a building permit. If the latter decided to confiscate a portion of the land to comply with Tanzim lines, then no compensation would be paid if this area was less than one-fifth of the total land area. However, if it exceeded one-fifth, then the Tanzim would pay the market price of the area in excess of one-fifth of the area.

THE 1866 DECREE CONCERNING WAQF

Seven years after this important decree had been issued, another significant decree was passed dealing specifically with the question of whether the *sharia* allowed for the possibility of exchanging *waqf* domains.[42] Since it was commonly believed that once a building had been designated as *waqf* it could never be dealt with as private property again, and therefore could never be appropriated or confiscated for urban planning purposes, the decree referred to *waqf* "as one of the most important obstacles to urban development (*'umariyya*)." In an attempt to get around this issue, Isma'il wrote to the Privy Council, and the council, in turn, wrote to 'Ali Afandi al-Baqli, the *mufti* of Majlis al-Ahkam (the highest court in the land), for an opinion. In response, al-Baqli gave a detailed *fatwa* in which he argued that if the originator of the *waqf* (*al-waqif*) had specifically ruled out the possibility of exchange (*istibdal*), then the *waqf* could never be exchanged. However, if the *waqf* domain had fallen into ruin over the years and no longer yielded income for upkeep or for its beneficiaries, it could be exchanged for another more profitable domain, or even for cash (*yajuz istibdalahu . . . wa-law bi'l-darahim*). In case the domain in question was not completely ruined, al-Baqli added, then according to the great jurist Abu Hanifa (d. 767) and his disciple Muhammad ibn al-Hasan, it should not be exchanged. But according to Abu Hanifa's other disciple, Abu Yusuf (d. 798), exchange was still possible in case a different domain could be found which could yield a higher income (presumably in case of agricultural land), or which was better located (in case of urban property). Al-Baqli went on to cite other leading religious authorities including the late-eighteenth early-nineteenth-century Palestinian jurist al-Ramli and the Damascene scholar Ibn 'Abidin to give weight to his argument that it was indeed lawful to exchange *waqf* domains even for cash.

With this unambiguous opinion at hand, the Privy Council issued a recommendation to the khedive to allow for the exchange of *waqf* "as this will lead to urban development and the public good (*kamal al-'umariyya wa al-manfa'a al-'umumiyya*)."[43]

THE 1866 TANZIM ORDINANCE

A few months later, in October 1866, a new decree contained further regulations about street widths, traffic laws, and building codes, and set new penalties for those who contravened these measures. Like the previous two decrees, it was issued by the Privy Council and came in response to an explicit order by the khedive. An order by Isma'il to his interior minister shows that an earlier draft had been prepared by the Ministry of Public Works. Isma'il, however, remarked that the stipulations of that earlier draft about street widths were not satisfactory, as they could not guarantee "the free circulation of air, which is the main reason for good public hygiene," nor were they enough to ease traffic congestion. Isma'il also remarked that he had recently viewed a report about "enclosures" (*hishan*) within the city in which "riffraff" (*ri'a'*) were packed on top of one another. "Given how crowded these enclosures are," Isma'il said, "and given their filthy, squalid nature, these enclosures pose a grave danger to the health of their inhabitants and to people residing close by." He ended by suggesting that the enclosures be emptied of their inhabitants, and that these people be moved to specially constructed buildings in each quarter, even if this entailed considerable expense.[44]

On receiving this order from the khedive, the Privy Council set up a committee composed of the Deputy of the Ministry of Public Works (Wakil Diwan Ashghal 'Umumiyya), the Chief Architect (Mi'mar wa Nazir Qalm al-Tanzim), the Deputy of the Architecture Authority (Wakil Qalm Handasa), the Chief Health Inspector of Cairo (Mufattish al-Sihha), the Chief Investigator of the Tanzim (Mufattish al-Tanzim), and the Buildings Supervisor (Ma'mur Kashf al-Amakin). The committee came up with a Tanzim Ordinance (La'ihat al-Tanzim) composed of six sections. Unlike the 1859 decree, which it effectively replaced, the 1866 decree was not only concerned with Cairo, but also set out to establish Tanzim councils in Alexandria and in other towns and cities (mudun wa banadir).[45]

One of the clear features of this decree was the importance given to maps. Section Two stipulated that general maps be made for each city to the scale of 1:1,000, which were to be used by the Tanzim councils of each city to demarcate the lines of new streets and midans, as well as the lines of old streets. Realizing that this process would necessarily take considerable time, the decree directed that "in order that the tasks of the Tanzim not be delayed until the completion of these maps, whenever a landlord requests to demolish or build his property overlooking public streets, the chief architect of the Tanzim has to draw a detailed map to the scale of 1:500 of the property in question extending to fifty meters on either side of the said building."[46] Like the 1859 decree, this one set down various widths for different kinds of street. And it argued that every effort should be made to straighten old streets and to make new streets absolutely straight. Old buildings "such as mosques, synagogues (hayakil), water fountains (sabils), and graveyards (maqabir) . . . were not to be demolished."[47] And, as in the previous decree, confiscated property should be paid for by the government if its size exceeded one-fifth of the original plot. One major deviation from the previous decree was the punishment system: the decree contains no mention of ta'zir, and, instead, a system of fines and administrative penalties are specified.

'UMARIYYA, SHARI'A, AND PUBLIC HYGIENE

While the above-mentioned decrees in no way represent an exhaustive list of laws and ordinances which were concerned with Cairo during the khedival period, they do help highlight a number of challenges to the traditional narrative of how Cairo was modernized.[48] The first is that the concern about the city and its development predated Isma'il's much-celebrated visit to Paris in 1867. As this small sample of city planning decrees shows, Egypt's rulers from the time of Muhammad 'Ali onward, and the countless officials and bureaucrats who worked for them, were acutely concerned about al-Mahrusa, i.e., the "Protected City"—the name by which Cairo was then known. And as explained further below, from as early as the 1830s decrees were issued to improve the status of the city's public health, security, markets, streets, and buildings. Therefore, it makes little sense to bemoan the fact that Cairo has always lacked an independent municipal body which would allow it to control its own destiny rather than be at the mercy of Egypt's rulers.[49] To do so is to concentrate on what André Raymond has called the Orientalist description of a "non-city," a city which is seen only as lacking in what is believed to have allowed Western European cities to develop—namely, the regularity and institutions of the cities of antiquity and the charts and communes of the medieval towns.[50] Such views (of which Gabriel Baer is an excellent representative[51]) overlook the significant effort of numerous administrative bodies established to improve the city's public hygiene, security, and economic development.

However, there are further problems with the "Paris-as-model-for-Cairo's-development" argument. As argued elsewhere, any critique of Eurocentrism that is satisfied with proving that the "East" beat the "West" in some of the latter's achievements ends up reiterating the same features of Eurocentrism it sets out to dispute.[52] Rather, the challenge is to decipher each city's unique, differentiating features. With regard to how Cairo was modernized, therefore, the task should not simply be to prove there were some planning measures undertaken by the khedives before 1867, but to uncover what motivated them to take these steps, and explain how these motivations might have been different from subsequent ones.[53] In other words, while the above-described city planning decrees dating from the late 1850s and early 1860s show a concern about straight lines and exhibit a clear understanding of the intricate connection between cartography and urban design, concerns that would assume paramount importance under 'Ali Mubarak and Grand Bey in the late 1860s and early 1870s, it would be erroneous to assume that they simply prefigured these.

So what did inform these concerns about city planning before Isma'il and his energetic Public Works minister visited Paris in 1867? Without ruling out aesthetic considerations altogether, it seems one major concern was urban growth and expansion. Evidence of this concern exists in the ubiquitous official use of the term 'umaríyya—which can be translated, at once, as "construction," "urban development," "urbanity," and even "civilization." The preamble of the April 1866 decree concerning waqf, for example, mentions that "since the khedival thoughts have always been directed to whatever would bring 'umaríyya and enhance it. . . ."[54] And the October 1866 decree states that "demolition permits are being given to tear down walls overlooking the public thoroughfares with the pretext of renovating property and therefore [these permits should be stopped as they] make it difficult to set streets straight and therefore prevent the enhancement of 'umaríyya."[55] Furthermore, a later decree issued by the Privy Council, approving a recommendation of the Legislative Assembly (Majlis Shura al-Nuwwab), states that "one of the prime objectives of the khedive is . . . the enhancement of progress (taqaddum) and 'umaríyya."[56]

Besides the obvious meaning of growth and expansion, *'umaríyya* also denotes productivity. As Timothy Mitchell has explained at great length, productivity and abhorrence of waste were concepts that were becoming increasingly important to Egyptian officials in the khedival period.[57] And we find them shaping much government policy, not only in regard to urban planning, but also in agriculture, education, the military, and in numerous other aspects of social life.[58] But in addition to these "modern" connotations of the term, it is clear that *'umaríyya* has strong echoes of Ibn Khaldun's famous term *'umran*, and it would not be farfetched to argue that it was directly influenced by it.[59] In fact, beneath the veneer of "modernity" connoted by the term may lie many concerns that have preoccupied Muslim thinkers in the field of city planning and urban growth from Ibn Khaldun's time and even earlier.

Moreover, the different city planning decrees and regulations passed in the nineteenth century paid close attention to *sharía* principles as elaborated in classical books of jurisprudence (*fiqh*). There are many examples in the decrees mentioned above that testify to the importance that town planners gave to *sharía*. I have already mentioned the extreme care given to finding a *sharía*-based solution to *waqf* domains seen as an obstacle to *'umaríyya*. Rather than declaring *waqf* an obsolete system not conducive to "modern" urban planning, nineteenth-century town planners and administrators in Egypt must have seen how it allowed Islamic cities to develop and grow over centuries. Hence, rather than dispensing with *waqf* altogether, they were keen to find a solution to the problem of unproductive, ruined *waqf* domains—a solution they eventually found in the notion of *istibdal*.

The stipulation that violations to building codes and traffic regulations should be punished by *ta'zir* rather than by a system of fines is another example of how *sharía*-based principles were not seen as inherently contradictory to the goals of "modern" city planning. A further example is contained in a stipulation in the 1859 decree that a religious scholar, Shaykh Isma'il al-Halabi of Majlis al-Ahkam, be included as a member of the Tanzim committee.[60] Lastly, that same decree of 1859 referred explicitly in Section Four, Article Fifteen, to the *sharía* when it said that only *sharía*, rather than the Tanzim, was competent to consider disputes arising from breach of privacy resulting from someone opening a window onto his neighbor's.[61]

It is common to argue that *sharía* was increasingly marginalized in nineteenth-century Egypt (and in the Ottoman Empire at large), and that it was losing ground to secular law in the fields of state organization and legislation. As in the process commonly referred to as "legal reform," which saw *sharía* as "a religious law largely inappropriate for a modern society," *sharía* is also seen as increasingly irrelevant to city planning and urban reform.[62] However, the many ordinances pertaining to city planning and the copious government correspondence related to it from the 1830s to the late 1870s clearly illustrate how *sharía* was not only upheld, but that it informed many city planning policies.

PUBLIC HYGIENE AND CITY PLANNING

Besides being informed by the concept of *'umariyya* and the principles of *sharīa*, many of the decrees, laws, and ordinances governing Cairo in the nineteenth century were also informed by a desire (one might even call it an obsession) to raise the level of public health. In fact, it can be argued that concern for public hygiene was the most important factor influencing urban planning, and that fears about epidemics and the measures taken to combat disease and improve public hygiene were far more significant than the aesthetic concerns implied in the "Paris-as-model" argument.

During Muhammad ʾAli's reign, and again contrary to Abu Lughod's arguments, there is compelling evidence that Cairo was subject to many ordinances aimed at improving public hygiene. In 1830, for example, the Superintendent of Cairo's Public Works (Maʾmur Ashghal al-Mahrusa) was ordered by the Department of Civil Affairs (Diwan Khidiwi) to implement a new ordinance aimed at improving health conditions in the city. "Due to the state of public safety that Cairo currently enjoys," the ordinance said, "its streets and alleyways should also be included by cleanliness and purity, as this will undoubtedly have its impact on the city's general appearance and its public hygiene. Accordingly, the residents will have to be ordered by *mashayikh al-athman* (heads of quarters) each to sweep and sprinkle with water the area in front of his house. Sentries will go on regular rounds to check on the cleanliness [of the city] and to punish the recalcitrant with light beating."[63]

Five years later a more detailed decree observed that in spite of the existence of latrines (*murtafaqat*) in the city's many mosques and *zawiyas*, rural migrants, as well as the poor and the blind of the city, were in the habit of easing nature in the streets.[64] "Since these nasty deeds," the ordinance went on to say,

> contribute to increasing stench and the emission of various miasmas, causing harm to the dwellers of the city, and since it has also been noticed that the dwellers of houses overlooking the Khalig are flushing their toilets in it, . . . it was decided to appoint a special police officer who will head a force of six soldiers and will pass regularly on the streets and alleyways of the city to make sure that they remain clean. On spotting anyone easing nature in the public way [he will be severely punished] and on catching anyone dumping rubbish either in the Khalig or on the streets he will have the door of his house nailed for three days.[65]

The ordinance added that seven years previously, the main road leading to Bulaq, which was flanked by fields, had become surrounded by rubbish as a result of people dumping their garbage there. A special police force composed of soldiers, each with a monthly salary of thirty piasters, was to be formed to stop this practice. It added that the protruding *mastabas* of shopkeepers had to be removed completely, as they were obstructing traffic. Finally, the ordinance called for engineers to make

sure that the water of the Khalig, the main waterway bisecting the city, ran smooth-
ly and continuously and did not stagnate. In order to undertake these tasks and to
implement them "to the letter" (*harf bi-harf*), a special council (*jam'iyyat mashura*) was
to be composed of the following officials: the Superintendent of Cairo's Public
Works (Ma'mur Ashghal al-Mahrusa); the heads of the districts (*nuzzar al-arbu'*); 'Ali
Agha, Cairo's Police Prefect; and Rashid Afandi, the head of the Department of
Public Buildings within the Civil Affairs Department (Nazir al-Abniyya al-Miriyya
Bi-L-Diwan al-Khidiwi).

As a further sign of the importance of sanitation to city planning matters,
Clot Bey, the head of the Health Council, was a regular member of the Tanzim
council, and when he did not show up for a number of subsequent meetings, he
was sent a stern letter by the head of the council requesting his attendance. In
response, he wrote back in a characteristic sardonic language:

> I have received your letter in which you request my presence next Tuesday,[66] . . . and
> that I had been missing a number of meetings. . . . It is therefore necessary to
> remind Your Excellency that the reason that I am counted among the members of
> the Tanzim Council [in the first place] is because of [my expertise in] health mat-
> ters. I have been attending several meetings in which we discussed matters pertain-
> ing to public hygiene such as removing tanneries, drying up lakes, and finding a way
> to make sure that the water of the Khalig flows regularly. . . . However, none of
> these matters has been resolved. So if there is some vital matter that requires my
> presence, then I will obediently be there. But to the best of my knowledge there
> are no public health matters more important than those that I have just men-
> tioned. And since we have already discussed these matters and our decisions have
> not been implemented, [there is no need for my presence], and if you request my
> presence to discuss such matters as straightening streets or organizing (*tanzim*)
> some shops, then this could be done by the engineers, as this is their specialty.[67]

In his capacity as member of the Tanzim council, and notwithstanding his sardonic language, Clot Bey would regularly suggest measures to improve public
hygiene, as when he proposed that all buildings in Cairo should be whitewashed "to
prevent stench and dirtiness" (*al-'ufuna wa-l-qadhurat*).[68] Other government bodies
concerned with sanitation were also vocal about city planning measures that had a
bearing on public hygiene. In 1845, for example, the Quarantine Board (Majlis al-
Kurantina) suggested that strict measures be implemented to clean the city's
cesspools. They stressed that the carriages that carry the city's solid waste should
be covered with tight lids, or that the clearing operation be done at night, when few
people would be in the streets, to minimize the danger of inhaling the dangerous
fumes. Once carried outside the city, the waste should be buried in holes specially
dug for that purpose.[69] During 'Abbas's reign, and contrary to traditional accounts,

Cairo's health conditions continued to receive official attention. In 1852, for example, a decree was issued by his deputy to the Cairo police ordering them to make sure that people stop watering the streets in winter. It said that:

> the streets and alleyways of Cairo are damp as it is now winter, but they are [still] being constantly sprinkled with water so much so that they have become dangerously slippery for pedestrians. This is [partly] the result of people throwing dirty water from their window. . . . And since all this causes stench (*'ufuna*) and harm as the winter sun is not strong enough to dry the soil . . . you have to issue your orders to stop people from watering the streets or throwing water [from windows]. Streets should only be swept and brushed. Only open areas which has a lot of dust that could not be settled except by watering it could be sprinkled with water according to the law as they are exposed to the sun.[70]

In 1859, during Sa'id's reign, another order was issued obligating those making renovations to their houses not to dump the rubble resulting from such operations in the streets, "since it has been noticed that doing so over the years has resulted in elevating the street level in relation to the ground floors of many buildings, which, in turn, has caused serious medical hazards to dwellers of these floors."[71]

These decrees and orders pertaining to public hygiene may strike the modern reader as somewhat quaint and even ridiculous. However, this distrust of water, humidity, and dampness, and this strong penchant for open spaces exposed to sunshine, belong to what was believed to be a scientific medical view and a compact theory of disease etiology. According to this theory, prevalent in the Qasr al-'Aini Medical School throughout much of the nineteenth century, disease was thought to be spread by inhaling "thick airs" or "miasmas" emanating from decomposing bodies. This quaint medical theory informed many public health measures taken in the nineteenth century. In particular, it prompted the authorities to pay attention to cesspools, slaughterhouses, cemeteries, marshes, and stagnant waters. These were all sources of putrid air which had been released from decomposing bodies, and which could spread disease if inhaled by, or absorbed by the skin of, healthy bodies.

Strongly adhering to this miasmatic theory, Cairo's health officials also advised city planners of the need to undertake numerous measures that would alter the shape of Cairo forever. Chief among these was the drying up of Azbakiyya Lake in 1848.[72] This was followed by the drying up of all other lakes which had dotted the Cairene landscape, and which had shaped the daily life of its inhabitants for centuries.[73] Of no less significance as far as Cairo's streets were concerned was the drying up of the Khalig, the main waterway bisecting the city from south to north, which, like the lakes, had long been part of Cairo's social life.[74] Of equal significance was the decision to prevent intra-mural burials and to move cemeteries beyond the city limits. Chief among these cemeteries was the Sayyida Nafisa, which stopped receiving bodies for burial in the 1870s, and which was replaced by the Imamein Cemetery south of the Aqueduct.[75]

SUBALTERN REACTION

As should be clear by now, public hygiene was a prime concern of Cairo's city planners throughout much of the nineteenth century. The concern about disease and the desire to raise the health standards in the city (as well as in the country in general) prompted them to alter the very shape of the city. These policies also affected the daily life of Cairenes, who found their neighborhoods, streets, and houses—and even their bodies—touched in unprecedented ways. New building codes, city planning ordinances, and numerous public health measures all made it increasingly difficult for Cairenes to exist beyond the reach of the khedival state.

So how did the residents of the city react to these new ordinances? Undoubtedly, and as illustrated by Fadl Wasi''s story, with which this chapter opened, there were many residents who were either oblivious to these new measures, or who preferred to ignore them. For example, the Egyptian National Archives report the case of someone called Mikha'il Kassab, who had a house overlooking Azbakiyya Lake in which he had been doing some construction work, leaving the resulting rubble outside so that it obstructed the street. He was repeatedly warned by the Cairo police commissioner to remove the rubble. Eventually, however, the Tanzim unit within the Department of Education wrote the Department of Civil Affairs requesting immediate action, as "this is a main street—and as thick airs may rise from this dust [that has been piling outside the house] causing harm to the residents of the area."[76] When Kassab still did not comply, he was ordered to pay twice the cost of removing the rubble.[77]

However, given the pervasiveness of the new urban planning and public hygiene measures, it would be safe to argue that they were becoming more and more difficult to evade altogether. So how were these unprecedented policies resisted and/or accommodated by the city's residents, especially the subaltern classes? Fortunately, the National Archives contains copies of petitions that Cairenes themselves presented occasionally to complain of particular decisions they thought unjust. At other times, such petitions could serve as a way to comply with the new regulations. In both types of cases, these petitions constitute a valuable source from which to gauge the public's reaction to the authorities' moves to alter the shape of their city.

One example of the second type of petition (i.e., those that represented people complying with regulations) was the case of Mustafa Agha, the *odabasi* of the school of Muhammad 'Ali's children, who presented a petition (*ardhal*) to build a house in the district of Qaysun, and who had to present the blueprint of the house with his petition to be reviewed and approved by the Tanzim engineers.[78]   In another case a certain Mustafa al-Gindi presented a petition pointing out that the wall separating his house from that of his neighbor, Shiha al-'Allaf, was unsteady, and requested that it be checked by the Tanzim.[79]

An example of the first type of petition—those complaining of particular administrative decisions and requesting amendments or annulments—is the interesting case of two brothers, Mahmud and Mustafa, who had a house in Harat al-Rum.   In their petition they insinuated that their neighbor, Hasan Bey al-Barudi, was bribing Tanzim officials to declare that their house was unsteady so he could enlarge his property and so drive his carriage all the way up to his house. They specifically complained of an earlier demolition order issued by the Cairo police (al-zabtiyya): "this in spite of the fact that our house is safe and sound. And since the khedival justice," they added, ". . . does not allow this assault and calls for equality among the subjects, we have dared to present this petition requesting a re-investigation of our case by unbiased people as His Excellency 'Ali Basha Mubarak, given that he is among the greatest architects (min akabir al-muhandesin), His Excellency 'Umar Bey [Lutfi], the Governor [of Cairo], [and] Linant Bey, Ma'mir Diwan al-Ashghal. . . ."[80] Their articulate petition notwithstanding, they did not manage to convince the authorities of the validity of their claim.

Complaints about the moving of cemeteries provided a further good example of the reaction to public hygiene measures that had a direct bearing on city planning. Cairo's inhabitants in the nineteenth century do not seem to have shared with the medical authorities the belief that cemeteries posed a grave danger to the living. The records of the Cairo Governorate contain many petitions from people requesting that they not be separated from their dead, and asking for an exemption from the general rule banning intra-mural burials.[81] For example, when it was declared that the Sayyida Nafisa Cemetery would be relocated outside the city, several residents living nearby presented petitions asking for the continued use of the cemetery in its present location.[82] The petitions were turned down.[83]

In short, the numerous petitions that Cairenes presented to complain of, or comply with, the new city planning and public hygiene measures show their acute awareness of the importance of these new activities of the khedival state. And, as might be expected, even though these new state policies might originally have been intended to bring tighter control and monitoring of the population, once they were put in place, they were used by subaltern classes (and others) to promote their own interests. Naturally, these new sites of power were not equally accessible to everyone, and, as exemplified by the case of the two brothers mentioned above, there were some who managed to manipulate them better than others. Nevertheless, it remains true that people used these same institutions to resist and challenge the new ordinances and policies, which they saw as affecting their lives. In other words, these new sites of power were simultaneously sites of resistance.

CONCLUSION

Historians of modern Cairo have traditionally privileged sight over smell. By highlighting Khedive Isma'il's trip to Paris to attend the Universal Exposition of 1867, and by stressing the subsequent activities undertaken by his energetic public works minister, 'Ali Mubarak, to transform Cairo into a "Paris along the Nile," they have overlooked the numerous measures that previous rulers and their city planners had taken to reform Cairo and to attend to its many needs. Fascinated by the glamour of the Exposition itself, by Baron Hausmann's revolutionary urban planning policies, and by the likely impact these spectacular Parisian achievements had on Cairo, many observers have ignored the significant role played by smell in shaping modern Cairo.

By stressing the impact that the anxiety about epidemics and disease had on shaping public hygiene policies, I have tried to challenge the elitist and Eurocentric assumptions inherent in this dominant "Paris-as-model" argument. Smell, I argue, was central to shaping these public hygiene policies, for before the discovery of germs and microbes at the end of the nineteenth century, the Egyptian medical establishment adhered to a theory of disease etiology which was suspicious of miasmas and "thick airs." At the same time, the concern about public hygiene was fundamental in shaping city planning policies. The subsequent evolution in the Cairene landscape was much more influenced by prevalent medical theories (which took the olfactory sense seriously), than by aesthetic sensibilities that were visually impressed by what went on in the French capital.

NOTES

1. Dar al-Watha'iq al-Qawmiyya, (The Egyptian National Archives), hereafter DWQ Zabtiyyat Misr (Cairo Police), Register L (Lam) 2/6/4 (old No. 2032), case No. 597, pp. 45–47, 21 Jumada I 1295 May 27, 1878. In this and similar cases the police would not convict the defenders; they would either charge them with a given offence or set them free, leaving for a higher legal authority, Majlis Misr, the task of convicting and sentencing them.

2. J. Marlowe, *Spoiling the Egyptians* (London: Andre Deutsch, 1974), p. 108.

3. See L. Kuhnke, *Lives at Risk: Public Health in Nineteenth-Century Egypt* (Cairo: American University in Cairo Press, 1990). See also K. Fahmy, "An Olfactory Tale of Two Cities: Cairo in the Nineteenth Century," in J. Edwards, ed., *Historians in Cairo: Essays in Honor of George Scanlon* (Cairo: American University in Cairo Press, 2002), pp. 155–87.

4. There have been may attempts to challenge this Eurocentric account, the most recent of which is, N. Hanna, *In Praise of Books: A Cultural History of Cairo's Middle Class, Sixteenth to the Eighteenth Century* (Syracuse, N.Y.: Syracuse University Press, 2003). See my critique of these attempts in "Hina kanat Misr tabhath 'an al-hadatha" ("When Egypt Was

Searching for Modernity"), *al-Kutub: Wijhat Nazar*, Vol. 6, No. 64, May 2004, pp. 64–67.

5. J. Abu Lughod, *Cairo: 1001 Years of the City Victorious* (Princeton: Princeton University Press, 1971), pp. 84–85. See also A. Raymond, *Égyptiens et Français au Caire, 1798–1801* (Cairo: Institut Français d'Archéologie Orientale, 1998), pp. 314–15.

6. Abu Lughod, *Cairo*, p. 87.

7. For a good analysis of the origins of 'Abbas's bad image, see E. Toledano, *State and Society in Mid-Nineteenth-Century Egypt* (Cambridge: Cambridge University Press, 1990), pp. 108–34. Strictly speaking, 'Abbas was the successor of his uncle, Ibrahim Pasha, and not his grandfather, Muhammad 'Ali. But given that Ibrahim ruled only for a few months, during which Cairo witnessed very little change, one can say that 'Abbas in effect succeeded his grandfather and not his uncle.

8. Abu Lughod, *Cairo*, pp. 99–100. On Abbasiyya, see N. Tamraz, *Nineteenth-Century Cairene Houses and Palaces* (Cairo: American University in Cairo Press, 1998), p. 48; 'Ali Mubarak, *al-Khitat al-Tawfiqiyya al-Jadida* (Bulaq, 1305 AH), Vol. 9, p. 23; H. al-Din Isma'il, *Madinat al-Qahira min Wilayat Muhammad 'Ali ila Isma'il (The City of Cairo from Mehmed Ali's Rule until Isma'il, 1805–1879)* (Cairo: Dar al-Afaq al-'Arabiyya, 1997), p. 205.

9. This is not the place to discuss the two-city model, which is often used to describe how Cairo evolved in the second half of the nineteenth century. For such a discussion, see Fahmy, "An Olfactory Tale."

10. Z. Celik, *Displaying the Orient: Architecture of Islam at Nineteenth-Century World's Fairs* (Berkeley: University of California Press, 1992).

11. Due to diplomatic problems with Istanbul, however, the opening ceremony was delayed for another year, giving the Khedive Isma'il the much-needed time to reform his capital city.

12. See his autobiography in *al-Khitat*, Vol. 9, pp. 37–61. For a lucid English-language summary of his character and life, see R. Hunter, *Egypt Under the Khedives: From Household Government to Modern Bureaucracy* (Pittsburgh: University of Pittsburgh Press, 1984), pp. 123–38. See also M. Reimer, "Contradiction and Consciousness in Ali Mubarak's description of al-Azhar," *International Journal of Middle East Studies*, Vol. 29 (1997), pp. 53–69.

13. 'Ali Mubarak, *al-Khitat*, Vol. 9, p. 49.

14. Celik, *Displaying the Orient*.

15. A. Raymond, *Cairo*, trans. Willard Wood (Cambridge, MA: Harvard University Press, 2000), pp. 276–79.

16. About the statues of Soliman Pasha and Mehmed Lazoughlu, see DWQ, Mahfuzat Majlis al-Wuzara', Nizarat al-Ashghal, Carton 4/4, folder No. 171 Ashghal, memorandum dated April 9, 1893. About the statue of Mustafa Kamil, see DWQ, Majlis al-Wuzara', Nizarat al-Ashghal, Carton 4/4, folder No. 471, memoranda dated November 8, 1908, November 10, 1908, and January 17, 1914.

17. On how accurate the *Khitat* is as a source of Egyptian history, see Gabriel Baer, "Ali Mubarak's *Khitat* as a Source for the History of Modern Egypt," in P.M. Holt, ed., *Political and Social Change in Modern Egypt* (London: Oxford University Press, 1968), pp. 13–27.

18. See, for example, A. 'Abdu 'Ali, *al-Qahira fi 'Ahd Isma'il (Cairo During Isma'il's Reign)*

(Cairo: al-Dar al-Misriyya al-Lubnaniyya, 1997); Isma'il, *Madinat al-Qahira*.

19. J. Arnaud, *Le Caire, mise en place d'une ville moderne, 1867–1907: Des intérêts du prince aux sociétés privées* (Aix-en-Provence: Actes Sud, 1998).

20. Arnaud, *Le Caire*, p. 365, n. 6.

21. Arnaud, *Le Caire*, p. 82.

22. DWQ, Majlis al-Wuzara'(Council of Ministers), Nizarat al-Ashghal (Ministry of Public Works), carton 1/5 titled "Lawa'ih wa qawanin khassa bi-l-ashghal," folder No. 17 titled "Qanun ta'ifat al-mi'mar." The plan was reproduced in facsimile in G. Alleaume, "Politique urbaines et contrôle de l'entreprise: Une loi inédite de 'Ali Mubarak sur les corporations du bâtiment," *Annales Islamologiques*, Vol. 21 (1985), pp. 147–88.

23. M. Clerget, *Le Caire: Etude de géographie urbaine et d'histoire économique* (Cairo: Schindler, 1934), Vol. 1, p. 256.

24. Alleaume, "Politique urbaines," p. 149.

25. Arnaud, *Le Caire*, p. 82.

26. Alleaume, "Politique urbaines et contrôle de l'entreprise," pp. 148–49.

27. Abu-Lughod, *Cairo*, p. 104.

28. Raymond, *Cairo*, pp. 227–28. But see also pp. 243ff., where he notes the problems ensuing from the lack of a centralized authority in charge of Cairo.

29. A. al-Rahman al-Jabarti, *'Aja'ib al-Athar fi-l-Tarajim wa-l-Akhbar* (Cairo: Dar al-Kutub, 1997), Vol. 1, p. 56 (events of AH 1106/August 1694–August 1695).

30. On the Alexandria Urnatu council, see M. Reimer, "Reorganizing Alexandria: The Origins and Development of the *Conseil de l'Ornato*," *Journal of Urban History*, Vol. 19, No. 3 (May 1993), pp. 55–83; G. Baer, "The Beginnings of Municipal Government in Egypt," *Middle Eastern Studies*, Vol. 4, No. 2 (January 1968), pp. 118–40; and H. Ahmad Shalabi, *al-Hukm al-Mahalli wa al-Majalis al-Baladiyya fi Misr Mundhu Insha'iha Hatta 'Amm 1918 (Local Government and Municipal Councils in Egypt Since Their Establishment Until 1918)* (Cairo: 'Alam al-Kutub, 1987), pp. 15–33. On the Tanzim, see Abu Lughod, *Cairo*, pp. 96, 147–49; and Arnaud, *Le Caire*, p. 98.

31. It is probably this unlikely location of the documents of the Tanzim from its early years that has confused previous researchers.

32. The following is only a brief account of the early history of this important council. A proper study of the activities and accomplishments of the Tanzim Council in the pre-Isma'il period requires a careful reading of the registers of Diwan al-Madaris, the Department of Education, and later, the registers of Diwan al-Ashghal, the Department of Public Works.

33. DWQ, Diwan Madaris (Department of Education), Register No. 2091, p. 14, correspondence dated 8 Dhu al-Hijja 1259/December 30, 1843.

34. DWQ, Ma'iyya Saniyya (Cabinet of the Khedive), Turki, Regsiter No. 376, February 1844; quoted in Shalabi, *al-Hukm*, p. 35.

35. DWQ, Diwan Madaris, Sadir (outgoing), Register M (Mim)/1/6 (old No. 6), correspondence No. 90, p. 3018, dated 28 Sah'ban 1261/September 1, 1845.

36. DWQ, Diwan Khidiwi (Department of Civil Affairs), Register S (Sin) 2/1/2 (old No. 506), correspondence No. 410, p. 48, dated 9 Jumada II 1261/June 15, 1845. See below for how this matter was eventually settled in subsequent legislation.

37. DWQ, Diwan Madaris, Sadir (outgoing), Register M (Mim) 1/6 (old No. 6), petition with no No., p. 2963, dated 22 Sha'ban 1261/August 26, 1845.

38. Order of Majlis Tanzim al-Mahrusa published in *al-Waqa'i' al-Misriyya*, issue No. 83, dated 29 Rajab 1263/July 13, 1847. The fifty-article order is reproduced in A. Sami, *Taqwim al-Nil* (Cairo: Dar al-Kutub, 1928), Vol. 2, pp. 547–52, and in Hasan 'Abd al-Wahhab, "Takhtit al-Qahira wa tanzimuha mundhu nash'atiha," (Planning and Organizing Cairo since its foundation) *Bulletin de L'Institut D'Égypte*, Vol. 37 (1955–1956), pp. 23–31. Abu Lughod is skeptical if this order was ever implemented, arguing that it does "not seem to have been followed very enthusiastically, if at all": *Cairo*, p. 96, n.42. However, 'Abd al-Wahhab says that he actually saw some of the street signs written in the same ink color stipulated in the order and installed on buildings that predate Muhammad 'Ali's reign, proving that they must have been hung there in implementation of this decree: "Takhtit al-Qahira," pp. 32–33.

39. DWQ, Majlis al-Khususi, Register S (Sin) 11/8/2 (old No. 1960), decree No. 40, pp. 38–48, dated 2 Jumada I 1276/November 27, 1859. On the Privy Council, see Hunter, *Egypt Under the Khedives*, pp. 49–50.

40. DWQ, Diwan Madaris, Register M (Mim) 1/1/3 (old No. 3), correspondence without No., p. 827, dated 6 Muharram 1261/January 15, 1845.

41. On the issue of *ta'zir* in nineteenth-century Egyptian criminal law, see K. Fahmy, "Justice, Law and Pain in Khedival Egypt," in B. Dupret, ed., *Law and the Person in the Modern Middle East* (London: I.B. Tauris, 2004), pp. 85–116.

42. DWQ, Majlis Khususi, Register S (Sin) 11/8/8 (old No. 71), decree No. 56, pp. 55–56, dated 4 Dhu al-Hijja 1282/April 20, 1866.

43. Ibid.

44. DWQ, Diwan Khidiwi, Awamir, carton No. 2, document dated 5 Rabi' II 1282/August 28, 1865.

45. DWQ, Majlis Khususi, Register S (Sin) 11/8/10 (old No. 73), order No. 6, pp. 9–16, dated 27 Jumada I 1283/October 7, 1866.

46. Ibid.

47. See, to the same effect, DWQ, Majlis al-Khususi, Register S (Sin) 11/8/14 (old No. 76), order No. 90, p. 97, dated 15 Rabi' II 1287/July 15, 1870, where it is explicitly stated that "the Khedival wishes are against the demolition of old monuments especially . . . shrine(s)."

48. While the title "khedive" was not officially granted by the Ottoman Sultan to Egypt's rulers until 1865, it was commonly used inside Egypt much before that year. By "khedival period," I mean the period extending from Muhammad 'Ali's ascension in 1805 to Isma'il's deposition in 1879.

49. This is, of course, a variation on the larger theme of the "Islamic city." See, I.

Lapidus, *Muslim Cities in the Later Middle Ages* (Cambridge, MA: Harvard University Press, 1967); A. Hourani, "The Islamic City in the Light of Recent Research," in A. Hourani and S. Stern, eds., *The Islamic City* (Oxford: Bruno Cassirer, 1970), pp. 9–24; and J. Abu Lughod, "The Islamic City," *International Journal of Middle East Studies*, Vol. 19 (1987), pp. 155–76.

50. André Raymond, "Islamic City, Arab City: Orientalist Myths and Recent Views," *BRISMES Bulletin*, Vol. 21, (1994), pp. 3–18.

51. Baer, "The Beginnings of Municipal Government."

52. Fahmy, "Hina kanat Misr tabhath 'an al-hadatha," (n. 4).

53. This is what Arnaud seems to be arguing. For another example, see 'Abd al-Wahhab, "Takhtit al-Qahira," pp. 17–18.

54. See note 42 above.

55. See note 44 above.

56. DWQ, Diwan al-Khususi, Register S (Sin) 11/8/14 (old No. 76), Decree No. 61, dated 12 Muharram 1287/April 14, 1870, pp. 66–69, commenting on an earlier decree by the Legislative Council dated 24 Dhu al-Qa'da 1285/March 8, 1869.

57. T. Mitchell, *Colonising Egypt* (Berkeley: University of California Press, 1990).

58. For an example of how these principles, productivity and abhorrence of waste, might have been influential in shaping the criminal justice system and specifically in affecting the shift from lashing to imprisonment, see Fahmy, "Justice, Law and Pain," p. 106.

59. It is noteworthy that Ibn Khaldun's *Muqaddimah* was published by Bulaq Press in the nineteenth century and was one of the books sent to be exhibited in the 1867 Paris Exposition. See A. Radwan, *Tarikh Matba'at Bulaq (History of the Bulaq Press)*, (Cairo: al-Matb'a al-Amiriyya, 1953), p. 204.

60. DWQ, Majlis al-Khususi, Register S (Sin) 11/8/2 (old No. 1960), decree No. 40, dated 2 Jumada I 1276/November 27, 1859, p. 48.

61. Ibid., p. 40. See, in this matter, K. 'Azab, *Takhtit wa 'Imarat al-Mudun al-Islamiyya* (Dawha: Wizarat al-Awqaf wal al-Shu'un al-Islamiyya, 1997), pp. 84–86.

62. T. Asad, *Formations of the Secular: Christianity, Islam, Modernity* (Stanford: Stanford University Press, 2003), p. 208. For a challenge to this view see K. Fahmy, "The Anatomy of Justice: Forensic Medicine and Criminal Law in Nineteenth-Century Egypt," *Islamic Law and Society*, 6 (1999), pp. 224–271; and Fahmy, "Justice, Law and Pain," pp. 91ff.

63. DWQ, Diwan Khidiwi, Turki, register S (Sin) 2/40/16 (old No. 764), letter No. 427, p. 164, dated 12 Safar 1246/August 2, 1830.

64. This was a practice recorded in Ottoman times as well: Jabarti quotes the sarcastic Azhari poet Hassan al-Hijazi saying that the streets of Cairo contain "seven evils: urine, wastes, mud, dust, rudeness, noise, and the inhabitants of the streets themselves, who resemble ghosts in a cemetery." Jabarti, quoted in Raymond, *Cairo*, p. 243.

65. DWQ, Majlis Mulkiyya, Sadir Khulasat, register 45, p. 22, correspondence no. 229, dated 3 Sha'ban 1251/November 24, 1835, as reproduced in al-Mihi carton, document No.

16, folder No. 8. A key word is unclear, making it difficult to know what the punishment was. It reads: "He who eases nature in the street . . . will have one of his ??? nailed on the spot till sunset as deterrent to others."

66. Tuesday seems to have been the day reserved for going through the backlog of work. See DWQ, Diwan Madaris, Sadir (outgoing), Register M (Mim) 1/6 (old No. 6), correspondence No. 90, p. 3018, dated 28 Sha'ban 1261/September 1, 1845.

67. DWQ, Diwan Taftish al-Sihha, Register M (Mim) 5/2 (old No. 167), correspondence No. 11, p. 52. dated 12 Jumada I 1268/March 4, 1852.

68. DWQ, Diwan Madaris, Register M (Mim) 1/1/4 (old No. 4), correspondence No. 269, pp. 2136, 2160, dated 16 Muharram 1261/January 25, 1845. As a further example of Clot Bey's sarcastic language, see DWQ, Diwan Jihadiyya, Sadir Shura al-Atibba, Register No. 440, correspondence No. 50, p. 49, dated 14 Dhu al-Hijja 1263/November 23, 1847, in which he was asking the other members of the Tanzim to approve his request to issue a circular forbidding people from taking his whitewashing guidelines too seriously, and asking them to desist from painting wood and marble columns in mosques. He said that this was like gold-plating diamonds. He added in a postscript that tourists might make fun of this practice.

69. DWQ, Diwan Madaris, Register M (Mim) 1/1/3 (old No. 3), correspondence No. 197, pp. 862, 872, dated 17 Muharram 1261/January 26, 1845.

70. DWQ, Majlis al-Ahkam, Register S (Sin) 7/33/1, p. 229, order dated 14 Rabi' I 1269/December 26, 1852.

71. DWQ: Muhafazat Misr (The Municipality of Cairo), Register L (Lam) 1/5/2 (old No. 185), document No. 51, p. 55, on 21 Jumada I 1277/December 5, 1860.

72. See Muhammad 'Ali's order to Edhem Bey, the head of the Department of Education, to investigate the source of stench of the Azbakiyya Lake and to take measures to eradicate it: DWQ, Diwan Madaris, Carton No. 3, document No. 135, dated 22 Sha'ban 1263/August 5, 1847.

73. According to Muhammad 'Ali Bey al-Baqli, head of the Medical School, 605 lakes had been dried up in Egypt during 1283/1866–1867: Ya'sub al-Tibb, issue No. 29, 4 Jumada I 1285/August 23, 1868, pp. 1–2, 6. This was the first medical journal to be published in Egypt. Its first editor was Muhammad 'Ali Bey al-Baqli.

74. For the history of the Khalig, see Raymond, Cairo, pp. 48, 125, 230, 246. For the health problems associated with it, see Fahmy, "An Olfactory Tale," pp. 171–73. On the eventual process of drying it up, see DWQ, Majlis al-Wuzara', Nizarat al-Ashghal, Carton, No. 1/3, folder 23–563 titled "Pertaining to the Khalig," dated 1882–1887.

75. DWQ, Majlis al-Khususi, Register S/11/8/22/, Order no. 10, pp. 13–16, Shawwal 1291/November 1874. This is a very significant decree by the Privy Council in which they compared the vital statistics of Cairo to those of leading European cities. The conclusion they reached was that one of the main reasons for the still high mortality figures of Cairo was population density, measured by the number of inhabitants per household. They also specified five areas which still needed to be worked on to improve the general level of sanitation of the city: the Khalig, the absence of a sewage system, the process of removing the

solid waste (which they estimated at 22,500 tons per year) beyond the city's limits, cemeteries, and slaughterhouses.

76. DWQ, Diwan Madaris, Register M (Mim) 1/1/3 (old No. 3), correspondence without No., p. 827, dated 6 Muharram 1261/January 15, 1845.

77. DWQ, Diwan Madaris, Register M (Mim) 1/1/4 (old No. 4), correspondence No. 278, p. 2184, dated 23 Rabi' I 1261/April 1, 1845.

78. DWQ, Diwan Madaris, Register M (Mim) 1/6 (old No. 6), p. 2959, petition dated 22 Rajab 1261/July 27, 1845.

79. DWQ, Diwan Madaris, Register M (Mim) 1/1 (old No. 1), p. 29, dated 28 Sha'ban 1260/September 13, 1844.

80. DWQ, Nizarat al-Dakhiliyya, Mukatabat 'Arabi, Carton No. 6, petition dated 12 Safar 1286/May 24, 1869.

81. See, for example, DWQ, Muhafazat Misr, Register L (Lam) 1/5/11 (old No. 209), document No. 22, p. 64, 29 Rajab 1286/November 4, 1869; and the interesting case of Shalabi Afandi who had Isma'il Pasha pull strings for him (Isma'il was not yet khedive) to have his infant son buried in the city. The Department of Health Inspection was furious when it was informed of the matter, saying that these health regulations were to be followed by elites and commoners alike: DWQ, Muhafazat Misr, Register L/1/5/2 (old No. 185), document No. 178, pp. 171, 184, 27 Safar 1278/September 4, 1861.

82. DWQ, Muhafazat Misr, Register M (Mim) 5/11 (old No. 226), documents No. 92, pp. 208, 211, dated 2 Dhu al-Hijja 1290/January 21, 1874.

83. DWQ, Nizarat al-Dakhilyya, Mukatabat 'Arabi, Carton No. 13, document dated 11 Rabi' I 1291/April 28, 1874.

10

Medievalization of the Old City as an Ingredient of Cairo's Modernization: Case Study of Bab Zuwayla

Nairy Hampikian

A comparative gaze at the 1:5,000 two-partite map of Historic Cairo printed in 1948 and the map prepared by the savants of Bonaparte around 1800 helps high-light some of what occurred in the city between these two dates concerning the search for its identity.[1] On the 1800 map, a sea of urban fabric is interrupted by streets and *birkas* (lakes), with some scattered numbers which correspond to the location of sites mentioned on a reference list to the side. On the 1948 map, no more lakes appear, and instead, precise borders of 622 "Muhammadan Monuments of Cairo," with the name and foundation date of each color-coded by period, are positioned carefully so as to interrupt a network of roads and a sea of urban fabric.

For the expansion of any city 150 years is quite an extended period, during which change is not only foreseeable but inevitable. But for Cairo, these years were critical in that the city witnessed the launch of an imported modernity followed by, or accom-panied with, an awakening of the desire to safeguard a special sector of the local and traditional city. Ironically, Cairo can be seen enthusiastically opening one arm to accept modern European architectural styles and urban methodologies, while using its other to shield, with the same enthusiasm, the privileged "selection of its old."

The major elements of the transformation of Cairo during the nineteenth and early twentieth centuries should be well known to anyone familiar with the city. The first important date was 1800, the year Jomard's volume on *L'état Moderne* was published as part of the *Description de' l'Égypte*. This volume established the notion of a historically acceptable and aesthetically distinguished Islamic legacy in Cairo, which allowed the city to gain recognition within heritage-conscious, East-loving Western societies. Then, in 1867, two years before the inauguration of the Suez Canal, Khedive Isma'il, determined to put Cairo on a matching position with the European cities he had visited, initiated the making of "a modern Cairo." As part of this initiative, the Tanzim (Alignment), founded in 1845, became the main planning institution in the city. In the years that followed, seeing the old quarters of Cairo as an obstacle to Isma'il's vision, it laid out new quarters equivalent in size to the old city, and planned new avenues that cut through the existing urban fabric.[2]

Next, in 1881, influenced by movements of heritage preservation around the world, Khedive Tawfiq established the Comité de Conservation des Monuments de l'Art Arabe.[3] Charged with protecting and restoring buildings of art-historical value, it soon became the preeminent body on all work dealing with the study and preservation of Islamic and Coptic monuments in Egypt.[4]

Following the above developments, from 1889 to 1907, the old city, now identified as "Historic Cairo" was used to represent Egyptian identity at major international exhibitions. In 1889, a street in historical Cairo was faithfully presented. And in 1900, "Le Palais de L'Égypte" featured two faces—one representing the "Arab" style, and the other the "ancient Egyptian." In the West, this signaled an acceptance that Egyptian identity was not only a matter of Pharaonic culture, but Arabic as well.[5]

The last important nineteenth-century development was a noticeable boom in neo-Islamic-style modern buildings. These were erected in different districts of Cairo and in its cemeteries. The movement was crowned by the creation of Heliopolis in 1904, a satellite city built entirely in the Moorish style.[6]

A key agent of change in the old city of Cairo during this period was the Comité de Conservation des Monuments de l'Art Arabe.[7] From its founding in 1881, it attempted to systematize the preservation of historical Islamic buildings in Egypt. According to this approach, once a building was identified as a "monument of Arab art," it was first listed.[8] It was then researched extensively and readied for a program of practical intervention, which might include structural consolidation, architectural conservation, replacement of deteriorated fabric, reconstruction of fallen ornament, and the addition of roofs, doors, etc. All these actions, and the whole process of planning them, would then be documented in the Comité's yearly publications, its *Bulletins*.

The basic task this institution set for itself was to save old buildings with enough historical merit to be tagged "monuments." At first, this only involved selecting practical interventions to ensure their safety and documenting these interventions; but the Comité's ambitions soon surpassed such conservation basics. As it discovered the huge amount of historic built fabric still *in situ*, it also started to categorize buildings, create parallels, define pure chronological architectural characteristics, and eventually apply these findings to the reconstruction of the monuments themselves. These efforts eventually came to include such extensive nonconservation activities as clearing space around the historical buildings, reconstructing their missing parts, and demolishing intrusions.

At the time, these activities were championed by enthusiasts of Arab art under the axiom "saving the historical buildings from peril." As such, they have normally been contrasted to the activities of the Ministry of Public Works and the fanatics of al-Tanzim, who were intent on introducing modern, Western architectural styles and urban concepts, destroying the old to make space for the "shiny and healthy" new quarters of Isma'il's Cairo. In fact, however, I believe it is impossible to evaluate these two movements in isolation. Only together can one see how they created a single modus operandi of change by which the multiethnic melange of nineteenth-century Cairo was separated into urban and cultural islands, allowing different quarters to establish individual identities.

This chapter considers these two seemingly contradictory interventions in nineteenth-century Cairo and questions whether they were really opposing policies, or one consistent strategy. To do this, it provides a case study of the Comité's actions with regard to Bab Zuwayla and the area around it from the 1880s right up to the 1950s.[9]

DIFFERENT WAYS OF EVALUATING THE ACTIVITIES OF THE COMITÉ

During the last ten years, investigators from a wide variety of fields have studied both the raison d'être and strategies adopted by the Comité. This is not surprising since the Comité was representative of a vital movement in the public life of Cairo. Researchers on the history of conservation of monuments, politics, art, and urban history have also been attracted to the Comité's work because it was an institution actively involved in the definition of Cairo's heritage and because it was composed of a cluster of prominent figures at the time. This has resulted in a variety of perspectives.

The first to tackle the work of the Comité at length was Speiser, whose scope of interest was limited to practical aspects of monument conservation.[10] His attempt to relate the Comité's activities to his own conservation projects in Cairo is typical of the interest among conservationists to know the history of interventions on sites where they are working. My own dissertation was likewise oriented. It provided an analytic survey of the Comité's actions in one sector of Historic Cairo—al-Salihiyya in Bayn al-Qasrayn.[11]

But not all scholars have taken this approach to the work of the Comité. Bierman was more interested in urban changes caused by the Comité's achievements; and El-Habashi and Warner have dealt with the history of mapping and listing of the Cairo's monuments—one of the Comité's main activities.[12] For his part, Reid concentrated on political analysis, linking the Comité's formation and its actions to cultural imperialism and nationalism.[13]

More recently, however, El-Habashi's dissertation has returned to the conservation issue, and extensively surveyed the technical methods and philosophy adopted by the Comité.[14] Finally, Ormos has given details on the strategy of Herz Pasha, a Hungarian architect and one of the chief directors of the Comité (1890–1914).[15]

Research on the Comité's activities is facilitated by the existence of the *Bulletins*. These provide a full documentation of all activities thought, planned, and/or executed by the Comité. The faithfulness of what was published to what really happened is a great tribute to the Comité.[16] And today the *Bulletins* offer both a detailed record of their interventions and also the opportunity to criticize and/or praise their actions based on their own understanding of them. This is a type of honesty worthy of imitation, and it is the facet of the Comité's work which most closely matches the highest standards for ethical conduct spelled out in the International Conventions for Conservation.[17] It is not an exaggeration to consider the *Bulletins*, which recount the history of preservation efforts in Cairo between 1881 and 1960, an encyclopedic masterpiece.

BAB ZUWAYLA AND ITS SURROUNDINGS FROM 1092 TO 1881 C.E.

To understand the Comité's actions with regard to Bab Zuwayla, one must first investigate how this structure (founded in 1092 as the southern gate of al-Qahira) and its immediate surroundings came to be as they were in 1881.[18]

In 969 C.E., upon the foundation of al-Qahira as a residential enclosure for the Fatimid ruling class, its southern gate, made of mud bricks like the rest of its enclosure wall, was called Bab Zuwayla. This Bab Zuwayla (Bab al-Qus) was located near the present-day mosque of Sam Ibn Nuh. Records indicate its remains could still be observed as late as the beginning of the fifteenth century.[19]

A stone-made second Bab Zuwayla replaced the old gate at a location one hundred meters to the south in 1092. The southern face of this structure was composed of two massive round towers connected by a bridge, which was carried on an entrance arch. This construction was in turn connected to the northern portion of the structure by a passageway covered by a semicircular dome supported by four pendentives and carried on four huge arches. Just past the entry arch, two massive wooden leaves controlled access to al-Qahira and separated the gate's outer fortified face from its inner friendly face. Access to the upper reaches of Bab Zuwayla was provided by means of an L-shaped staircase located at its northeastern corner. A food-storage area, called al-Ahra al-Sultaniyya, was also constructed on the northwestern side of the gate. This was destroyed in 1218, however, to provide space for a prison, called Shama'il's prison.[20]

In 1160, al-Salih Tala'i' Mosque was built, facing the southeastern corner of the eastern tower of Bab Zuwayla (FIGURE 10.1A).[21] Different commercial constructions and facilities were then built in the space between the old and the new Bab Zuwayla at the beginning of the thirteenth century. These included the Qaysariyyat (caravansary) Sunqur al-Ashqar, Darb (small alley) al-Saffira, and

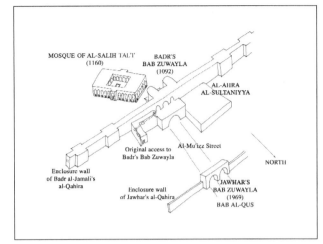

Figure 10.1a. Bab Zuwayla area until 1160 (construction of the mosque of al-Salih Tal'i').
(Source: Drawn by Author)

Qaysariyya Raslan on the western side; and Qaysariyyat al-Fadil (1135–1200) and two *hammams* (baths) on the eastern side.[22] It was during this period that a drinking trough for animals and people was also installed on the western half of the gate's southern wall. At this time the palatial complex of al-Qahira, which the gate had previously helped guard, was also opened to the rest of the city, as the ruling class established new dwelling and administrative spaces on the Citadel.[23]

In 1408, al-Sultan Faraj Ibn Barquq built a *zawiya* (small prayer hall) with an attached *sabil* (drinking fountain) only seven meters south of the western tower of Bab Zuwayla (FIGURE 10.1B). Then, between 1415 and 1422, al-Sultan al-Mu'ayyad Shaykh built a mosque on the ruins of Shama'il's prison and the two

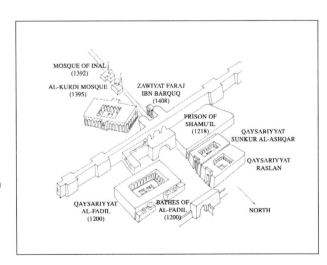

Figure 10.1b. Changes in the Bab Zuwayla area between 1160 and 1408. (Foundation of Sabil-kuttab of Faraj)
(Source: Drawn by Author)

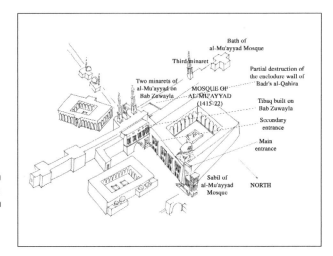

Figure 10.1c. Changes in the area of Bab Zuwayla until 1415–22 (construction of the mosque of al-Mu'ayyad Shaykh).
(Source: Drawn by Author)

qaysariyyas and *darb* on the west side of the street between the two gates. He also erected twin, identical minarets on Bab Zuwayla's two semicircular towers, constructed a *tibaq* (residential complex) on its upper platform, and carved out parts of its core to create the *bab sirr* (secondary door) to his mosque—using the vaulted space carved in the core as his *kitabkhana* (library). To provide access to this secondary door, he covered the drinking trough. He also built shops in the passageway through Bab Zuwayla as a continuation of the shops along the walls of his newly founded mosque, the revenue from which was endowed to cover the expenses of the mosque and its annexes (FIGURE 10.1C).[24]

One of the most important alterations to Bab Zuwayla at this time involved its transformation to "Bawwabat al-Mitwalli." This can be considered a climax of sorts to the process by which Bab Zuwayla slowly surrendered to the shifting city around it. Most significantly, alteration in name was accompanied by a change in personality, as the former military bastion was transformed into a holy space where people sought assistance from an imaginary saintly persona by the name of Mitwalli.[25]

The next change came in 1650, when Radwan Bey initiated a big construction project on the southern side of Bab Zuwayla. This consisted of the construction of Qasabat Radwan (an alley now called al-Khayyamiyya) and a palace for himself.[26] Most probably, it was also around this time that the walls of Bab Zuwayla and the minarets were plastered in red and white stripes.

During the eighteenth century, additional changes took place in the area. The northeastern side of Bab Zuwayla and the western portion of the original enclosure wall of al-Qahira were invaded by two residences (the houses of al-Ayati and al-Qayati), built on the remains of the city wall and around the original staircase leading to the upper sections of Bab Zuwayla. Meanwhile, urbanism had crawled around and inside the al-Salih Tala'i Mosque, which was nearly in

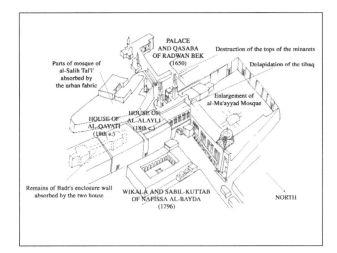

Figure 10.1d. The situation in the area of Bab Zuwayla prior to the intervention of the Comité (1881).
(Source: Drawn by Author)

ruins, and Zawiyat Faraj Ibn Barquq was encircled with the remains of a fruit market called Wikalat al-Tuffah. In 1798 the *sabil-kuttab* (drinking fountain and school) of Nafissa al-Bayda were constructed on the same site (FIGURE 10.1D).

In Pascal Coste's depiction of the ground plan of the al-Mu'ayyad Mosque, dated 1826, Bab Zuwayla is labeled 21. On a reference list to one side, this is identified as "*Grande porte, el-Soukkarieh, flanqués de deux tours, sur lesquelles s'élèvent deux minarets.*" On the same plan, the southernmost stretch of al-Mu'izz Street is called "Souk el-Soukkarieh."[27]

Prior to the inauguration of the Suez Canal in 1869, the red and white stripes of the facades were refreshed as a quick facelift to the old city. Probably, Bab Zuwayla was also replastered at this time (FIGURES 10.2 AND 10.3). Then, around 1880, the flat lintel under the monumental arched entranceway was deliberately destroyed because its low height blocked passage of *mahmal* (camels that carried the *qiswa* of the *ka'ba*)—which passed underneath the gate every year on its way to Mecca.[28] The tops of the minarets also collapsed sometime between 1860 and 1875 (REFER TO FIGURE 10.1D). Built in the eleventh century with strict military intent, the above summary shows how Bab Zuwayla never really functioned as such. On the contrary, it has consistently let neighboring buildings and surrounding urban fabric make use of its architectural elements for new purposes. Over the years these additions have, among other things, allowed it to serve as the landmark of a busy quarter, a background for commercial activities, a base for minarets, a foundation for a house, and a solid mass to be hollowed out to create a library.

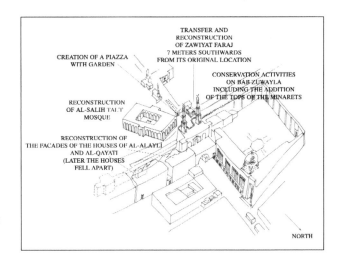

Figure 10.1e. Comité's intervention in the area of Bab Zuwayla.
(Source: Drawn by Author)

SURVEY OF INTERVENTIONS BY THE COMITÉ TO PRESERVE BAB ZUWAYLA AND ITS SURROUNDINGS

In 1881 Bab Zuwayla was "frozen in time" as the 199th "Muhammedan monument" of Cairo deemed worthy of special care by the Comité. Since then it has been studied, accessed, cleaned, caressed, reconstructed, conserved, stripped of encroachments, and watched carefully so that no harm could reach its walls.

I will now turn to a catalogue of actions taken by the Comité with regard to Bab Zuwayla (FIGURES 10.1E AND 10.4), recruited from all that is mentioned about Bab Zuwayla in the *Bulletins* of the Comité, the "Bab Zuwayla file" in Al-Mahfuzat (the Supreme Council of Antiquities' Department of Archives), and other related sources. Because of the limitations of this chapter, I have had to make a selection of the information gathered. I have also not presented the activities in strict chronological order.[29]   Instead, I have grouped the actions of the Comité according to categories which emerged as a result of decisions that members of the Comité made after their first visit to Bab Zuwayla in 1881. That visit was prompted by a police complaint concerning falling debris, which had killed two passersby. Following that visit, the Comité reported as follows:

Members of the Commission decided that the building and the two minarets were in relatively good condition and that as an emergency measure, the roof had to be cleared of the debris, which was falling to the street. Having secured the safety of the street, they had also decided:

1. To use iron ties on the upper layers to stop the enlargement of the cracks, 2. To exchange some of the blocks damaged because of the infiltration of the

Figure 10.2 (left). Eastern tower and minaret of Bab Zuwayla viewed from the south with the red and white stripes still on.
(Source: Courtesy of SCA's 'Abbasiyya archives–neg. 453)
Figure 10.3 (right). Southern facade of the gate before Comité's intervention.
(Source: Courtesy of SCA's 'Abbasiyya archives–neg. 603)

sewage or the leakage of the waste water from the latrines of the private houses constructed on the terrace of the monument, 3. To remove the shops built at the foot of the towers to make the monument regain its original appearance [*aspect primitive*], 4. To open the two side niches on the passageway under the gate, 5. To clean the facade, and, finally, 6. To redo [*refaire*] some reparation in cement on the parts where the surface is too damaged (color of repair should imitate the color of stone).

On the other hand, because of the more urgent things to be attended to on other monuments, the members decided that it was not necessary to reconstruct the lintel of the gate, which was destroyed in modern times, nor was it necessary to rebuild the upper parts of the minarets destroyed some years ago.[30]

In my opinion, the skeleton of a long-term conservation policy for Bab Zuwayla and its surroundings was already set during this first visit. It elements can be summarized as follows: ensure the safety of the passersby; consider con-

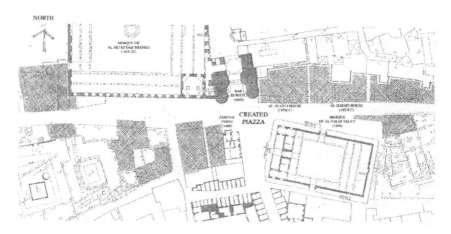

Figure 10.4. Plan prepared by the Comité clarifying their plan for urban conservation around Bab Zuwayla. Monuments are depicted as cross sections, cross hatched areas indicate zones that were planned for evacuation, while the rest is the urban fabric which was to be left untouched.
(Source: Courtesy of SCA's 'Abbasiyya archives).

servation/consolidation to be more advantageous than reconstruction; develop a system of expropriation to clear the facades and the interior of the monument so it could regain its "*aspect primitive*"; and deal with its urban context.

SAFETY AND EMERGENCY MEASURES FIRST

The first assignment of the Technical Bureau of the Comité with regard to Bab Zuwayla was to clean the rubble accumulated on the terrace, which was falling and harming passersby.[31] Following this, restoration work did not start until 1890, when the staircase leading to roof was reconstructed—again an emergency measure, since it secured safe access to the upper levels of Bab Zuwayla.[32]

In 1909, passersby were again threatened, when loose blocks at a height of two meters on Bab Zuwayla were on the verge of falling. As recommended, these were removed, and the stone walls were cleaned of ugly gypsum plaster that concealed the decorations underneath.[33]

In 1915, again as a security measure, hanging objects on the south wall of Bab Zuwayla were re-fixed.[34]

FROM CONSERVATION OR CONSOLIDATION TO RECONSTRUCTION

In 1890, a letter was sent to the Comité listing various construction works planned for Bab Zuwayla by the Ministry of Public Works and al-Awqaf.[35] But it was only in 1896 that a detailed bill of quantities was sent to the Commission for approval.[36] Today, the list demonstrates the type of interventions and degree of detail that were typical of Comité work. The event also illustrated how such responsibilities were shared between the Comité and other bodies. Thus, even when the Ministry of Public Works was responsible for work on Bab Zuwayla, the Comité dictated its conditions. In this case, the walls were not to be plastered, the cleaning was to be done by *la potasse*, and works were to be executed only with the consent of the Comité's architect.[37]

Between 1946 and 1953, LE 53,054 was spent to exchange some blocks and repoint joints with cement on the cross vault of the western side of the passageway. An additional LE 8,229 was spent for the consolidation of the blocks with iron anchors, and LE 27,091 was spent to fix the stone blocks of the portal and the joints of the eastern niche.[38]

These reports indicate how conservation and consolidation were considered a superior mode of intervention than reconstruction. Indeed, the Comité developed a style of work that emphasized making only the appropriate intervention at the appropriate moment. However, once conservation work had started, reconstruction activities were sometimes deemed unavoidable.[39] Such was the case with the repair of the damaged stone blocks on the soffit of the main arch and the reconstruction of the upper parts of the minarets, begun in 1892.[40] In such cases, members of the Comité were keen to explain their exact methods. For example, while working on the inscription above the entrance arch (which was discovered under the plaster), the chosen intervention was considered harsher than optimally desirable. But Herz was careful to give the following justification:

> . . . the bad state of the surrounding masonry constituted a continuous threat, which compelled us to operate a partial demolition followed by an immediate restitution. The inscription delicately removed, now occupies the same location as before, with no danger in the future.[41]

The Comité also took great pains to document Bab Zuwayla both before and after its interventions. Thus, before any work was undertaken, the Comité produced a full set of architectural drawings (plans, elevations, and sections) indicating its existing condition. Even the *tibaq* on its terrace and the shops at the street level, which it planned to expropriate and demolish, were depicted in great detail, and a short report was provided on the identity of their occupants.

As work progressed, the Comité was also careful to record all its aspects: the ingredients in the mortar used, the exact methods of anchorage between stone blocks, the agents used to strip the red and white plaster stripes from the walls, and the material used for repointing joints, etc. It goes without saying how precious this data can be to subsequent conservation teams working on the same building. In addition to information recorded in the *Bulletins* and the archives of the SCA, they also carved the years (in *hijriyya*) of the actual work on some of the blocks that were exchanged. Finally, two marble plates with inscriptions mentioning details of the repairs were placed on the remains of the western wall in 1899.[42]

As part of this work, members of the Comité were highly respectful of new historical discoveries. For example, during the cleaning of Bab Zuwayla's walls in 1897, a partial Kufic inscription was discovered on the large entrance arch surmounting the southern facade. This was deciphered, completed theoretically, and restored. It was then photographed and published in the *Bulletin*.[43]

Members of the Comité also showed great interest in how the work was executed, and in this regard, letters in the archives today record detailed discussions between Herz and contractors. These mention such things as corrections in financial statements, deadlines, permits to erect scaffolding, papers for occupying the street, requests to add to the budget for the removal of stone, etc. In one letter, Herz cautions that the iron rods used by the contractor to fix blocks in place were not long enough.[44] Another explains how to clean the walls.[45] And in another, Jusuf Jum'a, a contractor to the engineer of the antiquities, points out how new graffiti had recently appeared on the eastern side of Bab Zuwayla, and recommends that it to be washed with potash.[46] In 1919, the walls were finally cleaned at a cost of LE 6,800, done by *mu'allim* (master) Ahmad Sayyid.[47] Meanwhile, a sum of 700 milliemes was given to *mu'allim* Muhammad Husayn Shakkal to close the holes in the shops under Bab Zuwayla by using new wooden pieces, instead of the damaged old ones, and fixing their ends in gypsum.[48] Reading letter after letter, one is amazed by the number of details that members of the Comité had to look into and decisions they had to make.

TO DEVELOP A SYSTEM OF EXPROPRIATION SO THAT THE MONUMENT COULD REGAIN ITS "*ASPECT PRIMITIVE*"

In 1896 members of the Comité justified a policy of expropriation to clear the facades of Bab Zuwayla:

> Another more costly but absolutely necessary measure is the expropriation of the shops which adhere to the facades of a number of mosques because owners of these shops use the rear sides of the mosques as their waste disposal areas. . . . The internal and external appearances of the mosques have been tremendously harmed. Besides the fact that these heaps have narrowed the streets such as those on Suq al-Nahhasin, they have also crowded the traffic, and have obstructed the view of the passersby to appreciate the glamour and real proportions of the facades of these mosques.[49]

When nothing happened, the members repeated their demands in harsher tones:

> It is imperative that the facades of all structures against which the shops are placed be cleared indefinitely of the shacks which disfigure and attribute, slowly but surely, to their destruction. . . .

a) The first report of the second Commission, dealing with the conservation of Bab al-Mitwalli, called for the removal of the shops which lie at the foot of the towers. No follow-up action was taken on this decision.

b) In the 24th report of 11th of December 1886, the Comité re-demanded the removal of the shops built against Bab al-Mitwalli.

The problem is not new to the Comité; it has been the subject of several meetings and the second Commission has mentioned it in its reports, but to date nothing has been done. Two years have elapsed. . . . What has the General Direction of Waqfs done? Nothing.[50]

Eventually, such inaction led the Comité to systematize a method of expropriation. The second Commission proposed that: 1) the Waqf pursue the evacuation and demolition of the shops that belong to it, within a fixed time; 2) the expropriation of other shops be made obligatory after the publication of a decree declaring the public utility of the lands occupied; and 3) a certain sum, taken annually from the Comité budget, be allotted for the payment of those expropriations.

The Comité also prepared a study (FIGURE 10.5) to estimate the sums necessary to indemnify the owners of shops planned for expropriation. A total of

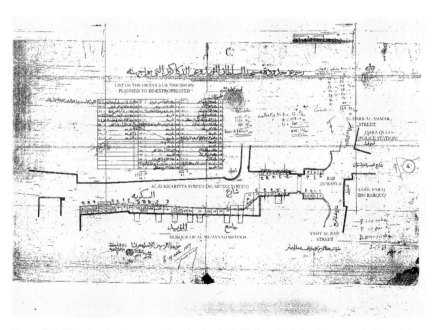

Figure 10.5. Plan showing the survey done by the Comité before finalizing the expropriation and demolition actions of encroachments around Bab Zuwayla and al-Mu'ayyad Shaykh Mosque.

(Source: Courtesy of SCA's 'Abbasiyya archives)

forty-one shops were counted built against the walls of the al-Mu'ayyad Mosque and Bab al-Mitwalli (Bab Zuwayla).[51] Of these, three were owned by the Waqf, seven were shared between the Waqf and individuals, and thirty-one were owned by individuals.[52] The Comité presumed the need to allot a sum of money equal to ten times the annual revenue of these shops to cover their expropriation.

Designation		No of boutiques expropriated	Revenue		Indemnity allotted for expropriation
			Monthly LE. M.	Annual LE. M.	LE. M.
Mosque of al-Mu'ayyad and Bab al-Mitwalli					
Boutiques	Waqfs	7	3. 485		
	Particulars	31	22. 215		
Total		38	25. 700	308. 400	3080. 00[53]

Expropriation soon became an obsession of members of the Comité, who believed that such commercial activities invaded the "*aspect primitif*" of the monument. But they faced a number of complications, the biggest of which was financial. In 1897, however, the Comité received an amount of LE 1,500 (LE 1,000 from the Waqf and LE 500 from the Ministry of Public Works). Accordingly, it was able to demolish twenty-two shops, plan for the demolition of two more, and purchase two others.[54]

Expropriations also always took longer than expected and led to endless discussions with the tenants. For example, in 1901, the Ministry of Public Health informed the Comité, in letter No. 1032 dated March 17, that the issue of the house ("*maisonette*") built under the gate of Bab Zuwayla belonging to the inheritors of 'Abd al-Wahid al-Tazi had been settled and that compensation had been paid to the *wakil* of the family. Thus, it was up to the Comité to take immediate possession of the house. But Mr. Herz noted that the house had been abandoned for years, so the Technical Section decided to act as necessary. Later, Herz presented the only offer he had received for the demolition of the house—from Yussuf Affandi Sirri (who promised to take the demolished debris, pay 700 milliemes, and finish the job in thirty days). The Technical Section approved, but there was a delay in the demolition because there was a shop attached to the house, which belonged to Rachel Cohen, and she was having problems with the Waqf concerning her share of the compensation. This matter was not finally settled until 1909.[55]

Despite this arrangement, additional letters on this property appeared in 1919. These included a request to rent a shop under Bab Zuwayla; another to rent a shop, which was a *makhba'a* owned by Hajj 'Abdu Taji; and a request from al-Fasakhani for a permit for *ishghal tariq* in front of his shop.[56] Then, in 1947, a petition was recorded from four tenants concerning complaints issued against them for showcases in front of their shops.[57] A record also exists of a complaint against a sign on a shop, which ended in an agreement by the tenant to reduce the size of the sign within fifteen days.[58]

Part of the problem with expropriation was that a number of bodies could become involved, which in some cases spoiled the arrangements. Basically, the process of expropriation was shared between al-Waqf, the Comité, and the Ministry of Public Works. Thus, as early as 1891, Grand Bey informed the Comité that the Minister of Public Works had already given instructions to al-Tanzim to prepare documents for the expropriation of shops along the walls of al-Mu'ayyad Mosque and Bab al-Mitwalli.[59] Tenants and owners of these properties were at first puzzled by the absence of clear laws governing the process of expropriation, the multiplicity of shared responsibilities, and the ambiguity of borders between governmental institutions; but they later used the chaos to their benefit. Thus, even though Mahmud 'Ali al-Qut wanted to rent the eastern niche in 1908 (and even had permission to do so), the Comité refused because it had previously petitioned to clear the walls there to restore an original feature of the gate.[60]

Typical of this confusion was a request in 1912 by Herz for a report on *al-kharjat* (protrusions) that one of the tenants had added to his shop. Yusuf Jum'a replied that the shop was *asfal* (under) Bab Zuwayla and had been rented to Muhammad Effendi Tawfiq by al-Maliyya (Finances), who had submitted a request to al-Muhafaza (the Governorate) for *rukhsat ishghal tariq* (a permit to occupy the street) (1x2 sq.m.) from al-Tanzim—but that this permit had not yet been granted. Meanwhile, Tawfiq had placed a *dulab* on the wall and a *dikka* in front, both touching the monument. Herz answered back that al-Muhafaza should ask permission from the Comité before giving a *tarkhis* (permit).[61]

There were other examples of such chaotic permitting. For example, in 1920, the Comité estimated LE 1,600 as rent for the shop along the northern wall of Bab Zuwayla. Meanwhile, Muhammad Qasim asked at *hikimdariyya* (the police station) for permission to put a display in front of his shop, but was told he should ask the *athar* (Comité).[62] In 1937, al-Tanzim issued a fine for the kiosk under Bab Zuwayla because it violated the alignment. It also requested the Comité to address the general issue of such shops. Accordingly, a decree was issued to demolish the kiosk because it had no permit. But this was accompanied by a request to the Comité to ask al-Tanzim to grant the owner a permit.[63] Such situations have only worsened nowadays.

The Comité also had to deal with temporary rentals. In 1918, a petition was sent from Husayn al-'Adli to set up *farsh halawa* (a table with sweets) during Mawlid al-Husayn (the feast celebrating the birthday of the Prophet). He was granted a permit from the Governorate for fifteen days, but only on east side of Bab Zuwayla.[64] In the same year, other requests to rent two meters of pavement next to Bab Zuwayla and to put up a display during the sales were also granted by the Comité.[65] But even such seemingly straightforward cases could be complicated. In 1924, for example, Muhammad Ramadan requested that he be able to temporarily rent a piece of land around Bab Zuwayla during Mulid al-Nabi. The Comité replied that it had no objection as long as doors and windows of the monument were not blocked, and as long as temporary structures were located at least one meter away from it. However, the same person then sent another request asking to rent the eastern niche for sweet stalls, mentioning that since the Comité did not object to it being rented during the Mulid, he would like to rent it all year round.[66]

Obviously, expropriation was the most costly, difficult, and time-consuming operation that members of the Comité engaged in. But in most cases it was essential, since no work on Bab Zuwayla could start until adjacent spaces were cleared and the walls made visible. Moreover, expropriation was the only Comité activity that impinged directly on the pulse of the street, where a hushed hostility existed toward all governmental bodies, including the Comité.

One becomes aware of this silent struggle when one observes how once-evacuated shops were reoccupied, temporary permit holders tried to get permanent permits, and shop owners appealed for stands or protrusions in front of their shops. Despite a plethora of difficulties, however, the Comité was able to expropriate and evacuate all the shops around the eastern and western towers and the two door leaves of Bab Zuwayla, the house on the western part of its northern wall, and the residential structure on its upper platform (the *tíbaq*) (FIGURE 10.6 AND REFER TO FIGURES 10.1D AND 10.1E).

TO DEAL WITH THE URBAN CONTEXT OF THE MONUMENT

In 1896 the Comité discussed the problem of monuments or parts of them being owned by individuals. A policy was articulated to evacuate residential structures by appropriately compensating their residents and making them leave the area.

> The Government had no authority to force the owners to maintain or conserve these historic places. Dwellers and tenants of houses could not be forced to sell them. Some of these surviving houses in the city of Cairo had more importance than the mosques which are under conservation by the Waqfs because these included unique forms which reflected Arab domestic architecture. Thus, it was desirable that these houses be under the supervision of the Comité. Moreover, if the appropriate compensation was given to owners, these would have nothing to complain about.[67]

In 1909, Fakhri Pasha demanded immediate removal of mobile stores along the walls of the al-Maridani, al-Mu'ayyad, and al-Aqmar Mosques under terms of the Khedivial Decree of December 18, 1881. This mentioned that no work or change, whatever its nature, was allowed to the facades of buildings classified as monuments without the consultation and the approval of the Comité.[68] In 1938, after a complaint was sent to Comité concerning a big sign hanging on the *mashrabíyya* next to Bab Zuwayla, the sign was taken down by force.[69] Finally, during a visit to the site

Figure 10.6. Northern façade of Bab Zuwayla during the destruction of the Tibaq from the upper platform.
(Source: Author's postcard collection)

between the years 1941–1945, the members observed that the showcases of the boutique situated on the western side of Bab Zuwayla "disfigured the site aesthetically." Riad Pasha then proposed replacing these with small open roofs with an "Arabic style, which will be in harmony with the surrounding environment."[70]

Other problems concerned the installation of new public infrastructure. In 1915–19, during the digging of sewers along the street which passed through Bab Zuwayla, Mr. Patricolo of the Comité and Mr. Pinson of the Drainage Department together decided on a course of action. This stipulated a number of things: that the Drainage Department would carry out excavations under the gate to the level of the original masonry; that the unearthed granite blocks would be put at the disposition of the Comité; that al-Tanzim should be informed that the Comité would be making pits with the Drainage Department; that a drawing would first be sent to identify the location of the pits; that meetings would be held during the progress of the work; and that the Comité would re-fix pavement removed during excavations. Accordingly, the Technical Service of the Comité and the Sanitary Service began the excavations under the door. Unfortunately, nothing of importance was found, because irreparable harm had already taken place when the Company of Water had installed its pipes there.[71]

Similar problems were encountered with the installation of electrical service. In 1946 a letter from the Director of al-Athar (Antiquities) complained that when tenants connected electricity to their shops, the wires were left running on the walls of the al-Mu'ayyad Mosque and under the *mashrabíyya* at the entrance to the house of al-Alayli. As these were dangerous, it was suggested that they be removed.[72] During the same year, one shop tenant requested that he obtain an electricity connection from the middle shop under the window at the entrance to Bab Zuwayla, provided that the tenant of that shop agreed. The administration allowed him to do that.[73] But in 1947 a request from a tenant to connect water to his shop was denied.[74]

Throughout this process, the Comité argued that the monument must be untouchable, and that the street must understand this. Thus, from 1894 to 1900, the Comité directed the Ministry of Public Works to remove posters glued to the eastern tower of Bab Zuwayla. It further asked the ministry to issue a formal interdiction so that "the monument is not exposed to such harm." It also directed the removal of a huge postbox hung directly on the masonry of the eastern tower using 8-cm. nails. A letter was then sent from the Egyptian Post Administration asking about the future location of the letterbox—which was eventually removed.[75]

A number of specific structures needed special attention. Two such projects involved the transfer of Zawiyat Faraj Ibn Barquq and the reconstruction of the al-Salih Tala'i Mosque. In 1904 the Comité discussed the *kuttab* built atop Faraj Ibn Barquq. They argued that its vulgar construction harmed the rest of the fifteenth-century facade. They agreed it would be desirable for this *kuttab* to be removed and for the *zawíyat* to be restored with the fountain. This would not only "free the monument from a late addition," but would also "free Bab Zuwayla."[76] A survey map (1:1000) dated 1913 showed Faraj Ibn Barquq before this took place (FIGURE 10.7).[77] Eventually, this work included the dismantling of the entire structure and its reconstruction seven meters to the south. Moreover, a slice of Wikalat al-Tuffah, which was not a registered monument, was demolished to widen the portion of Taht al-Rab' Street facing Bab Zuwayla and the southern wall of the al-Mu'ayyad Mosque.[78] Urban fabric was also removed and residences expropriated and then destroyed around the ruins of the al-Salih Tala'i Mosque—which were then examined and reconstructed to their original (1160 C.E.) appearance (FIGURE 10.9). As part of this work a minaret added during the Ottoman period was eliminated and never reconstructed.[79]

The house of al-Alayli was also a topic of ongoing concern (FIGURES 10.8A AND 10.8B). In 1920 the Technical Service placed a plate on this house at the eastern side of Bab Zuwayla, facing onto on al-Darb al-Ahmar Street, declaring it

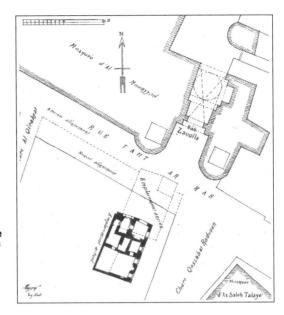

Figure 10.7. Urban plan showing the original and transferred positions of Faraj Ibn Barquq's zawiya.
(Source: From the bulletins of the Comité, available at the website of the Islamic Art Network: http://www.islamic-art.org/)

a registered building.[80]   Alarmed, its owners protested the action, asking the Comité to allow them to enjoy their dwelling, or else just buy it from them.

> The elements that interest the Comité are the *mashrabíyyas* of the facade. As for the building itself, there is no interest in conserving it; on the contrary, its demolition would be desirable as this will disengage the eastern end of the bastion of Bab Zuwayla and will highlight the remains of the adjacent fortification walls.[81]

Based on the fact that this clearing would also affect the public street, the Comité asked for the assistance of al-Tanzim.   In reply, al-Tanzim sent a letter to the Comité informing it about a counter-project which included the expropriation of a number of buildings between al-Darb al-Ahmar and the house of al-Alayli.   After examination, the members of the Comité decided this counter-project did not correspond to their point of view, which was limited and aimed at the reestablishment of the original alignment, marked by the remains of the city wall, which were detached from the bastion.[82]

Between the years 1930 and 1932 the estimate was made that one-quarter of the house (valued by the Committee of the Ministry of Public works at LE 1,545,725 mill, without the shops on the ground floor) belonged to al-Waqf, while the other three-quarters belonged to individuals.   Initially, the Comité bought 6 *kirats* from one of the co-owners and 2 2/3 *kirats* from another with money allotted by the government.[83]   Later, the rest of the house was purchased, and finally the Comité was allowed to work on it.[84]

Figure 10.8a (top), 8b (bottom). Facades of the houses of al-Alayli and al-Qayati before and after conservation.

(Source: Courtesy of SCA's 'Abbasiyya archives)

Figure 10.9. Southern facade of Bab Zuwayla when the area once occupied by al-Salih mosque was evacuated to start the reconstruction works of the mosque in its original location. Faraj Ibn Barquq's zawiya is already transferred, but al-Alayli house's facade is not yet restored. The angle of the picture clarifies how the sense of a piazza developed. *(Source: Courtesy of SCA's 'Abbasiyya archives)*

When the Comité started to set a strategy for the house, they declared:

The only interesting part is the eastern facade, which is worth restoring by re-establishing the composition of its *mashrabiyyas*. In this context, we need to mention the case of the Bab Zuwayla square, as an ensemble. It will be very interesting to have this facade restored.
1) The arrangement of the entrance to Qasabat Radwan,
2) The restoration of the facade of the house of Waqf Radwan Bey next to Qasabat Radwan,
3) The reconstruction of an appropriate facade to the house situated between Qasabat Radwan and sabil Faraj,
4) The reconstruction of the portico and façade of al-Salih Tala'i' mosque, and finally,
5) The summit of Sabil Faraj.[85]

Accordingly, the Technical Section asked the Bureau to prepare a project for the repair of the facades of all the buildings around the square of Bab Zuwayla, and the

Bureau asked Mr. Pauty to make the necessary study plan. It was also suggested, "It was possible to choose from the storage areas of the Comité *mashrabíyyas* that could suit the house."[86] Accordingly, new *mashrabíyyas* were installed on the house of al-Alayli and its external walls were plastered anew. But as the interior of the house, already in bad shape, was left untouched, the restored facade could not resist structurally, and soon cracks appeared that threatened its stability. At that point, the *mashrabíyyas* went back to their storage areas, and the house went back to its ruinous state.[87]

As a culmination to all the above efforts, during the years 1936 and 1940 the Comité was full of enthusiasm for the creation of a "*píazza*" in front of Bab Zuwayla (REFER TO FIGURES 10.4 AND 10.9). Thus, when it started the action on the house of al-Alayli, it decided to register the facades of adjacent houses, extending to the northern entrance of the al-Salih Mosque. Their rationale was to "salvage . . . the picturesque character of al-Darb al-Ahmar Street."[88] During this period, the Comité did not approve the clearing of the shops located on the left and right sides of Bab Zuwayla, because these protected it from direct exposure to traffic.[89] But in a 1937 letter, al-Tanzim agreed on construction of a park (600 sq.m., which contained 100 cu.m. of debris) around public latrines near "Midan" Bab Zuwayla. Statements of expenses for the construction and maintenance of the garden were detailed in a subsequent letter.[90]

In summary, the practical steps the Comité took to create a *píazza* and a garden in front of Bab Zuwayla can be recounted as follows: installation of a sewage main line through Bab Zuwayla; transfer of Zawiyat Faraj Ibn Barquq seven meters to the south of Bab Zuwayla; evacuation of the area around the remains of al-Salih Tala'i' Mosque and reconstruction of the mosque on its original borders; razing portions of Wikalat al-Tuffah overlooking Taht al-Rab' Street; reconstruction of the facade of the house of al-Alayli; rearrangement of the entrance to Radwan Street; restoration of the facade of the house of Waqf Radwan Bey next to Qasabat Radwan; and restoration of the facade of the house situated between Qasabat Radwan and Sabil Faraj.

I have deliberately included many minor details in the recapitulation of these activities of the Comité, because I believe they will help counter hasty conceptual and political judgments on its activities. Data collection of this kind is not only necessary to understand the history of Bab Zuwayla, but to understand the Comité's method of work. The love and care which was transmitted to these monuments through the work of the Comité, the meticulous professionalism by which its members worked, and the sincerity of their efforts is often underappreciated. Furthermore, the degree of seriousness with which these people approached their work is only really apparent when one follows its line of thinking with regard to a single structure over a number of years.

CONCEPTS BEHIND THE WORK OF THE COMITÉ IN AND AROUND BAB ZUWAYLA

As the preceding section has tried to indicate, when the Comité started its work on Bab Zuwayla in 1881 it faced a structure that had completely surrendered itself both on its exterior and interior to the city around it. Shops were built around the whole southern circumference of its towers, along both sides of the interior passageway, and along the exposed portions of its north wall. The interior of the gate had also been invaded by a house which was attached to the western portion of its north wall. And the alignment of the street to the south of its towers was only seven meters away—with Zawiyat Faraj Ibn Barquq and Wikalat al-Tuffah running westward, and urban fabric around the ruins of the al-Salih Tala'i' Mosque running eastward, leaving only a very narrow alley between the two blocks leading to Qasabat Radwan. There were other issues with the structure of Bab Zuwayla proper: the stonework was completely plastered in red and white stripes and was falling apart; the tops of the minarets were absent; and the upper platform was occupied by a residential unit, No. 9 'Atfit al-Hammam, which was reached by ascending the original interior stairs of Bab Zuwayla.

Considering these conditions, the situation of Bab Zuwayla was lamentable. The impressive twenty-meter-high towers were belittled by the encroachment of urban fabric. Bab Zuwayla itself was not visible from the street; it was chopped off on the top; and debris was falling on passersby, causing complaints from the police. It is not surprising that the Comité immediately became involved with Bab Zuwayla, first to ensure the safety of passersby, then through a series of preservation activities. These were followed by the simultaneous organization and execution of a succession of expropriations within the immediate surroundings of the gate, and finally by the implementation of a mini-urban conservation project. Considering the fate of much of historic Cairo in the past century, any conservation-conscious mind will affirm that the pattern of interventions detailed in the previous section was very successful. This is particularly true when one considers that most of what was planned was for the best of the monument, and that (except for some problems, such as with the house of al-Alayli[91]) most of what was executed was inevitable from a conservation point of view.[92]

The last section gave a sense of the type and volume of activities undertaken by the Comité; I would now like to consider more conceptual issues. Specifically, did the Comité have a vision, a concept, or a master plan for this area before starting? Or did things follow each other? I believe that the members of the Comité were vigorously motivated by a real desire to preserve the "Monuments of Arab art." A broad vision of how to do this developed as work progressed and as they gained experience. From individual monuments, to their immediate surroundings, to their neighborhoods, the Comité worked outward to develop a strategy that sought to link the monuments and create clusters. But I also think the members of the Comité learned from what had already gone on in other parts of Cairo, particularly in the quarters of Isma'il's new city.

On the basis of a detailed survey of the Comité's activities from 1881 to 1961, I believe it possible to arrive at a formulation of the Comité's philosophy with regard to Bab Zuwayla and its surroundings. This involved the elimination of all undesired layers (including the later addition of walls, dwellings, materials, or colors), and then the reconstruction of missing architectural elements (tops of the minarets, crenellations, etc.). The goal was to allow the gate to be selected from the rest of the urban fabric, and to restore its original (1092 C.E.) appearance as a fortification. This would allow it to assume a worthy position in the approved chronology set by the historical research that accompanied the practical interventions of the Comité. Ultimately, the criteria used to accomplish these goals depended on what the Comité considered to be original "Arab" or "Mohammedan" art.[93] All that did not meet these criteria was eliminated to free the monument of "the effect of time" and reestablish its "*aspect primitive*" (*li-i'adat halatiha al-asliyya*).[94]

The elimination of undesired layers from the area around Bab Zuwayla (mainly residential dwellings and shops from the eighteenth and nineteenth centuries) had several purposes. It allowed existing, reconstructed, or transferred monuments to be exposed to maximum visibility; it enabled the reconstruction of ruined monuments; it facilitated traffic; and it allowed construction of a central *piazza* and garden. In essence, the Comité was redefining the old city by eliminating the residential encrustations of the last two centuries. Because such buildings were believed to be intruders, they were categorically selected for demolition, and their residents evacuated from the old city. The Comité thus set out to create a "picturesque cadre" that would be pleasant and charming to a Western-oriented clientele. Such a vision valued a skyline carved by the silhouettes of existing and reconstructed minarets and domes and a procession of exposed "Arab" facades. But not only did the Comité create a "picturesque cadre" around Bab Zuwayla, it went even further to introduce the Western concept of "*la piazza*," which created the possibility for a "panoramic picturesque cadre."

In addition to the Comité's high standard for physical conservation activities, its work was thus accompanied by a unifying vision of its role as an agent of architectural and urban change. This involved the salvage of buildings and areas in Historic Cairo where some reminiscence of "Arab art" could be detected through the elimination of "undesirable layers" and the addition of "desired and yet missing layers." The effect was to create the appropriate patina that would allow structures under conservation to regain their "original appearance"—which meant their "medieval ambiance."

In their search for such an original appearance authenticity often had to be refabricated. The case of Bab Zuwayla shows how this was accomplished. It was gradually sculpted out from the old city, and the old city was tamed into a medievalized version of itself. By causing Bab Zuwayla and the other monuments around it to "regain their original appearances," and by creating a "picturesque urban cadre," the Comité artificially brushed out and retouched the area to reveal "a medieval authenticity" from the dirt of nineteenth-century Cairo.

CONCLUSION

[T]he safety of the noble Bab-ez-Zuweyleh has been seriously imperiled by the removal of its massive lintel-stone, and the substitution of a wooden beam. This was done because the level of the thoroughfare immediately under the gateway had to be lowered each year on the occasion of the procession of the Mecca pilgrims, the arch not being high enough to allow for the passing of the Mahmal, or scattered litter. As the street is not paved, it may be conceived how easily it was lowered and remade when necessary. To spare this trifling expense, however, the lintel stone was torn from its place a year or two ago. When too late the authorities were astonished to find that the structure overhead was giving way; so the stone was replaced by a temporary wooden beam. About 800 pounds is now required to repair the damage; and if that sum is not soon forthcoming, the Bab-ez-Zuweyleh will soon some day come down upon the heads of the passers-by. If left to the Egyptian Minister of Public Works, whoever he may chance to be, the money will in all probability never be forthcoming; in which case the gate is doomed.[95]

It was such intolerable destruction vis-à-vis historical buildings in the old city that initially triggered some French residents (among whom were Gabriel Charmes, Ambroise Baudry, and Arthur Rhoné) to plan for the foundation of an independent Comité des Monuments Historiques in 1881 to counterbalance the powers of the Ministry of Public Works. However, "To their great astonishment, the realization of this project was met with resistance."[96]

Such a confrontation between the defenders of historical buildings and modern urban planners of the time was implicit in the revolutionary "Hausmann-ization" of Cairo that had been initiated after Isma'il's visit to Paris in 1867 and the appointment of 'Ali Mubarak as director of the Public Works.[97] Indeed, Mubarak expressed his opinion of those who desired to preserve all historical buildings as follows: "Does one need so many monuments? When one preserves a sample, isn't that enough?" Bab Zuwayla, in particular, he noted, had once been used for hanging criminals. "We don't want to keep those memories; we ought to destroy them as the French destroyed the Bastille."[98] But when Mubarak proposed the removal of the *sabíl* near Bab Zuwayla because it obscured carriage and pack-animal traffic, members of the newly formed Comité protested, reminding Mubarak that their aim was preservation, not demolition.[99]

In 1882, Arthur Rhoné (one of those who cared most deeply about the preservation of the urban pattern of the old city) can also be heard protesting city officials' blind obedience to the imported idea of the straight alignment. He noted how luxurious *mashrabiyyas* and overhanging stories were being removed, leaving beautiful stone corbels protruding into emptiness as the sole witnesses to the lavishness and taste of the original buildings.[100] "*Et surtout ô bonheur! Pas un trot-toir, pas un alignement, rien enfin qui rapelle l'ennui des constructions urbaines d'aujourd'hui,*" he wrote. And, grieving over the advance of modernization, Rhoné described al-Muski Street in the following words: "*C'est donc fait! La ville plus merveilleuse du vieux monde oriental va devenir banale et européennne comme tant d'autres.*"[101]

The difficulty of implementing urban laws enforced by the Ministry of Public Works and executed by al-Tanzim in the old city was clarified by Pauty:

> . . . the 1889 law on alignment for the new city made by Lord Cromer, con-
> tained dangerous clauses concerning its realization on the old city. The law
> demanded that the alignment of the facades be straight and parallel to each
> other, prohibited protrusions, imposed that the vaults or ceilings over public
> roads be demolished gradually, regulated the balconies, etc.[102]

Obviously, the implementation of these regulations in the old city meant the destruction of the character of its streets and the architectural charm of its hous-es. "Already numerous cantilevered stories have disappeared in the turmoil. It is high time to put this into good order."[103]

Such sharp discrepancies often led to the failure of the two opposing sides to reach an agreement.[104] At these times the Comité's slogan "saving all the histori-cal buildings from peril" would certainly seem to have been in conflict with the spirit of "destroying the old to make space for the new" adopted by the Ministry of Public Works during the creation of Isma'il's Cairo. But, despite all the com-plications between these two institutions, they held much in common. In partic-ular, the Comité adopted a framework for urban conservation whose model echoed the imported modern strategies behind Isma'il's Cairo.

> The transformation of the city of Cairo from the aesthetic point of view
> required the filling in and the leveling of the waste land around the city, the
> opening up of main streets and new arteries, the creation of squares and open
> spaces, the planting of trees, the surfacing of roads, the construction of drains,
> and regular cleaning and watering. This spatial ordering in turn required the
> removal of certain human agglomerations from the interior.[105]

This declaration describing the procedure followed by the Ministry of Public Works to build the city's new quarters fits the description of the conservation procedures followed by the Comité around Bab Zuwayla. One only has to substitute the words "expropriation of the intruding structures on Bab Zuwayla and destruction of the nineteenth-century dwellings around al-Salih Mosque" for "filling in and the leveling of the waste land around the city" to make a perfect match between the two.

Therefore, despite the disagreements concerning the alignment laws (which continue today), the fact is that the Comité used many of the same strategies as the Ministry of Public Works to tame the neighborhoods around the monuments.

Finally, one might observe that, as all modern cities have museums located in their hearts, one of the Comité's aims was to turn the entire old city of Cairo into a museum.[106] The idea of considering the "whole of the old city as one monument" was affirmed by Pauty; he even went so far as to plan its borders, naming it "Historic Cairo" and dividing it into working zones, each to be approached with a different strategy.[107] Thus, the Comité dealt with the old city in the same way it handled individual monuments. Using a sieve, it selectively highlighted "desirable" from "undesirable" structures. It worked both on monuments so they could "regain their original appearance," and on the city so it could display "picturesque cadres." Year after year, intruding layers were eliminated from the old city to expose representatives of "Arab art"—or to be replaced by modern imitations of it. As a result, a city in Arab style was penciled into the old city, and the intrusions were erased.

This was what the Comité was trying to do: tame the old to be appropriately presented beside the new, shiny, and modern Cairo. The Comité thus recreated a medieval city—a monument. This was precious merchandise to the clientele of the shiny Cairo, the modernity of which would be accentuated by the existence of the medieval at its center. An old heart to a modern city is always attractive to the tourist.

"A medieval Cairo—an open museum for modern Cairo" was the dream of the Comité.

NOTES

1. The 1800 map is in Jomard's portion of *l'Etat Moderne*, pp. 113–535, in the second edition of the *Déscription de l'Égypte* known as the Panckouke edition, Paris 1821 and 1829 (26 volumes). The 1948 map is nearly identical to another brought together in 1924. A. El-Habashi and N. Warner, "Recording the Monuments of Cairo: An Introduction and Overview," *Annales Islamologiques*, Vol. 32, 1998, pp. 81–99.

2. J.L. Arnaud, *Le Caire mis en place d'une ville moderne* (Arles: Sinbad/Actes Sud, 1998), pp. 9–17.

3. Reid considers France's Commission des Monuments Historiques the model for the Egyptian Comité. See D. Reid, "Cultural Imperialism and Nationalism: The Struggle to Define and Control the Heritage of Arab Art in Egypt," *International Journal of Middle East Studies*, Vol. 24, No. 1, 1992, pp. 57–76.

4. Activities of the Comité are published by the French Institute of Oriental Archaeology (IFAO) in volumes under the title "The Bulletins of the Comité de Conservation des Monuments de l'Art Arabe" (*Bulletins*). These stretch from 1882 to 1961, when the Comité stopped its activities and changed its name several times, finally becoming today's Supreme Council of Antiquities (SCA), Sector for Islamic and Coptic Monuments. The entire collection of the *Bulletins* is online as a separate section of the Islamic Art Network site. The unpublished material of the Comité, mainly the correspondence and technical and financial spreadsheets, is kept in the archives of the Supreme Council of Antiquities (Al-Mahfuzat), separately filed for each monument.

5. J.M. Humbert, *L'Égypte à Paris* (Paris: Action artistique de la Ville de Paris, 1998).

6. Other examples are the Awqaf Ministry Building (1898) and the Islamic Museum (1903). This trend continued to be practiced to the twentieth century as surveyed by Tarik Sakr in *Early Twentieth-Century Islamic Architecture in Cairo* (Cairo: American University in Cairo Press, 1993). A new version of Heliopolis is Khan al-Aziziyya, a satellite quarter imitating historic Cairo, founded in 1998 on the road to Alexandria, near 15 of May City.

7. From this point on, it will be referred to as the Comité.

8. The lists were modified in the early years of the Comité. The list accompanying the 1948 map mentioned above is considered to be more or less the final list of registered Islamic monuments in Cairo. See El-Habashi and Warner, "Recording the Monuments of Cairo."

9. Most of the material presented here was compiled during the five-year Conservation Project on Bab Zuwayla (1998–2003), funded by a USAID grant (Grant No. 263-G-00-93-00089-00) and executed in cooperation between the Supreme Council of Antiquities (SCA) and the American Research Center's Egyptian Antiquities Project (ARCE-EAP) under the direction of Dr. Nairy Hampikian.

10. P. Speiser, *Die Geschichte der Erhaltung arabischer Baudenkmäler in Ägypten* (Heidelberg: Abgandlungen des Deutschen Archäologischen Instituts Kairo, Islamische Reihe: Bd. 8, 2001).

11. N. Hampikian, "Al-Salihiyya Complex through Time," Ph.D. Diss., Archaeology Program, University of California at Los Angeles, 1997. See chapter on activities of the Comité on al-Salihiyya Complex (forthcoming publication with same title).

12. I. Bierman, "Urban Memory and the Preservation of Monuments," in J.L. Bacharach, ed., *The Restoration and Conservation of Islamic Monuments in Egypt* (Cairo: American University in Cairo Press, 1995), pp. 1–11; and El-Habashi and Warner, "Recording the Monuments of Cairo."

13. D. Reid, "Cultural Imperialism and Nationalism: The Struggle to Define and Control the Heritage of Arab Art in Egypt," *International Journal of Middle East Studies*, Vol. 24, No. 1, 1992, pp. 57–76.

14. El Habashi, "Cairo of the Comité," Ph.D. Diss., University of Pennsylvania, 2001.

15. I. Ormos, "Preservation and Restoration, The Methods of Max Herz Pasha," in J. Edwards, ed., *Historians in Cairo* (Cairo: American University in Cairo Press, 2002), pp. 123–53.

16. This point is verified by comparing the information published in the *Bulletins* with that kept in Al-Mahfuzat (SCA's Department of Archives) where the correspondence of every monument is accumulated. In the case of Bab Zuwayla, most of what is mentioned in the letters kept in the archives also appeared, naturally in fewer details, on the published pages of the *Bulletins*.

17. B.M. Feilden, "Every intervention must be documented during the conservation work in detail," *Conservation of Historic Buildings* (Oxford: Butterworth Architecture, 1994), p. 6.

18. A full account is presented in N. Hampikian, "Final Report, Conservation Project of Bab Zuwayla," in Archives of ARCE-EAP, Vol. 1, 2004.

19. al-Qalqashandi, *Subh al-A'sha fi sina'at al-'Insha*, Vol. 3 (1964), pp. 348–49; and al-Maqrizi, *al-Khitat*, Vol. 1, (1853), p. 361, and Vol. 2 (1853), p. 92.

20. al-Maqrizi, *al-Khitat*, Vol. 1 (1853), p. 373.

21. al-Qalqashandi, Vol. 3 (1964), p. 362.

22. al-Maqrizi, *al-Khitat*, Vol. 1 (1853), p. 373.

23. This was discovered during the 1998–2003 Conservation Project of Bab Zuwayla.

24. F. 'Abd al-'Alim, *Jami' al-Mu'ayyad Shaykh* (Cairo: Printing House of the Supreme Council of Antiquities, 1994); and results of the investigations during the 1998–2003 Conservation Project on Bab Zuwayla.

25. See the results of the excavations conducted during the 1998–2003 Conservation Project of Bab Zuwayla under the wooden door leaves in the final report of the conservation project (2003).

26. A. Raymond, *Cairo: City of History*, trans. W. Wood (Cairo: American University in Cairo Press, 2000), p. 237.

27. Comité VII (1890), Plate 2.

28. A.B. Edwards, *The Destruction of Cairo*, Vol. XXII (London: The Academy, 1882).

29. For a chronologically arranged and complete survey of all that the Comité has planned and/or executed on Bab Zuwayla and its surroundings see N. Hampikian, "Final Report, Conservation Project of Bab Zuwayla," in Archives of ARCE-EAP, Vol. 1, 2004.

30. Comité I (1882–3), pp. 39–40.

31. Comité I (1882–3), p. 33.

32. File Bab Zuwayla, Al-Mahfuzat, letter No. 8 (20.12.1890).

33. Letter signed by Herz. See File Bab Zuwayla, Al-Mahfuzat, letter No. 16 (5.1.1909).

34. Four letters from the technical inspector of al-Tanzim, who was afraid that the hanging objects, might fall. The inspector assured that there was no such threat. Nevertheless, Muhammad 'Abd al-Rahman reinforced their fixations at the cost of 400 milliemes. File Bab Zuwayla, Al-Mahfuzat, letter Nos. 70 (October 1915), 71 (9.9.1915), 72 (15.9.1915) and 73 (11.10.1915).

35. Comité VII (1890), p. 7. See also the list of the works, File Bab Zuwayla, Al-Mahfuzat, letter No. 7 (3.7.1890).

Letter No. 7:

Works to be carried out by *nizarat al-a'mal al-'amma* (Ministry of Public Works)

1. Cleaning the stairs leading to the lower roof and replacing the missing steps and installation of doors at the end of the corridors.

2. Demolition of all walls on the lower roof and replacing the screen situated in the middle shop with an iron screen.

3. Removing the thick plaster and the thin coating covering the entire monument and plastic repair for the damaged stone using mortar. (The corner stones should be replaced using natural stone.)

4. Repair of the top of the roof from the mosque side and installation of crenellations on the top of the roof.

Works to be carried out by al-Awqaf

1. Construction of staircase leading to the roof and the minarets.

2. Rebuilding the minaret bulbs using stone carved to the design of the old and restoring damaged balustrades.

3. Demolition of the building above the shop located under the Bab, which cannot be done until the shop itself is demolished.

4. Demolition of shops.

Signed Herz, Manicolo in Arabic—3.7.1890.

36. File Bab Zuwayla, Al-Mahfuzat, letter No. 22 (21.2.1896).

No.	Item	Quantity	Franks
1	Re-pointing using cement mortar (1 sand: 1 cement)	3000 m.	1500
2	Plastic repair using cement mortar including removal of old plaster and indentations on old stone surface	400 sq. m.	2000
3	Stone exchange by 1st quality 'Abbasiyya red stone from including removal of old stone & building cost.	20 cu. m.	1800
4	Stone exchange cornice all inclusive—same design as existing cornice on north-eastern facade	22 m.	1320
5	Blocking 3 windows & 3 openings in the houses above gate and latrines slopes & all openings from street using rough stone & mortar (lime, sand & brick dust)		195
6	Plastic repair of stone to make it regain its original state "*li-'adat halatiha al-asliyya*"		15
7	Exchange of solid stone column with base and capital located at the eastern jamb of the entrance passage		200
8	Repair of the door leaves including the iron cladding, nails, etc.		150
9	Placing flat cement stalactites similar to the existing ones on the western side of the passage		80
10	Three layers of oil painting including plaster blocking of all stones on the NE and SW facades and the interior facades of the passage imitating the color of stone in its natural state	1000 sq. m.	2500
11	Scaffolding around the building and in the passage		1000

37. Comité X (1893), p. 74.

38. Comité XXXX (1946–53), pp. 139, 198, and 281.

39. During the execution of the works, a letter in Arabic from the Health Department was sent to the officer of al-Awqaf where it was mentioned that dust and old plaster was constantly falling from Bawwabat al-Mitwalli, and described it to be *fi ghayit al-wasakha* (extremely dirty). As an answer to this letter, Herz sent a message in French to the chief engineer asking him to tear down the house on the upper roof and make a project to restore it. See File Bab Zuwayla, Al-Mahfuzat, letter Nos. 18 (7.8.1893) and 20 (21.8.1893).

40. LE 1.006 was spent for the repair of the blocks of the soffit of the arch and LE 350 (LE 200 from the Waqfs and LE 150 from the Comité) was spent for the reconstruction of the minaret tops. See File Bab Zuwayla, Al-Mahfuzat, letter No.s 9 (16.7.1892) and 10 (21.9.1892); and Comité VII (1890), p. 70.

41. Comité XIV (1897), pp. x–xii.

42. LE 3 and 900 milliemes were paid for the preparation of these marble plates. See Comité XVI (1899), p. 54.

43. Comité XIV (1897), pp. x–xii.

44. File Bab Zuwayla, Al-Mahfuzat, letter Nos. 26–34 (Nov. 1898–Jan. 1899).

45. File Bab Zuwayla, Al-Mahfuzat, letter No. 76 (24.5.1916).

46. File Bab Zuwayla, Al-Mahfuzat, letter No. 103 (24.12.1919).

47. File Bab Zuwayla, Al-Mahfuzat, letter No. 104 (24.12.1919).

48. File Bab Zuwayla, Al-Mahfuzat, letter No. 106 (3.8.1920).

49. Comité XIII (1896), pp. 107–8. This is part of a report sent by Stanley Lane-Poole about the conservation of Islamic monuments presented in a report by Lord Cromer concerning Affairs of the Egyptian Government.

50. Comité VI (1889), p. 121; and IX (1892), p. 104.

51. Seventy-three shops were counted in front of Barquq, al-Nasir Muhammad, and Qalaun on a 140-meter stretch, forty-one shops in front of al-Ashraf, etc. (see same report).

52. Shops belonging to individuals were extended toward the interiors of the mosques, such as the No.s 21, 26, 29 and 34.

53. For or all five monuments surveyed a total of LE 7368.840 was needed for expropriation (facades of Qalaun-Barqu-al-Nasir, al-Ghuri complex, Bab al-Mitwalli, al-Mu'ayyad Mosque, al-Ashraf, and Qijmas mosque). "Probable funding sources for the LE 7368 might be the Waqf, the Ministry of Public Works, and the Governorate. This money will be employed as usefully as that which is used for consolidation works. The Comité must not hesitate in taking this decision, though this sum appears to be a bit high." Comité VI (1889): 127–28.

54. Comité XI (1894), p. 34; and XIV (1897), p. 15.

55. Comité XVII (1901), pp. 46 and 59; and Bab Zuwayla File, Al-Mahfuzat, letter Nos. 47 (17.3.1901), 49 (2.5.1901), 50 (11.5.1901), 51 (6.2.1901), 52 (29.7.1901), 54 (24.5.1901), 55 (3.11.1902), 56 (16.6.1903), 57 (20.6.1903), and 60 (4.3.1909).

56. Bab Zuwayla File, Al-Mahfuzat, letter Nos. 97 (11.12.1919), 98 (4.2.1919), 100 (24.1.1918), 101 (28.8.1919), and 99 (26.2.1919).

57. Bab Zuwayla File, Al-Mahfuzat, letter Nos. 136 (28.11.1940), and 151 (17.5.1947).

58. Bab Zuwayla File, Al-Mahfuzat, letter Nos. 153 (6.10.1947), 154 (6.10.1947), and 156 (20.11.1947).

59. Comité VIII (1891), p. 108.

60. Bab Zuwayla File, Al-Mahfuzat, letter Nos. 62 (12.12.1908), and 63 (19.4.1909).

61. Bab Zuwayla File, Al-Mahfuzat, letter Nos. 67 (6.11.1912), 68 (9.11.1912), and 69 (9.11.1912).

62. Bab Zuwayla File, Al-Mahfuzat, letter Nos. 105 (21.4.1920), 107 (7.7.1920), and 108 (1.9.1920).

63. Bab Zuwayla File, Al-Mahfuzat, letter Nos. 122 (21.4.1937), 123 (2.6.1937) and 125 (June 1937).

64. Bab Zuwayla File, Al-Mahfuzat, letter Nos. 79 (28.1.1917), and 92 (28.1.1918).

65. Bab Zuwayla File, Al-Mahfuzat, letter Nos. 93 (16.5.1918), and 94 (9.11.1918).

66. Bab Zuwayla File, Al-Mahfuzat, letter Nos. 114 (Sept 1924), 115 (8.9.1924), and 121 (26.1.1936).

67. This is a part of a report sent by Stanley Lane-Poole about the conservation of Islamic monuments presented in a report by Lord Cromer concerning Affairs of the Egyptian Government. Comité XIII (1896), pp. 107–8.

68. Comité XXVI (1909), p. 52.

69. File Bab Zuwayla, Al-Mahfuzat, letter Nos. 128 and 129 (24.2.1938).

70. Comité XXXIX (1941–45), pp. 32–33. The drawings proposed for these shops in "Arab style" are in the archives of the SCA.

71. File Bab Zuwayla, Al-Mahfuzat, letter Nos. 84–88 (Feb. to May 1917) and Comité XXXII (1915–19), pp. 511 and 531.

72. File Bab Zuwayla, Al-Mahfuzat, letter Nos. 145 and 146 (27–30.6.1946).

73. Bab Zuwayla File, Al-Mahfuzat, letter Nos. 147 (17.7.1946) and 148 (10.8.1946).

74. Bab Zuwayla File, Al-Mahfuzat, letter No. 152 (18.10.1947).

75. Comité XI (1894), pp. 42–43 and 74–75; and File Bab Zuwayla, Al-Mahfuzat, letter No. 21 (30.6.1897).

76. Comité XXI (1904), p. 44.

77. File Bab Zuwayla, Al-Mahfuzat, letter No. 110.

78. The razed tunnel vaults of the ground floor rooms of this *wikala* are still noticed in ruins behind the signs of the shops.

79. I. Bierman, "Urban Memory and the Preservation of Monuments."

80. House of Mounib near Bab Zuwayla, end of eighteenth century. Darb al-Ahmar quarter.

81. Comité XXXIII (1920–24), pp. 70–71.

82. Ibid.

83. Comité XXXVI (1930–32), pp. 24–25.

84. Comité XXXVII (1933–35), pp. 319 and 417.

85. Comité XXXVI (1930–32), pp. 146 and 176–77.

86. Comité XXXVI (1930–32), p. 164.

87. The house left then in ruins is still left with no remedy under the mercy of nature, man, and time.

88. Comité XXXVIII (1936–40), pp. 224–25.

89. Comité XXXVIII (1936–40), p. 338.

90. File Bab Zuwayla, Al-Mahfuzat, letter Nos. 128 (3.10.1937) and 126–27.

Letter #126	
Item	Cost LE
worker 365 days	18.25
plants flowers	2.18
fertilizer	1.00
extra compensation for holidays	1.83
tools	5.00
transfer	1.25
administrative fees—10%	2.95
contingency	3.55
TOTAL	36.00

Letter #127	
Item	Cost LE
remove 120 m debris	6.00
200 m mud	22.00
500 workers on a daily basis	25.00
tools	1.5
trees, plants, etc.	9.00
extra compensation for holiday workers	2.50
water supply, connecting pipes, etc.	20.00
administrative fees—10%	8.60
contingency	5.40
TOTAL	100.00

91. The problem in this house was to restore a facade without touching what was behind it. Not only was this unethical conservation-wise, but it was also unsafe, since the facade became a wall without any real support. This was exactly what happened in the case of the house of al-Alayli. It is a good lesson to learn, since first, it is not right to register only the facade of a structure as a monument and ignore the interior; and second, that conserving only a facade provides only a temporary plastic surgery. In the West, when facades are kept with completely new interiors, a whole new set of new structural elements are added to create new connections between the preserved old facade and the reconstructed interior.

92. In my opinion, the Comité's activities in this area must be a starting point for any conservation practice in historic Cairo because they represent a whole bouquet of preservation experiences. When digested properly, these can serve as a first step toward local adaptation to the international concepts and ethical obligations of conservation.

93. The Comité used some repetitive architectural details, which were reproduced on different parts of buildings with similar or close functions and/or which fell in the same chronological order. Some of these were the wooden balustrades of balconies on the minarets, the parapets and sheds hanging over the *sabíls*, the unified details of the *mashrabíyyas*, details of the moldings, the wooden railings, the wooden staircases, the crenellations adorning the tops of the buildings, and the missing stucco windows inside the buildings. Born for a practicality, this has affected the reinforcement of what the Comité believed to be "Arab art." See Hampikian, *Al-Salíhíyya Complex Through Time* (forthcoming).

94. Needless to say, this philosophy is the most undesirable form of intervention, and is done only for strict reasons. A building is justified as being historical by the presence of all the layers it gained through time, so privileging some layers over others, and destroying the unprivileged ones, is not acceptable in the conservation discipline today.

95. Edwards, *The Destruction of Cairo* (courtesy of 'Ala' al-Habashi).

96. E. Pauty, "Rapport general sur la defense de l'ancienne ville du Caire et de ses monuments," *Bulletin de l'Institut Français d'Archéologie Orientale*, Vol. XXXI, 1931, p. 136.

97. Fahmy, "An Olfactory Tale of Two Cities," in J. Edwards ed., *Historians in Cairo* (Cairo: American University in Cairo Press, 2002), pp. 160–63.

98. D. Reid, "Cultural Imperialism and Nationalism: The Struggle to Define and Control the Heritage of Arab Art in Egypt," *International Journal of Middle East Studies*, Vol. 24, No. 1, 1992, p. 65; quoted from Clerget, *Le Caire*, Vol. 1 (Cairo: E. and R. Schindler, 1934), p. 337.

99. Comité I, (1882–83), p. 16.

100. A. Rhoné, "Coup d'oeil sur l'état present du Caire," in *Gazette des Beaux Arts*, Vol. 24, 1881, pp. 9 and 12.

101. A. Rhoné, *L'Égypte à petites journées: Le Caire d'autrefois* (Paris: Société Générale d'Édition, 1910), pp. 30 and 33.

102. Pauty, "Rapport general sur la defense de l'ancienne ville du Caire et de ses monuments," pp. 141–42.

103. Ibid.

104. The Ministry of Public Works and the Comité have changed their names, but still a wide gap exists between those in charge of the urban fabric around the monuments in Historic Cairo and the general urban laws of the City of Cairo, which will only be settled when the historic core of Cairo develops its own urban laws which respect its traditional architectural forms and urban planning.

105. T. Mitchell, *Colonising Egypt* (Cambridge: Cambridge University Press, 1988), p. 65; quoted from Abbate-Bey, "Questions hygiéniques sur la ville du Caire," *Bulletin de l'Institut Égyptien*, 2nd series, Vol. 1, 1880, p. 69.

106. Objects of Arab art were collected in the ruins of al-Hakim Mosque and then were transferred to the Islamic Museum in Bab al-Khalq in 1903. Meanwhile, there was a plan to build a museum inside the courtyard of al-Mu'ayyad Shaykh Mosque, which was not realized because of financial problems. This is also an indication of how important this plot around Bab Zuwayla was for the Comité.

107. Pauty, "Rapport general sur la defense de l'ancienne ville du Caire et de ses monuments," pp. 135–75.

11

The Cemeteries of Cairo and the
Comité de Conservation

May al-Ibrashy

The historic cemeteries of nineteenth-century Cairo were a sprawling expanse of desert, tombstones, solitary canopies, shrines, walled graveyards, imposing ruins, and squatter huts that ran along the foot of the Muqattam hill, east and south of the city. Occupying a huge area that stretched from the Bab al-Nasr Cemetery outside the northern gate of Fatimid al-Qahira, down to the village of al-Basatin in the south, they were almost the last zone in Cairo to come under the normative efforts of the new, modernizing administration of the city. Urban design tools such as the 1874 Grand Bey map stopped at the cemeteries, and the jurisdiction of the Tanzim did not extend there.[1] Likewise, efforts to control burial practice, such as the 1876–77 regulations of the Conseil Sanitaire, were designed more to organize new, unbuilt cemeteries outside the city, than to impose a new sense of order on the older cemeteries of Cairo.[2] While recognizing that Cairo's cemeteries (known popularly as al-Qarafa) were also in need of regulation, modernizers felt that, with their vast area, built-up zones, residential clusters, and walled family graveyards (*hawshs*), they represented a special zone that had to be studied further before being addressed by new legislation.[3]

The cemeteries were, however, very much within the focal center of the movement to conserve the city's historical buildings, a movement that culminated in the establishment of the Comité de Conservation des Monuments de l'Art Arab in 1881.[4] In particular, the buildings of the cemeteries' most picturesque zones—the quarter of Qaytbay in the east, and the cemetery zone of Sayyidi Jalal al-Suyuti in the south (referred to, respectively, as "the Tombs of the Caliphs" and "the Tombs of the Mamluks" in travelers' guidebooks)—were repeatedly used in the writings of European connoisseurs of "Arab Art" as quintessential examples of an architectural heritage direly in need of preservation.[5] Beautifully proportioned, partially ruined buildings, standing within a field of tombstones, with the hill of al-Muqattam as backdrop, they lent themselves easily to the artist's brush, and, later, to the photographer's lens. In fact, the two images of Cairo that European artists depicted most frequently were its narrow streets filled with bustling crowds below a forest of domes, minarets, and *mashrabiyyas*, and its serene, melancholy cemeteries with the odd solitary figure or funerary procession in the foreground.

The two cemetery zones noted above were specifically satisfying, both aesthetically and conceptually, since they catered to the romantic inclinations of nineteenth-century Europeans and conformed to their perception of the beautiful, mysterious, yet declining Orient. But they were not representative of Cairo's cemeteries as a whole, which contained many spaces of very different character—as can be seen from Edward Lane's mid-nineteenth century description of a walk through the "Cities of the Dead." Lane told how the Bab al-Nasr Cemetery north of al-Qahira contained only modest tombs, mostly whitewashed or decorated with red and green paint. He described the Eastern cemetery as a desert with "not a trace of verdure," and with many roads and squalid residential settlements around Qaytbay and Barquq. He explained how the section closest to the Citadel contained the tombs and cenotaphs of the Mujawirin arranged close together. And he noted that although the Southern Cemetery did not contain as many sepulchural Mamluk mausolea as the Eastern Cemetery, it did contain many walled family enclosures with accommodations and trees, and many decorated tombs of the Beys of the Ottoman period. In particular, Al-Imam al-Shafi'i was the spiritual center of this cemetery, Lane wrote; and west of it, he noted how the lake of 'Ayn al-Sira was visited for its healing powers, in part because of its proximity to al-Shafi'i.[6]

The shrine of al-Shafi'i was, indeed, the foremost spiritual center in Cairo's cemetery complex at this time. In fact, the Southern Cemetery as a whole was known as Qarafat al-Imamayn, or "the two Imams" after the shrines of al-Shafi'i and al-Layth. Yet these buildings were not depicted in any European gravures, possibly because they lay within residential clusters that were not picturesque, but more importantly because they were not accessible to non-Muslims.[7] The Comité's first task was, therefore, not just to research the monumental and historical ruins of the two clusters the Europeans knew and admired, but also to try to extract the "monument" from the "shrine" across Cairo's entire cemetery zone, and create a new narrative that emphasized art history over cultic memory.

EXISTING PATTERNS OF PATRONAGE AND CONTROL

These shrines were, of course, the focus of a tradition of maintenance and preservation that preceded that of the Comité. This tradition functioned within a framework of private patronage both through endowment and use. The patrons of these shrines maintained them both practically through setting up *waqfs* for the maintenance of their buildings and activities, and spiritually through visiting them, participating in their religious ceremonies, and augmenting their cultic stature through the perpetuation, or even the embellishment, of memory. Overseeing these processes was the Awqaf organization, an administrative body in charge of cultural buildings throughout the city, their *waqfs*, and the activities carried out in them.

While patronage of shrines was practiced by Egyptians of all classes, the royal family and the new aristocracy were, by virtue of the magnitude of their donations and their position as leaders of the society, the most visible representatives of this tradition. Likewise, the Comité had only been founded after extensive lobbying of Khedive Isma'il by the European community, and its continuity was partially a function of it maintaining the goodwill and support of the ruling family and its court. Moreover, the Comité also fell under the jurisdiction of the Awqaf, which administered some of these *waqfs* directly, and supervised the *nazírs* (*waqf* overseers) of the rest of them. The Comité was also dependant on the Awqaf for financial support, especially during its formative years. It was, therefore, in the unenviable position of being under the yoke of the two main representatives of the very framework it wished to replace.

The visitors to these shrines (*za'irs*) and the worshippers and sufis in their mosques and *takíyyas* were also a force to be reckoned with by the Comité. But many of their needs were considered secondary by the Comité when a new competitive "consumer," the Western cultural tourist, became interested in their shrines as monuments. Such changes were bound to be met with resistance. Yet this category of patrons were largely invisible in the Comité records, as their direct dealings with the Comité were limited. Nevertheless, in the long run, by virtue of their sheer numbers and the frequency of their use of cemetery buildings, they constituted a movement that would derail many of the policies the Comité sought to develop for "restoring" the shrines to their original appearance and thus freezing them in time.

While the Comité was not initially conversant with the scale of difficulties it would encounter dealing with this existing framework of patronage and administration of cultic sites, this was nothing compared to the problems it would have in dealing with the real "masters" of the cemetery, the *turabí* community. As caretakers of its funerary structures and enclosures, undertakers and grave-diggers, the *turabís* both lived and worked in the cemetery. Each cemetery was sectioned off into zones, under separate jurisdiction and of different size and degree of importance, and *turabís* were granted these as concessions by the Supreme Judge, or the Qadi of Misr, and subsequently registered by the Governorate (Muhafaza).[8] The *turabís*, then, though not technically employees of the Muhafaza, reported to it, and were its representatives in the cemetery.

Furthermore, as the walled *madfan* or *hawsh* became the funerary structure of choice for the upper and middle classes, open expanses of desert within the cemetery zone started to shrink, and the cemeteries became more and more built-up. With the rise in Cairo's population, the cemeteries also started to house excess population from the city. Existing residential pockets grew in size, and new ones also appeared, especially in the vicinity of the Mahajir railway, which was originally established to service the sand and stone quarries on the outskirts of the cemetery, and where a new community of stone-cutters and quarry workers settled. The occupancy rate of the built-up *madfans* also grew, as did the number of resident *turabis* and their assistants.[9]

Therefore, the cemeteries' high concentration of shrines—where the city's *walis*, sufis, and *'ulama* were buried—already functioned as monuments (in this case, to a degree or variation of the sacred), and were cared for accordingly. As part of this awareness of heritage, a proper sense of their importance was perpetuated through *ziyara* (pious visitation) and a corresponding literature, and special care was taken to preserve and protect them from harm (not necessarily as physical structures, but most certainly as sites of memory) for the *ziyara* tourist.[10]

The Comité, on the other hand, worked to understand and therefore identify certain buildings as "*monuments de valeur artistique et historique*." Across Cairo it sought to preserve and protect such structures, and then re-form them and their surroundings with the Western cultural tourist in mind. This meant transforming these buildings from mosques, schools, hospitals, or homes to "monuments." The Comité was consequently in the position of "re-inventing" the cemeteries according to a new cultural framework. And this ultimately meant developing a strategy that contended with the existing patterns of use, patronage, maintenance, and care. With regard to this effort, the Comité viewed the cemetery's main function, as a funerary zone, as relatively harmless. But the constant presence of the *turabis* and the proliferation of walled family *hawshs* soon led to problems that would prove extremely hard to handle. Meanwhile, the stream of new residents trickling into the cemetery zone would become a steady flow by the end of the nineteenth century, and would further complicate the matter.

Over time, these conditions necessitated that the Comité develop a strategy for intervention that was particular to the cemetery. Indeed, the Comité bulletins show that during its first four decades (until the 1918 monuments law endowed it with new legal powers), it experimented with several different strategies. From the 1880s to the 1920s, the Comité was still trying to understand the buildings of the cemetery, learning about its own limitations—and more importantly, learning how to maneuver around them. But by the 1920s the Comité had identified most of the cemetery buildings in need of conservation; its powers had been normalized; and its position vis-à-vis the older framework of patronage, use, and administration was clearer. Moreover, the 1920s saw the formation of the

Cemeteries Committee and its active involvement, along with the Tanzim, in the organization of cemetery spaces, the regulation of *turabi*, and the growth of residential clusters.[11]   Since these two governmental bodies were organized along "modern" European principles, the extension of their authority to the cemeteries brought the Comité important allies in its struggle against the old guard.

This study, however, focuses on the formative first forty years of the Comité's work in the cemetery areas, and its early attempts to understand and contend with the status quo there.   Above all, this was a period during which the Comité struggled to identify buildings, partners, and adversaries, and during which it tried to formulate a comprehensive system of reorganization to deal with the issues mentioned above—namely, working to identify and understand; to contend with an existent framework of patronage and administration; to curb the powers of the *turabis*; and, finally, to control the increase in urban sprawl due to the proliferation of built-up family *madfans* and the growing cemetery community.

ACTIVITIES OF THE COMITÉ: IDENTIFICATION, STUDY, AND LISTING

As no intervention could take place without some form of understanding of the buildings, the first task of the Comité de Conservation was to list buildings, *waqf* or otherwise, that it felt were in need of preservation and protection. Changes to this list were published in its bulletins.[12]   Parallel to the identification of buildings to be listed came efforts to understand their history (their original patron and construction date, for instance), and legal status.[13]   Toward this end, the Comité produced a number of lists, until it finally settled on the monuments list and map of 1948—a map used to this very day with a few additions.

Identification of the legal status of buildings—though important during the first decades because it determined how the restoration work would be funded— was not easy.[14]   Inquiries addressed to the Awqaf organization, then to the *turabis* and the Governorate, were often fruitless.   In terms of legal status, for example, cemetery buildings could be owned in many ways: privately (as in the case of the complex of Inal in the Eastern Cemetery);[15] as *waqf* under the supervision of the Awqaf administration (as in the case of all the major shrines, such as al-Shafi'i and al-Sayyida Nafisa); as *waqf* under supervision of a *nazir* (as in the case of the Mausoleum of the Abbasid Caliphs[16] or Zayn al-Din Yusuf); by the state when structures were abandoned or of unknown ownership (as in the case of most of the "Tombeaux des Mamlouks"); or by the public (as in the case of the aqueducts).

The history of major shrines, such as al-Imam al-Shafi'i, did not need identification, of course, because this was well known and their *waqf* established.   Yet, the Comité still needed to pinpoint sections of historical and artistic importance within such shrine complexes. Thus, in the case of al-Shafi'i, the mausoleum was listed and conserved, while the 'Abd al-Rahman Katkhudha mosque adjacent to it was not. This was the reason, for example, that the Comité did not oppose the demolition of the Ottoman structure to make room for a new mosque sponsored by Khedive Tawfiq.

While some buildings of monumental importance (such as the Qaytbay complex) were well known, with active *waqfs*, others (such as al-Sultaniyya) had no known *waqf*, and many of its surrounding buildings, though a regular feature in tourist guidebooks and travelers' descriptions of Cairo, had yet to be placed historically. Of these, some, such as the mausoleum known as Abu Sibha, whose founder was identified as Sudun Amir Majlis, had also acquired new popular identities that had been retained in the collective memory. The names of others, such as the Mausoleum of Azdumur had mutated (in this case to al-Zumur) through time. Meanwhile, a last group of buildings were abandoned, unnamed, and unidentified.

In identifying buildings, the Comité was working with two levels of awareness, which, despite feeding into each other and often coinciding, were quite distinct. The first was local, based on Awqaf documentation and Governorate records, but further fed by historical and religious books that were still in use—such as al-Maqrizi's work; al-Jabarti's chronicle; and, in the case of the cemetery, *ziyara* literature, especially the work of Ibn al-Zayyat and al-Sakhawi.[17] Such local awareness represented a continuum of knowledge that had remained on the surface for cultic and religious purposes, but also to assist in the administration and organization of the cemetery. The second level of awareness was related to what caught the attention of a Western eye trying to make sense of buildings that were interesting because of their "*valeur artistique and historique.*" On this level, picturesque clusters, such as those around Qaytbay or al-Sultaniyya, were more important (or of more immediate relevance) than al-Shafi'i or al-Layth, which were living structures of varying degrees of historicity and beauty not accessible to foreigners.

In its attempt to understand such structures, the Western eye had to begin from scratch. This often meant ignorance of a good deal of what the locals knew, but it also led to a rereading of the buildings and the clearing up of misconceptions concerning their history (as can be seen from the reidentification of Abu Sibha and Azdumur). The Comité was, therefore, engaged in a fundamental reassessment of these buildings according to different measures of significance. For example, whereas the area southeast of Bab al-Qarafa was known locally as Sayyidi Jalal after Jalal al-Din al-Suyuti, the fifteenth-century writer and religious figure, it was called the "Tombs of the Mamluks" in the Western tradition—and its core was perceived to be the unnamed, unidentified Mamluk Sultaniyya complex, with its impressive double dome, rather than the modest, yet well-frequented and locally famous Ottoman shrine of Jalal al-Din al-Suyuti.[18]

THE COMITÉ'S ATTEMPTS TO MODIFY EXISTING PATTERNS

Although the Awqaf was the mother organization and financial backer of the Comité, it seems the latter envisioned a situation where the acquiescence of the Awqaf to its conservation strategy was a matter of course. The Comité would soon discover otherwise. Right from the beginning, the funds available for its work were never enough, but it was only when it started to widen the scope of its work to include the modification of environments around monuments that real trouble started. This was a problem in both city and cemetery; but since the Comité had higher expectations for the cemetery due to its relatively open, unbuilt morphology, the compromises it had to make there were bigger.

Around the turn of the century, the Comité started concerning itself with freeing the "monuments" from their urban surroundings, both to protect them from encroachment and to facilitate a better appreciation of their beauty. It was particularly ambitious in imagining the size of protection zones around cemetery buildings. In this regard, it felt that the dead (further burials of whom it wished to prohibit) and the few who lived in such buildings would be less formidable as adversaries than the occupants of monuments in the city-proper. Therefore, while protection zones in the city-proper did not exceed two meters on average, protection zones of up to twenty meters were recommended around cemetery monuments.[19]

In order to carry out its wishes, the Comité required funds to compensate the owners of expropriated structures and an executive body to implement its expropriation plans. The likely candidates for these two jobs were the Awqaf, its mother organization and funder; and the Tanzim, which due to its work organizing and widening the city streets, was well versed in expropriation. The Comité met with obstacles on both counts.

With regard to the Awqaf, the 'ulama ruled that it was illegal to use *waqf* money for an operation that would, in essence, deprive the *waqf* of part of its income (in addition to the fact that such use had not been specified in the *waqf*). The ruling recognized the reality that the shops and houses targeted for removal tended to be property endowed as a source of revenue for the neighboring charitable or religious building. This problem was resolved when the government allocated, in 1897, a sum of LE 20,000 for the Comité to use for its demolition projects and for the maintenance of buildings without *waqf* or with insufficient *waqf.*[20] On the other hand, when the Comité asked the Tanzim to remove buildings encroaching on the Mausoleum of al-Imam al-Shafi'i, it was informed by the Ministry of Public Works that this "*endroit n'est pas soumis aux reglements du Tanzim.*"[21]

It was left to the Comité to redesign the urban fabric of the cemetery unaided, and it began by using part of the LE 20,000 for freeing its most important buildings. It also took preventive measures to avert further complications, and its first step here was to ask the Governorate not to give permits for restoration or construction work in the cemetery without referring them first to the Comité.[22] This strategy sometimes worked; but often it did not, as can be seen from the Azdumur incident to be discussed below. Moreover, if private citizens managed to build, the Comité still did not have the powers to demolish their structures. For example, the Awqaf was of the opinion that the Comité's 1908 request to tear down a structure built by a Daramalli Bey in the *haram* (protection zone) it had proposed around the Mausoleum of Tashtamur in the Eastern Cemetery was not legally binding and could only be processed and implemented by the Ministry of Public Works.[23] Attempts to prevent restoration of existing buildings around monuments were also often unsuccessful. Thus, in 1912, the Comité's request to stop the rebuilding of a house adjacent to the Qaytbay complex was ignored.[24]

The Comité, as it grew more ambitious, also started to antagonize the *waqf nazirs*, the administrators of *waqfs* not directly run by the Awqaf organization. In the Comité's development phase these people did not pose that much of a threat, and in the nineteenth century the relationship with the *nazirs* was fairly cooperative in spirit. The *nazirs*, at this stage, were generally ordered to restore historic buildings using funds from their *waqfs*, and the Comité was often asked to oversee the restoration of unlisted *waqf* buildings. Nevertheless, the two sides did not always see eye to eye concerning duties and responsibilities. For example, the *nazir* of the Mausoleum of the Abbasid Caliphs restored it, but refused to comply with the Comité's request to restore the passageway to it since this was a public passageway that also led to many *hawshs*. On the other hand, the *nazir* of the adjacent Sabil al-Yazji sought the Comité's advice about restoration strategies, and the Comité, while not interested in the *sabil* as a historical building, decided to oversee the conservation anyway since the *sabil* was of "pleasing aspect and humanitarian function."

In a similar instance, the petition of the *nazir* of the Mausoleum of Mustafa Jaliq (southeast of Bab al-Qarafa) to the Comité for help tearing down a wall encroaching on the property (since the forty *waqf* beneficiaries were widows and minors) shows that the Comité, as the body in charge of the implementation of all Awqaf construction work on both listed and unlisted buildings, was often regarded as a caretaker of sorts in the cemetery. In this instance, the Comité responded, and ordered that the wall be torn down.[25] But by the beginning of the twentieth century, its relationship with the *nazirs* was becoming generally less smooth. For example, a difference in opinion concerning responsibilities with the *nazir* of the *waqf* of Inal in the Eastern Cemetery, and the refusal of the Awqaf administration to take responsibility for the management of the *waqf*, led the Comité to declare that it would go to court if it found the *waqfs* being managed in an unsatisfactory manner.[26]

The Mausoleum of Zayn al-Din Yusuf south of Bab al-Qarafa exemplified both the souring of the relationship with the *nazirs* and an inherent conflict of interest with the *turabis*, to be discussed below. This building was listed in 1892, but in

1905 the *nazir* refused to allocate a budget of LE 500, proposed by the Comité. As the Awqaf could not afford it, the Comité was left to look elsewhere for the money. In the same year, the request of the Mausoleum's *turabi* to build a house adjacent to it was denied, and he subsequently filed a complaint with the Sayyida Zaynab Court.[27] The atmosphere of antagonism and acrimony was such that when, in 1907, a fire erupted in the building, the Comité suspected that it was the result of arson.[28]

The Comité, probably out of respect for religious feeling, was more tolerant of patronage of shrines through financial sponsorship or use. At the beginning, accord- ing to the Comité, it was not necessary to preserve all buildings and freeze them in time, particularly if they were active cultic sites with structures dating no earlier than the Ottoman period. Thus, permission was given to replace the eighteenth-century baldaquin shrine over the grave of Shaykh Mustafa al-Bakri in the Eastern Cemetery with a modern structure more suited for the sufi activities of his followers.[29]

The funding of renovations and the construction of new shrines over cultic centers was also tolerated. Thus, a request from Muhammad al-Maghrabi to ren- ovate the dome of 'Abd Allah al-Manufi, one of the Eastern Cemetery's most pop- ular shrines, was approved by the Comité, as long as the work was done under their supervision.[30] In a more extreme case, the reconstruction of the shrine and mosque of al-Sayyida Nafisa and its surrounding buildings also met no opposition.[31] In this case, it only documented the older structures and moved some of their decorative elements to the museum, but allowed everything else to be demolished in the mid- 1890s. As part of the rebuilding, the mosque and mausoleum were reoriented cor- rectly toward the *qibla*, although the Comité did remark that it was "regrettable" that the new mosque obscured the western facade of the Mausoleum of the Abbasid Caliphs.[32] It should, however, be noted that al-Sayyida Nafisa was listed in the 1890 monuments list, while 'Abd Allah al-Manufi was not.[33]

Yet by the beginning of the twentieth century, the Comité was also becoming less tolerant of cultic activities in listed monuments. In 1904, for example, it sug- gested that the cultic activities of the Qadiri Sufis be moved from the Mausoleum of al-Ashraf Khalil north of al-Sayyida Nafisa to a nearby plot of land.[34]

The Comité's conservation activities were different from earlier restorations because they were triggered by the appreciation of a building for its historic and artistic merit and not its religious or cultic significance. Western cultural tourists were the new user group which had to be accommodated, and their tastes often clashed with those of religious tourists. After the Mausoleum of al-Imam al-Shafi'i was restored, the Comité asked its Shaikh to remove the shroud from the cenotaph in order to uncover its beautiful twelfth-century carvings. The Shaikh refused, giv- ing the excuse that the *maqsura* surrounding the cenotaph was also obscuring it from view. The Comité, on examining the *maqsura*, found it not worth preserving, and replaced it with a less elaborate one whose construction it insisted the *waqf* of al- Shafi'i fund. The tables were turned on the Comité, however, when Khedive

Tawfiq visited the shrine and found the *maqsura* too simple and not worthy of a shrine of this cultic weight. The Comité had to redo the *maqsura*.[35]

This story exemplifies the tug-of-war in the cemetery between protectors of its historic buildings and visitors and supporters of its shrines. Reid, in his discussion of the work of the Comité within the framework of cultural imperialism and nationalism, cited devotion to shrines and sites of cultic visitation as an example of the kind of interest shown by the Egyptians in their historic sites:

> But where were the modern Egyptians? The European officials, architects, Orientalists, and amateurs of Islamic art on the *Comité* tended to blame Egyptians for neglecting their monuments while assuming that their own motives were self-evident, scientific and pure. Things were not so simple, however. Egyptians from many walks of life were devoted to the shrines of al-Azhar, Sayyidna al-Husayn, Sayyida Zaynab, Imam al-Shafi'i and Sayyid Ahmad al-Badawi. These attachments were more to the religious associations of a holy site, however, than to the artistic or historical value of particular structures. Devotion to the text and message of the Quran and other Islamic classics outshone attachment to the specific architecture or decoration of a building, however old or beautiful it may be. Such mosques were living centres of worship and study, not museums to represent a dead past for Western tourists.[36]

These two approaches clashed in their understanding of what was acceptable in terms of the aesthetics of conservation and the type of activities and rituals that prompted people to visit them. Thus, a *maqsura* that was perfect to the Comité because it was simple and did not obscure the historic cenotaph within was not elaborate enough to befit the shrine of a major cultic figure important to the religious visitor.

For the Comité, restoring monuments, removing buildings that obscured them, guaranteeing access via good roads, publishing art-historical studies about them—these were all ways of encouraging the "right" tourism. Indeed, other more elaborate schemes were devised but often not implemented. For example, after the major conservation project of the Khanqah of Faraj ibn Barquq in the Eastern Cemetery in the 1930s, a suggestion was made to turn its courtyard into a kind of open-air museum to display the Islamic Museum's collection of funerary stelae.[37]

DEATH, LIFE, AND THE *TURABI* COMMUNITY

In 1910, the Ministry of Public Works, during the implementation of the project of organizing the streets of the Eastern Cemetery, reported a problem with the protection zone of twenty meters requested by the Comité around the monuments. According to the ministry, this required that tombs be disinterred, an un-Islamic practice according to the *fatwa* of the Mufti of Egypt. The Comité responded that the protection zone was intended only to prevent new constructions and burials, not to remove existent tombs. However, even this was found unacceptable by the Mufti, who was against preventing burial in a zone declared as cemetery, and, according to tradition, made *waqf* for burial.

When it felt its intentions were being misunderstood, the Comité next appealed to the Governor of Cairo. All it wished was to find "the practical method to put an end to the abusive dealings of the *turabis* (*fossoyeurs*) and other individuals on the surroundings of the monuments of the cemetery."[38]

This is a typical example of the methods of the Comité at the time. Not fully conversant with its limits, it over-reached. Then, on meeting an obstacle related to one of the issues it could not touch (in this case, religion), it transferred its reformist strictures to a more vulnerable adversary—in this case, the *turabis* and *madfan* residents. Here, its attack on the *turabis* came despite the fact that it had, in the course of the first twenty years of work, set up a system in which each *turabi* was paid a fee to guard the monuments in his area.[39] Thus, an uneasy alliance was gradually transformed into enmity.

The Comité, therefore, came to identify the *turabi*—who both lived in the cemetery and made his livelihood from burials in structures encroaching on monuments—as its "enemy number one." In 1911 it went a step further and used the Mufti's *fatwa*, initially not in its favor, against the *turabis*. It stated that, as the cemetery land was designated for burial, it should not be used for any other purpose—residence, for example. It also stated that the *turabis*, by virtue of their profession, should respect the dead and not build houses and residences over them. Therefore, it directed that a plan of the status quo should be sent to the Governorate, who should then make sure it did not change—i.e., that all new construction should be forbidden.[40]

The tomb of Azdumur in the Eastern Cemetery provides a paradigmatic example of the rocky Comité/*turabiyya* relationship. In 1893 the *turabi* in charge built a wooden structure near the tomb; and the structure grew in size until a full-scale residential building was finally erected in 1898. A second structure with running water was then built in 1916. All attempts of the Comité to prevent these building activities failed. The disagreement finally escalated into a full-fledged court case, in which the Comité even accused the *turabi* of removing decorated stones from the monument to reduce its historic value and sabotage the Comité's case.[41]

It should be noted that while the Comité had fixated on the *turabis* as the primary source of trouble in the cemetery, the problems it faced in the cemeteries were not the work of the *turabis* alone. Other individuals who worked in other professions lived around the cemetery buildings, and their homes were also torn down, as can be seen from the work of the Comité in freeing the surroundings of the Shafi'i shrine. Moreover, the walled family *madfans* or *hawshs*, while guarded by the *turabis*, were owned by Cairenes from all walks of life.

All these issues were summed up in a report discussing the cemetery from "the trifold view of history, religion and archaeology" in the 1915–19 bulletin.[42] In it, the Comité tried to use historical and religious arguments to support its ongoing campaign against new structures and unacceptable activities in the cemetery. In the process, it divided the cemetery into two legal categories: al-Qarafa al-Kubra, made *waqf* by 'Umar ibn al-Khattab, for the burial of the Muslim dead;[43] and the rest of the cemeteries, which were traditionally treated as *waqf* land too. It also described the practice of outlawing structures over tombs as the "Islamic" way, attributing the introduction of structures on cemeteries (especially nonfunerary ones, such as markets or houses) to the Fatimids. Different accounts of protests against cemetery buildings were also cited from primary sources of the late-medieval period, and according to the Comité, these protests had been effective. Thus, in the Mamluk period, only structures related to religious practice were built there; and even that custom was no longer popular under the Ottomans, who only built small tombs within simple enclosures. As the Comité argued:

> The invasion of the cemetery by these *hochs* (sic) is purely the product of the indifference of the authorities in charge and the arbitrary power of the gravediggers (over the cemetery). This invasion is . . . very recent and photographic evidence from about four decades points to how far they (the *hawshs*) have increased to the detriment of what had been one of the most characteristic charms of this suburb of Cairo from the artistic point of view.[44]

The report then cited a paper presented by Muhammad Yusuf Bey in the Premier Congres Egyptien of 1911 advocating the return to the "orthodox" burial practices of early Islam, i.e., those practiced in the Hijaz, Turkey, and Syria, where the private funerary *hawsh* did not exist. In a move that cleverly turned to its advantage the earlier injunction of the Mufti against its practices, the Comité then reiterated the illegality of establishing a private *hawsh* on land made *waqf* for Muslim burial—thereby appropriating for itself the mantle of protector of religion. Finally, it reviewed the new law of February 6, 1911, for the regulation of the cemeteries of Alexandria by the new Cemeteries Committee as a good example to follow. This law recommended the reorganization of the cemetery into registered lots and passageways; specified certain days for visitation; prohibited overnight stays in the cemetery (even for the *turabis*); prohibited new burials in ancient cemeteries except under special circumstances; required a planning permit for private *madfans*; and limited the powers of the *turabis*.[45] The Comité wished to present this law to the Tanzim as an option that was, as it had shown, not a violation of Islamic law, but actually in accordance to it.[46]

A NEW ERA ARRIVES

In 1918 the Comité was finally given a law more suited to its overall conservation and protection efforts. This was Law No. 8 for the protection of monuments of the Arab period, which expedited the expropriation process for encroachments, and which regulated the trade in antiquities. It declared as "*monument de l'époque arabe*" all buildings of artistic, historic, or archaeological importance from the Arab conquest to the death of Muhammad 'Ali.[47] All such monuments were to be expropriated for public utility (*manfa'a 'amma*) to become public property; they could not be modified or demolished except after permission from the Comité; and their restoration was to be made the financial responsibility of the Awqaf organization.[48]

A report presented to Majlis al-Nuzzar dated March 1913 shows that this law was the result of extensive lobbying on the part of the Comité. In it, the case of the cemetery was used to show the inadequacy of the existing legal framework. For example, it agreed that the family *madfans*, which the Comité had found unacceptable, were being torn down by a greater evil, the "*qasrs*" of the turabis and the residences of their assistants (*atba'*). Historic cenotaphs and tombstones were being removed and sold in the process, and many of them were making their way out of the country.[49] This was in addition to the continued establishment of funerary *hawshs* in the cemetery's more open zones—for example, the "Tombs of the Mamluks," where, but for the vigilance of the Director of the Awqaf, access to listed monuments would only have been possible via these *hawshs*.[50]

As this chapter has tried to show, however, during the development phase that preceded passage of this law, the Comité was aware that it had limited powers to contend with a restrictive status quo. It did the most it could within these limits, and tried to increase its effectiveness both directly by lobbying for more legal powers, and indirectly through subversion. It, therefore, tolerated the reconstruction of major shrines, many of which dated from the Ottoman period, (due to the fact that they were constantly being upgraded and restored) and therefore were not within the Comité's immediate scope of interest. Yet it also worked to define sections within these major shrines to be placed under its control. In the case of minor shrines such as Abu Sibha, it stripped them, whenever possible, of most of their cultic attributes and gradually discouraged cultic activities in them. It also worked to endow them with a new identity that was art-historical rather than religious or cultic.

Originally a subsidiary of the Awqaf, the Comité tried to find circumspect ways of achieving its ends—sometimes, as can be seen from its creative interpretations of *fatwas* concerning the legal status of cemetery buildings and land, using religious arguments. Therefore, the *fatwa* that all cemetery land was *waqf* for burial—initially used by the religious establishment to prevent the Comité from banning burial in protection zones—was used over and over again by the Comité for its own purposes. It first argued that such land could not be used for residence, and therefore people should not live there. It then decided that since all buildings were on *waqf* land, they belonged to the Awqaf, and it had a responsibility to restore all of them, even those of unknown ownership. Therefore, the Comité—as a representative of the Awqaf, owner of all cemetery land, and consequently of all the cemetery—could demolish any building it found unsuitable and restore any building it found worthy of listing. A champion of the unbuilt cemetery (except where its own buildings were concerned), it also used religious arguments concerning the illegality of building over graves and examples from outside Cairo to advocate a ban on all funerary structures.

The 1918 Monuments Law heralded a new era where the Comité's powers were clearer. It was now the responsibility of the Tanzim to expropriate listed monuments and their surroundings as *manfaʿa ʿamma*.[51] And with the establishment of a Cemeteries Committee, or Lajnat Jabbanat al-Muslimin bi-Madinat al-Qahira, in 1922, of which the Comité was a member, the regulation of the cemetery as a whole and its *turabis* became a more straightforward affair. The law establishing this committee also outlawed all nonfunerary activities in the cemetery, allowing people to live in only a handful of residential clusters.

Yet, paradoxically, at the same time that a legislative framework for the regulation of the cemetery according to these new norms was being established, a new adversary, more powerful than any of the above, had appeared. The lack of burial ground, the trend of walled *madfans* (many of which were inhabited), and the growth of residential pockets all combined to attack the monuments from new directions. The Comité had reached a level of sophistication whereby it could formulate plans for the urban reshaping of the zones around important monuments. Legally and conceptually, the Comité and its new partners had developed the powers and the abilities to reshape the cemetery completely. But, practically, they could no longer control what happened there.

Figure 11.1. Map of Cairo showing the location of the cemeteries of Cairo.
(Source: Drawn by author based on the Description de l'Égypte *Map)*

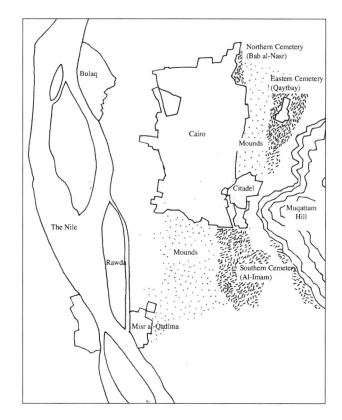

Figure 11.2. The so-called "Tombs of the Caliphs" or the Eastern Cemetery in the early twentieth century.
(Source: Author's Collection)

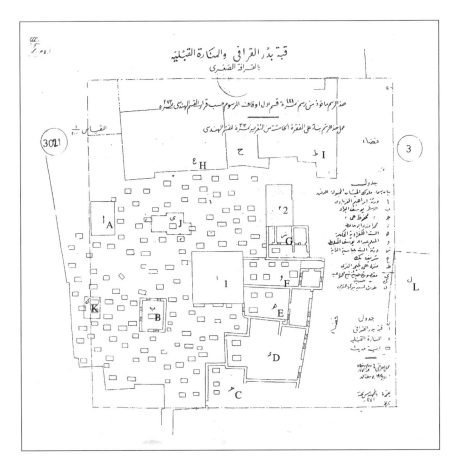

Figure 11.3. The cemetery, its spaces, and users as encountered by the Comité: A survey of a section of the so-called "Tombs of the Mamluks" drawn by a Comité architect in 1903.

1-2: Listed monuments, the Mausoleum of Badr al-Qarafi, and an unidentified minaret dating from the Mamluk period.

A-H and J-L: Private family *hawshs*

I: House of the turabi 'Ali Bulayha

(Source: Courtesy of the Archives of the Supreme Council of Antiquities, Egypt)

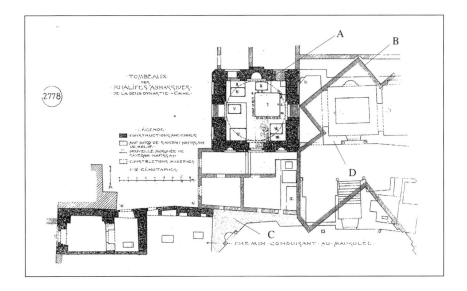

Figure 11.4. Protection of monuments versus private patronage: Plan approved by the Comité for the rebuilding of the Nafisi shrine in the beginning of the twentieth century using *waqf* money from an endowment set up by Khedive Isma'il.

A: The Dome of the Abbasid Caliphs; Historic building to be conserved

B: New mosque and shrine to be built

C: Mosque of al-Sayyida Nafisa; Historic building to be demolished

D: Shrine of al-Sayyida Nafisa; Historic building to be demolished

(Source: Courtesy of the Archives of the Supreme Council of Antiquities, Egypt)

NOTES

1. The Grand Bey map was used to help the government plan the new wide, straight roads and European squares it proposed to cut through the city's dense urban fabric. In fact, some of the roads drawn on the map were never implemented. See A. el-Habashi and N. Warner, "Recording the Monuments of Cairo: An Introduction and Overview," *Annales Islamologiques*, Vol. 32, 1998, pp. 81–99. The Tanzim (Alignment) was founded in 1845 and revitalized as an institution in 1879–80. Its responsibilities extended to replanning Cairo's streets in the late 1880s. See J. Abu Lughod, *Cairo: 1000 Years of the City Victorious* (Princeton: Princeton University Press, 1971), pp. 147–48.

2. The following are its salient points. Cemeteries should be downwind—at a distance of at least 500 meters from the city borders, and 200 meters from habitation. They should be on elevated ground, and should be fenced without undermining air circulation. The area of the cemeteries should be three times the area needed for the burial of five years. And they should not be located near bodies of water and not in a location in danger of inundation. Moreover, modifications to existing cemeteries should be set after investigation, when the need arises. In the meantime, all burial would be prohibited in gardens, mosques, churches, temples, synagogues, or other places dedicated to the practice of religion, public monuments, and generally in all locations other than the nonabandoned cemeteries. See P. Gelat, *Repertoire général annoté de la législation et de l'administration Égyptiennes*, Part I, Vol. 1 (Alexandria: Impr. J. C. Langoudakis, 1908), pp. 598–601, Part II, Vol. 5, pp. 103–5; V. Sisto, ed., *Repertoire permanent de législation Egyptienne*, Vol. 2 (Cairo: n.p., 1968), "cimetieres," pp. 1–2; and M.R. Basyuni and R. Farjun, eds., *Al-majmu'a al-da'ima l'il-qawanin w'al-qararat al-misriyya*, Vol. 2 (Cairo: Bulaq Press, n.d.), "jabbanat," pp. 1–3.

3. The term "Qarafa," originally the name of the southern cemetery only, was being used generically to mean "cemetery," by the mid-nineteenth century. A draft for a high decree—related to the transfer of graves in unsanitary cemeteries to new cemeteries planned according to modern specifications—dating to 1893, states: "In Alexandria and Cairo there are built *madfans* (graveyards) belonging to prestigious families—The Ministry of Interior is allowed to make exceptions in their case while maintaining the general law that no burial is allowed inside these two cities." The final decree dating to January 24, 1894, and a later one dated March 12, 1898, concerning enclosing the cemeteries, maintain: "This present decree is not applicable to public cemeteries that exist in Cairo or Alexandria. A later decree will determine the formalities to be followed for transfer of cemeteries in these two cities." See Archives of Dar al-Watha'iq al-Misriyya, Mahfaza 2 3 2, Nizarat al-Dakhiliyya Majlis al-Wuzara; Gelat I 1, pp. 601–2; Sisto, *Repertoire permanent de législation Egyptienne*, pp. 2–3; and H. al-Fakahani, *Al-mawsu'a al-tashri'iyya al-haditha*, Vol. 9, Part III (Cairo: Bulaq Press, n.d.), "jabbanat," pp. 4–5.

4. For a history of the Comité, see A. el-Habashi, "Athar to Monuments: The Interventions of the Comité de Conservation des Monuments de l'Art Arabe," Ph.d Dissertation, University of Pennsylvania, 2001. The Comité bulletins were published

regularly for the years between 1881 and 1953. They are referred to here by the year(s) they report on, rather than by their date of publication. They were put online at http://www.islamic-art.org/ in 2002 by the Islamic Art Network. The site includes a history of the Comité written by 'Alaa el-Habashi.

5. For an account of the first calls made by Europeans for the preservation of monuments of the Islamic Era in Cairo, many of which cited cemetery buildings as examples, see el-Habashi, "Athar to Monuments," pp. 61–65.

6. E.W. Lane, *Cairo Fifty Years Ago*, edited by S. Lane-Poole (London: J. Murray, 1896), pp. 117–27.

7. De Forbin, writing in the early nineteenth century, could only enter mosques if he pretended to be a Muslim. Se L. de Forbin, *Travels in Egypt* (London: Printed for Sir R. Phillips and Co., 1819), p. 25. These restrictions would gradually decrease, but would not disappear. By the end of the nineteenth century, while the mosque of Qaytbay was easily accessible to Westerners, the Mosque of al-Imam al-Shafi'i, could only be visited with "a special order from the Wakfs (sic.) Administration, not easily obtained." See Black's Guidebook, *Cairo of Today* (London: Adam & Charles Black, 1898), pp. 94–97. By 1911, entry to al-Shaf'i', while possible, was still difficult as tickets had to be bought beforehand from Cook's travel company. See D. Sladen, *Oriental Cairo: The City of the Arabian Nights* (London: Hurst & Blackett, 1911), p. 171.

8. These concessions were registered in ledgers called *taqarir al-nazar*, some of which are still held in the Dar al-Watha'iq archives. See, for example, Archives of Dar al-Watha'iq al-Misriyya, Taqarir al-Nazar 1, No. 187, p. 21, 1138 H.

9. This railroad, established in the mid-nineteenth century, drew even more people to the residential zone of 'Arab Quraysh immediately south of Bab al-Qarafa. Afterward, a new planned settlement, arranged in blocks of buildings oriented parallel to the railway line was introduced south of 'Arab Quraysh. This development must have been built between 1874 and 1897, as it is not drawn on the Grand Bey Map of 1874, but is featured in the Ministry of Public Works map of 1897. See Ministry of Public Works 1:10,000 Map of Cairo and its Environs (1897), Available at the Archives of Maslahat al-Misaha, Giza, Egypt. The presence of lime kilns in its vicinity and its orientation parallel to the line shows that it was a development directly linked to the new facilities for the production of lime, stone, and sand. According to El Kadi and Bonnamy, this settlement, called al-Kharta, was built by Khedive Tawfiq to house the quarry workers squatting illegally in a shantytown that had sprung up in the same area. See G. El Kadi and A. Bonnamy, *La cité des morts: Le Caire* (Paris: Institut de Recherche pour le Developpement, MARDAGA, 2001), p. 258.

10. The literature on *ziyara* included a genre of guidebooks that offered to lead the reader through sites of pious visitation in the Islamic world. A subsection of them dealt exclusively with the cemeteries of Cairo. Yusuf Raghib has produced a list of these books, some of which we know of only through citations in later manuscripts, while others still exist. The earliest extant *ziyara* manuscript dealing with the cemeteries of Cairo is Ibn 'Uthman's

(d. 1213) *Murshid*, recently published in 1995. The most comprehensive *ziyara* book is Ibn al-Zayyat's (d. 1412) *Kawakib*. See Y. Ragib, "Essai d'inventaire chronologique des guides a l'usage des pelerins du Caire," *Revue des Etudes Islamologiques*, Vol. 41, 1973, pp. 259–80; Muwaffaq al-Din, *Murshid al-zuwwar ila qubur al-abrar*, edited by M.F. Abu Bakr (Cairo: Al-Dar al-Misriyya al-Lub naniyya, 1995); and Shams al-Din Muhammad Ibn al-Zayyat, *Al-kawakib al-sayyara fi tartib al-ziyara*, edited by A. Taymur (Cairo; rprt., Baghdad, 1907).

11. Law 1 for the formation of a *lajna li-jabbanat madinat al-qahira* was passed on March 6, 1922, and its regulations were approved on December 14, 1922. Finally, on March 4, 1926, a final list of all approved Muslim cemeteries was prepared. See Sisto, *Repertoire permanent de législation Egyptienne*, pp. 8–12; and Basyuni and Farjun, *Al-majmu'a al-da'ima l'il-qawanin w'al-qararat al-misriyya*, "jabbanat," pp. 6–9.

12. See, for example, the monuments lists of 1890, 1903, 1910, 1914, 1922, 1924, and 1948. For a discussion of the activities of the Comité in listing the city's buildings, see el-Habashi and Warner, "Recording the Monuments of Cairo." It should be noted that as long as the Comité was a subsidiary of the Awqaf, it did not limit its conservation work to listed buildings. El-Habashi has shown that, especially in its early years, it was responsible for the repair of any *waqf* building in need of conservation. See El-Habashi, "Athar to Monuments."

13. See, for example, the studies of the Mausoleum of the Abbasid Caliphs, the Basatin Aqueduct, the Mausoleum of Shajar al-Durr, the Domes of al-Sab' Banat, Mausoleum of 'Uthman Qazdughli. See Comité bulletins, Vol. II, 1884, pp. 21–28; Vol. X, 1893, pp. 58–61; Vol. XVII, 1900, pp. 112–18; Vol. XXVII, 1910, p. 131; Vol. XXVIII, 1911, pp. 122–25; and Vol. XXX, 1913, pp. 145–46.

14. The buildings were funded using money from their *waqfs*. Some buildings did not have *waqfs*, and other sources of funding had to be found for their conservation. Therefore, for purely administrative reasons, it was often easier for the Comité to list its conservation projects, first by legal status then by geographic zone. See Comité bulletins, Vol. XII, 1895, pp. 10–13; and Vol. XIII, 1896, p. 9.

15. Comité bulletins, Vol. X, 1893, p. 54.

16. Comité bulletins, Vol. X, 1893, p. 30.

17. T. al-Maqrizi, *Al-mawa'iz wa'l-i'tibar bi-dhikr al-khitat wa'l-athar* (Bulaq: n.p., 1877, rprt: Beirut: Dar Sadir, n.d.); A. Al-Jabarti, *'Aja'ib al-athar fi'l-tarajim wa'l-akhbar* (Beirut: Dar al-Jil, n.d.); al-Zayyat, *Al-kawakib al-sayyara fi tartib al-ziyara*; and N. Al-Sakhawi, *Tuhfat al-ahbab wa bughyat al-tullab fi'l-khitat w'al-mazarat w'al-tarajim w'al-biqa'al-mubaraka*, edited by M. Rabi' and H. Qasim (Cairo: al-Ulum wa-al-Adab, 1937).

18. It is telling that the first time the Comité visited the double dome of al-Sultaniyya it called it al-Suyuti. This shows that they knew the local name for the zone as a whole, but preferred to use the European appellation. More importantly, according to their logic, the quarter's most monumental building should be its center after which it is known. They, therefore, identified al-Sultaniyya as the shrine of al-Suyuti. The latter was actually a small Ottoman building annexed to it. See Comité bulletins, Vol. V, 1887–88, p. 27.

19. See, for example, Comité bulletins, Vol. XXVII, 1910, p. 27.

20. See el-Habashi, "Athar to Monuments"; Comité bulletins, Vol. XIII, 1896, pp. 9–11; and Vol. XVI, 1899, p. 117, for a discussion of this point.

21. Comité bulletins, Vol. XIV, 1897, p. 164. The buildings on the city's cemetery fringe, such as those around Bab al-Wazir or on the city side of Bab al-Qarafa, on the other hand, were under Tanzim jurisdiction. For example, the 1898 bulletin mentions that it planned to move the Sabil of Aytmish al-Bajasi. See Comité bulletins, Vol. XV, 1898, pp. 99–100.

22. See, for example, the request to build close to the Mausoleum of Zayn al-Din Yusuf, which was denied by the Comité. It should be noted that this was a general ruling for all of Cairo. See Comité bulletins, Vol. XXII, 1906, p. 25.

23. Comité bulletins, Vol. XXV, 1908, p. 99.

24. Comité bulletins, Vol. XXIX, 1912, p. 29.

25. Comité bulletins, Vol. X, 1893, p. 30; Vol. VIII, 1891, p. 70; and Vol. XVI, 1899, p. 105.

26. Comité bulletins, Vol. XXI, 1904, p. 35.

27. Comité bulletins, Vol. IX, 1892, pp. 70–71; and Vol. XXIII, 1906, pp. 25 and 53.

28. Comité bulletins, Vol. XXIV, 1907, p. 70.

29. Comité bulletins, Vol. III, 1886, p. xxviii. The grave is marked today by a modern shrine and mosque.

30. Comité bulletins, Vol. IX, 1892, pp. 81–82, and 94.

31. After it was partially damaged by fire. See Comité bulletins, Vol. XXVII, 1910, p. 132, footnote 1.

32. Comité bulletins, Vol. XIII, 1896, p. 183; and Vol. XXVII, 1910, p. 132, footnote 1. A number of *hujjas* that register the purchase of this land exist in the records of the Awqaf. They date from the years 1319–21/1901–4. See, for example, Awqaf 1879, 1890, 1911, 1923, 1929, 1931, 1973, and 1986 in the Daftarkhana of the Ministry of Awqaf, Cairo.

33. Comité bulletins, Vol. VII, 1890, p. 147.

34. Comité bulletins, Vol. XXI, 1904, p. 80. This suggestion came during the course of the project for the expropriation and demolition of buildings around Umm al-Salih and al-Ashraf Khalil.

35. Comité bulletins, Vol. XXIV, 1907, pp. 67–68, and 77; Vol. XXV, 1908, p. 77; Vol. XXVII, 1910, pp. 5 and 11; Vol. XXVIII, 1911, p. 38; and Vol. XXIX, 1912, pp. 25–26.

36. D. Reid, "Culture, Imperialism and Nationalism," *International Journal of Middle-East Studies*, Vol. 24, 1992, p. 58.

37. Comité bulletins, Vol. XXXVIII, 1938–40, p. 313.

38. Comité bulletins, Vol. XXVII, 1910, pp. 27, 83, and 92.

39. This was particularly important for what was termed "*environs du Caire*" by the Comité. This was the zone closest to al-Muqattam (the Eastern Cemetery and the eastern section of the Southern Cemetery). Piecemeal commissions to *turabis* to guard certain buildings were regularized, when, in 1902, a more structured system for supervising the *turabis* was devised. Ten *turabis* were put in charge of the thirty-two listed monuments, and two caretakers were employed by the Awqaf administration to oversee them. See

Comité bulletins, Vol. V, 1887–88, p. 28; Vol. VI, 1889, pp. 28 and 83; Vol. VII, 1890, p. 20; Vol. VIII, 1891, p. 10; and Vol. IX, 1892, p. 55.

40. Comité bulletins, Vol. XXVIII, 1911, pp. 33 and 40.

41. This case is also of significance for another reason. When the Awqaf administration argued that it could not interfere, as this case did not affect an Awqaf-administered building, a previous Awqaf ruling that all cemetery buildings, because they stand on *waqf* land, was used by the Comité as a counter-argument—albeit to no avail. Moreover, this case brought out the need for a legal mechanism of intervention that might depend on the Ministry of Public Works, not on the Awqaf—as according to the Comité, "*il doit bien exister une autorité qui régisse ces terrains ainsi que ses bâtisses.*" See Comité bulletins, Vol. XV, 1898, p. 102; Vol. XVI, 1899, pp. 45–46, and 77–8; and Vol. XXXII, 1915–19, pp. 558–59.

42. Comité bulletins, Vol. XXXII, 1915–19, p. 589.

43. This observation was wrong on two counts. First, al-Qarafa al-Kubra was wrongly identified by the Comité as the older cemetery at the foot of al-Muqattam. In reality, it was the western section of the Southern Cemetery, now nonexistent except for the Mausolea of al-Sab' Banat and al-Khadra al-Sharifa, and was called al-Qarafa al-Kubra in the Mamluk period. When this zone fell into ruin in the Ottoman period, the Eastern Cemetery, previously called al-Sahra', was often called al-Qarafa al-Kubra. Second, medieval sources such as al-Maqrizi's *Khitat* tell us that it was al-Qarafa in general (this term was only used to denote the Southern Cemetery until the Ottoman period), and not just al-Qarafa al-Kubra, that 'Amr ibn al-'As made *waqf* for burial. See al-Maqrizi, *Khitat*, Vol. 2, pp. 443–64, for a discussion of the history of cemeteries until the Mamluk period.

44. Comité bulletins, Vol. XXXII, 1915–19, p. 237.

45. Sisto, *Repertoire permanent de législation Egyptienne*, "cimetieres," pp. 4–9.

46. Comité bulletins, Vol. XXXII, 1915–19, pp. 235–40.

47. This law also applied to Coptic monuments from the birth of Christianity to the death of Muhammad 'Ali.

48. Sisto, *Repertoire permanent de législation Egyptienne*, "Art Arabe," pp. 1–2.

49. The Comité was buying what it could of these historic objects and transferring them to the museum. For example, it bought the *shahid* of 'Abd Allah ibn Luhay'a al-Hadrami, dated 175 H, and as such the oldest tombstone in the museum. It also bought part of the cenotaph (*tabut*) of Ahmad ibn al-Sada Tabataba.

50. Archives of Dar al-Watha'iq al-Misriyya, Mahfaza 163, 'Abdin.

51. The Tanzim had started to get involved in the organization of the cemetery some ten years earlier, but had lacked the proper legal framework for expropriation of buildings for the Comité.

SELECTED BIBLIOGRAPHY

Abu Lughod, J. *Cairo: 1001 Years of the City Victorious.* Princeton: Princeton University Press, 1971.

Ahmed, L. *Edward William Lane: A Study of His Life and Works and of British Ideas of the Middle East in the Nineteenth Century.* London: Longman, 1978.

Allen, R. *A Period of Time: A Study and Translation of Hadith Isa Ibn Hisham bu Muhammad al-Muwaylihi.* Oxford: Ithaca Press, 1992.

Bacharach, J.L., ed. *The Restoration and Conservation of Islamic Monuments in Egypt.* Cairo: American University in Cairo Press, 1995.

Baedeker, K., ed. *Egypt: Handbook for Travellers.* Leipsic: Karl Baedeker, fourth edition, 1898.

Baer, G. *Studies in the Social History of Modern Egypt.* Chicago: University of Chicago Press, 1969.

Buzard, J. *The Beaten Track: European Tourism, Literature and the Ways to "Culture" 1800–1918.* Oxford: Oxford University Press, 1993.

Celik, Z. *Displaying the Orient.* Berkeley: University of California Press, 1992.

Choay, F. *The Invention of the Historic Monument.* Trans. by Lauren M. O'Connell. Cambridge: Cambridge University Press, 2001.

Crabbs, J. *The Writing of History in Nineteenth-Century Egypt.* Detroit: Wayne State University Press, 1984.

Darby, M. *The Islamic Perspective: An Aspect of British Architecture and Design in the Nineteenth Century.* London: Leighton House Gallery, 1983.

de Forbin, L. *Travels in Egypt.* London: Printed for Sir R. Phillips and Co., 1819.

de Leon, E. *The Khedive's Egypt.* New York: Harper & Brothers Publishers, 1878.

Duff-Gordon, Lady. *Letters from Egypt.* London: Macmillan and Co., 1865.

Duncan, J., and D. Gregory, eds. *Writes of Passage: Reading Travel Writing.* New York: Routledge, 1999.

Edwards, J., ed. *Historians in Cairo: Essays in Honor of George Scanlon.* Cairo: American University in Cairo Press, 2002.

El-Shayyal, G. *A History of Egyptian Historiography in the Nineteenth Century.* Alexandria: University of Alexandria, 1962.

Fahmy, K. *All the Pasha's Men: Mehmed Ali, His Army and the Making of Modern Egypt.* Cambridge: Cambridge University Press, 1997.

Feilden, B.M. *Conservation of Historic Buildings.* Oxford: Butterworth Architecture, 1994.

Flaubert, G. *Flaubert in Egypt: A Sensibility on Tour.* Trans. Francis Steegmuller. London: Bodley Head, 1972.

Frith, F. *Photographs of Egypt and the Holy Land.* Introduction by C. Williams. Cairo: American University in Cairo Press, 1999.

Galal, M.N. *Dynamics of the Egyptian National Identity.* Lahore: Sang-e-Meel, 1998.

Gillispie, C.C. and M. Dewachter, eds. *Monuments of Egypt: The Napoleonic Edition: The Complete Archaeological Plates from la Description de l'Égypte.* Princeton: Princeton University Press, 1987.

Goldschmidt, A. *Biographical Dictionary of Modern Egypt.* Boulder, CO: Lynne Rienner, 2000.

Hanna, N. *In Praise of Books: A Cultural History of Cairo's Middle Class, Sixteenth to the Eighteenth Century.* Syracuse, N.Y.: Syracuse University Press, 2003.

Hunter, R.F. *Egypt under the Khedives, 1805–1879.* Pittsburgh: University of Pennsylvania Press, 1984.

James, T.G.H. *Egypt Revealed: Artist-Travellers in an Antique Land.* London: The Folio Society, 1997.

Kabbani, R. *Imperial Fictions: Europe's Myths of Orient.* London: Pandora, 1994.

Kalfatovic, M.R. *Nile Notes of a Howadji: A Bibliography of Travelers' Tales from Egypt, from the Earliest Time to 1918.* London: The Scarecrow Press, 1992.

Lane, E.W. *An Account of the Manners and Customs of the Modern Egyptians Written in Egypt During the Years 1833–1835.* London: Charles Knight, 1836.

Lane, E.W. *Cairo Fifty Years Ago.* Edited by S. Lane-Poole. London: J. Murray, 1896.

Lane, E.W. *Description of Egypt.* Edited by J. Thompson. Cairo: American University in Cairo Press, 2000.

Lane-Poole, S. *The Englishwoman in Egypt: Letters from Cairo.* London: Charles Knight, 1844; rprt. Cairo: American University in Cairo Press, 2003.

Lane-Poole, S. *Cairo: Sketches of its History, Monuments and Social Life.* London: J. S. Virtue, 1898.

Lane-Poole, S. *The Story of Cairo.* London: J.M Dent & Co., 1924; first edition, 1902.

Lowenthal, D. *Possessed by the Past: The Heritage Crusade and the Spoils of History.* London: Viking, 1997.

Marlowe, J. *Spoiling the Egyptians.* London: Andre Deutsch, 1974.

Mitchell, T. *Colonising Egypt.* Berkeley: University of California Press, 1991.

Raymond, A. *Cairo: City of History.* Trans. Willard Wood. Cambridge, MA: Harvard University Press, 2000.

Raymond, A. *The Glory of Cairo: An Illustrated History.* Paris: Editio-Editions Citadelles & Mazenod, 2000.

Reid, D. *Whose Pharoahs?* Berkeley: University of California Press, 2002.

Sattin, A. *Lifting the Veil: British Society in Egypt 1768–1956.* London: J.M. Dent & Sons Ltd, 1988.

Sladen, D. *Oriental Cairo: The City of the Arabian Nights.* London: Hurst & Blackett, 1911.

Smith, A.C. *The Attractions of the Nile and its Banks.* London: John Murray, 1968.

Smith, J.V.C. *A Pilgrimage to Egypt.* Boston: Gould and Lincoln, 1852.

Starkey, P. and J. Starkey, eds. *Travellers in Egypt.* New York: I.B. Tauris, 1998.

Thompson, J., ed. *Egyptian Encounters.* Cairo: The American University in Cairo Press, 2002.

Toledano, E. *State and Society in Mid-Nineteenth-Century Egypt.* Cambridge: Cambridge University Press, 1990.

Warburton, E. *The Crescent and the Cross: Romance and Realities of Eastern Travel.* London: Colburn, 1844.

Warner, N. *An Egyptian Panorama, Reports from the 19th Century British Press.* Cairo: Zeitouna Press, 1994.

Wilkinson, I.G. *Handbook for Travellers to Egypt.* London: John Murray, 1858.

Williams, C. *The Islamic Monuments of Cairo: The Practical Guide.* Cairo: American University of Cairo Press, 2002.

INDEX

'Abbas Pasha, 52, 181
Abbasid, 29, 239, 242–243, 251
Abu Lughod, Janet, 52, 56, 178, 181, 188
Ahmed, Leila, 147, 151, 168
Alexandria, 31, 35, 38, 53, 55, 57, 59, 70, 97,
    105, 132, 134, 176, 181, 185, 246, 252
'Ali Mubarak, 50–53, 55, 59, 61–62, 153,
    157, 176–180, 182, 186, 193, 225
'Ali Pasha 'Ali Pasha Mubarak, 35, 49, 60
AlSayyad, Nezar, 1, 3, 5, 169
American, 16, 69, 76, 82, 86–88, 91–92,
    95, 125, 152
antiquity, 10, 14–15, 25, 46, 130, 133, 186
Arabian Nights, 69–71, 76–79, 81–85, 87, 90,
    147, 150, 154–155, 159, 165–166, 170
Arabic: accounts, 153; literature, 30, 163, 171
archeology/archeological, 11, 127, 130, 133,
    140, 246–247
architectural: descriptions, 33, 37; drawings,
    13, 98, 211; heritage, 175, 235; history,
    32, 38–39, 43; origins, 37; tradition, 35,
    37, 39, 46
Arnaud, Jean-Luc, 178–179
art: criticism, 127; dealer, 95, 108, 116; his-
    torical, 26, 128, 202, 244, 247; historri-
    cism, 126, 131; historicist, 126; history,
    126–127, 131, 138, 236; market, 95;
    Orientalist, 112
awqaf, 171, 182, 228, 237, 239–243, 247–248,
    254–256
Ayyubid, 31, 105, 143

Azbakiyya, 56–57, 60, 87, 97, 104, 108, 122,
    155, 161, 171, 176–178, 190–191, 198
Bab Zuwayla, 9–10, 21–22, 72, 81, 99,
    203–219, 221–225, 227–229, 234
Baer, Gabriel, 50, 57, 186
Baghdad, 29–30, 79, 154
Bierman, Irene, 1, 3, 5, 49, 203
Birkat al-Fil, 97, 99, 101
boulevards, 130, 134–135, 155–156, 171, 174,
    176
British: colonialism, 128; colonization, 55;
    occupation, 55, 57, 152, 160
Bulaq, 59, 80, 83, 96, 99, 104, 133, 138, 188

Cairene/Cairenes, 35–36, 39, 60, 77, 80,
    82, 101, 105, 111–112, 115, 118, 129,
    144–146, 149–151, 154, 158, 160, 162,
    164, 166–167, 169, 190–193, 245
Cairo: architecture of, 35; contemporary, 9,
    24, 82, 98; European, 159–161, 165;
    historic, 24, 201–203, 223–224,
    227–228, 233–234; history of, 13,
    32–33, 35, 42, 50, 144, 175; Islamic, 9,
    11–12, 17, 24, 40; medieval, 2–3, 10,
    16–17, 19, 22, 24, 36, 38, 69, 85, 102,
    121, 227; modern-day, 40; monu-
    ments of, 32, 35, 119, 201; nineteenth-
    century, 1, 3–5, 24, 98, 128, 144, 147,
    166, 174, 203, 225, 235; Orientalist, 87
Cairo National Archives, 156

Cairo's: development, 179; modernization, 161, 174–175, 177; streets, 182, 190; transformation, 179
caliph/caliphs, 40, 59, 76, 92, 104, 129, 143, 235, 239, 242–243, 249, 251
caliphate, 29, 31, 59
cemetery/cemeteries, 22, 31, 104–105, 175, 190–192, 197, 199, 202, 235–250, 252–256
Chicago, 17, 22–24, 117, 134
Christianity, 29, 77, 256
city: dual, 143, 145, 149, 166; medieval, 3, 21–22, 57, 101, 178, 227; modern, 14, 129, 133–134, 155, 227; planners, 179, 190–191, 193; traditional, 201
Clot Bey, 78, 181, 189
collective memory, 13, 49, 240
colonial: project, 34
Columbian Exposition, 17, 21–22, 24, 134
Comité, 17–19, 21–22, 24, 26, 49, 60, 129
Cook, Thomas, 149–150, 157
Copt/Coptic, 2, 20, 29, 110, 132, 135, 202, 228, 256
Coptic Museum, 19, 134–135
cosmopolitan, 2, 11, 49, 129, 143, 163
Coste, Pascal, 4, 34–35, 80, 90–91, 97–101, 119–120, 207
Crabbs, Jack, 50, 59
Creswell, K.A.C., 36–37, 39
Crystal Palace, 131, 134, 136–137

De Leon, Edwin, 152, 155, 161–162, 166, 171
de Nerval, Gérard, 85, 89
Description de l'Égypte, 13–14, 34, 45, 95–96, 101, 132, 147, 171
Deutsch, Ludwig, 95, 117, 124
dragoman, 149, 154, 161
dual city, 143, 145, 149, 166
dualistic, 130, 143
Duff-Gordon, Lady, 152, 154–155, 157, 161, 165–166, 170

East, 3, 51, 54–55, 63, 79, 82, 102, 117, 144, 147, 151, 153, 158–161, 165–167, 170, 186
École des Beaux-Arts, 13, 116
Egypt: ancient, 133; colonization of, 55; history of, 2–3, 29, 50, 134, 146, 153; modern, 2, 16, 50–51, 175; of the nineteenth century, 35, 159, 187; Pharaonic, 13, 40, 133; public works in, 56
Egyptian: ancient, 29, 202; citizen, 38, 46; civilization, 50; contemporary, 14, 80, 108,

169; culture, 134, 164–165; government, 16–17, 178; landscape, 146; natives, 134; novel, 50; people, 16; ruler, 16, 52, 174; society, 108, 147, 153, 169; writer, 148
Egyptian Museum, 19, 133–134, 138
Eiffel Tower, 125–126, 172
Enlightenment, 34, 127
European: artist, 96; consumer, 166; literature, 49; writer, 153
exotic, 104, 112, 117, 126, 147, 150, 165
expropriate/expropriation, 210–216, 218–219, 223, 227, 231, 241, 247–248, 255–256

Fahmy, Khaled, 4
Fatimid: caliphate, 29, 31
foreign, 3, 15, 17, 59, 62, 108, 130–131, 133, 136, 144, 146, 160, 166–167, 178–179
foreigner/foreigners, 42, 60, 77, 130, 143–145, 159–161, 163, 165–166, 240
France, 12, 15, 17–18, 25, 34–35, 43, 50, 54–55, 61, 95, 119, 125, 132, 134, 153, 162, 169–170
French: architect, 34
Frith, Francis, 105–107, 114
Fustat, al-, 30–31

Galland, Antoine, 78–80, 82, 84, 90
Gérôme, Jean Léon, 112–118
government: Egyptian, 16–17, 178; khedival, 58, 159; offices, 56
governmental: authorities, 54
Grand Bey, 179, 186, 215, 235, 252–253
Gregory, Derek, 3, 5, 12, 49
guidebooks, 12, 21, 76, 134, 149–151, 167, 235, 240, 253

Hampikian, Nairy, 4, 228
harem, 77, 98, 100, 109–110, 150
Hausmann/Baron Hausmann, 3, 5, 56, 134, 176–177, 193
Hay, Robert, 4, 80, 90–91, 97–104, 110, 117, 119
historiography, 2, 37, 174–175
history: architectural, 1, 32, 38–39, 43; pre-Islamic, 31; topographic, 41; urban, 1, 13–15, 30–33, 35, 39–41, 144, 167, 203

Ibn Khaldun, 32–33, 43–44, 187
imperialist/imperialism, 126, 203, 244
Irwin, Robert, 69, 151
Islam, 29, 31–32, 40, 46, 77, 119, 130, 152, 169, 246

Islamic: architecture, 35–36, 98; Cairo, 2–3, 9, 11–12, 17, 24, 40; civilization, 132; culture, 95, 117, 130; heritage, 40; monuments, 35, 102, 119, 228, 231–232; period, 30; society, 109, 116; urbanism, 98
Isma'il/Isma'il Pasha, 2, 10, 16, 35–36, 52, 56–57, 99, 144, 152–153, 155–157, 160–162, 165–166, 174, 176–181, 184–186, 193, 199, 201–203, 224–226, 237
Isma'ilya, 53, 56, 155, 161, 165, 177

khedival: entourage, 52; government, 58, 159; period, 185, 187, 196; state, 191–192
khedive, 52–53, 56–57, 62, 171, 177, 180, 182, 184–186, 196, 199
khitat, 3, 13, 30–42, 50–51, 54, 57–63, 153, 159, 178–179

Lane, Edward William, 3, 16, 54–55, 70–91, 97, 101–102, 108, 110, 115, 120, 147–148, 150–153, 165, 168–169, 236
Lane-Poole, Stanley, 41, 82–83, 88, 152–154, 156–157, 159–161, 165–166, 171
Le Bon, Gustave, 135–136
Lewis, John Frederick, 90, 108–112, 117, 122
lieu de mémoire, 32, 85
literature: Arab, 148; Arabic, 30, 163, 171; European, 49

Mamluk, 2, 18–19, 29, 31–33, 35, 40–41, 44–45, 58, 76, 114, 144, 235–236, 240, 246–247, 256
medieval: Cairo, 2–3, 10, 16–17, 19, 22, 24, 36, 38, 69, 85, 102, 121, 227; city, 3, 21–22, 57, 101, 178, 227; heritage, 42; period, 14, 17, 30–31, 246
medievalization, 2, 4
medievalizing, 2
Middle East, 102, 106, 122, 128
Ministry of Public Works, 178–179, 181, 184–185, 202, 210–211, 214–215, 218–219, 225–227, 230–231, 234, 241–242, 244, 253, 256
Mitchell, Timothy, 1, 49, 129, 168, 187
modern: Cairo, 2, 10, 174–177, 179–180, 193, 201, 227; city, 14, 129, 133–134, 155, 227; development, 39; historians, 38, 50; lifestyle, 155; transport, 178
modern Egyptians, 16, 70, 75, 82, 88, 244

modernity: imported, 201; project of, 144, 152–153, 160, 167; urban, 157
modernization: program, 161
modernizing: the city, 165
monumental, 34, 152, 207, 236, 240, 254
Muhammad 'Ali: Boulevard, 57, 60, 158, 161, 171, 178; Pasha, 34, 97, 103, 181
museum/museums, 3–4, 12–13, 17, 19–21, 26, 126–128, 130–139, 148, 161, 227, 234, 243–244, 256
Muslim/Muslims, 11, 24, 31, 36, 55, 62, 115, 133, 135, 159–160, 166, 187, 246, 253–254
Muwaylihi, Muhammad al-, 153, 162–165, 169, 172

national, 12, 14–15, 24, 31, 37–38, 40, 43, 45–46, 50, 57, 63, 127–129, 133
nationalist/nationalism, 29, 37–39, 42–43, 46, 125, 159, 167, 174, 203, 244
Nile, 2, 29, 59, 70, 72, 85, 99, 105, 133, 148, 150, 157, 160, 165–166, 173, 176–177, 193
nineteenth-century: Cairo, 1, 3–5, 24, 98, 128, 144, 147, 166, 194, 203, 225, 235; development, 202; image/images, 3, 95; travelers, 144–145; writings, 49
Nora, Pierre, 17, 32
North Africa, 26, 117, 125, 128, 135
Nubia, 70

Orient, 3–4, 34, 75, 79, 84, 87, 98, 118, 121, 147, 150, 153, 162, 165, 168, 236
Oriental: character, 76, 150; historian, 83; life, 76, 87, 150; scenes, 150; tales, 79
Orientalism, 37, 130, 149, 166
Orientalist: art, 4, 112; Cairo, 87; culture, 86, 89; discourse, 143; image/images, 117; painter, 111–112, 116; power, 87
Ottoman, 1, 18, 22, 40, 58, 98, 111–112, 117, 124, 130, 180, 187, 196–197, 218, 236, 240, 243, 246–247, 254, 256

Palestine, 29, 105, 130, 166
Paris, 2, 5, 12, 14–17, 22, 26, 34, 49, 52–54, 56, 64, 89, 112–113, 116–117, 129, 134, 148–149, 153–154, 156–157, 161, 165, 171, 174–180, 185–186, 193, 197, 225
Paris-as-model, 179, 186, 188, 193
performance/performances, 52, 54, 73–75, 77, 85–87, 90
Pharaonic, 2, 10, 13, 29, 34, 40, 98, 108, 119, 132–133, 202

photographer photographers, 5, 11, 105–106, 115, 121, 236
photography, 3, 105, 117, 127–128, 166
Pitt-Rivers, 137–139
planning: city, 179–180, 182, 185–187, 189, 191–193; decrees, 185–187; street, 176, 178, 180–182
Poole, Sophia, 106
preservation, 1, 4, 60, 202, 204, 223, 226, 233, 235–236, 239, 253
Preziosi, Donald, 4–5
Privy Council, 182, 184–186, 198
public: health, 174–175, 186, 188–191; hygiene, 174–175, 181, 184, 186, 188–193; infrastructure, 217; life, 33, 203; property, 162, 247; works, 56, 177, 179, 193

Qahira, al-, 30–31, 40–41, 129, 135, 204–206, 235–236, 248
Qasr al-Nil, 57, 157, 173–174, 176

Rabbat, Nasser, 3, 5
Raymond, André, 1, 180, 186
representation representations, 1–4, 12–14, 16–17, 22, 97, 106, 118, 126, 128, 135–136, 143, 147, 151, 166
Roberts, David, 4, 90, 97, 102–106, 110, 112–113, 117, 122, 147
Ruskin, John, 105, 108, 126

Seine, 125, 148
Shayyal, Gamal al-, 153
Shepheard's Hotel, 86
Suez Suez Canal, 53, 59, 130, 155, 157, 174, 176–177, 201, 207

Tahtawi, Rifa'a al-, 54, 148–149, 153, 157–158, 169
Tanzim, 60, 179–183, 185, 187, 189, 191–192, 195, 198, 202–203, 215, 217, 219, 222, 226, 229, 235, 239, 241, 246, 248, 252, 255–256

technocratic, 158
tourism, 90, 152, 244
tourist tourists, 3, 11, 19, 21–22, 25, 69, 76–78, 83, 86, 88, 92–93, 120, 130–131, 133, 134, 143, 145, 148–150, 152, 159, 198, 227, 237–238, 240, 243–244
transnational, 5, 51, 63
transportation, 160
traveler travelers: European, 146, 149, 159; nineteenth-century, 144–145
Trocadero Palace, 125
Turkish, 53, 74, 77, 104, 112, 117, 157, 169, 177

Universal Exposition, 125–126, 176–177, 180, 193
urban: amenities, 157, 160; context, 30, 105, 210; culture, 158; design, 186, 235; development, 15, 36, 167, 184, 186; expansion, 32; fabric, 156, 201–202, 207, 218, 223–224, 234, 241, 252; geography, 11, 147; growth, 186–187; history, 1, 13–15, 30–33, 35, 39–41, 144, 167, 203; modernity, 157; museum, 130; property, 184; quarter, 30; redevelopment, 134; reform, 187

Victorian Victorians, 105, 108–109, 111–112, 137
Viollet-le-Duc, 15, 17–18, 26

waqf, 57, 169, 181, 183–184, 186–187, 213–216, 219, 221–222, 231, 237, 239–243, 245–248, 254, 256
Williams, Caroline, 3–4
World's Exposition, 147

CONTRIBUTORS

HEBA FAROUK AHMED is Assistant Professor of Architecture and Architectural History in the Faculty of Engineering at Cairo University.

NEZAR ALSAYYAD is Professor of Architecture and Planning and Chair of the Center for Middle Eastern Studies at the University of California, Berkeley. He is also director of the International Association for the Study of Traditional Environments.

MAY AL-IBRASHY is currently finishing a Ph.D. on Cairo in the Department of Art, Architecture, and Archaeology at the School of Oriental and African Studies in London.

IRENE A. BIERMAN is Professor of Art History and Chair of the Islamic Studies Program at the University of California, Los Angeles.

KHALED FAHMY is Associate Professor of History in the Department of Middle Eastern Studies at New York University.

DEREK GREGORY is Professor in the Department of Geography at the University of British Columbia, Vancouver.

NAIRY HAMPIKIAN is a restoration specialist and is currently Director of the Bab Zuwayla conservation project for the American Research Center in Cairo.

DONALD PREZIOSI is Professor of Art History at the University of Oxford in England.

NASSER RABBAT is Associate Professor of Islamic Architectural History at MIT. He has also been Director of the Aga Khan Program of Islamic Architecture at MIT since 1999.

CAROLINE WILLIAMS is a Lecturer of Islamic Art at the University of Richmond, Virginia. Previously, she was a Lecturer at the College of William and Mary in Williamsburg, Virginia.